Descent and Return

Descent and Return

THE ORPHIC THEME
IN MODERN LITERATURE

Walter A. Strauss

DISCARDED

Harvard University Press
Cambridge, Massachusetts
1971

For Nancy

Acknowledgments

Research on this study was made possible through the generosity of the John Simon Guggenheim Memorial Foundation, the Bollingen Foundation, and the Emory University Research Committee, to whom I am profoundly grateful. Particular thanks are also due to my friend and ex-colleague Professor Thomas J. J. Altizer for his persistent and insistent encouragement; to Professor Victor Brombert, for reading the manuscript and making valuable suggestions as to its improvement; and to my wife, Nancy, for her patience and fortitude in helping me at various stages of the writing and revision.

Sections of this study, in modified form, appeared in the *Emory University Quarterly* of Spring 1965 and in the *Centennial Review* of Spring 1966.

I wish to thank Editions Gallimard for permission to use copyrighted material from Stéphane Mallarmé's *Correspondance*, Maurice Blanchot's *L'Espace littéraire* and *Thomas l'obscur*, Saint-John Perse's *Oeuvre poétique* and *Poésie*; the *Mercure de France* for material from Pierre-Jean Jouve's *Poésie*; Librairie Plon for material from Georges Poulet's *Les Métamorphoses du cercle*; Librairie Universelle de France for material from Pierre Emmanuel's *Poésie raison ardente* and *Tombeau d'Orphée*; Mrs. Ruth Fritzsche-Rilke and the Insel-Verlag for material from Rainer Maria Rilke's *Sämtliche Werke* and *Briefe*; Harvard University

Acknowledgments

Press and Basil Blackwell, Ltd., for material from Kathleen Freeman's *An Ancilla to the Pre-Socratic Philosophers*; Princeton University Press for material from Saint-John Perse, *On Poetry* (trans. W. H. Auden); Holt, Rinehart and Winston, Inc., for material from Martin Buber's *Daniel: Dialogues on Realization* (trans. Maurice Friedman).

The translations are all my own unless otherwise noted. They serve the purpose of providing the reader unacquainted with French or German with the closest possible English equivalent of the original: they are *transpositions* into English and claim to be no more.

The May 1970 issue (no. 22) of the *Cahiers de l'Association Internationale des Etudes Françaises*, which contains a long section (seven essays) entitled "Le Mythe d'Orphée au XIXe et au XXe siècle" (pp. 137–246), reached me too late for consideration and possible inclusion; the interested reader will find that the various discussions of the Orphic theme in that volume can be situated in a more traditional context from the one that I am setting forth in the present study.

WALTER A. STRAUSS

November 1970

Contents

Descent and Return

In an age in which disbelief is so profoundly prevalent or, if not disbelief, indifference to questions of belief, poetry and painting, and the arts in general, are, in their measure, a compensation for what has been lost. Men feel that the imagination is the next greatest power to faith: the reigning prince. Consequently their interest in the imagination and its work is to be regarded not as a phase of humanism but as a vital self-assertion in a world in which nothing but the self remains, if that remains. So regarded, the study of the imagination and the study of reality come to appear to be purified, aggrandized, fateful. How much stature, even vatic stature, this conception gives the poet! He need not exercise this dignity in vatic works. How much authenticity, even orphic authenticity, it gives to the painter! He need not display this authenticity in orphic works. It should be enough for him that that to which he has given his life should be so enriched by such an access of value. Poet and painter alike live and work in the midst of a generation that is experiencing essential poverty in spite of fortune.

Wallace Stevens, The Necessary Angel

Wer nur weiss was er weiss, kann es nicht aussprechen;
erst wenn Wissen über sich selbst hinausreicht wird es zum Wort,
erst im Unaussprechbaren wird Sprache geboren.
Und es muss der Mensch, da ihm das Göttliche auferlegt ist,
stets aufs neu die Grenze überschreiten und hinabsteigen
zu dem Ort jenseits des Menschhaften, ein Schatten
am Ort des wissenden Vergessens, aus dem Rückkehr schwer wird
und nur wenigen gelingt.
Aber die Gestaltung der Irdischkeit ist jenen aufgetragen,
die im Dunkel gewesen sind und dennoch sich losgerissen haben
orphisch au schmerzlicher Rückkehr.

Hermann Broch, "Vergil in des Orpheus Nachfolge"

Il s'agit là bien plus d'une métamorphose que d'une métaphore.

Georges Braque, Cahier de Georges Braque, 1917–1947

I

Introduction:
The Metamorphosis
of Orpheus

Orpheus, seer and bard in one, weaned savage forest-tribes from murder and foul living; whence the legend that he tamed tigers and fierce lions. It was said, too, that Amphion, founder of Thebes, moved stones by the sound of his lyre and drew them where he would by the magic of his entreaty. This was the poets' wisdom of old—to draw a line between the Man and the State, the sacred and the common; to build cities, to check promiscuous lust, to assign rights to the married, to engrave laws on wood. Thus did praise and honour come to divine poets and their lays.[1]

Thus Horace celebrated the power of Orpheus in his *Art of Poetry* and invested him with the noblest attributes reserved by antiquity for poetry: the force of magic and the strength of wisdom. This Latin Orpheus, consecrated not only by Horace, but also by Vergil and Ovid, has prolonged the sound of his lyre and of his voice across the ages, modulating his song to accord with the deepest needs and desires of men in their troubled histories. And, in his journey through history, this mythical figure has himself been modulated and modified.

Three fairly distinct stages define present-day notions about the Orpheus myth. The first of these, of course, is antiquity, from the sixth century B.C. to the Hellenistic period, in which the figure of Orpheus first appears and becomes the center of a cult that arises in conjunction with the cult of Dionysus; this cult was revived during the decline of antiquity, the original Orphic doctrine having by that time been supplemented and ramified by all sorts of parallel doctrines such as Neoplatonism and Gnosticism. The first phase of Orphism is the classical scholar's domain: despite the paucity of available and reliable documents there has been vigorous research activity from the end of the nineteenth century to the present, resulting in our current knowledge of the Orphic cosmogony and the ritual practices of various Orphic sects.[2] The second phase, the Renaissance, is derivative in its special manner: the themes of antiquity are imitated, but in such a way as to provide new forms for a new kind of art. The poets of the fifteenth to the eighteenth centuries, from Poliziano to Pope, drawing primarily on Vergil's *Fourth Georgic* and on Ovid's *Metamorphoses* as sources, look upon Orpheus as the archetypal poet—the "sacer interpresque deorum," as Horace designated him, who celebrates in song a cosmic harmony that philosophers and scientists were then demonstrating in their own disciplines. But more original than this traditional attitude was the role allotted to Orpheus as a patron saint of opera. The first known opera is Peri's *Euridice* of 1600, which was followed by Monteverdi's more familiar *favola in musica, Orfeo* (1607). Between this *Orfeo* and Gluck's *Orfeo ed Euridice* (1762) the opera grew and developed into a superbly expressive art form under the patronage, so to speak, of Orpheus.

A splendidly original and sensitive study by Elizabeth Sewell[3] uses as its point of departure the Renaissance juncture of poetry and science, defining the Orphic voice primarily in terms of poetry and natural history. Its impact comes from treatment of the Orpheus myth as exemplary—it is "myth thinking about myth." Miss Sewell develops a morphology of thinking for the period from Shakespeare and Bacon to Wordsworth and Rilke, establishing a framework of relationships for science, myth, and poetry that sheds a great deal of light on the transformations which took place in intellectual history between 1600 and 1800. But she treats the modern period as a continuation of the earlier period, without taking into account the most recent ramifications of the Orphic theme such as the impact of new forms of Gnosticism and especially nihilism upon this mythological material. It is this particular situation that not only justifies but even necessitates a study of the third phase of Orphism, the central concern of the present study. What is this new sense of the Orphic myth? How and why did it come into being? And what is its final significance for literature and the study of ideas?

Understanding of the meaning of the "modern" Orpheus is dependent upon a grasp of the importance of the theme of metamorphosis and on the realization that Orpheus himself is its most powerful embodiment and emblem. It seems strange that a number of recent studies of the Orphic theme in modern literature have not emphasized this point;[4] after all, Orpheus has been traditionally associated with the power of transformation, especially since Ovid, who devoted an extended and crucial portion of his *Metamorphoses* to a recounting of the Orpheus myth. In view of the fact that, since the late eighteenth and early nineteenth centuries, ideas about myth (as well as most other ideas) have been located in a context of change, and have actually been tantalized by the problem of change, it is to be expected that the Orphic myth and other classical myths should provide a rich occasion for reassessment and reinterpretation.

The use of the term myth, as it is understood here, needs clarification. The very fact that since the beginning of the eighteenth century, but more particularly since the end of that century, modern man—be he anthropologist, historian of religions, or artist—has been a collector, analyst, and consumer of myths and mythologies indicates something more than an antiquarian interest in the subject. Mircea Eliade has perhaps understood the deeper reasons for this preoccupation better than anyone else. "The life of modern man proliferates with half-forgotten myths, with lapsed hierophanies, with symbols fallen into disuse. The uninterrupted desacralization of modern man has altered the content of his spiritual life, yet it has not shattered the matrix of his imagination: a heap of mythological waste products survives in poorly controlled zones of his being."[5] In the poets this receding flotsam and jetsam has been to some extent salvaged and reassembled, often in very bizarre arrangements. What has been seen and understood by now is that the rationalistic age that succeeded the Middle Ages and found its most transparent formulation in the eighteenth century was an attempt—which has turned out to be unsuccessful—to demythologize thinking. As Eliade maintains: "Symbol, myth and image belong to the substance of the spiritual life . . . they can be camouflaged, mutilated, degraded, but . . . they will never be rooted out."[6] What is now known as the Romantic period is in effect the prolonged effort at a new stock-taking based on a more acute sense (and a more intense self-consciousness) of the altered historical, theological, philosophical reality of modern man. The Romantics, particularly the German Romantic movement centering around Friedrich Schlegel, Schelling, and Novalis, were intoxicated with mythological and symbolic thinking.

But immediately an important distinction must be made: all modern myth-making, no matter how broad its scope or universal its ambition, is doomed to be artificial. Primitive myth exists first in close conjunction with religion itself and cannot be fully understood apart from it; it contains the germs of what will later be categorized as narrative (for that is the basic *form* of myth) and idea or concept (its basic *content*). Whenever a religious cult becomes reflective and self-conscious, that is, when it moves from what is conventionally called a "lower" to a "higher" status, this dissociation takes place, and from that point on it seems legitimate to speak of "myth" or "mythology." In this way, a psychic distance from religion has been created, which is subsequently elaborated: the formal aspect develops into epic narration or is transmuted into lyrical rhapsody or dramatic enactment, whereas the content furnishes the basis for ratiocination, whether the direction of inquiry be scientific, metaphysical, theological, ethical, or political. This schematization does not sufficiently take into account the slow and often erratic progression of the development; it is given here primarily to argue that the genesis of myth out of religion constitutes also the origin of artistic forms and logical structures. Myth, then, is here understood as the matrix out of which issues the life of mental forms, logical as well as imaginative. It is a movement toward abstraction and artifice, but a movement that strives to remain in contact with its source and, indeed, seeks by a process of creation-in-reverse to rejoin it. The greater the distance, the more arduous the effort. Modern myth-making, however, takes place in or across the void created by the progressive decline of symbolic perception beginning with the end of the Middle Ages[7] and reaching its nadir in the "enlightened" simplifications of the eighteenth century. This void can no longer be bridged or filled by communal creeds, because such creeds have, for the most part, decomposed to such an extent that re-composition is possible only by the mythical imagination of the individual. In terms of the above analysis of primitive myth, modern mythopoeia tends to be a private fabrication utilizing traditional personae and details (though this is not necessarily the case) to protect a personal vision of the world that expresses a certain notion about man and his "reality," the world, and some power or destiny that lies beyond or within.

As far as the myth of Orpheus is concerned, the materials are utterly confusing —and not merely to the nonspecialist in classical studies. In his discussion of Orpheus and Orphism within the context of Greek culture, E. R. Dodds throws up his hands in despair at the proliferation of theories concerning Orphic cults. Speaking of the "edifice reared by an ingenious scholarship," he remarks: "I am tempted to call it the unconscious projection upon the screen of antiquity of certain unsatisfied religious longings characteristic of the late nineteenth and early twentieth centuries."[8] But what may be reprehensible in the field of historical scholarship becomes the earmark of a great deal of poetry of the modern age: the very fact that Orpheus serves as a screen or medium necessitates a different order of investigation from that required of the study of Orpheus in antiquity or in the Renaissance.

Nevertheless, the choice of Orpheus as a screen suggests that there are certain particularities in the Orpheus myth that make it eminently suitable to a certain kind of modern mentality. When the myth itself is looked at and the points where it lends itself to the modern imagination analyzed, it is clear that the screen is in reality a prism.

In its raw outline, the myth runs like this: Orpheus was a native of Thrace (whether he was a historical figure has been the subject of lengthy scholarly disputes, but his historicity is inconsequential here), the son of a local king, Oiagros, or, according to some accounts, of Apollo. His mother was one of the Muses, presumably Calliope, the Muse of epic poetry. It is generally believed that the mythological figure of Orpheus appeared in the sixth century B.C., since there is no mention of him in Homer and Hesiod; and as a native of Thrace he was from the very beginning associated with the cult of Dionysus. As a shaman-figure, he possessed magic powers and prophetic vision; his special attribute was that of a lyrist of such magnificent seductive force that all nature, animate and inanimate, was subdued by and followed him. In his many wanderings he introduced the cult of Dionysus wherever he went. Later traditions include him among the list of heroes and prophets who set out on the Argonautic journey; one of his achievements on that voyage was to charm the Sirens by the power of song so that the Argo and its crew could pass unscathed. Orpheus married the dryad Eurydice and lost her soon after his marriage; Aristaeus pursued her, and in flight she was bitten by a snake and died. Orpheus set out to rescue her from the underworld and succeeded in charming Pluto and Persephone by the powers of his song, so that permission was granted to Eurydice to return to life on condition that Orpheus not turn back to look at her before they had crossed the edge of the underworld. Nevertheless, near the mouth of Hades, he turned back toward Eurydice (for reasons which are variously interpreted), lost her, and returned to the upper world disconsolate and alone. After this point the accounts diverge once more. Some have it that Orpheus shunned the company of women altogether and is thus credited with the introduction of homosexuality into Greece; the female followers of Dionysus, the Maenads (Bacchantes), took vengeance upon him and tore him asunder. Other legends have it that, upon his emergence from Hades, he was set upon by the Maenads and torn apart. In any case, according to the myth, his head floating down the river Hebros continued to sing and prophesy, and his lyre continued to sound, until both were finally washed ashore on the isle of Lesbos, subsequently the site of an oracle of Orpheus.

There are three major "moments" in this myth: (1) Orpheus as a singer-prophet (shaman) capable of establishing harmony in the cosmos (his apocryphal participation in the journey of the Argo elaborates this motif); (2) The descent into Hades (the *katábasis*): the loss of Eurydice, the subsequent subterranean quest, and the second loss (here all the accounts are in agreement except for the problem of motivation, and this is certainly the best known and most popular portion of the myth); (3) The dismemberment theme (*sparagmós*), which suggests a possible deviation from Dionysus or a friction between bacchantic Dionysus-worship and Orphic practices; it is particularly important that the conclusion of the myth reaffirms more strongly than before, in the "other" Orphic journey beyond death (that is, as a force transcending death), the Orphic power of song.

A problem which remains fundamental to an analysis of the myth is the position occupied by Orpheus with respect to Apollo and Dionysus. It is altogether possible that Orpheus was first thought of as the son of Oiagros and that he only later "became" the son of Apollo, who directly bequeathed to him, or taught him, use of the lyre. It must be remembered that the Olympian gods belong to an older tradition, and also that (as in Homer and Hesiod) they are the product of aristocratic imagination and reflection about the nature of the forces that govern the universe. Popular religion was certainly a good deal less ironic about the gods than Homer, or less cosmological in its objectives than Hesiod. The introduction of Dionysus worship—whatever the broader historical origins of Dionysus may be—in the sixth century had much wider popular appeal. It spoke to the "darker," more "irrational" side of the Greek religious sensibility and came to be understood only beginning with the Romantic period (that is, after the sunny-serene-rational view of the Greeks, in vogue since the Renaissance and culminating in Winckelmann, had run its course), finding its most incisive apologist in Nietzsche (*Die Geburt der Tragödie aus dem Geiste der Musik*, 1872) and more recently in scholars like E. R. Dodds (*The Greeks and the Irrational*, 1951). The famous Nietzschean antithesis of the Apollonian and Dionysiac also sheds light on the position of Orpheus, for he resembles Apollo in certain ways, as a patron of the arts, for instance. Nevertheless, Orpheus is virtually always associated with the cult of Dionysus, though he would often appear to be Dionysus' adversary. Jane Harrison declares that "Orpheus reflects Dionysos, yet at almost every point seems to contradict him."[9] This situation accounts for the general ambivalence in the various explanations of the Orpheus-Dionysus-Apollo relationship and in the discrepancies found in the versions of Orpheus' death. Orpheus was ideally suited to bridge the gap between two modes of looking at the world; Eva Kushner states in her study of the Orpheus myth in France since the end of the nineteenth century that "The myth of Orpheus represents precisely the symbolic expression par excellence of the fusion of the Apollonian dream and of Dionysiac intoxication, in music, as well as poetry . . ."[10] F. M. Cornford's formula is even more attractive: "a Dionysus tamed, and clothed, and in his right mind—in a word, Apollinised."[11]

On another level, since Orpheus is at the beginning as much a religious phenomenon as an artistic one, the fusion may be expressed thus: the Apollonian way designates essentially a separation from the gods, making possible the "principle of individuation" and of human autonomy, primarily through enlightened Reason; the Dionysiac way designates, essentially, nonseparation, indeed, union with the gods, through the darker and irrational powers of the body and the soul, in close conjunction with the "chthonic" elements of the earth. Orpheus serves as a mediator between the two orientations—without, however, losing his identification with the followers of Dionysus.

This Orpheus-Dionysus alliance is stressed by the followers of the Orphic cult in the sixth and fifth centuries B.C., who also draw on the teachings of mystical philosophers, particularly Pythagoras and Heraclitus. The central tenets of the doctrine are, in its simplest outline, a cosmogony rivalling Hesiod's and a doctrine of the soul that links Orphism with Gnostic traditions as well as with Christian theology.

The Orphic cosmogony has its origin in Hesiod's, but departs from it to make room for the pre-eminence of the force of Eros as well as for the central importance of Dionysus. According to Orphic accounts, Zeus's offspring (by Persephone) Zagreus is identified with Dionysus: the Titans devoured Zagreus and were in turn annihilated by Zeus's thunderbolts; from their corpses sprang the human race, a compound of the divine and the Titanic (evil). Athena, however, had preserved the heart of Zagreus from the Titans and offered it to Zeus, who swallowed it and thus was able to beget Zagreus a second time, via Semele, under the name of Dionysus.

The other central tenet, the notion of the double composition of man, is closely related to the Orphic notion of the soul and its reincarnations; indeed, this cosmogony is an attempt to explain mythically the good-evil dichotomy in the human being. According to this notion, the soul is immortal and divine but imprisoned in a mortal, Titanic body; therefore it becomes the duty of the follower of Orpheus to liberate the divine, ecstatic, and pure soul from the shackles of an evil body by living a life of progressive ritual purification oriented toward the attainment of immortality. Thus, the ethical ideal of Orphism has interesting points of correspondence with the Hebraic and Christian idea about man's fall and builds an elaborate doctrine of the soul and its salvation upon it. But it must be stressed that, unlike the Jewish and Christian doctrines of redemption, Orphism was from its very beginnings an esoteric cult (and in this way not open, or popular, like the cult of Dionysus) requiring certain practices of initiation and instruction and an ascetic discipline, such as vegetarianism. Gertrude Rachel Levy defines Orphism in *The Gate of Horn*: "Orphism replaced the emotional ecstasy, which has been engendered in the thiasos through a realization of unity with the dynamic energies of wild lives, by the rapture of the individual aspirant acquired through long discipline and purification, both ritual and moral, which conserved its vitality to face higher power; to know it, and therefore to be at one with it. To accomplish singly and permanently what the Dionysiac thiasos had attained at moments, was the Orphic way of redemption."[13]

The doctrine of successive reincarnations of the soul, which Orphism has in common with virtually all forms of Gnosticism, is the attempt to account for the indestructibility of the divine element in man and to justify the requirements imposed on his ethical behavior to liberate his soul progressively from the evil element, which resides in matter. The old Gnostic idea of the body as a prison or a tomb (*sōma-sēma*), in which the soul is held captive, appears in full strength in Orphic thinking and accounts for cathartic practices as well as for the ascetic nature of the doctrine—indeed, it accounts for the general puritan cast of Orphism. It must nevertheless be pointed out that the purpose of all this *askēsis* is not simply to assure the reincarnated soul a higher form of existence, but to strive toward total liberation of the soul from its prison to enable it to reacquire its resting place within the Divine Soul. In brief, the ultimate aim of Orphism is to "escape from the unending cycle of reincarnation—to abolish, in other words, the periodic return to life."[14]

Another interesting feature of Orphism, again in comparison with the monotheistic religions, is its reliance on sacred books and hymns, most of them apocryphally attributed to Orpheus. This is quite at variance with official Greek religion, which recognized no sacred texts at all. There are obvious correspondences with Gnosticism (the principal common ground being that of

Pythagoreanism, with which Orphism is all too easily confused); or, at least, Orphism can be seen as a *gnōsis*, a special way of obtaining knowledge of the cosmos and of salvation.

The nineteenth century found the Orpheus myth intriguing in a new way. The Romantic movement is not, as some have claimed, a reaction against classicism, but a reaction to a particular way of looking at the art of the past. The Romantics, despite their medievalism and exoticism, were practically without exception lovers of antiquity, but in a new and different way. German Romanticism in particular is full of Romantic Hellenism, and the same phenomenon can be observed in France, England, and Italy. One may say that the Apollonian view of Greece was being replaced by an Orphic-Dionysian view. In this respect, the religious underpinnings of Romanticism are of particular importance, since the end of the so-called Age of Reason coincides with growing awareness of a religious void created, in part by the rationalistic and scientific energies released since the Renaissance, but more particularly by the gradual corrosion and erosion of Christianity. It is for this reason that the anti-Newtonian modes of thinking at the end of the eighteenth century, despite their eccentricities and aberrations, ought to be given serious attention within the context of scientific and philosophical thought. On the one hand, Goethe's insistence on the organic structure of the world can be cited as a levelheaded attempt to stem the tide of encroaching mechanism; on the other hand, the theosophical and illuministic revivals of the eighteenth and early nineteenth centuries can be regarded, despite their perverseness, as genuine attempts to restore to a mechanized universe its proper symbolic, even magical, perspective.[15] Here again, not so much the Orphic myth but the Orphic cult made its contribution; it coincided neatly with the magical preoccupation of the illuminists and neo-alchemists. And, the figure of Orpheus played a considerable role in the esoteric literature of the seventeenth and particularly the eighteenth centuries, thus merging with all sorts of other currents from Hellenistic Orphism through all varieties of neoplatonism, the Kabbala, and the alchemistic, theosophical, and Swedenborgian movements and their multitudinous variants, up to the beginning of the twentieth century.

With the new and syncretistic attempts to renovate religious attitudes came new formulations in philosophy and in the arts, indeed in all areas of intellectual endeavor. For the redefinition of the poet and poetry, the Orphic myth provided supports that were eagerly seized upon by theorists and by poets themselves.

Was it not tempting to think of the poet, dispossessed by ages of cold reason, recovering his own domain as soothsayer, harmonizer, even legislator—"être nécessaire," as Claudel said in a slightly different context? All the poets with whom this study is concerned stress, in one way or another, the irreplaceability of poetry, the need for symbolic expression, the perpetuity of the poetic voice. Their approaches differ sharply; but in this one sense, they are all "symbolists," makers of metaphors.

Though the Orphic mission of the poet is generally agreed upon, each of these poets handles the materials of the myth, particularly the Eurydice-Hades theme, in his own way. In keeping with the new sensibility, the Eurydice theme gives some (Nerval, Jouve, Emmanuel) the opportunity to formulate their convictions about the nature and place of the erotic, usually in the context of the descent motif—interpreted with varying stress as a plunge into the unconscious (Nerval), a confrontation with death and night (Nerval, Novalis, Rilke), and a coming face to face with Nothingness (Mallarmé, Blanchot). Consequently, it becomes evident that the decisive factor in appraising the nature of the modern Orphic is not so much in the magical mission of the poet, but in the account and interpretation of his experience as reflected in his poetry—the nature of his Orphic journey, that quest for a dark but "pure" center. These journeys are made more poignant by the fact that the poets, in their own descent into Hades, are directly conscious of their "ancestor" and model, Orpheus.

Because the modern world abounds in myths, the myth of Orpheus can be expected to collide and amalgamate with other myths. The connection between Orpheus and Dionysus has been pointed out; the antithesis to the Orpheus myth is the Prometheus theme. Certain Romantic poets are classifiable as Promethean (Shelley, Byron, Hugo) and others as Orphic (Novalis, Wordsworth, possibly Keats); in Nerval's case, the Orphic struggles against the pressure exerted by the Promethean. The differences can be summarized in this fashion: Prometheus and Orpheus are readily contrastable as half-gods and as mythological culture-heroes. Prometheus defies Zeus in behalf of mankind and is martyred for his deed; as a fire-stealer, he is at the same time the eternal rebel (joining forces with Faust, Satan, and Cain) and the representative of a "progressive" Romantic humanism. Orpheus does not rebel; he refuses to accept the world as it is; he does not lead the people, he charms them. Prometheanism aims for an outer transformation of society; it proposes to ameliorate man's lot by external action. Orphism proposes to transmute the inner man by a confrontation with himself and to alter society only indirectly, through the changes that man can effect within himself. All of modern literature tends to fall within the area delimited by these two points of reference, rebellion and refusal. From the end of the eighteenth to the middle of the nineteenth century the Orphic and Promethean remained in conflict; thereafter the Promethean retreated gradually, with the result that the second half of the nineteenth and the early twentieth centuries remained largely under the Orphic spell. M. H. Abrams, in discussing August Schlegel's concept of a "creative" nature, remarks that "through the displacement, as creative principle of both Jehovah, Demiurge and Prometheus by an indwelling Soul of Nature, the role of a deliberately supervisory artisan, whether *deus* or *alter deus*, dwindles: the real and poetic worlds alike become self-originating, autonomous, and self-propelling, and both tend to *grow* out into their organic forms."[16]

From about 1750 the idea of art as *mímēsis* began to be replaced, or at least transformed, by the idea of art as *poíēsis*. In this development the accent shifts gradually from the Prometheus-figure, creator in a *natura naturata*, to the Orpheus-figure, creator in and through a *natura naturans*. This represents, in effect, a discovery of the dynamic principle of nature-as-organic, over and against the idea of nature-as-organized; it ushers in an age of process, rather than progress.

Herbert Marcuse, who contrasts the Promethean and the Orphic in his provocative *Eros and Civilization*, also points out that the theme of Narcissus plays a role in the modern self-consciousness that is closely related to the Orphic. Orpheus and Narcissus both reconcile Eros and Thanatos; they are ways of liberating the self through self-contemplation and death.

They have not become the culture-heroes of the Western world: theirs is the image of joy and fulfillment, the voice which does not command but sings; the gesture which offers and receives, the deed which is peace and ends the labor of conquest; the liberation of time which unites man with god, man with nature. Literature has preserved their image . . . The Orphic Eros transforms being: he masters cruelty and death through liberation. His language is song, and his work is *play*. Narcissus' life is that of *beauty*, and his existence is *contemplation*. These images refer to the *aesthetic dimension* as the one in which their reality principle must be sought and validated.[17]

Two important and related themes emerge from this discussion: first, the Orphic transformation of being, the ontological refusal of the Promethean existence; second, the attempt to struggle against limitations set by time and history. Here again there is an interesting correspondence between the strivings of the Orphic sects of antiquity to break out of the eternal cycle of reincarnation, out of historical Being. This progressive attempt at liberation from Being as defined by the post-Renaissance world provides a kind of sequence for the present study. The first Orphics of the Romantic period, formed by certain rationalistic modes of thought of the Age of Enlightenment, are characteristic in wanting to replace rationalism by something missing in it—the imagination, the intuition, *Gemüt*. In this they appear to be more interested in extending the definition of man as rational animal to man as imaginative-and-rational animal in the late nineteenth century; for a really antirational program one must wait until Rimbaud and Lautréamont. But it is also significant that Romantic Orphism frequently attempts (as was true of Gnostic sects in the third and fourth centuries) to reconcile Orpheus and Christ;[18] an early illustration is in catacomb frescoes and, subsequently, in Milton's *Lycidas*, as well as in Calderón's remarkable *auto sacramental*, *El divín Orfeo*. The best example of the synthesis is Novalis, with whom I shall begin my study. The same phenomenon occurs in Nerval but collides with a more acute consciousness of the incompatibility of antiquity and Christianity, of the pantheistic and the transcendent, and on occasion it shades off into Satanic-Promethean rebellion.

It is only after the collapse of the Romantic ideal, around 1848 (Nerval can be said to have prolonged the Romantic Orphism by a few years) that, in a sense, poetic Orphism is partially relieved of its Gnostic baggage and that problem of the new Orphic attitude emerges more clearly. The question is no longer one of reconciling Orpheus and Christ, but one of a world vision that makes the sacred possible at all. In Mallarmé the essential question is whether the poet can even exist in the modern world—even the nocturnal vision of Hölderlin's "Dichter in dürftiger Zeit" is no longer valid—whether the modern world is any longer subject to poetic comprehension and treatment. The Orphic poet is, once more, at the beginning of a journey, confronted with the task of sacralizing time, space, and language before the Orphic spell can take place. His task is to face the Nothingness, to overcome (abolish) it in order to make poetry once more possible. In religious terms, what has come about is the creation of an immanent Orphic reality as it developed out of the unstable tensions of Romantic Orphism. Like Mallarmé, Rilke creates an immanent Orphic space-reality in which *Wandlung* (transmutation of the self) and a poetics of praise and lament are infinitely possible.

Two other themes, regeneration and memory, should be pointed out. All modern poetry has been a quest for self-renewal, and the Orphic poet seeks to regenerate himself particularly by means of the voyage downward, with its attendant self-recognition through remembrance and its mandatory self-transformation, followed by return to the world that will become the ground of a vaster metamorphosis. The context of this new Orphic era is the modern pathos of time and history, coinciding with the Romantic period, with its quest for the lost or forgotten self—the legacy of Jean-Jacques Rousseau. Moreover, the nucleus of all varieties of Gnosticism (and this includes the major part of Orphic doctrine) is the quest for the lost, dimly-remembered or forgotten, repressed self—recovery of the authentic self underneath the incrustation of material and historical existence. In the orbit of modern Orphism the themes of regeneration and reminiscence go hand in hand. Seen in this perspective, the new Orphics are comparable to the Dante of the *Vita Nuova*, who experienced his renewal through the love and death of Beatrice very much in the way Orpheus "renews" himself (at least, according to the moderns) through his loss of Eurydice and his descent into hell. Because the *Vita Nuova* offers such a convenient counterpoise to the modern Orphic quest for rebirth it will be frequently invoked in subsequent pages, particularly since a number of poets directly refer to it. Furthermore, the reference point it provides enables one to see the vast differences between an age that could conceive regeneration in Christian terms only, and an age that feels impelled to create its own universe of redemption because the other, Dante's, is no longer felt to be valid.

This raises another point: the terms transformation and transmutation, so frequently used above, designate one of the key features of modern literature, again in contrast with literature before the end of the eighteenth century. Whereas in classical literature (that is, from the Greeks to the eighteenth century) the relationships of parts to whole revolve around a fixed center, a kind of closed aesthetic universe (like Ptolemy's, or Newton's), the nature of literature since the Romantic days has come increasingly to revolve around an imaginary center (or, more recently, around a point off center or even "around" no center at all). This patterning of shifting relations characteristic of modern literature was heralded by Coleridge as "organic," a term that has served well until the twentieth century. This term points toward an organic world view such as Goethe proposed and Darwinian biology actualized. The present age, however, looks back on the nineteenth century as a series of antitheses that call for a dialectical resolution, a kind of coincidence of opposites.

What are the wider implications of this coincidence of opposites for the modern Orphic mind? In a period like the nineteenth century, in which old, exhausted values are being replaced by new value schemes and by radical patterns of thought and action, one of the major problems that invariably demands revaluation is that of the One and the Many. Not only the domain of professional philosophers after Kant, this was also a concern of the poet in his attempt to measure the new world in which he was living and writing. From the beginning of the nineteenth century on, the poet was impelled to become a thinker in a somewhat different way: he meditated not only upon his craft, or the subject matter of his discourse, but upon the relation of poetry to the world and to reality. New poets found themselves confronted with the necessity of retraversing the terrain originally occupied by philosophy and theology into which earlier poets, such as Dante, Shakespeare, Donne, Milton, and Pope, had made significant and successful sallies. By the end of the eighteenth century, Goethe, Blake, Hölderlin, and Wordsworth were writing a kind of poetry that, to be sure, proceeded from a tradition, but that bore witness to a new spirit and a new quest.

Isaiah Berlin's classification of thinkers into hedgehogs and foxes acquires particular relevance when applied to this situation and, at the same time, points up a possible alternative solution whose impact on Orphic thinking is of paramount importance. In some ways, it is as if there were a need to recapitulate the essential orientation points of the pre-Socratic philosophers all over again.[19] The modern thinker is required to orient his thought in relation to one of the three exemplary pre-Socratic minds. First is Parmenides, the perfect hedgehog, the philosopher of absolute being and of intransigent monism: "Being has no coming-into-being and no destruction, for it is whole of limb, without motion, and without end. And it never Was, nor Will Be, because it Is now, a Whole all together, One, continuous; for what creation of it will you look for?" (fragments 7 and 8). This mode of thinking is completely intellectual and depends on an ontological identity of Being and Thinking. ("For it is the same thing to think and to be" [fragment 3].) It accords no reality either to nonbeing or to becoming. The next model is Empedocles, the representative fox:

I shall tell of a double [process]: at one time it increased so as to be a single One out of Many; at another time again it grew apart so as to be Many out of One. There is a double creation of mortals and a double decline: the union of all things causes the birth and destruction of the one [race of mortals], the other is reared as the elements grow apart, and then flies asunder. And these [elements] never cease their continuous exchange, sometimes uniting under the influence of Love, so that all become One, at other times again each moving apart through the hostile force of Hate. Thus insofar as they have the power to grow into One out of Many, and again, when the One grows apart and Many are formed, in this sense they come into being and have no stable life; but insofar as they never cease their continuous exchange, in this sense they remain always unmoved [unaltered] as they follow the cyclic process (fragment 17).

Here there is a double principle of Being, a polarity, whose interactions or mixtures account for Becoming. An antithesis within Being thus generates the antithesis between Being and Becoming.

In Heraclitus the dynamism remains, but the antitheses are overcome in a new unity—a concert of Being and Becoming: "That which is in opposition is in concert, and from things that differ comes the most beautiful harmony" (fragment 8). In Heraclitean metaphysics the principle of contradiction is expressly abnegated; the logical basis for this kind of thinking has much in common with Oriental modes of thought and with mystical theology. Since Western thought, particularly after Aristotle, has generally moved along the paths of syllogistic thinking, which proceeds by identities and equations and thus rules out all contradictions, Heraclitean inroads into its mainstream up to the end of the Enlightenment have been sporadic and to some extent ineffectual. To the classical, medieval, or Renaissance mind such Heraclitean assertions as "they do not understand how that which differs with itself is in agreement: harmony consists of opposing tension, like that of the bow and the lyre" (fragment 51) or "and what is in us is the same thing: living and dead, awake and sleeping, as well as young and old; for the latter (of each pair of opposites) having changed becomes the former, and this again having changed becomes the latter" (fragment 88) would, generally speaking, have made little philosophical sense.

The Heraclitean concert of opposites does, however, take on a new guise in the writing of Nicholas of Cusa (1400–1464), but in a completely new context. Briefly, a different logic and a different theology must be dealt with from the medieval one current before his time. Nicholas Cusanus is theologically the heir of the mystics, such as Dionysius the Areopagite and Meister Eckhart, who were visionaries and also formulators of the intellectual order implicit in their intuitions. The fact that both Dionysius and Eckhart frequently defined God's unity in *negative* terms is of particular interest; Rudolf Otto's juxtaposition of S'ankara and Meister Eckhart as virtually identical examples of Eastern and Western mysticism suggests that the problem of a dialectical theology is not to be dismissed simply on the grounds that it is nonrational or nontraditional.[20] What Cusanus attempted was to replace the logic of the Scholastics by a more comprehensive mode of thinking that would be applicable to a vision of the infinite. The solution, in his case, was a new mathematical logic: he was eager to ground mystical theology in a system of reflections that would bridge the gap between the finite and the infinite, and that system was mathematics. Cassirer observes in *Individuum und Kosmos in der Philosophie der Renaissance:* "[Cusanus' doctrine of God] requires a new type of mathematical logic, which does not exclude the coincidence of opposites, but rather one which needs this coincidence itself, this convergence of the Absolute Maximum and the Absolute Minimum, as a consistent principle and a necessary vehicle of progressive cognition."[21] Without going into the detailed proofs of the *coincidentia oppositorum* in Cusanus as they are found in *De docta ignorantia*, it is possible to simply summarize by saying that, for Cusanus, the *coincidentia oppositorum* is a dialectical form of thought in which all possible contradictions are resolved and annulled in God. The dynamics of this dialectic involve a constant polar tension between *explicatio* and *complicatio*, between *alteritas* and *unitas*. "The one truth, inapprehensible in its absolute sense, can be represented to us only in the sphere of otherness; but similarly there is for us no otherness that does not in some way point toward Unity and participate in it."[22]

The relevance of this digression about the coincidence of opposites points up a peculiar affinity of modern Orphic exploration with the Orphism of antiquity. The earliest forms of ancient Orphism had a strongly monistic tendency; the late Hellenistic version was marked by a strong influence of Gnostic-dualistic doctrines. As a consequence of certain correspondences between the Gnosticism of late antiquity and the dualism of the modern epoch,[23] the phenomenon of the Orphism of modern poets recapitulates the tensions of earlier epochs. Novalis and particularly Nerval stand under the spell of an Orpheus who bridges, rather than fuses, Gnostic dualities of spirit and body. It was Coleridge and Hegel who proposed, in their different ways, synthetic or concordant methods to establish unity rather than polarity. Coleridge emphasized the unity that grows out of diversity—a "reconciliation of opposite or discordant qualities."[24] Put in another way, Hegel's and Coleridge's concepts are also evidence of a new shift in emphasis in nineteenth-century thinking, a movement toward historical and biological ways of exploring the nature of reality.

It may be asked, in this connection, why my study is concerned primarily with Continental authors, despite the fact that Wordsworth and Coleridge figure in the preceding discussion and the names of Keats and Yeats might also be cited as relevant. The answer is that the theme of Orpheus does not figure prominently or decisively in modern English literature. Miss Sewell's *The Orphic Voice* crosses the Channel after discussing Wordsworth, and this is as it should be. The spirit of Orpheus in its contemporary form comes to haunt British poetry again only after the expansion of French poetic ideas and ideals at the end of the nineteenth century. But there is a more fundamental distinction involved here, which helps account for the difference between the English view of poetry in its relations with science and philosophy and the Continental view, particularly as it was elaborated in Germany between 1795 and 1825. This difference explains why poetry in England has tended to remain more distinct from these other areas of intellectual inquiry than has poetry on the Continent.[25]

My aim is not to inquire what Orpheus was in antiquity, or what he is at the beginning of the nineteenth century, but what he *becomes* in the modern age; the aim is to examine the metamorphosis of Orpheus, seen in the context of lyrical reflection and reflective lyricism—the poet-as-thinker. Orpheus is not only poetry; he has become, in modern times, the agony of poetry—a sort of ambassador without portfolio of poetry. He is the figure, the myth, entrusted with the burden of poetry and myth. His metamorphosis is the change in poetic climate itself, placed against an ever-darkening sky in which poetry recedes more and more toward secret and unexplored spaces, spaces that are obscure and must be illuminated by constellations of the mind ever threatened by disaster and extinction.

The first two authors, Novalis and Nerval, attempt to derive their Orphic vision within a setting of the Gnostic dualities. Novalis manages this feat by an almost total negation of the realm of light in favor of a nocturnal reality. Nerval pursues a similar path but finds himself at the end ambiguously suspended between affirmation and negation. Mallarmé, the third author, discovers in an anguished moment of his life that negation of the created world can also lead to affirmation of the creative act, which recreates the negated world by poetic affirmation. He develops a poetry that is both absence and presence, nothing and everything. Through him the paradox of the coincidence of opposites has taken root in modern poetry. With Rilke, this paradox is heightened and deepened, and to a large extent humanized. Orpheus becomes the mythical figure who affirms death-within-life, being-within-becoming. Mallarmé and Rilke bring the modern poetic paradox of language as silence and silence as language to a point of incandescence.

This shift in modern Orphism from an uneasy dualistic polarity to a paradoxical unity parallels also, in a peculiar way, the movement of modern thought toward a constructive nihilism in theology, the quest for a new ontology, and, finally, a resurgence of the mathematical and abstract over the biological and concrete. This may sound like an oversimplification; the problem is, in fact, a good deal more complex. But the changing Orphic vision over the last hundred and fifty years or so reflects in its own particular way the preoccupation and hesitations and audacities of modern thinking—thinking that has questioned the nature of reality, the nature of being, the nature of God, the nature of nature, and the nature of poetry and thought themselves.

And so Orpheus journeys down and up: down to the depths of the psyche, to the depths of being, to death's realm, and back up to life and creation and thence into death and song—this servant of Dionysus and pupil of Apollo, architect of the troubled soul and peacemaker for the distressed mind. For Orpheus is truly a reconciler of opposites: he is the fusion of the radiant solar enlightenment of Apollo and the somber subterranean knowledge of Dionysus. Indeed, this is what J. J. Bachofen demonstrates in his analysis of the Orphic myth and of the cosmological structure of Orphic thought, which rests on a dualism dividing the upper (uranian) from the lower (telluric) hemisphere: "Dionysus is recognized as the lord of the telluric sphere, and the uranian half is conceded to Apollo; and thus the highest domain of light relinquished by Apollo is restored to that god which the oldest form of Orphism had worshipped in its purer form." But Dionysus does not lose his luminosity thereby; on the contrary, the eclipse serves to affirm the principle of light and he becomes, as Macrobius describes him, "*sol in infero hemisphaerio.*" Thus "Apollo becomes the upper complement of Dionysus, Dionysus becomes the downward continuation of Apollo. A Bacchic Apollo, an Apollonian Dionysus emerge from this conjunction, restoring in a double incarnation the unity of the principle of light."[26]

Karl Kérenyi, from a different perspective, draws a similar conclusion, which emphasizes the concordance of Dionysus and Apollo under the aegis of Orpheus: "Orphic living and thinking is Dionysiac living and thinking, but in an atmosphere dominated by the Apollonian desire for purity, in an existence which is no longer so primitive that it can endure the contradictions of being that the Delphic cult still permitted by a fraternal juxtaposition of Apollo and Dionysus."[27]

The most eloquent commentary on the quest of my study—an account of the modern poetic vision in its varied struggles to recover the true mythical meaning of Orpheus—is to be found in Erich Heller's *The Disinherited Mind*. What Heller says about German literature applies, mutatis mutandis, to French poetry as well.

The attempt of scholars to unravel the complex of historical reminiscences, the images, insights, feelings that make up the story of Dionysus, Apollo and Orpheus in modern German literature and thought, and then to relate it to what may be the Greek reality of these divine creatures, is as heroic as it is doomed to failure. For a scholar's guarded steps cannot possibly keep pace with the rush and dance of the passions of the mind swirling around those names and arrested only for brief moments in innumerable figurations. Nietzsche, from *The Birth of Tragedy* onwards, is seeking spiritual employment in the service of a god who is a synthesis of Dionysus and Apollo. In this composite Nietzschean deity, Apollo, it is true, more and more loses his name to the other god, but by no means the power of his artistic creativeness, for ever articulating but the Dionysian chaos in distinct shapes, sounds and images, which are Dionysian only because they are still aglow with the heat of the primeval fire.[28]

II

Novalis:
Orpheus the Magician

Modern literature begins in the last decade of the eighteenth century: the spirit
of this literature is characterized by an intense self-consciousness, undergirded
by a complex sentiment of duality—the divorce of self from cosmos and the
division of self from self—along with a desire to heal the breach and usher in a
new age of the spirit. William Blake's *Songs of Innocence and Experience* and *The
Marriage of Heaven and Hell*, Wordsworth's and Coleridge's *Lyrical Ballads*,
Schiller's *Naïve and Sentimental Poetry*, the odes of Hölderlin, and Novalis' *Hymns*
—all fall within the period 1790–1800 and delineate the new spirit in literature,
the central current of which would be called Romanticism during the first half
of the nineteenth century. But the physiognomy that this new literature gradually acquired goes considerably beyond that of Romanticism. The new way of
seeing and feeling was shaped by a new, organic pattern of thinking; its content
was predominantly "mythical"; and its mode of perception was ironical and
paradoxical. It is Friedrich Schlegel, Novalis' contemporary and close friend,
who strikes the keynote at the turn of the eighteenth century. For him all poetry
is mythology, the modern counterpart of religion, and consequently profound,
real, and unifying:

Der Kern, das Zentrum der Poesie ist in der Mythologie zu finden, und in den Mysterien
der Alten. Denn Mythologie und Poesie, beide sind Eins und unzertrennlich. Alle
Gedichte des Altertums schliessen sich eins an das andere, bis sich aus immer grössern

Massen und Gliedern das Ganze bildet; alles greift ineinander, und überall ist ein und derselbe Geist nur anders ausgedrückt. Und so ist es wahrlich kein leeres Bild, zu sagen: die alte Poesie sei ein einziges, unteilbares, vollendetes Gedicht. Warum sollte nicht wieder von neuem werden, was schon gewesen ist? Auf eine andere Weise versteht sich. Und warum nicht auf eine schönere, grössere?[1]

The core, the center of poetry is to be found in mythology, and in the mysteries of the ancients. Mythology and poetry—both are one and indivisible. All poems of antiquity are interlinked, so that the whole is formed from the accumulation and its connections; everything interpenetrates, and one and the same spirit is expressed throughout in different ways. And thus it is truly no empty formula to say: ancient poetry is a single, indivisible, complete poem. Why should not that which has once existed exist anew? In a different manner, to be sure. And why not more beautiful, and more magnificent?

Despite the aphoristic form and enthusiastic manner of these pronouncements, one is struck here by a new seriousness regarding mythology, as well as what might be called the deepening of the mythological consciousness. At the same time, Schlegel was clearly aware of the artificial aspects of the new mythology— his ironic sensibility told him that it is not, in any sense, like the mythology of the ancients, but that it is a creative enterprise of the modern intellect: mythopoeia, rather than mythology. Thus Orpheus came once more to occupy the position he had held in the Renaissance. But this is a different Orpheus, only superficially resembling the Renaissance and the operatic Orpheus; he has been radically transformed into an instrument of the imagination whereby the poet can assess himself and his mission in a new way; the myth, losing its classical and neo-classical grounding, now becomes *the* myth of regeneration, and it is interpreted so as to account for the modern situation of the poet (that is, his growing alienation from the world) and for the experience of his psyche (his inner self-division and his quest for self-integration).

The Renaissance revitalization of the Orpheus myth from the sixteenth through the eighteenth centuries, as manifested in literature, opera, and the fine arts, had taken over the figure of Orpheus as a patron saint of song, placing its various emphases on the triumph and apotheosis of an Orpheus who emerged victorious, though without Eurydice, from the underworld. This treatment of the myth eschewed the tragic confrontation of poetry and the universe, and of the soul with its own abyss, that may have been implicit therein. As a matter of fact, as Elizabeth Sewell's study *The Orphic Voice* shows, the Orpheus theme can be increasingly identified during that period with the progress of the biological sciences and the optimism that generally marks the epoch of the Renaissance through the Enlightenment. Nor does this element of affirmation disappear during the new phase of Orphism that is of concern here: the context and emphasis have changed and become undermined with all sorts of paradoxes and contradictions, so that it may be said that in all the instances of the Orphic to be examined in the nineteenth and twentieth centuries, the affirmations themselves turn out to be paradoxical and to a certain extent ambiguous.

This ambiguity is certainly not present in Goethe's "Urworte Orphisch" of 1817. Enthusiasm for classical antiquity inspired this sequence of five stanzas which express Goethe's version of Orphic wisdom in a poetic compendium that is of great power in terms of the drama of the individual soul in its struggle with the world. The stanzas are superscribed with the names of the forces that act within and upon the individual: *daimon*, chance, *eros*, necessity, and hope. Goethe's commentary notes his intention to present older and more recent Orphic doctrines in a concentrated manner.[2] Of the titles of the strophes, the use of *daimon* presents the major difficulty. Goethe explains that he means

die notwendige, bei der Geburt unmittelbar ausgesprochene, begrenzte Individualität der Person, das Charakeristische, wodurch sich der einzelne von jedem andern bei noch so grosser Ähnlichkeit unterscheidet . . . Deshalb spricht diese Strophe die Unveränderlichkeit des Individuums mit wiederholter Bedeutung aus. Das noch so entschieden Einzelne kann, als ein Endliches, gar wohl zerstört, aber, solange sein Kern zusammenhält, nicht zersplittert noch zerstückelt werden, sogar durch Generationen hindurch.[3]

the necessary individuality of the person, fixed and limited at birth; the characteristic endowments which make one individual differ from another, no matter how great the resemblance . . . For this reason this strophe asserts with repeated emphasis the immutability of the individual. Even a clear-cut unit, being finite, can be destroyed; yet so long as its core remains intact, it cannot be shattered or fragmented, not even in subsequent generations.

Here is the text of the *daimon* stanza:

> Wie an dem Tag, der dich der Welt verliehen,
> Die Sonne stand zum Grusse der Planeten,
> Bist alsobald und fort und fort gediehen
> Nach dem Gesetz, wonach du angetreten.
> So musst du sein, dir kannst du nicht entfliehen,
> So sagten schon Sibyllen, so Propheten,

Und keine Zeit und keine Macht zerstückelt
Geprägte Form, die lebend sich entwickelt.

Just as on that day on which you came into the world
The sun stood in relation to the planets,
From that day on you began to develop
According to the law that made you take your appointed place.
Such must you be, you cannot escape from yourself,
Thus sibyls and prophets have declared,
No time, nor any force can destroy
Form impressed, which, living, develops.

Goethe here asserts the unity and indivisibility of the individual as subject to a developmental law of growth, a law that is a form stamped upon his being. The arena in which the development takes place is that of Nature, where chance and necessity are operative, and where *eros*—ardor, passion—serves as a crucible for polarized forces, the power of metamorphosis itself. The final strophe is the flight of the self beyond its limitations, beyond space and time: the elevating virtue of hope.

Aus Wolkendecke, Nebel, Regenschauer
Erhebt sie uns, mit ihr, durch sie beflügelt;
Ihr kennt sie wohl, sie schwärmt nach allen Zonen—
Ein Flügelschlag—und hinter uns Äonen.

Past the ceiling of clouds, past mists, past rainstorms
[Hope] lifts us along, by her wings;
You know her well, she swarms toward all zones—
One beat of the wings—and aeons are left behind us.

These primordial Orphic words are, as Miss Sewell points out, not only a synthesis of subject matter, but also a synthesis of method: "Here a mind passionately interested in the dynamics of life, in the individual organism, in nature at large, in human beings and in his own thinking and feeling and acting self, having tried to evolve a dynamic of nonmathematical thought as a means of interpreting life, brings this home, centrally and finally, to words, poetry and myth . . . Metamorphosis was for Goethe not just a phenomenon; it was a working discipline."[4]

Much of the preceding paragraph could be applied to Goethe's Romantic contemporaries, but the emphasis would be wrong. The common elements are there: the new dynamism of becoming, that drive toward biological and historical thinking that gave the nineteenth century its unique and novel profile; the new organicism that became the hallmark of the new literature; the corollary concept of metamorphosis, variety-in-unity, that is the seal of the new Orphic dispensation itself. But Miss Sewell is right—for Goethe metamorphosis was a fact of the real world, as well as a dimension of the inner experience; and because of this correspondence he was able to maintain a continuous though ever-shifting equilibrium within the systolic-diastolic rhythm of nature without and within. A way of life, a mode of understanding. Note his "Parabase" of 1820:

> Freudig war vor vielen Jahren
> Eifrig so der Geist bestrebt,
> Zu erforschen, so erfahren,
> Wie Natur im Schaffen lebt.
> Und es ist das ewig Eine,
> Das sich vielfach offenbart:
> Klein das Grosse, gross das Kleine,
> Alles nach der eignen Art,
> Immer wechselnd, fest sich haltend,
> Nah und fern und fern und nah,
> So gestaltend, umgestaltend:
> Zum Erstaunen bin ich da.

> Joyfully many years ago
> Eagerly the spirit strove
> To explore, to discover
> How nature lives in creating.
> And it is that which is eternally One
> That reveals itself manifold:
> Smallness as great, greatness as small,
> Everything according to its own manner,
> Always changing, holding fast,
> Near and far and far and near,
> Thus forming, transforming:
> I exist for the sake of wonder.

Goethe's sense of wonder and his sense of creativity remain firmly planted in the soil of *this* world; the Romantics began to shift the focus of astonishment to worlds behind, beneath, or beyond, and the shift was accomplished by progressive devaluation of the visible world. Particularly in German Romanticism, and most notably in Novalis, there is a cultivation of the inner world that results, perhaps unwittingly but nevertheless inescapably, in a blurring and distortion of the outer world.

Goethe kept his distance and voiced his disapproval, but perhaps he did protest too much: a man of his great sensitivity was also tempted by the dark side of experience. Passages in the second part of *Faust* illustrate the problem—and circumnavigate it. When, during the Classical Walpurgisnacht, Faust in quest of Helen asks to be conducted to Hades, Manto welcomes the task by saying

> Den lieb' ich, der Unmögliches begehrt (l. 7488)
>
> I love him who desires the impossible.

and before entering the underworld adds

> Hier hab' ich einst den Orpheus eingeschwärzt;
> Benutz es besser! frisch! beherzt! (ll. 7493–7494)
>
> Here I once sneaked Orpheus in;
> Make better use of it! Take heart!

Manto's reference to Orpheus is jocular because she places higher hopes (subsequently fulfilled) in Faust's success; it is worth noting that Goethe refrains from depicting the actual descent despite the dramatic, lyrical, and philosophical possibilities inherent in the theme. Significantly, in Act I of *Faust II*, the hero's descent to the Mothers, an event of decisive importance to his growth, is described only externally. Mephistopheles' use of the word "Mütter" brings on a kind of fear and trembling in Faust, an intimation of the uncanny:

> FAUST: Das Schaudern is der Menschheit bestes Teil;
> Wie auch die Welt ihm das Gefühl verteure,
> Ergriffen, fühlt er tief das Ungeheure. (6272–6274)
>
> The sense of awe is man's noblest faculty;
> No matter how difficult the world makes the feeling for him,
> Enraptured, he deeply feels the uncanny.

One might expect to accompany Faust on this journey into his own depths, but again Goethe gives only the effect:

> Mein Schreckensgang bringt seligsten Gewinn.
> Wie war die Welt mir nichtig, unerschlossen!

Was ist sie nun seit meiner Priesterschaft?
Erst wünschenswert, gegründet, dauerhaft!
Verschwinde mir des Lebens Atemkraft,
Wenn ich mich je von dir zurückgewöhne! (6489–6494)

My dreadful journey is most happily rewarded.
How empty and unknown the world used to be!
And what is it now since I assumed my priestly office?
Only now it has become desirable, well-founded, durable!
May my breath fail me,
If I ever turn back from thee!

It is evident that the descent to the Mothers has radically transformed Faust: he is altered in his relationship to the world, he is passionately attached to his new being, and he even uses a term dear to the Orphics, priesthood. But the nature of this mission is not elaborated here or in subsequent passages of the drama. Goethe contents himself with the observation that the way down is terrifying and that the self is "tremendously" altered. The exact geography of the way down is left obscure; and just as there is in *Faust*, and indeed in all of Goethe's work, an avoidance of the tragic, as Erich Heller has shown,[5] so there is an avoidance of the subterranean and infernal. Such investigations would have betrayed a will to thaumaturgy, to black magic—to all that tempts Faust but upon which he must learn to turn his back.

The Romantics, and in particular the Orpheus-centered Romantics, rushed in where Goethe feared to tread. Novalis not only offers no resistance to the nocturnal powers, he passionately embraces them. He reads his own pitifully brief life as an Orphic experience and structures all of his thought and work around this experience. At approximately twenty-seven—the age at which Dante wrote his own mystical interpretation of his encounter with the living Beatrice and her death—Novalis wrote his own *vita nuova*, the *Hymnen an die Nacht*.[6] There are a number of parallels in the two poets' experiences and a number of significant differences. Both lost the girls they loved: Beatrice died at eighteen and Sophie von Kühn at fifteen. Each poet considers the event so crucial that he is prompted to reinterpret his existence with the beloved's death at the center, so that his own life history is thenceforward understood as a renewal (meeting with the beloved) that is followed by death (the axial event) and that leads to a regeneration (spiritual recovery of the beloved, along with a new resolve to conceive all future activity in her image).

With Dante, this spiritual regeneration takes the form of an analogy with Christ, as Charles Singleton shows;[7] with Novalis the analogy is with Orpheus, or with Orpheus-Christ. But Novalis' ties with this world are progressively weakened, whereas with Dante the opposite is true. In effect, Dante acquires a new vitality which animates and radiates through his great tribute to Beatrice, the *Divine Comedy*. Novalis remains, and *wills to remain*, under the shadow of death, despite his evidently sincere resolution to accept and perform his daily tasks after surmounting the initial grief over Sophie's death. But the death wish is there, in his letters and writings, so intense and voluptuous that it becomes evident that his resolution meant no more than willingness to bide cheerfully and purposefully the time allotted to him—barely three years. But even in view of this essential difference between Dante and Novalis, it can be said that Novalis' work after the *Hymnen*—particularly the romance *Heinrich von Ofterdingen* and the project of a universal encyclopedia—are monuments, albeit fragmentary ones, in celebration of Sophie: they are Novalis' Magic or Orphic Comedy.

Novalis' interest in Orpheus dates back to his early years, when he made three translations of the passage from Book IV of Vergil's *Georgics* in which Orpheus descends into Tartarus.[8] More intriguing is the verse epic in hexameters which he began, probably at the same time (about 1789), on the subject of Orpheus.[9] In his invocation (to the Muse Calliope, Orpheus' mother) Novalis passes in review the great epic poets of the past: Homer, Vergil, Ariosto, Milton, Klopstock, and Glover (Dante is not mentioned, probably because Novalis was not familiar with him), and continues:

> Vater wie lächeltst Du, wie mich die Mutter geboren
> Nicht mit erhabenem Blicke, Du weihtest mich lächelndem Scherze
> Und den sanfteren Grazien, ländlich mit Blumen gekränzet,
> Sieh drum wählt ich mir auch zu singen den sanfteren Orpheus
> Welcher die Leier zuerst mit zärtlichen Tönen begabet
> Und mit harmonischen Liedern die Sitten der Hirten gebildet
> Singend zum schrecklichen Orkus hinabstieg, welchen noch niemals
> Sterbliche Füsse berührt, von klagender Liebe getrieben;

> Father, how thou didst smile when my mother bore me,
> Not with sublime glance, thou didst ordain me for smiles and mirth
> And for the gentler Graces, with pastoral flower wreaths;
> Behold, therefore, I chose to sing the gentler Orpheus
> Who first endowed the lyre with tender notes

And with harmonious songs formed the shepherds' way of life,
And who, singing, descended to dreadful Hades, never before
Touched by mortal feet, yet was he moved by lamenting love;

When Eurydice dies, Novalis breaks the flow of hexameters to insert eight short stanzas of Orpheus' lament, demonstrating the "gentler graces" of his poetic art. This particular quality of delicacy and seductive charm is to be found in all of Novalis' subsequent work, poetry and prose alike.

About ten years later, two years after Sophie's death, Novalis composed the *Hymnen an die Nacht*. The work exists in two versions, the one printed in the *Athenäum*, in prose and verse, and a manuscript version entirely in free dithyrambic verse. Despite a number of discrepancies between the two, the prose passages generally make use of the same wording as the dithyrambic poems and can therefore be considered early examples of a poetic prose style. If Novalis had been familiar with the *Vita Nuova*, one would be inclined to say that he was attempting to adapt the prose-verse alternation of Dante's book to Romantic purposes. But actually the six hymns begin (in the *Athenäum* version, the text used here) in prose and at certain points "overflow" into verse, so that portions of the fourth and fifth hymns are in (rhymed) verse and the sixth is entirely rhymed.

This remarkable work is the *locus classicus* of the voluptuous mystique of the night and the ultimate expression of the nostalgia of death; it is the indisputable source of many of the best and most seductive passages in Wagner's *Tristan und Isolde*. The first hymn begins with what appears to be a celebration of light as "König der irdischen Natur" (lord of earthly nature), whose presence manifests the splendor of the world. But the second paragraph turns away from the luminosity of the world toward the deeper and more mysterious reality of the night: "Abwärts wend ich mich zu der heiligen, unaussprechlichen, geheimnissvollen Nacht. Fernab liegt die Welt—in eine tiefe Gruft versenkt—wüst und einsam ist ihre Stelle." (Downward I turn to the holy, ineffable, mysterious Night. The world lies remote—sunk into a deep tomb—a lonely desert in its place.) Whereas the domain of light made its appeal to the senses, the domain of night appeals to the *Gemüt*, that mysterious disposition of the soul that, with Novalis, is enthroned as the principal faculty of the Romantic sensibility, a faculty that is in contact with—indeed, in tune with—the mysterious and magic reality of the cosmos. "Wie arm und kindisch dünkt mir das Licht nun—wie erfreulich und gesegnet des Tages Abschied ... Himmlischer, als jene blitzenden

Sterne, dünken uns die unendlichen Augen, die die Nacht in uns geöffnet."
(How paltry and childish the light now seems to me—how joyous and blessed
the parting of day . . . More heavenly than those flashing stars seem to us the
infinite eyes which Night has opened in us.) As the language becomes more and
more voluptuous, Novalis identifies the encounter with the night as a reunion
with the beloved ("liebliche Sonne der Nacht," lovely nocturnal sun) and an
eternal nuptial night.

The second hymn laments the intrusion of daylight: "Muss immer der
Morgen wiederkommen? Endet nie des Irdischen Gewalt?" (Must morning
always return? Will the earth's violence never end?) The answer is suggested a
moment later: "Zugemessen ward den Lichte seine Zeit; aber zeitlos und raum-
los ist der Nacht Herrschaft." (To Light was allotted its time; but Night's
dominion is timeless and spaceless.) The night is infinite and therefore infinitely
greater than finite day. Sleep is eternal and holy and is therefore a capacity and a
seal that those consecrated to night ("der Nacht Geweihte") possess as a sign of
their election.

The first two hymns propose a kind of uneven dialectic between day and
night, outer world and inner world, surface and depth, sense and *Gemüt*. It is
uneven because for Novalis night is infinite and therefore comprises day. One
expects a cosmogonic myth here but must wait for it until the fifth hymn. The
third and fourth are intensely personal; they grow out of the very center of
Novalis' own regeneration after Sophie's death and must be understood in light
of that experience. Novalis' diary, begun a month after Sophie's death, is helpful.
On May 13, 1797, he writes:

Abends ging ich zu Sophien. Dort war ich unbeschreiblich freudig—aufblitzende En-
thusiasmusmomente—das Grab blies wie ein Staub vor mir him—Jahrhunderte waren
wie Momente—ihre Nähe war fühlbar—ich glaubte, sie solle immer vortreten.[10]

In the evening I went to Sophie. There I was indescribably joyous—flashes of enthusiasm
—the grave fell apart before me, like dust—centuries were like moments—her nearness
was tangible—I thought she was always about to appear.

This is the axial moment in Novalis' life: Sophie's death is, as it were, annihilated, time is compressed into a mystical moment of vision. Later entries evidence a deepening sense of indissolubility with Sophie, accompanied by a greater
spiritual calmness but always the quiet resolution to join her in death. But the
emphasis shifts from planned suicide to a quiet longing for death. A number of
diary entries document this development.

Ich muss nur immer mehr um Ihretwillen leben—für Sie bin ich nur—für mich und keinen anderen nicht. Sie ist das Höchste—das Einzige. Wenn ich nur in jedem Augenblick ihrer wert sein könnte. Meine Hauptaufgabe sollte sein—alles in Beziehung auf ihre Idee zu bringen.

Die Welt wird immer fremder. Die Dinge um mich her immer gleichgültiger. Desto *heller* wird es jetzt um mich und in mir.

An S. hab ich fleissig gedacht—besonders ist mir lebhaft geworden, dass mich die schönsten wissenschaftlichen und anderen Aussichten nicht auf der Welt zurückhalten müssen. Mein Tod soll Beweis meines Gefühls für das Höchste sein, echte Aufopferung —nicht Flucht—nicht Notmittel.

Sie ist gestorben—so sterb ich auch—die Welt ist öde. Selbst meine philosophischen Studien sollen mich nicht mehr stören. In tiefer, heitrer Ruh will ich den Augenblick erwarten, der mich ruft.

Christus und *Sophie.*

Verbindung, die auch für den Tod geschlossen ist—ist eine Hochzeit—die uns eine Genossin für die Nacht gibt. In Tode ist die Liebe am süssesten; für den Liebenden ist der Tod eine Brautnacht—ein Geheimnis süsser Mysterien.

Liebe, vom Herzen unabhängige, auf Glauben gegründete Liebe, ist Religion.[11]

I must live for her sake more and more—I live only for her—not for myself or anyone else. She is the highest, the only thing. If I could only be worthy of her every instant. My chief task ought to be: to relate everything to what she stands for.

The world is becoming more and more alien. Things around me [are] more and more indifferent. Yet around me and within me everything is becoming *brighter.*

I have thought a great deal about S.—I have become vividly aware that the most valuable scientific and other projects must not be allowed to bind me to the world. My death is to be the proof of my sentiment for what is highest, genuine sacrifice—not escape—not an expedient.

She has died—thus I too will die—the world is a desert. Not even my philosophical studies will hinder me. In deep and joyous tranquillity I shall await the moment when I am to be called.

Christ and *Sophie.*

A union that has been contracted even unto death is a true marriage—it gives us a companion for the night. In death love is sweetest; for the lover death is a wedding night—a secret of sweet mysteries.

Love, independent of the heart, love founded upon faith, that is religion.

These diary notes reveal Novalis' incipient and willed alienation from the world and, finally, his curious identification of Sophie with Christ. This, in turn, explains the redefinition of his relationship with Sophie as a religious engagement: absolute love is religion.

The third and fourth hymns transpose the tombstone vision into its symbolic equivalent: the new life in Sophie.

. . . mit einemmale riss das Band der Geburt—des Lichtes Fessel. Hin floh die irdische Herrlichkeit und meine Trauer mit ihr—zusammen floss die Wehmuth in eine neue, unergründliche Welt—der Nachtbegeisterung, Schlummer des Himmels kamst über mich—die Gegend hob sich sacht empor; über der Gegend schwebte mein entbundener, neugeborner Geist. Zur Staubwolke wurde der Hügel—durch die Wolke sah ich die verklärten Züge der Geliebten . . . Es war der erste, einzige Traum—und erst seitdem fühl ich ewigen, unwandelbaren Glauben an den Himmel der Nacht und sein Licht, die Geliebte.

. . . suddenly the umbilical cord snapped—the rope of light which shackles us. Earthly splendor vanished, and with it my sorrow—melancholy fused into a new, infathomable world—that of night-enthusiasm; heavenly slumber, thou didst take hold of me—the landscape rose gently; above the landscape there soared a new-born spirit. The hill turned into a cloud of dust—through the cloud I saw the transfigured features of the loved one . . . It was the first and only dream—and only since that moment I feel an eternal and changeless faith in the heaven of night and its light, the loved one.

The new element introduced by Novalis into this synthesis of the vision of Sophie is the "dream"—the amplification of the notion of sleep in the second hymn that is provided by endowing it with a content which is in contact with the deeper reality of the imagination. At this point Novalis joins hands with Coleridge, and of course with his friend Friedrich Schlegel, in regard to the primacy of the imagination—and with Keats in his meditation on sleep and poetry. Novalis discovers the link between dream and poetry; and the path is cleared for Romantic, symbolist, and surrealist verse.

The vision leads to a conversion: what was formerly consecration now becomes mission. The poet rejects totally the realm of daylight and envisages a new, apocalyptic era in which day will dissolve into night and sleep into dream. And the Sophie-Christ theme hinted at in the diary becomes more explicit in Novalis' identification of holy tomb and holy sepulcher:

Nun weiss ich, wenn der letzte Morgen seyn wird—wenn das Licht nicht mehr die Nacht und die Liebe scheucht—wenn der Schlummer ewig und nur Ein unerschöpf-licher Traum seyn wird. Himmlische Müdigkeit fühl ich in mir. Weit und ermüdend ward mir die Wallfahrt zum heiligen Grabe, drückend das Kreutz.

Now I know when the last morning will be—when the light no longer banishes night and love—when sleep is eternal and but one inexhaustible dream. I feel heavenly weari-ness in myself. Long and wearisome grew the pilgrimage to the holy sepulcher for me, oppressive grew the cross.

The language becomes more and more sensual as Novalis meditates enthusi-astically upon the ravishments of night, that great mother who has sent the poet into the light so that he may serve as an apostle to night among the children of light. ("Zu bewohnen deine Welt / Und zu heiligen sie / Mit Liebe. / Zu geben / Menschlichen Sinn / Deinen Schöpfungen"—To dwell in thy world and to consecrate it with love. To give human meaning to thy creations.) Now Novalis breaks into rhyme with a canticle celebrating, erotically and swoon-ingly, the sweetness of death and regeneration in death.

The fifth hymn leaves behind the personal experience, translating it into a cosmological-apocalyptic myth. As is frequently the case with Gnostic cos-mogonies (and, interestingly enough, nineteenth-century historical thought), the first of three aeons is ruled by the iron law of fate, presided over by the gods dwelling on earth and illuminated by the rays of the sun. Nevertheless, it is a happy period of mankind—the springtime, the childhood of the human race—in which the gods communicate freely with each other and nature is attuned to man. But this paradisaic infancy of the world is shattered by the nightmarish appearance of death. (One must refrain from asking detailed explanations of Novalis: this cosmogony has all the characteristics of a romantic *Märchen*.) The aeon ends with the retreat of the gods, man's loss of innocence, the dereliction of nature; destiny is superseded by mere necessity (number and measure), belief and imagination vanish from the earth, and the gods return to night and slumber.

The transition from the second to the third and final phase is effected in the East with the birth of Christ and infused with poetic and prophetic significance by the Orphic singer. Nowhere in the *Hymnen an die Nacht* is Orpheus mentioned by name, but the Orphic characteristics of the bard are unmistakable: Novalis adapts for his own uses the hermetic myth of the coincidence of Greek-Palestinian-Eastern Gnostic revelation:

Von ferner Küste, unter Hellas heiterm Himmel geboren, kam ein Sänger nach Palästina und ergab sein ganzes Herz dem Wunderkinde:

> Der Jüngling bist du, der seit langer Zeit
> Auf unsern Gräbern steht in tiefen Sinnen;
> Ein tröstlich Zeichen in der Dunkelheit—
> Der höhern Menschheit freudiges Beginnen.
> Was uns gesenkt in tiefe Traurigkeit
> Zieht uns mit süsser Sehnsucht nun von hinnen.
> Im Tode ward das ewge Leben kund,
> Du bist der Tod und machst uns erst gesund.

Der Sänger zog voll Freudigkeit nach Indostan—das Herz von süsser Liebe trunken; und schüttete in feurigen Gesängen es unter jenem milden Himmel aus, dass tausend Herzen sich zu ihm neigten, und die fröhliche Botschaft tausendzweigig emporwuchs.

From distant shores, born under the happy sky of Hellas, a bard wandered to Palestine and offered his entire heart to the wonder-child:

> Thou art the youth who since long ago
> Has stood on our tomb in deep thought;
> A sign of consolation in the darkness—
> The joyful beginning of a higher humanity.
> Whatever has plunged us into deep sadness
> Now draws us away with sweet longing.
> In death was eternal life proclaimed,
> Thou art Death and now makest us healthy.

The bard joyfully wandered to Hindustan—his heart drunk with sweet love, and poured it out in fiery songs under that clement sky, so that a thousand hearts turned toward him, and the joyous gospel sprouted a thousand branches.

Thus the Orphic bard becomes a magus from the North on his eastward journey (a reversal of the Dionysiac myth in which Dionysus journeys west), whose wisdom concerning the renovating power of death will coincide with and be confirmed by the Resurrection. In this sense, both the Orphic singer and

Christ are "healers": consequently, it is the Resurrection that ushers in the final phase of redemption. Instead of continuing the prose fable, Novalis concludes the hymns in a lyrical outburst very close in style to the *Geistliche Lieder* written after the hymns. All that is indicated is a utopian resolution of the divisions and disharmonies introduced by death:

> Die Lieb ist frey gegeben,
> Und keine Trennung mehr.
> Es wogt das volle Leben
> Wie ein unendlich Meer.
> Nur eine Nacht der Wonne—
> Ein ewiges Gedicht—
> Und unser aller Sonne
> Ist Gottes Angesicht.

> Love has been set free,
> No more division.
> Full life surges
> Like an infinite sea.
> Only one night of rapture—
> One eternal poem—
> And our own sun
> Is God's countenance.

Is it to be understood, then, that the annihilation of death would restore the first age, the age of childhood and sunlight and the presence of the gods? Evidently not, since Novalis casts this redemption in the form of nocturnal bliss and, somewhat unexpectedly, introduces (for the first time) God's countenance as a "nocturnal sun." The convergence of opposites that Novalis is striving for—the union of night and day, mother and father, death and life—implies an age prior to the first age, barely hinted at in a passage of the fifth hymn that implies a shackling of the Titans prior to the advent of the gods. ("Fest unter Bergen lagen die Ursöhne der Mutter Erde. Ohnmächtig in ihrer zerstörenden Wuth gegen das neue herrliche Göttergeschlecht und dessen Verwandten, die fröhlichen Menschen." Fixed beneath mountains lay the primal sons of Mother Earth. Impotent in their destructive wrath against the new magnificent race of the gods and their kin, happy mankind.) But this smacks of Hesiodic and Orphic cosmogonies, rather than of the Romantic Golden Age that Novalis' apocalypse suggests. In some respects, it looks as if Novalis were about to parallel Blake's perception that a New Jerusalem cannot be identical with the primordial Garden of Eden, and then develop an original Orphic-Christian *eschaton*, a cosmogonic sequence: gods—Mother-Father, in which God the Father is to reveal himself, or become manifest, only in the final aeon. But all this remains a matter of speculation because Novalis has not worked out the question in any detail; moreover, he continues to be intoxicated by night and death to such an extent that a true convergence of opposites cannot possibly result.

The sixth and final hymn, subtitled "Sehnsucht nach dem Tode" (longing for death), only compounds the difficulty. Here are some lines from the beginning stanzas:

> Hinunter in der Erde Schooss,
> Weg aus des Lichtes Reichen . . .
>
> Gelobt sey uns die ewge Nacht,
> Gelobt der ewge Schlummer . . .
> Zum Vater wollen wir nach Haus.

> Downward into the womb of the earth,
> away from the realms of the light . . .
>
> Praised be for us the eternal night,
> Praised be eternal slumber . . .
> We want to return home to the Father.

The four central stanzas deal with what Novalis calls "die Vorzeit"—the suggestion is therefore that he did imply a primordial age intentionally and that this age resembles the first phase of mankind in most respects, except for the fact that it is described monotheistically:

> Die Vorzeit, wo die Sinne licht
> In hohen Flammen brannten,
> Des Vaters Hand und Augensicht
> Die Menschen noch erkannten.
> . . .
> Wir müssen nach der Heymath gehn,
> Um diese heilge Zeit zu sehn.

35

> Primeval time, when the senses brightly
> Burned in tall flames,
> When men still recognized
> Their Father's hand and eye
>
> . . .
>
> We must return home
> To see this holy time.

So all redemption is a "homecoming," as Novalis insisted again in *Heinrich von Ofterdingen*. This is traditional apocalyptic thinking, according to which what will be is an identical repetition of what once was. The final stanza points in this direction, though it is obfuscated by the Jesus-Sophie and Mother-Father equation:

> Hinunter zu der süssen Braut,
> Zu Jesus, dem Geliebten—
> Getrost, die Abenddämmrung graut
> Den Liebenden, Betrübten.
> Ein Traum bricht unsre Banden los
> Und senkt uns in des Vaters Schooss.

> Downward to the sweet bride,
> To Jesus the Beloved—
> Take heart, twilight darkens
> For lovers, for the dejected.
> A dream shatters our bonds
> And draws us down into the Father's lap.

The confusion in Novalis is due to an excessive Dionysiac intoxication with night and death that threatens to disrupt whatever Orphic balance he set out to present in his thought and poetry. The Romantic mind, despite its rage for order and equilibrium, was persistently in danger of losing its perspective. Another example of this precarious balance between the demands of the diurnal and the nocturnal, written practically at the same time as Novalis' *Hymnen*, is Hölderlin's elegy "Brot und Wein" (1800). At a glance, Novalis' and Hölderlin's treatment of the night may appear quite similar; Hölderlin, too, is concerned with a consecration of the night, its power to arouse enthusiasm, its mystery. And yet, he maintains an intelligible balance between the powers of daylight and the powers of darkness:

Wunderbar ist die Gunst der Hocherhaben und niemand
  Weiss von wannen und was einem geschiehet von ihr.
So bewegt sie die Welt und die hoffende Seele der Menschen,
  Selbst kein Weiser versteht, was sie bereitet, denn so
Will es der oberste Gott, der sehr dich liebet, und darum
  Ist noch lieber, wie sie [die Nacht], dir der besonnene Tag.
Aber zuweilen liebt auch klares Auge den Schatten
  Und versuchet zu Lust, eh' es die Not ist, den Schlaf,
Oder es blickt auch gern ein treuer Mann in die Nacht hin,
  Ja, es ziemt sich, ihr Kränze zu weihn und Gesang,
Weil den Irrenden sie geheiligt ist und den Toten,
  Selbst aber besteht, ewig, in freiestem Geist.
Aber sie muss uns auch, dass in der zaudernden Weile,
  Dass im Finstern für uns einiges Haltbare sei,
Uns die Vergessenheit und das Heiligtrunkene gönnen,
  Gönnen das strömende Wort, das, wie die Liebenden, sei,
Schlummerlos und vollern Pokal und kühneres Leben,
  Heilig Gedächtnis auch, wachend zu bleiben bei Nacht.

Marvelous is the favor of that sublime one on high [night], and no one
  Knows from where [she comes] and what happens to us because of her.
Thus she moves the world and the hopeful soul of men,
  And not even a wise man understands what she has in store for us, for such
Is the will of the supreme God, who loves you greatly, and therefore
  You value more highly than her [night] the lucidity of day.
But at times even a clear-seeing eye prefers shadow
  And attempts, for pleasure's sake and before it is necessary, to sleep,
Or a loyal man likes to look into the night,
  Indeed, it is fitting to consecrate wreaths to her and song,
For she is sacred to those erring and to the dead,
  Yet endures herself, eternally, in the utmost freedom of spirit.
But she must grant us, so that in the instant of hesitation,
  So that there might be something for us to cling to in the darkness,
She must grant us oblivion and sacred rapture,
  Grant us the word rushing forth, so that it may be, like lovers,
Sleepless, so that the cup may be fuller and life more daring,
  And she must grant us also holy remembrance, to remain waking at night.

Hölderlin's night, unlike Novalis', is a consecrated time of waiting and attention; it offers some stability in the dark, and demands wakefulness. How different—despite superficial resemblances—from Novalis' wilting swoons, his erotic *frissons*! The real difference between the two poets is a matter of historical consciousness and the resultant mythical interpretation given to it. Both live in a time of darkness—something like the second phase of Novalis' tripartite pattern —awaiting an eschatological transformation of the aeon. Hölderlin in "Brot und Wein" understands the situation in cyclical terms: the gods have receded (as in Novalis), and we are living in darkness. But the darkness is a preparation for a new coming; night will yield to day once more; the tension between day (divine presence) and night (divine absence) remains fruitful and mysterious— whereas in Novalis the effort is solely directed toward the abolition of day or, rather, its absorption into the night. Hölderlin's historical thinking is cyclical, in the tradition of antiquity; Novalis' thought is essentially transhistorical (reinforced by certain Christian features), that is, utopian and apocalyptic.

The essay *Die Christenheit oder Europa* of 1799 is a case in point because it is concerned with a historical problem, Christian community versus secularized multiplicity. This effusive bit of historiography, quintessentially romantic in its "enthusiasm," begins with an idealization of the Middle Ages:

Es waren schöne glänzende Zeiten, wo Europa ein christliches Land war, wo *eine* Christenheit diesen menschlich gestalteten Weltteil bewohnte; *ein* grosses gemeinschaftliches Interesse verband die entlegensten Provinzen dieses weiten geistlichen Reichs.[12]

Those were beautiful, splendid times, when Europe was a Christian land, when *one* Christendom inhabited this continent shaped by men; *one* great common interest bound together the most farflung provinces of this vast spiritual domain.

The pattern of historical thinking is, again, tripartite. At the beginning there was a religious utopia ("echtkatholisch oder echtchristlich,"[13] arch-Catholic or arch-Christian), but mankind was not ready for it; then came the fragmentation, the Reformation, which Novalis takes to task here only for having divided Christendom. This in turn led to the Enlightenment and the suppression of enthusiasm, which resulted in perverting

die unendliche schöpferische Musik des Weltalls zum einförmigen Klappern einer ungeheuren Mühle, die vom Strom des Zufalls getrieben und auf ihm schwimmend, eine Mühle an sich, ohne Baumeister und Müller und eigentlich ein echtes Perpetuum mobile, eine sich selbst mahlende Mühle sei.[14]

the infinite creative music of the universe into the uniform rattle of a monstrous mill turned by the currents of chance and swimming in it, a mill in itself, without architect or miller; in fact, a real perpetuum mobile, a mill grinding itself.

The image of the mill grinding itself is a striking image, with its perpetual rattle and aimless monotony: it is an image of the world bereft of Orpheus. Only the third phase, the promise of a reawakening following upon the heels of the French Revolution, promises a restoration of a new Middle Ages, a metamorphosis of secularized Europe into a new Christendom.

Nur die Religion kann Europa wieder aufwecken und die Völker sichern, und die Christenheit mit neuer Herrlichkeit sichtbar auf Erden in ihr altes, friedenstiftendes Amt installieren.[15]

Only religion can reawaken Europe and give security to its peoples, and install Christendom visibly on earth in its ancient, peacemaking mission, in a new kind of glory.

In brief, Novalis' historical thinking is in the traditional form of romantic Christianity: paradise, the interregnum of disorder, the new Jerusalem. This scheme works better as myth (in *Hymnen an die Nacht*) than as history (in the present example), but it does show the tenacious quality of paradisaical nostalgia in Novalis and other Romantics. Mircea Eliade notes the persistence of this theme, particularly in certain authors whose intellects have been bent on discovering a convergence of opposites: "From a certain point of view, it might be said that a number of beliefs involving the *coincidentia oppositorum* reveal a nostalgia for a lost Paradise, a nostalgia for a paradoxical state of affairs in which contraries coexist without, however, getting in each other's way, and where multiplicity makes up the facets of a mysterious Unity."[16] Any number of passages in Novalis could be used to demonstrate the aptness of this observation; here is a characteristic example.

Das Paradies ist gleichsam über die ganze Erde verstreut—und daher so unerkenntlich usw. geworden—seine zerstreuten Züge sollen vereinigt—sein Skelett soll ausgefüllt werden. Regeneration des Paradieses.[17]

Paradise is, as it were, dispersed over the entire earth—and for this reason has become so unrecognizable, and so forth—its scattered features must be reunited—its skeleton must be fleshed. Regeneration of Paradise.

The final aim of Novalis' historical vision is the abolition of time and history

(history becomes the "Traum einer unendlichen, unabsehbaren Gegenwart,"[18] the dream of an endless, boundless present), but not the displacement of a dark cycle by an illuminated cycle.

> Aber das Irrsal
> Hilft, wie Schlummer, und stark machet die Not und die Nacht,
> Bis dass Helden genug in der ehernen Wiege gewachsen,

> But error
> Helps, like sleep, and need and night make strong,
> Until enough heroes have grown in the brazen cradle,

writes Hölderlin: even the nocturnal confusion serves a constructive purpose. The poet's task in these times of deprivation ("wozu Dichter in dürftiger Zeit?" —why be a poet in a time of destitution?) is to be like those priests of Dionysus who celebrated the god in anticipation of his return and who prepared the *kairos* itself. The god to come in Hölderlin's theophany bears the features of Dionysus, Hercules and Christ; his task is to restore the balance of night and day ("Ja! sie sagen mit Recht, er söhne den Tag mit der Nacht aus"), the sense of the divine to mankind, until the divine Father is once more recognized by men and belongs to them. The word "recognize" is the key word. Whereas Novalis strives for mystical annihilation, Hölderlin strives for theophany, epiphany:

> . . . aber so vieles geschieht,
> Keines wirket, denn wir sind herzlos, Schatten, bis unser
> Vater Äther erkannt jeden und allen gehört.

> . . . but so many things happen,
> None of them effective, for we lack hearts, we are shades, until our
> Father Aether, once recognized, belongs to each and all.

Novalis' work from 1800 to his death in 1802 was a courageous, tenacious, and utterly excessive attempt to construct a romantic synthesis, the kernel of which lies in the Sophie experience and its allegorization in the *Hymnen an die Nacht*. This frenzy for synthesis and "symphilosophy," as Novalis called it, had its intellectual equivalent in his post-Kantian contemporaries such as Fichte, Franz von Baader, Schelling, and Hegel. Fichte was perhaps the most influential, but Novalis' closest affinity was with von Baader, for whom the notion of philosophical systems was a matter of organic inter-relationships rather than a composite sequence of propositions.[19] Novalis' project was no less than the compilation of an encyclopedia of universal knowledge, related in theme to the *Encyclopédie* of the eighteenth century, yet vastly different in method and scope—the work of one man, one sensibility, rather than a team of experts. With the aid of voluminous reading (which he had done all his life) and intensified studies of all sciences, Novalis proposed a romantic synthesis of all fields of knowledge— philosophy, mathematics, the natural sciences, the biological sciences, philology and aesthetics, history and politics, the human sciences and ethics, and the crowning "magische Wissenschaft," culminating in cosmology and religion. It is obvious that even if he had lived twice as long as he did, he would not have been able to complete such a work—the word "complete" seems altogether meaningless in such a context of cosmic integration. Here, truly, is a striking instance of a human attempt to equal, or at least to reproduce, the totality and intricacy of Creation itself.

Novalis thought of his encyclopedia as a bible, a revelation of reality theretofore inadequately glimpsed. "Mein Buch soll eine szientifische Bibel werden— ein reales und ideales Muster—und Keim aller Bücher"[20] (my book is to be a scientific bible—a real and ideal model—and germ of all books). The achievement, despite its fragmentary character, is remarkable; Novalis left some eighteen hundred scattered notes and aphorisms that encompass at least microcosmically the grand design. The aphorism serves, as Theodor Haering points out,[21] the purpose of a part that has its place, its function, in the overall organism, in contrast with the lapidary aphorisms of Schlegel, which suggest or solicit elaboration in the mind of the reader. Perhaps it would be better to think of Novalis' fragments as fractions, or segments, that would have taken their allotted place in the completed whole. This encyclopedic totality is consistent in its thoroughgoing attempt to dissolve the distinction between objective and subjective, between science and magic, between the natural, the human, and the divine. Although the enterprise does not really make Novalis into the consistent philosopher Haering believes him to be, it does point up the unifying thrust of his thinking. "Den Satz des Widerspruchs zu vernichten ist vielleicht die höchste Aufgabe der höheren Logik"[22] (to annihilate the law of contradiction is perhaps the highest task of higher logic).

But this higher logic is really poetry conceived as magic, a religious instrument capable of transforming the world: "Die Poesie ist das echt absolut Reelle. Das ist der Kern meiner Philosophie. Je poetischer, je wahrer."[23] (Poetry is that which is genuinely, absolutely real. That is the core of my philosophy. The more poetical, the truer.) In other words, Novalis' notion of poetry, religion, and philosophy is thoroughly Orphic. Michael Hamburger puts this succinctly when he says: "Although he is rarely mentioned by name, the invisible hero of [Heinrich von Ofterdingen] and of all Novalis' work is Orpheus."[24] As a matter of fact, just as the encyclopedia was to reveal reality just as it is (by an abolition of contraries and a demonstration of their unity), so the novel-romance *Heinrich von Ofterdingen* was to reveal the identity, or interchangeability, of dream and world ("Die Welt wird Traum, der Traum wird Welt"). The romance acquires more and more Orphic density as it moves from outward to inner life; and although the completed portions of *Ofterdingen* represent only a portion of the projected romance, which in turn was probably to have constituted only one unit in a larger series of interconnected units (in this respect a parallel to the encyclopedia), there is some indication that the conclusion of *Ofterdingen* was planned as an Orphic apotheosis. In terms of the work's structure, this means that the progress of poetic revelation and vatic prophecy was to be marked by an ever-increasing utilization of the "fabulous," the *Märchen*. *Heinrich von Ofterdingen* was conceived of as a counterpart and corrective of Goethe's *Wilhelm Meisters Lehrjahre*—which Novalis regarded, despite his unmistakable admiration for the novel, as a " 'Candide,' gegen die Poesie gerichtet" and "durchaus prosaisch—und modern" (*Candide* aimed at poetry . . . thoroughly prosaic—and modern) because it was antithetical to the romantic: "Das Romantische geht darin zugrunde—auch die Naturpoesie, das Wunderbare"[25] (whatever is romantic in it perishes—as well as nature poetry, the marvelous). Accordingly, *Ofterdingen* was to be the romantic and poetic rejoinder to Goethe's antiromantic "prose." This accounts for the strongly didactic and exemplary nature of Novalis' novel-romance, which proceeds from *Erziehungsroman* to *Kunstmärchen* and in which fables serve as pedagogical and initiatory culminations of Heinrich's progress from outer to inner, from ordinary existence to Orphic mission; in brief, the work begins as a novel, becomes increasingly a romance, and ends in myth. The following fragments from the encyclopedia are illustrative of Novalis' conviction:

Ein Roman muss durch und durch Poesie sein. Die Poesie ist nämlich, wie die Philosophie, eine harmonische Stimmung unseres Gemüts, wo sich alles verschönert, wo jedes Ding seine gehörige Ansicht—alles seine passende Begleitung und Umgebung findet. Es scheint in einem recht poetischen Buche alles so natürlich—und doch so wunderbar— Man glaubt, es könne nicht anders sein und als habe man nur bisher in der Welt ge-

schlummert—und gehe einem nun erst der rechte Sinn für die Welt auf.
Im Märchen glaub ich am besten meine Gemütsstimmung ausdrücken zu können.[26]

A novel must be poetry through and through. Poetry is, like philosophy, a harmonious attunement of our disposition, where everything becomes embellished, where every object finds its appropriate perspective and everything its suitable accompaniment and environment. In a really poetic book everything seems so natural—and yet so wonderful —you feel it could not be otherwise, as though you had up to now been asleep in the world, and only now your eyes were opened.
I think I can best express the temper of my disposition by means of the fable.

The first part of *Ofterdingen*, entitled "Erwartung" (anticipation), is high-lighted by three such *Märchen* (fables). The first, a retelling of the myth of Arion, sets the Orphic mood (already implicit at the very beginning when Heinrich recounts his dream of the "blaue Blume") for the later ones (not *directly* Orphic but closely related to the poetic *Stimmung* of the whole) and specifically for the second part, "Erfüllung" (fulfillment), which remains uncompleted. The merchants, who collectively tell the first *Märchen* to Heinrich, preface their narration by alluding to the greater vitality and symbolic richness of nature in olden times. Speaking of ancient Greece, they report the existence of poets

die durch den seltsamen Klang wunderbarer Werkzeuge das geheime Leben der Wälder, die in den Stämmen verborgenen Geister aufgeweckt, in wüsten, verödeten Gegenden den toten Pflanzensamen erregt, und blühende Gärten hervorgerufen, grausame Tiere gezähmt und verwilderte Menschen zu Ordnung und Sitte gewöhnt, sanfte Neigungen und Künste des Friedens in ihnen rege gemacht, reissende Flüsse in milde Gewässer verwandelt, und selbst die totesten Steine in regelmässige tanzende Bewegungen hinge-rissen haben. Sie sollen zugleich Wahrsager und Priester, Gesetzgeber und Ärzte gewesen sein, indem selbst die höheren Wesen durch ihre zauberische Kraft herabgezogen worden sind, und sie in den Geheimnissen der Zukunft unterrichtet, das Ebenmass und die natürliche Einrichtung aller Dinge, auch die innern Tugenden und Heilkräfte der Zah-len, Gewächse und aller Kreaturen, ihnen offenbart. Seitdem sollen, wie die Sage lautet, erst die mannifaltigen Töne und die sonderbaren Sympathien und Ordnungen in die Natur gekommen sein, indem vorher alles wild, unordentlich und feindselig gewesen ist. Seltsam ist nur hiebei, dass zwar diese schönen Spuren, zum Andenken der Gegenwart jener wohltätigen Menschen, geblichen sind, aber entweder ihre Kunst, oder jene zarte Gefühligkeit der Natur verloren gegangen ist.[27]

who by means of the strange sounds of wonderful instruments awakened the secret life of forests and the hidden spirits in the treetrunks; in desert regions brought to life the

dead plant seeds and caused flowering gardens to grow; tamed cruel beasts and habituated savage men to order and morality, activated gentle inclinations and the arts of peace in them; transformed rushing torrents into gentle streams; and incited even the most inert stones to regular dancing movements. They are thought to have been soothsayers and priests, legislators and physicians, by virtue of the fact that even the higher beings were invoked by their magic power and instructed them in the secrets of the future, in the arts of proportion and the natural organization of all things, and revealed to them the virtues and healing powers of numbers, plants, and all creatures. According to reports, only since that time did the manifold sounds and the particular sympathies and orders come into nature, whereas formerly everything was wild, disorderly, and hostile. The only strange aspect of all this is that, though the lovely vestiges that would help us remember the presence of those benevolent men have faded, either their art or that tenderness of nature has been lost.

The second *Märchen*, based on the myth of Atlantis, deals with the love story of a poet and stresses once more the Orphic interpenetration of art and nature. The final one, which concludes the first part of *Ofterdingen*, is a culminating allegory (a *Kunstmärchen*) of Eros and Fable, cosmological in scope and setting and extremely complex in organization; it deals with the interaction of love and the poetic imagination and goes through a fantastic series of metamorphoses in which—as in the *Hymnen*—the old is abolished and renewed under the aegis of peace, the poetic imagination, and wisdom, here conceived of as Hagia Sophia: Sophie the woman and her abstract symbolic meaning: "Sophie ist ewig Priesterin der Herzen"[28] (Sophie is forever the priestess of hearts).

In the second part of the romance, Heinrich's beloved Mathilde has died and he has become a pilgrim. In the course of his wanderings and by virtue of his experience he has now become the Orphic poet:

Es dünkte ihm nunmehr alles viel bekannter und weissagender als ehemals, so dass ihm der Tod wie eine höhere Offenbarung des Lebens erschien, und er sein eigenes, schnell vorübergehendes Dasein mit kindlicher, heiterer Rührung betrachtete. Zukunft und Vergangenheit hatten sich in ihm berührt und einen innigen Verein geschlossen; er stand weit ausser der Gegenwart, und die Welt ward ihm erst teuer, als er sie verloren hatte und sich nur als Fremdling in ihr fand, der ihre weiten, bunten, Säle noch eine kurze Weile durchwandern sollte.[29]

Henceforth everything seemed to him more familiar and more prophetic than before, so that death seemed to him like a higher revelation of life; and he contemplated his own fleeting existence with a childish and gay emotion. Future and past had touched within him and concluded an intimate union; he stood far outside the present, and the world became precious to him only after he had lost it and found himself in it merely as a stranger who was to wander only for a brief while through its spacious and colorful hallways.

At this point the fantasies of the first part, and in particular of the Eros-Fable *Märchen*, become realities: everything is metamorphosed, earlier figures reappear in different guises, departed souls are reincarnated. In this final "homecoming," this ultimate fulfillment, the true significance of Novalis' poetics is disclosed as an instrument for attaining the cosmic poem (*Weltgedicht*):

Wie sich die Religion zur Tugend verhält [says Heinrich], so die Begeisterung zur Fabellehre, und wenn in heiligen Schriften die Geschichten der Offenbarung aufbehalten sind, so bildet in den Fabellehren das Leben einer höheren Welt sich in wunderbar entstandnen Dichtungen auf mannigfache Weise ab. Fabel und Geschichte begleiten sich in den innigsten Beziehungen auf den verschlungensten Pfaden und in den seltsamsten Verkleidungen, und die Bibel und die Fabellehre sind Sternbilder *eines* Umlaufs.[30]

As religion is to virtue, so is enthusiasm to fabulation; and just as the sacred scriptures conserve the histories of revelation, so the fables reflect variously the life of a higher world in marvelous poetic creations. Fable and history move hand in hand in the most intimate manner and along the most entangled paths and in the strangest guises; and the Bible and the fable are the constellations of *one single* cycle of rotation.

The two creations, the encyclopedic "bible" and the fabulous revelation, reflect each other allegorically because for Novalis they are actually aspects of the same reality, and this reality will finally be revealed as single and unique. Sylvester, the sage of this chapter, declares:

Euch wird alles verständlich werden, und die Welt und ihre Geschichte verwandelt sich Euch in die Heilige Schrift, so wie Ihr an der Heiligen Schrift das grosse Beispiel habt, wie in einfachen Worten und Geschichten das Weltall offenbart werden kann.[31]

Everything will become meaningful to you, and the world and its history will be transformed for you into Holy Scripture, just as the Holy Scripture is your great example of how the universe can be revealed in simple words and stories.

A page later the text breaks off. Wilhelm Tieck made fairly extensive notes concerning the plans for continuation based on conversations with Novalis and notes that the poet left behind; also extant is a sheaf of notes in the poet's own hand. It is somewhat risky to assume that these jottings or reports represent Novalis' full-fledged plans. There is reason to believe that in the two years during which he worked on the continuation of *Ofterdingen*, while suffering from a fatal illness, he changed his mind several times as to specific details and would no doubt have continued to modify them further. However, a few points are worthy of attention. Tieck reports: "Hier ist die christliche Religion mit der heidnischen ausgesöhnt, die Geschichte des Orpheus, der Psyche, und andere werden besungen" (here Christianity and paganism are reconciled; the story of Orpheus, Psyche and others are celebrated). The same notation occurs in Novalis' papers.[32] An interesting idea is projected in the following notebook entry, in which the Orpheus-Eurydice pattern is reversed:

Heinrich gerät unter Bacchantinnen—Sie töten ihn—der Hebrus tönt von der schwimmenden Leier. Umgekehrtes Märchen. Mathilde steigt in die Unterwelt und holt ihn. Poetische Parodie auf Amphion.[33]

Heinrich strays among the Bacchantes—They kill him—the river Hebrus resounds with the floating lyre. The fable reversed. Mathilde descends to the underworld and brings him back. Poetic parody of Amphion.

Apparently one of Heinrich's final exploits was to have been the destruction of the sun's empire, followed, according to Tieck, by a long poem celebrating the nuptials of the seasons. Tieck quotes the twenty-four lines that were completed. The poem, in elegiac meter, is quite evidently an Orphic hymn in which time and suffering are negated in a new synthetic unity:

> Wären die Zeiten nicht so ungesellig, verbände
> Zukunft mit Gegenwart und mit Vergangenheit sich,
> Schlösse Frühling sich an Herbst, und Sommer an Winter,
> Wäre zu spielendem Ernst Jugend mit Alter gepaart:
> Dann, mein süsser Gemahl, versiegte die Quelle der Schmerzen,
> Aller Empfindungen Wunsch wäre dem Herzen gewährt.[34]

> If the times were not so unsociable, if
> Future were joined to present and to past,
> If spring were joined to fall, and summer to winter,
> If for playful seriousness youth and age were paired:
> Then, my sweet bridegroom, the source of sorrow would dry up,
> The desire for all sentiments would be granted to the heart.

What makes Novalis so fascinating is that he is radically different from his predecessors, despite certain superficial resemblances, and, in this sense, he is distinctively "modern"; his only real counterpart is William Blake. With Novalis one can take the measure of modern literature, not merely because he wanted to romanticize the world, or "Orphicize" it, but because there is present in his work a quest for a primeval innocence ("Jeder geliebte Gegenstand ist der Mittelpunkt eines Paradieses,"[35] every loved object is the center of a paradise) so intense and frenetic that it constantly threatens to weaken even the precarious hold on brute reality with which all intellectual and artistic creation must begin. In the beginning of the chapter Goethe was invoked; let me return to him once more. The continuation of the second part of *Ofterdingen* was to have contained another "magic" poem consecrated to the celebration of death. Its last stanza reads as follows:

> Helft uns nur den Erdgeist binden,
> Lernt den Sinn des Todes fassen
> Und das Wort des Lebens finden;
> Einmal kehrt euch um.
> Seine Macht muss bald verschwinden,
> Dein erborgtes Licht verblassen,
> Werden dich in kurzem binden,
> Erdgeist, deine Zeit ist um.[36]

> Help us but to bind the earth-spirit,
> Learn to grasp death's meaning
> And to find life's word;
> *Once* make the reversal.
> Its power will soon disappear,
> Thy borrowed light will fade,
> [We] shall bind you soon,
> Earth-spirit, thy time is over.

Although Novalis does not seem to mean quite the same thing that Goethe means by "Erdgeist," there is no doubt that Novalis' primary objective is to repudiate the energies that bind us to the earth and to unweave—at least, to reweave—the warp and woof of nature whose ceaseless activity Goethe exalted in *Faust*. "Einmal kehrt euch um": reverse, convert yourselves, and you will be romantically redeemed. No amount of romantic speculation about the natural sciences can hide the fact that Novalis' magic idealism is basically an expression of alienation.

And when Novalis is compared with Hölderlin, with whom he had more in common temperamentally than with Goethe, his enthusiasm knew no bounds, whereas Hölderlin's was subjected to the most agonized self-criticism. Michael Hamburger writes:

> Both Hölderlin and Novalis were thinkers as much as poets; and their different visions could not have arisen but for a common predicament, the tyranny of philosophical and scientific systems based on the opposition between world and mind, between outward and inward reality. Both Hölderlin and Novalis were deeply and dangerously affected by the extreme intensification of this opposition in their own time; by Fichte's solipsism on the one hand, purely mechanistic interpretations of nature on the other . . . Novalis continually reverted to Fichte's solipsism, with the result that his poetry is exceptionally poor in concrete imagery derived from the observation of nature.[37]

Novalis appears to have been free from a sense of guilt, whereas Hölderlin impaled himself on his conscience. On the one hand, solipsism; on the other, madness.

Alienation, solipsism, and madness: the Wandering Rocks and the Scylla and Charybdis of modern literature. And yet there is another hazard of modern literature, hovering over all three: the temptation of *hubris*. It can be seen lurking behind Novalis' ambition to conjure up a solipsistic and magical equivalent of Creation itself. No doubt he saw his office as that of the unveiling prophet-priest, the new Orpheus, who was to disclose the cosmos as it really was; but in doing so he had to appropriate the world in such a way that it lost its independent and integral being, and thus became available to arbitrary and "ironic" (in the Romantic sense) constructions. Here again, a parallel with Dante can be established by pointing out the correlation *Hymnen an die Nacht* : *Heinrich von Ofterdingen* = *Vita Nuova* : *Divina Commedia*. *Ofterdingen* usurps the function of Scripture and Revelation (becomes identified with it) more and more, whereas the *Divine Comedy* remains stable and unchanging in maintaining its allegorical correspondence with Revelation and therefore a symbolic and metaphorical balance with Scripture.

The fact remains that Novalis' religion is more Gnostic than Christian; its pietistic underpinnings are all but knocked apart by an excessive addiction to Böhme, to the illuministic and alchemical traditions of the Renaissance and post-Renaissance epochs. The *coincidentia oppositorum*—the major touchstone of Novalis' thought, which can be characterized as a central ingredient of all modern Orphic creativity—reveals itself in his work more as a device to cancel out polarities than as a dialectical means of bringing them into a resolvable conflict. The drama of the interaction and reconciliation of these polarities is the drama of the new Orphic dispensation in modern literature. It is fought out in solitude and alienation, its setting is the descent into the dark night of the psyche, its terminus is the ambiguous triumph of the return. But its true significance, its truly Orphic aspect, is that reconciliation of opposites in which Orpheus stands exalted as the mediator between the dark forces of Dionysus and the radiant power of Apollo. The Orphic journey is a quest for the dark center of being, followed by a return in which this dark center, once it is apprehended, absorbed, and transmuted, is made to shine forth in its own new and intense light.

III

The Seasoning of Hell: Nerval

The Orphism of Novalis, elaborated in the years 1798 to 1801, and that of Nerval, in 1852 and 1855, invite comparisons that do not merely emphasize the continuity of interest in the "new" Orpheus, but that considerably widen the scope of its significance. Nerval, the only French Romantic of his generation to be genuinely *outre-Rhin* (through his wanderings in Germany, his firsthand knowledge of much German contemporary literature, and his translations of *Faust* and of Heine), appears nevertheless to have been unfamiliar with Novalis' work, despite his personal friendship with Heine. The Orphic correspondences between Nerval and Novalis are significant enough: the quest for the lost Eurydice by a descent into Hades, confrontation with the powers of darkness and death, the attempt at regeneration through this experience that culminates in a vision of a universe once more under the spell of the power of song. At the same time it should be noted that the conflict generated within Nerval was waged on more precarious terrain, failing to achieve anything like the simple Sophie-Christ equation that stabilized Novalis' vision. This difference between the Orphism of Novalis and that of Nerval is mainly due to a difference in temperament or background (German Romantic versus French Romantic sensibility); moreover, it was subject to the transformations effected by history in the fifty years which separate the major creative moments of the two writers. Both these arguments have their partial validity; for example, something could be made of the fact that, whereas Novalis overcomes his suicidal anguish by a real regeneration resulting in an unexpected though short-lived creative burst, Nerval's experience fluctuates back and forth uneasily between suicidal depressions and periods of madness, interspersed with moments of admirable lucidity during which the great works of his last period (*Les Filles du feu, Le Voyage en Orient, Aurélia,* and *Les Chimères*) are created.

Most importantly, the Orphic ideal of Novalis is, in effect, a new cosmology in which poetry and science, dream and reality, religion and philosophy are reconciled; the glorification of this new era was to have been, on the one hand, a fusion of encyclopedia and Bible, and, on the other hand, the convergence of lived reality and fable (*Märchen*). Despite his failure to achieve anything even approximating this ideal, Novalis deserves admiration for realizing the gravity of the danger inherent in divorcing the sciences from poetry and religion; and despite his exasperating tendency to indulge in wild, though sometimes perspicacious, fabrications regarding the connections between science and poetry, there is no doubt that his knowledge of the natural sciences was substantial and diversified. The failure lies rather in his method than in his objectives.

It can hardly be claimed that Nerval's scientific knowledge was equal to that of Novalis. Nerval, working with the occult, not the natural sciences, was not only limited in his scope of endeavor, but also hampered by a mode of speculation that emulated the ambitions but not the discipline of Pythagoras. Moreover, there is something incurably literary in Nerval's intellectual lucubrations, in contrast to the fantastic but genuinely speculative constructions of Novalis. But that is not the main question here. The motivation of both men was toward an integration of dream and reality by means of magic, poetry, and religion; in Novalis' case the effort led to confusion, in Nerval's to diffusion. The quest for a missing center, the crucial problem of modern poetry, which is still governed by a centripetal impulse in Novalis, shifts its focus and deteriorates into a centrifugal flight in Nerval, with consequences detrimental to his psyche and ultimately his life; and this phenomenon marks a radical failure of romantic Orphism. Thus the way opens after 1855, between 1865 and 1925, for the second avatar of the new Orpheus in the work of Mallarmé and Rilke.

The difference between Novalis and Nerval in a nutshell is the question they both raise in their writings: "Where am I going?" The former answers "immer nach Hause" (ever homeward-bound) and the latter "vers l'Orient" (toward the East).[1] The two answers denote the essential similarity of and difference between the two writers. Both replies are capsule definitions of a *patrie intérieure,* but in Nerval's case the East, by virtue of its religion and its magic, constitutes a spiritual homeland that presupposes a long, outward-bound journey. This simple juxtaposition of "homelands" illustrates the contrast between the centripetal and the centrifugal momentum, respectively, of the two authors. We know from bitter experience that the vagabond-voyager finds the return difficult, like Odysseus, or even impossible, like Kafka's protagonists. And so it may be said that Nerval never quite returned from the East.

But in a sense this very experience makes Nerval distinctively the more modern of the two, the precursor of Rimbaud as well as Proust; he reveals a more anguished and more divided Orpheus than does Novalis. If one considers Novalis' critique of the modern world and his program for a regeneration of Christendom (as presented in *Die Christenheit oder Europa*) in conjunction, with Nerval's remarks on the religious situation (scattered throughout his later work), it is clear that Nerval's critique of the collapse of Western religion is more devastating and the problem of regeneration consequently more exacting. These reflections on religion appear in most concentrated form in the essay on Quintus Aucler, an eighteenth-century predecessor of Nerval (*Les Illuminés*), in "Isis" (*Les Filles du feu*), and in a group of "pensées" published under the title *Sur un Carnet de Gérard de Nerval*. Meditating near the temple of Isis at Pompeii, Nerval writes:

Enfant d'un siècle sceptique plutôt qu'incrédule, flottant entre deux éducations contraires, celle de la révolution, qui niait tout, et celle de la réaction sociale, qui prétend ramener l'ensemble des croyances chrétiennes, me verrais-je entraîné à tout croire, comme nos pères les philosophes l'avaient été à tout nier?[2]

As the child of a skeptical rather than unbelieving century, and at sea between two contradictory educations, that of the Revolution which denied everything and that of the social reaction which claims to be bringing back the body of Christian beliefs— should I see myself impelled to believe everything, as the *philosophes*, our ancestors, had been impelled to deny everything?

The problem is only partially stated, however, because Nerval, in reaction to the eighteenth-century *philosophes*, aligned himself with the "illuminists" of that age; this orientation throws light on his early interest in utopian socialism, particularly the religious or pseudo-religious elements inherent in the Fourierist movement. But this early interest was more a characteristic of the atmosphere of French Romanticism and the imprint that Victor Hugo had left upon the movement during its years of growth than anything else; in his later years the illuministic and religious interests took the upper hand.

Il y a certes, quelque chose de plus effrayant dans l'histoire que la chute des empires, c'est la mort des religions . . . Le croyant véritable peut échapper à cette impression, mais, avec le scepticisme de notre époque, on frémit parfois de rencontrer tant de portes sombres ouvertes sur le néant.

. . . L'art de la renaissance avait porté un coup mortel à l'ancien dogme et à la sainte austérité de l'Eglise avant que la révolution française en balayât les débris. L'allégorie succédant au mythe primitif, en a fait de même jadis des anciennes religions . . . Il finit toujours par se trouver un Lucien qui écrit les *Dialogues des dieux*—et plus tard, un Voltaire qui raille les dieux et Dieu lui-même.[3]

There is certainly something more frightening in history than the fall of empires, and that is the fall of religions . . . The true believer may escape this impression, but, the skepticism of our epoch being what it is, a person sometimes trembles when he finds so many dark doors open upon nothingness.

. . . The art of the Renaissance had delivered a mortal blow to the old dogma and to the holy austerity of the Church before the French Revolution came and swept away the debris. When allegory came upon the heels of primitive myth, it did the same thing to the old religions . . . In the long run there is always a Lucian to write the *Dialogues of the Gods*—and afterwards, a Voltaire who mocks the gods and God himself.

The essential question for Gérard de Nerval becomes the task of rebuilding upon the ruins of skepticism, a task which necessitates the closing of the "doors of nothingness." For Nerval the answer is protracted commitment to the il-luministic tradition, from Pythagoras and the Neoplatonists by way of the Kabbala and the alchemists to the more recent Swedenborgians and Martinists. In this quest he was both aided and hindered by the rapidly developing interest in archeology and comparative religion during the late eighteenth and early nineteenth century. Whereas, on the one hand, the materials of ancient civiliza-tions and cults became more readily available to Nerval, the tendency of such accumulations of facts is to lead the reader into a still more devastating skepti-cism ("me verrais-je entraîné à tout croire"). But the problem does not end there. Nerval maintained throughout his life an attachment to the Christian faith and consequently felt more than once that his skepticism, as well as his experiments with magic, were rebellious or sinful. In other words, he had moments of remorse for his Faustian-Promethean curiosity: the magic synthesis of religions toward which his thinking gravitated appeared to him like a violent transgression into a forbidden world.

Since Nerval saw in his religious syncretism not only an intellectual structure but an attempt to reconstruct his personal life in harmonious relation to an

ordered cosmos—that is to say, a renewal of self through a renewal of vision—
the figure of Orpheus becomes increasingly the model to which he relates his
experience. But, it must be added, not merely Orpheus is to be included here,
but all the heroes of myth and literature who have descended into the underworld. Nerval's list is very large, reflecting the syncretic method of his thought
and his obsession with finding as many multiple personae for himself as possible
—Aeneas, Dante, Faust, to mention the most significant ones. The Orpheus
figure can be taken as exemplary because it combines the themes of the downward journey, love, death, and poetry in a context which is simultaneously
cultic and artistic. Jean Richer is correct in speaking of the "Orpheus complex"
that afflicted Nerval: "Up to the very end Nerval seems to have been the victim
of a lacerating 'Orpheus complex': divided, scattered, like the dying Orpheus,
did he perceive in his own flesh that Orpheus was the figure of the death and the
resurrection of Christ?"[4]

The problem, of course, is right here. Nerval, unlike Novalis, does not go so
far as to identify Sophie with Christ but with all sorts of mother goddesses,
notably Isis; yet there are occasional hints of a self-identification with Christ, and
Nerval was certainly conscious of the blasphematory aspects of this temptation.
Here is an example:

Il me semble que je suis mort et que j'accomplis cette deuxième vie de Dieu.

It seems to me that I have died and that I am fulfilling this second life of God.

The wording is somewhat ambiguous; moreover, the statement is followed by a
more anguished interrogation:

L'Ecriture dit qu'un repentir suffit pour être sauvé, mais il faut qu'il soit sincère. Et si
l'événement qui vous frappe empêche ce repentir? Et si l'on vous met en état de fièvre,
de folie? Si l'on vous bouche les portes de la rédemption?[5]

The Scriptures say that repentance is sufficient for salvation, but it must be sincere.
What if the event which befalls you prevents you from repenting? And what if you are
put in a state of fever, of folly? If the doors of redemption are closed off to you?

And it is not only mental illness that casts doubt on the sincerity of repentance
and precludes access to redemption; it is also the temptation of paganism, of
illuminism—the temptation, in brief, of the *libido sciendi*—that undermines
Nerval's search for his own paradise. A revealing note included in the aphorisms

appropriately entitled *Paradoxe et vérité* (1844) allows us to glimpse his Promethean and Satanic side, in spite of the gentleness and restraint of the wording:

Je ne demande à Dieu de rien changer aux événements, mais de me changer relativement aux choses; de me laisser le pouvoir de créer autour de moi un univers qui m'appartienne, de diriger mon rêve éternel au lieu de le subir. Alors, il est vrai, je serais Dieu.[6]

I am not asking God to change events in any way, but to change me in relation to things; to allow me the power to create around me a universe that would be mine, to direct my eternal dream rather than be subject to it. If that were the case, it is true, I would be God.

Nerval's fascination with the Orphic descent, in conflict with a Satanic obstacle within his psyche, raises the question of the nature and purpose of his religious syncretism.

Despite Nerval's encyclopedic hunger for the writings of the mystics and illuminists,[7] one must not be led into excessive source-hunting. Nerval, like Yeats some seventy years later, found in occult writings a partial confirmation and explanation for his own experiences and aspirations: he transposed old myths into Nervalian myths beginning with the declaration, quoted above, that the nineteenth century found itself faced with the death of religion. Nerval sees himself, as a man and as a poet, confronted with a fragmented cosmos, whose pieces he tries to reassemble. The quest for unity of cosmos, through the correspondence of microcosm and macrocosm, begins first of all with an awareness of the dichotomies *here and now*. The most pervasive of these is that of the divided self, long an appanage of the Romantics, consecrated particularly by *Faust I*, by Heine's "Doppelgänger," and by E. T. A. Hoffmann and echoed and amplified by virtually all writers of the first half of the nineteenth century. Nerval, translator and ardent champion of *Faust*, went beyond the personal "double" and arrived at the typology of the human race into "les enfants du limon" (the damned, those who cannot liberate themselves from the earth) and "les enfants du feu" (those who are open to redemption, through art, through magic, through the dream)—a reinterpretation of the Abel-Cain dichotomy. The activity of the "enfants du feu" has its origins in the center of the earth, underground, in the presence of the forgers and alchemists, and thus operates within the framework of black magic. But redemption cannot take place without Woman. Here Nerval, following the theosophists once more, elevates the figure of the goddess-mother-beloved into the figure of redemption, identifying her variously as the idealized form of all beloved women (Jenny Colon, Aurélia, Adrienne) plus the divine figures of the Virgin, Aphrodite, Demeter, and finally Isis:

> ... plutôt n'est-il pas vrai qu'il faut réunir tous ces modes divers d'une même idée, et que ce fut toujours une admirable pensée théogonique de présenter à l'adoration des hommes une Mère céleste dont l'enfant est l'espoir du monde?[8]

> ... as a matter of fact, is it not true that all these different modes of the same idea must be combined, and that it has always been an admirable theogonic idea to take a celestial Mother whose child is the hope of the world and offer her to the adoration of men?

Belief in the reality of the unified, redemptive Eternal Feminine, who is simultaneously wife, mother, and goddess, guarantees the integration of the "double" in man: if the Eternal Feminine is allowed to lead, she will unify and redeem her lover-worshipper. But since the image of Isis must be recovered through a lost beloved, such as the actress Jenny Colon, the lover must needs become Orpheus: he must make the descent into the darkness of deprivation and dereliction to reclaim his Eurydice, who, though she cannot accompany him back to earth, at least gives meaning and direction to his terrestrial life, precisely because she has opened to him the vistas of celestial life. Such is the general pattern of Nerval's Orphic experience.

The design of *Aurélia*, Nerval's last work, is indebted to several other works, all of which deal with the theme of initiation or regeneration. In Apuleius' *The Golden Ass*, or more appropriately, *Metamorphoses*, Lucius is redeemed from animal existence and initiated into the cult of Isis; Francesco Colonna's *Hypnerotomachy* presents the conflict of dream and love and the victory of the beloved; Emmanuel Swedenborg's *Memorabilia*, or spiritual diaries, are specifically evoked in *Aurélia*, as is Dante's *Vita Nuova*. A comparison of the latter two throws considerable light upon the quest for Orphic redemption, which in *Aurélia* ends in partial failure.

The first part of *Aurélia* describes an oneiric curve that extends the horizon of the dream into the very substance of waking life and engulfs it; this extension intensifies the visionary, the shamanic faculties of the dreamer, but because of its all-pervasiveness it intensifies the integrity of the self by alienating it from the processes of the world, even to the point of folly. The self becomes further and further divided, and Part I ends on a note of damnation and loss. The second part begins in anguish, describes the same curve as the first but with greater awareness of the error committed, then rises to a new and more complete vision —whose final outcome, however, is not integration of the self but madness, not the achievement of redemption but merely a vision of it glimpsed from a distance.

In the sense that *Aurélia*, like the *Vita Nuova*, is a spiritual diary, a book of memory read retrospectively for signs, a discipline and initiation into the true way of salvation, the analogy of the two books is apparent. So is the role played by Beatrice in Dante's work and the role played by the beloved, who becomes indirectly identified with Eurydice, in Nerval. But Beatrice leads Dante to the Trinity and eventually to Paradise in the *Divine Comedy*; Eurydice becomes identified, in Nerval, with all the mother-goddesses, most specifically Isis, and leads Nerval upward as well as downward, into an ambiguous Gnostic purgatory whose dimensions are those of a no-man's-land. The essential difference between the two works is that Dante moves from a zone of illumination through darkness into greater and greater luminosity, while Nerval moves through darkness occasionally touched by a radiance that never succeeds in abolishing it. And whereas in Dante the function of dreamer is distinctly placed in a context of experience that assigns reality and dream their proper respective places, in Nerval the dream tends at every point to obliterate reality and make it oneiric. But the main difference between Dante and Nerval can be seen in Nerval's vision of the *soleil noir* that occurs at crucial points in both sections of *Aurélia*.

The beginning of *Aurélia* is justly famous for the simplicity and power found throughout the work:

Le rêve est une seconde vie. Je n'ai pu percer sans frémir ces portes d'ivoire ou de corne qui nous séparent du monde invisible. Les premiers instants du sommeil sont l'image de la mort; un engourdissement nébuleux saisit notre pensée, et nous ne pouvons déterminer l'instant précis où le *moi*, sous une autre forme, continue l'oeuvre de l'existence. C'est un souterrain vague qui s'éclaire peu à peu, et où se dégagent de l'ombre et de la nuit les pâles figures gravement immobiles qui habitent le séjour des limbes. Puis le tableau se forme, une clarté nouvelle illumine et fait jouer ces apparitions bizarres: le monde des Esprits s'ouvre pour nous.[10]

Dream is a second life. Not without trembling have I been able to enter those gates of ivory or horn that separate us from the invisible world. The first moments of sleep are the image of death; some nebulous numbness takes hold of our minds, and we cannot determine the exact moment when the self, in another form, continues the work of existence. It is a vague underground which gradually becomes brighter, and out of its shadow and night arise the gravely immobile pale figures inhabiting their region in limbo. Then the picture falls into shape, a new brightness illuminates and animates these bizarre apparitions: the world of the Spirits opens for us.

Though he accepts the validity of the dream life, along with the other Romantics, in the context of total experience, Nerval here shows himself more akin to the Keats of the "Sonnet to Sleep" and the Proust of the opening pages of *Du Côté de chez Swann*. But even then his apprehensions intrude for a moment, announcing, *en sourdine*, the tensions to come: "je n'ai pu percer sans frémir." It is as though he (or in any case the "je" of *Aurélia*) were aware of the transgression involved in the attempt to break across the barrier separating dream and waking life.

Then follow the references to Swedenborg, to Apuleius, and to the *Divine Comedy* as exemplars for his work:

Je vais essayer, à leur example, de transcrire les impressions d'une longue maladie qui s'est passée tout entière dans les mystères de mon esprit . . . Cette *Vita nuova* a eu pour moi deux phases.

Following their lead, I am going to try to transcribe the impression coming out of a long illness that took place entirely in the mysteries of my mind . . . This *New Life* for me had two phases.

The first phase begins with Nerval's declaration that Aurélia is henceforth lost to him. A number of omens convince him that either her death or his own is being mysteriously announced to him; these events produce a prophetic dream-vision in which he loses himself in the corridors of a building and encounters a giant androgynous winged figure that resembles Dürer's *Melancholia*. The terror of this figure causes him to waken from his dream.

The effect of the dream is crucial for Nerval's experience: the next day he is already saying goodbye to his friends, mentally, and discoursing eloquently on mystical subjects ("il me semblait que je savais tout, et que les mystères du monde se révélaient à moi dans ces heures suprêmes," it seemed to me that I knew everything, and that the mysteries of the world revealed themselves to me in those supreme moments). He tells his friend Paul that he is not going home but toward the Orient, and he looks for a familiar star in the sky to guide him. At a crossroad he stops, sees his friend grown into a superhuman Paul the Apostle, and says to him,

Non! Je n'appartiens pas à ton ciel. Dans cette étoile sont ceux qui m'attendent. Ils sont antérieurs à la révélation que tu as annoncée. Laisse-moi les rejoindre, car celle que j'aime leur appartient et c'est là que nous devons nous retrouver!

No! I do not belong to your heaven. In that star over there are those that expect me. They are anterior to the revelation that you have announced. Let me join them, for the woman I love belongs to them and she and I must meet there!

—a clear indication that his impulsion toward the Orient is also a quest for the one archaic source of religion to which the star is to lead him. With this splitting of the religious intelligence into the Christian and the pre-Christian, or trans-Christian, we enter into the particular dichotomy of Nerval's experience:

Ici a commencé pour moi ce que j'appellerai l'épanchement du songe dans la vie réelle. A dater de ce moment, tout prenait parfois un aspect double—et cela sans que le raisonnement manquât jamais de logique, sans que la mémoire perdît les plus légers détails de ce qui m'arrivait. Seulement, mes actions insensées en apparence étaient soumises à ce que l'on appelle illusion selon la raison humaine.

This was the beginning for me of what I shall call the expansion of the dream into real life. Dating from that moment everything at times took on a double aspect—and in such a way that my reasoning was never devoid of logic, nor did my memory lose the slightest detail of what was happening to me. Only, my actions, senseless in appearance, were subject to what is called illusion according to human reason.

This "other" existence gives rise to a number of visions, the most notable of which is a descent into the underworld realm of fire inhabited by his ancestors. Here Nerval is initiated into the first aspect of metempsychosis: "nous conservons ici les images du monde que nous avons habité" (here we preserve the images of the world we have inhabited).

Le néant . . . n'existe pas dans le sens qu'on l'entend; mais la terre est elle-même un corps matériel dont la somme des esprits est l'âme. La matière ne peut pas plus périr que l'esprit, mais elle peut se modifier selon le bien et selon le mal. (766–767)

Nothingness . . . does not exist in the sense in which it is generally understood; but the earth is herself a material body the sum of whose spirits is the soul. Matter can no more perish than spirit, but it can modify itself according to good and evil.

After this preliminary revelation of the cabalistic-theosophical transmutation of matter into spirit, Nerval receives his second visionary glimpse into the arcane, this time the mystical homeland. This confirms his belief in God's existence. The first vision confirmed immortality, the second God's existence; the third reveals to Nerval the existence of the feminine archetype, but under the sign of death:

Chacun sait que, dans les rêves, on ne voit jamais le soleil, bien qu'on ait souvent la perception d'une clarté beaucoup plus vive. (772)

Everyone knows that in dreams one never sees the sun, even though one often has the perception of a much more vivid brightness.

This observation is followed by the description of a dream in which a lady guides Nerval through a park and enfolds a stem of hollyhock (*rose trémière*); then she becomes transfigured into the garden itself and recedes from the dreamer's sight, leaving the impression in him that the park has become a cemetery and that nature has died with her. The dream turns out to be prophetic, like so many other omens: Aurélia had actually died, although Nerval learned this only later.

At this point Nerval has his first cosmogonic vision, one compounded of a number of esoteric readings and the firsthand contact he had had with several of these traditions during his trip to the East. Two important details are the emergence of the archetypal mother-goddess, "l'image souffrante de la mère éternelle," 719 (the suffering image of the eternal mother), and the cause of her suffering, the spectacle of carnage and evil represented by another archetypal symbol, that of the serpent Ouroboros—"Ce sont les tronçons divisés du serpent, qui entoure la terre . . . Séparés par le fer, ils se rejoignent dans un hideux baiser cimenté par le sang des hommes." (780) (They are the divided segments of the serpent clasping the earth . . . Separated by iron, they come together again in a hideous kiss cemented by the blood of men.) But this vision is soon succeeded by a more intensified dream awareness of the fundamental dichotomy within the self, with the growing conviction that Aurélia has in reality been appropriated by the other, hostile self. "Un mauvais génie avait pris ma place dans le monde des âmes." (784) (An evil genie had taken my place in the world of souls.) The sensation is thenceforth one of slipping, a downward movement ("je déscendis par un escalier" [784], I went down a staircase) into the Cainite city of fire that contrasts sharply with the earlier descent, which culminated in a vision of paradise. Here, in this realm of alchemy, perfection of the craft has led to construction of an artificial nature. The awaited bride and groom now seem to Nerval to be Aurélia and his own double; he loses control of himself, becomes violent, and is appeased only by a magic gesture and the voice of a woman, Aurélia's voice, which causes him to awake from the nightmare. But the conviction of transgression subsists and closes Part I on a note of contrition that links the opening and the final paragraphs under the shadow of guilt:

Qu'avais-je fait? J'avais troublé l'harmonie de l'univers magique où mon âme puisait la certitude d'une existence immortelle. J'étais maudit peut-être pour avoir voulu percer un mystère redoutable en offensant la loi divine; je ne devais plus attendre que la colère et le mépris! Les ombres irritées fuyaient et jetant des cris et traçant dans l'air des cercles fatals, comme les oiseaux à l'approche d'un orage. (787)

What had I done? I had disturbed the harmony of the magic universe from which my soul was drawing the certainty of immortal existence. I was perhaps accursed for having wanted to penetrate a formidable mystery by violating the divine law; all I could now expect was wrath and scorn! The irritated shadows fled, emitting cries and describing fatal circles in the air, as birds do before a thunderstorm.

Why the feeling of transgression? Is there a wrong Orphic journey and a right one? Nerval suggests that the journey can be carried out only by the integral, not the divided, self and that any attempt of the double to penetrate the realm of darkness is sinful so long as the inharmonious self attempts to violate the secrets of the magic cosmology.

The reference to Orpheus, though only implied in the first part, becomes explicit in the epigraph to Part II: "Eurydice! Eurydice!" This part tells of the second loss of the Eurydice-Isis archetype: "Une seconde fois perdue!" (788)— Lost a second time! In the remorse that follows his sense of transgression, Nerval reproaches himself for not having thought of God—because the pantheism of his philosophy made the idea of God superfluous. "Le système fatal qui s'était créé dans mon esprit n'admettait pas cette royauté solitaire . . . ou plutôt elle s'absorbait dans la somme des êtres: c'était le dieu de Lucretius, impuissant et perdu dans son immensité." (788) (The fatal system that had taken shape in my mind did not admit that solitary kingship . . . or rather it became absorbed in the totality of beings: that was the god of Lucretius, impotent and lost in his immensity.) Here is the clearcut recognition of the dilemma which syncretism and occultism produced in Nerval's intelligence: the pantheistic and immanent notion of Deity sharply clashes with the Christian and transcendent idea, paralleling on a theological plane the fissure and conflict that he was experiencing on a psychological plane.

Two paragraphs follow that address themselves directly to this problem, beginning with the declaration that when the soul floats uneasily between life and the dream, religion offers succor. But at this point Nerval's critique of the religious situation reasserts itself once more:

Mais pour nous, nés dans des jours de révolution et d'orages, où toutes les croyances ont été brisées—élevés tout au plus dans cette foi vague qui se contente de quelques pratiques extérieures, et dont l'adhesion indifférente est plus coupable peut-être que l'impiété et l'hérésie—il est bien difficile, dés que nous en sentons le besoin, de reconstruire l'édifice mystique dont les innocents et les simples admettent dans leurs coeurs la figure toute tracée. "L'arbre de science n'est pas l'arbre de vie!" (788–789)

But for us, who were born in the days of revolutions and upheavals, in which all beliefs were shattered—brought up at the most in that vague faith that is satisfied with a few outward practices, demanding an indifferent loyalty that is perhaps more guilty than impiety and heresy—it is very difficult, once we feel the need, to reconstruct the mystical edifice whose outlined shape the innocent and naive recognize in their hearts. "The Tree of Knowledge is not that of Life."

That final quotation, appropriately from Byron's *Manfred* (I, 12) reiterates the Faustian dilemma and its aggravation as the nineteenth century progressed. Nerval is led to speculate whether it is not necessary to become Doubting Thomas—then he immediately feels that he has been blasphemous, Satanic.

Again a succession of crises follows due to Nerval's sense of guilt and dereliction, culminating in the overwhelming realization that it is now too late to repent; yet he discovers that the image of Aurélia continues to be alive in him, prompting his meditations about immortality, helping him to resist the temptation of suicide and to perform charitable acts. During one of his suicidal spasms he feels that the apocalypse is near, sees the *soleil noir*, has the certainty that Christ exists no longer, and finally falls prey to madness again.

This second *glissement* into darkness and madness is brightened by a new apparition of Isis—after another attempt by Nerval to relate himself charitably to mankind. Isis now reveals to him that:

Je suis la même que Marie, la même que ta mère, la même aussi que sous toutes les formes tu as toujours aimée. A chacune de tes épreuves, j'ai quitté l'un des masques dont je voile mes traits, et bientôt tu me verras telle que je suis. (805)

I am the same as Mary, the same as your mother, the same also whom you have always loved in all shapes. At every one of your trials I have taken off one of the masks with which I conceal my features, and soon you will see me as I really am.

But the effect on Nerval is contrary to the humble one the revelation was intended to produce: the Satanic, Cainite *hubris* asserts itself once more, this time in the guise of a Napoleonism ("ce soir j'ai en moi l'âme de Napoléon" [806], tonight I have the soul of Napoleon within me) and, finally, a somewhat different form of Satanism: "L'idée que j'étais devenu semblable à un dieu et que j'avais le pouvoir de guérir me fit imposer les mains à quelques malades, et, m'approchant d'une statue de la Vierge, j'enlevais la couronne de fleurs artificielles pour appuyer le pouvoir que je me croyais." (807) (The idea that I had become like a god and that I possessed the power to heal made me place my hands upon several sick persons, and, approaching a statue of the Virgin, I took the wreath of artificial flowers to strengthen the power I believed I possessed.)

The tension between *hubris* and humility, pagan and Christian, the Satanic and the angelic sets the pace for the remaining pages of *Aurélia* and for its ambiguous resolution. On the one hand, Nerval becomes convinced that it is his task to restore harmony—an undertaking that is no doubt laudable but partakes, again, of exorbitant pride and intensifies the scission within his own personality. A regeneration of the universe is not possible without regeneration of the self, and if that regeneration is effectuated by cabalistic means, it runs the danger of compounding the Gnostic fallacy—it reinforces a basic dualism in the world (and the self) out of which a real harmony cannot grow.

Une erreur s'était glissée selon moi, dans la combinaison générale des nombres, et de là venaient tous les maux de l'humanité . . . Mon rôle me semblait être de rétablir l'harmonie universelle par l'art cabalistique et de chercher une solution en évoquant les forces occultes des diverses religions. (808–809)

An error had, in my opinion, slipped into the general combination of numbers, and from it resulted all the woes of humanity . . . It seemed to me that my role was to re-establish universal harmony by means of the cabalistic arts and to try to find a solution by calling on the occult forces of the different religions.

The first major step along the path of self-regeneration, significantly experienced under the sign of the rising sun, is a clear formulation of the self as shamanic hero-priest—as Orpheus:

Du moment que je me fus assuré de ce point que j'étais soumis aux épreuves de l'initiation sacrée, une force invincible entra dans mon esprit. Je me jugeais un héros vivant sous le regard des dieux; tout dans la nature prenait des aspects nouveaux, et des voix secrètes sortaient de la plante, de l'arbre, des animaux, des plus humbles insectes, pour m'avertir et m'encourager. Le langage de mes compagnons avait des tours mystérieux dont je comprenais le sens, les objets sans vie se prêtaient eux-mêmes aux calculs de mon esprit—des combinaisons de cailloux, des figures d'angles, de fentes ou d'ouvertures, de découpures de feuilles, des couleurs, des odeurs et des sons je voyais ressortir des harmonies jusqu'alors inconnues. "Comment, me disais-je, ai-je pu exister si longtemps hors de la nature et sans m'identifier à elle? Tout vit, tout agit, tout se correspond; les rayons magnétiques émanés de moi-même ou des autres traversent sans obstacle la chaîne infinie des choses créées; c'est un réseau transparent qui couvre le monde, et dont les fils déliés se communiquent de proche en proche aux planètes et aux étoiles. Captif en ce moment sur la terre, je m'entretiens avec le choeur des astres, qui prend part à mes joies et à mes douleurs!" (810)

From the moment I had become convinced of the fact that I was subject to the trials of sacred initiation, an invincible strength entered my mind. I considered myself a hero living in the sight of the gods; everything in nature took on new features, and secret voices came out of plants, trees, animals, the lowest insects, in order to show me the way and urge me on. The language of my friends has mysterious inflections whose meaning I understood, lifeless objects became part of the operations of my mind—from combinations of stones, shapes of angels, from cracks and openings, from newspaper clippings, from colors, odors and sounds I observed how unknown harmonies emerged. I said to myself, "How could I have existed for so long out of nature without identifying myself with it? Everything lives, everything acts, all things correspond to one another; magnetic rays emanating from myself or from others cross unhindered the infinite chain of created things; a transparent network covers the world whose loosened strands relay themselves step by step to the planets and stars. Though at this moment a captive on earth, I am conversing with the choir of stars, which shares my joys and sorrows!"

Worth noting in this paragraph are the sense of sacred initiation, or prelude to rebirth; the idea of the Pythagorean Orphic hero rather than the earlier self-comparison with a god; the illuministic doctrine of correspondences, already enunciated in "Vers dorés" of *Les Chimères* and given wider currency by Baudelaire's famous sonnet a few years later; and the Neoplatonic-Gnostic notion of the captivity of the authentic self on earth, which is a corollary to the notion of correspondences. Subsequently, the figure of the double becomes incarnated in a fellow inmate of the sanatorium he is in, whom Nerval fraternally calls Saturnin. With this new access of charity it seems that the period of Nerval's trials is at an end, and the final vision of Isis appears once more ("une des étoiles que je voyais au ciel se mit à grandir, et la divinité de mes rêves m'apparut souriante" [816], one of the stars I was looking at in the sky began to grow in size, and the divinity of my dreams appeared to me, smiling). Isis-Aurélia tells him this:

L'épreuve à laquelle tu étais soumis est venue à son terme; ces escaliers sans nombre que tu te fatiguais à descendre ou à gravir, étaient les liens mêmes des anciennes illusions qui embarrassaient ta pensée, et maintenant rappelle-toi le jour où as imploré la Vierge sainte et où, la croyant morte, le délire s'est emparé de ton esprit. Il fallait que ton voeu lui fût porté par une âme simple et dégagée des liens de la terre. Celle-là s'est recontrée près de toi, et c'est pourquoi il m'est permis à moi-même de venir et de t'encourager. (816–817)

The trial that you have undergone is now at an end; these numberless staircases that you wearily went down or up were the very bonds of former illusions encumbering your mind; and now remember the day when you implored the holy Virgin and when, believing her dead, madness seized your mind. Your vow had to be borne by a naive soul and detached from the bonds of the earth. That soul appeared close by you, and that is why I myself am permitted to come and encourage you.

At this point Nerval inserts his own Memorabilia into a work which is already a spiritual diary in the manner of Swedenborg and Dante. There are no new themes in this diary; there is, rather, a recapitulation of all the preceding vision-ary moments, this time clearly steeped in the aura of a Christianized form of reconciliation and redemption. In a passage reminiscent of the Ancient Mariner's blessing offered to the slimy creatures of the deep, Nerval concludes with a blessing of the Ouroboros serpent: "Le serpent qui entoure le Monde est béni lui-même, car il relâche ses anneaux et sa gueule béante aspire la fleur d'anxoka, la fleur soufrée—la fleur éclatante du soleil!" (820) (The serpent clasping the World is itself blessed, for it loosens its rings, and its gaping jaw breathes upon the anxoka flower, the sulfur flower—the flower dazzling with sunlight!)

It appears thus that with the final act of love, the blessing accorded to Evil, Nerval has surmounted the Gnostic tensions within himself and become the microcosm that harmoniously reflects the macrocosm. ("Le *macrocosme*, ou grand monde, a été construit par art cabalistique; le *microcosme*, ou petit monde, est son image réfléchie dans tous les coeurs" [820], The *macrocosm*, or great world, was constructed by cabalistic art; the *microcosm*, or little world, is its image re-flected in all hearts.) But *Aurélia* does not end on this note. There is instead an insidious return of the "double," who disrupts the integrity of the *moi* and leaves Nerval, as before, in a state of suspension. Nerval's besetting difficulty is the attempt to *possess* the magic knowledge proffered to him in his dreams, to make the dream overflow into life and to dominate it. In order to achieve this, he all too readily gives in to his Faustian-Cainite penchants; not content with being the Orphic shaman, he also wants to be the Promethean god snatching fire from the deities:

Je résolus de fixer le rêve et d'en connaître le secret. Pourquoi, me dis-je, ne point enfin forcer ces portes mystiques, armé de toute ma volonté, et dominer mes sensations au lieu de les subir? N'est-il pas possible de dompter cette chimère attrayante et redoutable, d'imposer une règle à ces esprits des nuits qui se jouent de notre raison? . . . Qui sait s'il n'existe pas un lien entre ces deux existences et s'il n'est pas possible à l'âme de le nouer dès à présent? (823)

I made up my mind to pin down the dream and to know its secret. I told myself, why not crash those mystic gates, armed with all my willpower, and why not rule my sensations instead of being ruled by them? Is it not possible to tame that attractive and formidable chimera, to impose a law upon these nocturnal spirits that mock our reason? . . . Who knows whether there isn't a link between these two existences, and whether it isn't possible for the soul to piece it together here and now?

The phrase "percer les portes" of Part I has now been intensified to read "forcer ces portes"; and the extent of Nerval's desperate urge can be measured by that alone. Orpheus did not force entry, he simply entered; his counterpart Prometheus used force and aggression in his attempt to over-reach the human. The doctrine of correspondences is in this passage suspended for seizure of the means of *direct* relationship and control, and the urge for possession of the chimeric truth is *here and now*. It is as if Nerval were momentarily on the threshold of Rimbaud's infernal-angelic kingdom. But with this baleful new resolution—with the attempt to "chercher le sens de mes rêves" (823) (seek out the meaning of my dreams), anxiety insinuates itself once more, and with it comes the oppressive triumph of Narcissus, death-doomed, over Orpheus-Prometheus. Richer observes that in the last chapter of *Aurélia* there is "an offensive return of the 'double'; The reconciliation of opposites was only momentary and Nerval, once more confronted with the 'other,' would be tempted to kill his enemy, thus destroying himself."[11] Yet the final page of *Aurélia* has a tenderness that comes directly from Nerval's perception of the true way. Once more, there is a friendly identification with the double, Saturnin, who reciprocates the tenderness this time but also utters the fateful words for Nerval:

Pourquoi, lui dis-je, ne veux-tu pas manger et boire comme les autres? C'est que je suis mort, dit-il; j'ai été enterré dans tel cimetière, à telle place . . . —Et maintenant, où crois-tu être? . . . —En purgatoire, j'accomplis mon expiation. (824)

"Why," I said to him, "do you not want to eat and drink like the others?" "The fact is that I am dead," he said, "I have been buried in such and such a cemetery, in such and such a spot" . . . "And now, where do you think you are?" "In purgatory, I am doing my expiation."

This is also Nerval's destiny. The entrance into the "patrie mystique" is blocked by the sense of transgression; and yet, the "descente aux enfers" (824) has at least promoted him from the damnation of his hell or even the exclusion of his limbo into a zone of expiation—a zone which is not necessarily the step toward ultimate redemption, as is Dante's purgatory, but which is at least a partial liberation from the shackles of the earth.

Aurélia is the culmination of Nerval's prose; *Les Chimères,* a collection of twelve sonnets, marks the zenith of his poetry. The stages leading up to *Aurélia* were Jenny Colon's death in 1842 and Nerval's subsequent trip to the East, experiences that were transmuted into *Le Voyage en Orient, Les Illuminés,* and *Les Filles du feu.* Of these works the first two, in part, sketch out fragmentary cosmogonies and archetypal characters (Caliph Hakem and Queen Balkis, in two stories narrated in the *Voyage*). Moreover, the *Voyage* is in many ways the baptism of fire of the "new" Nerval: in that work he discovers his own particular blend of autobiography, fiction, mythology, and *rite de passage,* creating the prose that characterizes his late works. *Les Filles du feu* (1854) moves one step closer to *Aurélia,* particularly by its inclusion of "Isis" among the gallery of elect women and through the two closely autobiographical stories "Octavia" and "Sylvie." The latter especially is of major importance as a stepping-stone toward *Aurélia*; as Georges Poulet has shown in his penetrating study of the work, "the greatest human suffering consists not so much in losing one's illusion but in losing the means for bringing it back to life."[12] In this sense, *Aurélia* can be regarded as a new attempt to effect the recovery of illusion, though at the price of sanity.

The poems of *Les Chimères* are contemporaneous with this phase of Nerval's development; they all fall between the years 1843 and 1855; "Vers dorés," the sonnet-sequence "Le Christ aux Olivers," and "Delfica" were published in 1844 and 1845; the five others, "El Desdichado," "Myrtho," "Horus," "Antéros," and "Artémis" must be situated in the years 1853 to 1855. The interesting relation of these sonnets to the prose works is that, just as there is a parallel movement in the prose along lines of the cosmogonic (sections of *Voyage, Les Illuminés*—particularly the "Quintus Aucler" chapter—and "Isis" of *Filles du feu*) and the personal ("Octavie," "Sylvie"), with the two currents fusing in *Aurélia*, the poems can be grouped in accordance with the function accorded the "je." Significantly enough, the first person is not mentioned in the three earlier ones, "Vers dorés," "Le Christ aux Oliviers," and "Delfica": these sonnets are generally cosmological and theosophical; of the remaining five, "Horus" continues the cosmological speculation of "Delfica" and the other four utilize the first person centrally—in "Myrtho" the "je" is primarily the observer and thus essentially nonparticipating, whereas in "Antéros," "El Desdichado," and "Artémis" the self is central, and these three poems are at the same time hermetic cosmologies and confessions.

These relationships suggest a deeper connection between Nerval's prose and his poetry and indirectly throw light on the shifting emphasis between the genres during the Romantic period. The two modes of expression are no longer separable: they complement each other in a way reminiscent of, yet different from, Dante's form in *La Vita Nuova*, in which the prose controls the verse and provides glosses upon it.[13] This conscious and reasoned process of reminiscence in Dante does not, of course, find its counterpart in Nerval, although it does find its echo: all works of Nerval's later period are works of reminiscence, even when they are concerned with discovery and revelation—in every case the discovery or the revelation lays bare some *forgotten* fragment of the past, Nerval's or mankind's. (It is precisely this quest and experience in Nerval that made Proust list him as one of the ancestors of the involuntary memory.) If Nerval's last prose and verse works are viewed as one synthetic *Vita Nuova* (in a sense, this is the deeper meaning of his reference to Dante in *Aurélia*), one notes that, as in Dante and as, indeed, in virtually all poetry, the sonnets provide an intensification and a resonance, a kind of *stretto* treatment, to the materials more broadly presented in the prose works. Thus the movement from dream to reality in "Sylvie" and *Aurélia* operates along still descernible frontiers of separation although, as pointed out above, the effect of *Aurélia* is to obliterate the "signs." In the poems the levels of the personal, the historical, and the mythical are fused into an alchemical whole that is the more difficult to analyze because its meaningfulness grows out of their intricate multilayered structures.

Nerval's statement in the preface to *Les Filles du feu* (to which *Les Chimères* was originally joined) has justly become famous. Speaking of these sonnets "composés dans cet état de rêverie *supernaturaliste*" (composed in that state of *supernaturalistic* reverie), he insists that they are hardly more obscure than Swedenborg or Hegel and "perdraient de leur charme à être expliqués, si la chose était possible"[14] (would lose some of their charm by being explicated, if such a thing were possible). The key word in this sentence is "charme," in the sense in which Baudelaire and the symbolists and particularly Valéry liked to use the word—as enchantment, incantation. Although the poems have received numerous exegeses (some rigorously narrow, such as Georges Le Breton's, others more flexible—Richer, Moulin), the danger, which the exegetes are not always aware of, lies in the sundering of things that ought not to be sundered, the breaking of the "charm" of the poems. But, whatever one makes of this somewhat cryptic statement of Nerval's about the poems, how far it is from the critical and intellectual clearsightedness of Dante in his *Vita Nuova*! Dante's work is built around a center. It is not accidental that Nerval's "Delfica" and Yeats' "Second Coming" are analogous poems (though there is no direct "influence" of Nerval over Yeats); both are poems about a missing center.

But where are the specifically Orphic aspects of the *Chimères* to be found; and what are the Orphic qualities of "El Desdichado," "Artemis," and, to a lesser extent, "Antéros" in contrast to the more objective, cosmological sonnets that complete the cycle? The answer is not simply that they are "personal" and the other sonnets are not. Rather, they point toward the creation of a personal myth that the poet embodies, and this myth is Promethean in "Antéros" and Orphic in the other two. In "El Desdichado" the poet looks back to the Orphic descent and his successful return in the past; in "Artémis," he remains suspended in his underworld as he had been in *Aurélia*. The struggle of the three poems is played out between Promethean and Orphic temptations, and the framework for it is provided by the other *Chimères*: "Vers dorés" presents the general Pythagorean-Swedenborgian vision of the panpsychic world; "Le Christ aux Oliviers" provides a setting of dark night of the universe, a pivotal revolution in which an old religion dies and a new one is born; "Delfica," "Myrtho," and "Horus," continuing in this vein, treat axial transformations, past or future. The technique that Nerval utilizes characteristically and movingly after the last sonnet of "Le Christ aux Oliviers" is that of a fusion of various religious elements, a sort of lyrical syncretism. For example (Nerval is speaking of Christ in section V):

> C'était bien lui, ce fou, cet insensé sublime:
> Cet Icare oublié qui remontait les cieux,

> Ce Phaéton perdu sous la foudre des dieux,
> Ce bel Atys meurti que Cybèle ranime!

> It was indeed he, that fool, that sublime madman:
> That forgotten Icarus who flew back into the skies,
> That Phaeton lost beneath the gods' lightning bolt,
> That fair wounded Attis, whom Cybele revives!

and in "Horus," Isis becomes identified with Cybele and Aphrodite and, by a more remote analogy, with all the divine mothers whose offspring herald a transformation of the world.

From a stylistic point of view, these sonnets attempt—and generally achieve—the maximum of transmutation in a minimum of space; they are indeed an "alchimie du verbe," though this does not mean they can be explained with reference to alchemy alone. The major characteristic, then, of *Les Chimères* is the metamorphic style—a style of transformations and incarnations which corresponds in some way to the illuministic beliefs in metempsychosis held by Nerval and which, on another level, expressed itself in a historical syncretism of religion and, still on another, in a parallel syncretism of the female archetype ("poursuivre les mêmes traits dans les femmes diverses," to pursue the same features in different women). In a sense, this Protean-metamorphic style is the style of virtually the entire Romantic period, with its attempt to provide, simultaneously, maximum variety (of experience) and maximum unity (of organization) by means of various styles of motivic repetition and transformation (compare Berlioz, Wagner, "cyclical" style in symphonic writing): it is the new organic style of the nineteenth century, replacing the older, externally balanced symmetrical and rational style of the preceding three hundred years. This new aesthetic prefers the geometric figures of the circle and the sphere and cultivates analogies to music rather than architecture and geometry. In Nerval the predilection for the circle, the *ballet des heures* (analyzed by Georges Poulet[17]), accounts for a certain form given to his works but also for a failure to impose this form on anything other than his mind and its operations.

Something else needs to be said about Nerval's attitude toward Orpheus. From his preface to the translation of *Faust II* of 1840,[18] it is evident that the theme of Orpheus interested him before the traditionally assigned cleavage in his personal life and literary career (1841, first psychotic break; 1842, death of Jenny Colon; 1843, departure for the East). But in *Le Voyage en Orient*, published in 1851, there is a strangely ambivalent passage about Orpheus. In discussing various paradise myths with a fellow traveler in Egypt, Nerval follows astrological and neo-Pythagorean tradition in equating Moses, Triptolemus, Orpheus, and Pythagoras as shamanic founders of religions. According to this notion, Moses absorbed Egyptian religion and incorporated it into the biblical tradition. At this point, Nerval's interlocutor voices an important criticism of Orpheus; the fact that Nerval did not place this statement in his own mouth only complicates the problem:

Orphée eut encore moins de succès que Moïse; il manqua la quatrième épreuve, dans laquelle il fallait avoir la présence d'esprit de saisir les anneaux suspendus au-dessus de soi, quand les échelons de fer commençaient à manquer sous les pieds . . . Il retomba dans le canal, d'où on le tira avec peine, et au lieu de parvenir au temple, il lui fallut retourner en arrière et remonter jusqu'à la sortie des pyramides. Pendant l'épreuve, sa femme lui avait été enlevée par un de ces accidents naturels dont les prêtres créaient aisément l'apparence. Il obtint, grâce à son talent et à sa renommée, de recommencer les épreuves et les manqua une seconde fois. C'est ainsi qu'Eurydice fut perdue à jamais pour lui et bu'il se vit réduit à la pleurer dans l'exil.[19]

Orpheus was even less successful than Moses; he failed the fourth test, in which he needed the presence of mind to get hold of the rings suspended above him, when the iron rungs began to give way under his feet . . . He fell into the canal, from which he was rescued with difficulty, and instead of reaching the temple, he had to go back to the exit of the pyramids. During the test, his wife had been abducted from him by one of those natural accidents which the priests know so well how to simulate. He received permission, thanks to his talent and renown, to start the trials all over again and failed them a second time. Then Eurydice was forever lost for him, and he saw himself reduced to lament her in exile.

This fantastic version of the Orpheus story is a good indication of the apocryphal distortions it underwent. It is curious to encounter the notion of Orpheus as a failure in Nerval's work, even though one cannot be sure that Nerval in any way subscribed to it. In any event, he makes no attempt to refute it in the story, contenting himself with this casual (though appropriate) remark: "Avec ce système il est possible d'expliquer matériellement toutes les religions. Mais qu'y gagnerons-nous?" (With that system all religions can be materially explained. But what will we gain from it?) Nerval's interlocutor does not answer. But in view of a certain ambivalence in Nerval's treatment of Orpheus in some of the *Chimères* to be discussed, one may legitimately wonder whether the idea of Orpheus as a failure did not haunt him—in addition to all the other mythological labyrinths into which he constantly ventured. If Orpheus bungled, who is the real archetypal model? Christ? Faust? Or Prometheus? From this the deep contortions in Nerval's psyche can be sensed: the problem for him was not only Prometheus versus Orpheus, but the "good" versus the "bad" Orpheus. No wonder that his delicate personality could not ultimately stand the strain of this ferocious identity crisis. For it is precisely here that he was destined to founder; the integration of his religious passion and the unification of all the incarnations of the redemptive Female required, as a final complement, integration of the self into the archetypal Male. The tragedy of Nerval's quest is the insistence of the Nervalian double and the further fragmentation into a multiple Nerval.

Albert Béguin points out that Nerval was neither very rebellious nor blasphemous: "However, his rebellion is short-winded; he does not belong to the race of great blasphemers."[20] But the Promethean temptation does exist in him, and—as is the case with the other Romantics, such as Shelley and Byron—it becomes linked to the Faustian, and through Faust to Satan, in a way that is not true of the anti-Romantic Goethe. Nerval's *Pandora*, composed of two short chapters intended to prolong the "Amours de Vienne" section of *Le Voyage en Orient* and immediately preceding *Aurélia*, had already touched on the Promethean-Faust motif directly. (The epigraph is the famous "Zwei Seelen leben, ach! in meiner Brust"—"Alas! two souls dwell in my breast"—of *Faust I*; and, without doing violence to the general meaning of the passage, which needs no analysis, it can be added that the basic conflict between the two souls is also that of Prometheus and Orpheus.) The fact that Nerval in this story purposely confounds Prometheus with Epimetheus is of minor importance; as observed earlier, he had a predilection for the game of doubles, although in this story the doubling is not explicit. Jean Richer's comment is perceptive: "Whereas Gérard used his dreams in *Aurélia*, he made *La Pandora* into an anthology of his nightmares."[21] What does matter is that Nerval, confronted with a Pandora, (the anti-Aurélia), slips into an identification with Prometheus: "Je lui rappelais les souffrances de Prométhée, quand il mit au jour une créature aussi dépravée qu'elle"[22] (I reminded her of the sufferings of Prometheus, when he put into the world so depraved a creature). The final meeting with Pandora takes place in Northern Europe:

"Te voilà encore, enchanteresse," m'écriai-je, "et la boîte fatale, qu'en as-tu fait?"

"Je l'ai remplie pour toi," dit-elle, "des plus beaux joujoux de Nuremberg. Ne viendras-tu pas les admirer?"

Mais je me pris à fuir à toutes jambes vers la place de la Monnaie. "O fils des dieux, père des hommes!" criait-elle, "arrête un peu. C'est aujourd'hui la Saint-Sylvestre comme l'an passé . . . Où as-tu caché le feu du ciel que tu dérobas à Jupiter?"

Je ne voulus pas répondre; le nom de Prométhée me déplaît toujours singulièrement, car je sens encore à mon flanc le bec éternel du vautour dont Alcide m'a délivré.

"O Jupiter! Quand finira mon supplice?"[23]

"There you are again, enchantress," I exclaimed, "and what did you do with the fatal box?"

"I filled it with the most beautiful toys from Nuremberg for you," she said. "Aren't you coming to admire them?"

But I began running full speed toward the Place de la Monnaie. "O son of the gods, father of men!" she shouted, "Stop a moment. Today is Saint Sylvester's day, like last year . . . Where did you hide the fire from heaven that you stole from Jupiter?"

I could not bring myself to answer; the name of Prometheus always gives me a strange displeasure, for I still feel at my side the eternal vulture's beak from which Hercules delivered me.

"O Jupiter! When will my torment end?"

In the sonnet "Antéros" this theme receives the kind of expansion already noted in the *Chimères*. The title has a double meaning: the "race of Antaeus" refers to the giant who retained his strength only so long as he was in touch with the earth (here there is also a relation to the Adamite race, "les enfants du limon"); and Anti-Eros refers to the offspring of Mars and Venus, a vindictive and destructive principle. This Antaeus figure is equated in the poem with Cain and the accursed and disinherited races: Cain, Esau, Amalec, ultimate avengers of the gods Baal and Dagon, over whom Jehovah once triumphed.

But the Anteros figure can exist only momentarily—as a gesture of protest— in the context of the "esprit nouveau" presided over by Isis. Isis, as Aphrodite, makes Eros meaningful and confers purpose as the existence of Aurélia, or Adrienne, or whatever name Nerval might choose to give human incarnation to the archetype; whereas the setting of Prometheus and Cain permits only the existence of Pandora. Thus the true culmination points of *Les Chimères* are "El Desdichado," which exalts the reborn Orpheus and the regained Eurydice, and "Artémis," which places Eurydice in the total constellation of the archetype.

El Desdichado

Je suis le ténébreux—le veuf—l'inconsolé,
Le prince d'Aquitaine à la tour abolie:
Ma seule *étoile* est morte—et mon luth constellé
Porte le *soleil* noir de la *Mélancholie*.

Dans la nuit du tombeau, toi qui m'as consolé,
Rends-moi le Pausilippe et la mer d'Italie,
La *Fleur* qui plaisait tant à mon coeur désolé,
Et la treille où le pampre à la rose s'allie.

Suis-je Amour ou Phébus? . . . Lusignan ou Biron?
Mon front est rouge encor du baiser de la reine;
J'ai rêvé dans la grotte où nage la sirène . . .

Et j'ai deux fois vainqueur traversé l'Achéron:
Modulant tour à tour sur la lyre d'Orphée
Les soupirs de la sainte et les cris de la fée.

I am the shadowy one—the widowed—the unconsoled,
The Prince of Aquitania of the ruined tower:
My only *star* is dead—and my starred lute
Bears the black *sun* of *Melancholy*.

In the night of the tomb, you who consoled me,
Give me back Posilippo and the Italian sea,
The *Flower* that pleased my desolate heart so much,
And the arbor where the vine and the rose are entwined.

Am I Eros or Phoebus? . . . Lusignan or Biron?
My brow is still red with the kiss of the queen;
I have dreamed in the cave where the mermaid swims . . .

And twice victoriously have I crossed the Acheron:
Modulating in turn on the Orphic lyre
The sighs of the saint and the cries of the fairy.

One alternate title of the poem (in a manuscript version) is "Le Destin." The sonnet stands under the shadow of a black destiny, the destiny of misfortune (*desdichado* meaning unfortunate), the disinheritance ("ténébreux, morte, soleil noir, Mélancolie, tombeau"), and the extraordinary dark resonances that abound in the first part of the poem until they are gradually dissipated in lines 6–8, giving way to the brighter colors (especially lines 7–8 and 10) and ending in a note of triumph (12–14).

Without attempting to use extraneous aids, such as alchemical lore or the tarot pack of cards (reflected in this poem, but only to illuminate facets of secondary importance), one notes that in this sonnet the poet defines his present state (widowerhood, disconsolateness) in relation to his past: the death of his beloved (the "seule étoile"), the memory of a consoling figure in a previous "nuit de tombeau" (identifiable with "Octavie" and reflected once more in the "Myrtho" sonnet). Confrontation of present with past gives rise to the crucial question that opens the first tercet: What sort of lover am I? What sort of poet am I? The first inquiry is in terms of Amour-Eros-Bacchus against Phoebus-Apollo; it poses the question of relationship between the experience of love and transmutation of the experience into beauty. The Lusignan-Biron contrast connects with the (presumed) "prince d'Aquitaine" ancestry and with Nerval's actual roots in Valois. (Biron is one of the heroes of Valois legends; a possible cross-reference is intended to the Biron in *Love's Labour's Lost*, an apposite title in this context.) But the point is not so much geographical: the question is rather whether the disinherited Nerval of the "tour abolie" (a symbol of dispossessed nobility) is to find his identification in legendary living persons of the past, or in the gods. The answer is, I think, that neither set of contrasts or dilemmas predominates, but that the final identification, as a kind of coincidence of opposites, is to be found in Orpheus—who is at the same time divine (the subject of a cult) and human; who is, as well, the subject of legends; and who in the descent (as a "veuf," and "ténébreux") recovers not so much Eurydice herself as the power of song that she vouchsafes.

The three lines that follow the double inquiry are significant in their assertions. First, there is still imprinted on the poet's forehead the memory and proof of the experience of love, the Eros-mark. Second, the dream (the Apollonian) is, or has been, equally present all along (the poetic disposition has always been there: the experience prolongs itself into the present to activate the poetic urge). And finally, the role of Orpheus has been assumed before, on two occasions (which suggest, perhaps, that the *modern* poet must descend several times), with victorious results: the metamorphosis into song of the quintessence of the Feminine, in its sacred ("les soupirs de la sainte") and its secular and magic ("les cris de la fée") aspects. In brief, Orpheus transmutes Eurydice into song.

Attempts to identify the "sainte" as Adrienne or Aurélia and the "fée" as Sophie Dawes or Sylvie lead away from the real contextual significance of the line, which, in terms of the interpretation given to the crucial line 9, is the double aspect of Eurydice corresponding to the double aspect of the poet. What matters here *poetically* is the poetic density of the sonnet. The "fée" harks back to Melusina, implied by the Lusignan reference: the elusive nymph whose husband was Lusignan (and Nerval, here as elsewhere, lets his allusion do double duty—the name Lusignan also designates a feudal family of Angoulême, strengthening the aristocratic references at the beginning of the sonnet). Thus the opposites secular-sacred, successful lover-bereaved lover, and defeat-victory are constantly being played off against each other in an attempt to effect a coincidence and transcendence. If Nerval's ambivalence toward Orpheus hinted at in *Voyage en Orient* is recalled, it may even be possible to see an element of elated triumph (*hubris?*) in the "deux fois vainqueur": this is not only an autobiographical allusion to Nerval's two "crises de folie" (1841 and 1853) prior to the writing and publication of the sonnet, but also a declaration of Orpheus surpassed, Orpheus as equal to the Pythagorean sages, having at last accomplished his rites of initiation. Once again, it is well to insist on the essential unity of the Orpheus figure as presented in the sonnet: the mediator between Dionysus and Apollo, the divine and the human, the contemporary and the legendary, the defeated and the victorious, the widower and the husband.

Against "El Desdichado," with its resonances of *Les Filles du feu,* must be set "Artémis," which belongs to the orbit of *Aurélia.* "El Desdichado" inquired into the destiny of the poet by inspecting the past with relation to the present; "Artémis" (whose alternate title in another manuscript version is "Ballet des heures") is the existential collapse of Orpheus in a confrontation of the actual present with an eternal present. Considering the two sonnets, Jean Richer notes that "'El Desdichado' is the triumph of Destiny, 'Artémis' the Triumph of Love, which is also Death, and the two sonnets are at the same time epitaphs of the Poet. In this way they complete and illuminate each other mutually and, like 'Sylvie' and *Aurélie,* make up a single *imaginary autobiography.*"[24] Whereas the movement of "El Desdichado" was down and then up and out (from "ténébreux" to "vainqueur")—the Orphic victory—the movement of "Artémis" is, simply, downward, the words "tombez" and "abîme" absorbing the poem's downward impact.

Artémis

La Treizième revient . . . C'est encore la première;
Et c'est toujours la seule—ou c'est le seul moment;
Car es-tu reine, ô toi! la première ou dernière?
Es-tu roi, toi le seul ou le dernier amant? . . .

Aimez qui vous aima du berceau dans la bière;
Celle que j'aimai seul m'aime encore tendrement:
C'est la mort—ou la morte . . . Ô délice! Ô tourment!
La rose qu'elle tient, c'est la rose trémière.

Sainte napolitaine aux mains pleines de feux,
Rose au coeur violet, fleur de sainte Gudule:*
As-tu trouvé ta croix dans le désert des cieux?

Roses blanches, tombez! vous insultez nos dieux,
Tombez, fantômes blancs, de votre ciel qui brûle:
—La Sainte de l'abîme est plus sainte à mes yeux!

The Thirteenth returns . . . It is still the first;
And it is still the only one—or it is the only moment:
For are you queen, O you! the first or the last?
Are you king, you [who are] the sole or the last lover?

Love the one who loved you from the cradle in the grave;
Her whom I alone loved still loves me tenderly:
She is death—or the dead one . . . O delight! O torment!
The rose that she holds is the hollyhock rose.

Neapolitan saint with hands full of fires [lights],
Rose of the violet heart, Saint Gudula's flower:
Did you find your cross in the desert of the heavens?

White roses, fall! You insult our gods,
Fall, white phantoms, from your burning sky:
—The saint of the abyss is holier in my eyes.

The interrogation is placed at the end of the first quatrain; here again, as in

---

* A variant has "soeur de sainte Gudule"—St. Gudula's sister.

line 9 of "El Desdichado," the convergence of opposites ("première ou derni-ère," and so on) provides the answer, in this particular case clearly affirmed by the words "seul" and "seule." But the poem is more complex, just as *Aurélia* is more complex than the prose works that precede it. Lines 1 and 2 are concerned with the circularity of time, and a note in the Eluard manuscript (as well as its title, "Ballet des heures") makes this clear: "la XIIIᵉ Heure (pivotale)"—the thir-teenth is the hour designating repetition of the cycle, or the pivot, from the standpoint of which time is arrested, suspended. The key word "moment" is also axial: it pivots from the experience *of* time to the experience of love *in* time and, by an analogous movement, sets up a suspension of the lovers into one archetypal unit, queen and king.

The second quatrain pursues the feminine archetype across this suspension of time and space by expanding the image of the queen into the mother-spouse; that is, if I may exceed the confines of the poem for a moment, Aurélia-Isis. This excursus is all the more justifiable because the hollyhock is specifically associated with Aurélia (I, 773), but also, as Nerval indicates in a note of the Eluard manuscript, with Sainte Philomène (the "beloved"), a Neapolitan saint repre-sented as holding a (hollyhock) rose.

This saintly essence of the archetypal Beloved accounts for the two other saints, one southern (St. Rosalie, associated with Palermo), one northern (St. Gudula, associated with Brussels). These three incarnations of the saintly woman bring the poet to the all-important question: "As-tu trouvé ta croix dans le désert (a variant has l'abîme) des cieux?" The question is a challenge, and the negative answer is foreshadowed by the word "désert" (abîme). The final tercet marks the lapse and collapse of the poet's vision: the conflict between the deities on high, in the upper "abysses" of the saints, and "*nos* dieux," the deities down below—a conflict between the Christian version and the pantheistic-magic version of the world—culminates in the final desperate challenging assertion that the Eurydice of the downward way is holier to the poet than the trans-figured Aurélia-Isis.

There is, as it were, a gap between "El Desdichado" and "Artémis": it is as though Nerval had written "El Desdichado" in preparation for another Orphic descent, trying to assure himself of the victorious outcome by recalling the two earlier plunges. With "Artémis" the poet remains fixed in the underworld; just as time is suspended in the poem, so the Orphic is suspended at the edge of Hades. Whereas in "El Desdichado" the poet underwent the spell of Aphrodite-Eros, the later sonnet is under the ban of Artemis, the virgin and moon goddess. The scene has shifted from an impending eclipse (le soleil noir) beyond the eclipse (the realm of night). Whether the final commitment to a dark Eurydice constitutes in itself an admission of failure, or a realization that only the way down is the way out—that in a state of darkness the poet can only sing the darkness—is difficult to say. Going by Nerval's biography, one must conclude that "Artémis" ends in a recognition of failure.

Tout est accompli. Je n'ai plus à accuser que moi-même et mon impatience qui m'a fait exclure du *paradis*. Je travaille et j'enfante désormais dans la douleur.[25]

All is fulfilled. I have only myself to accuse and my impatience which made me to be excluded from *paradise*. From now on I toil and give birth in pain.

But biographical criteria are never quite reliable: biography treats the outer life of a man and merely conjectures about the inner. The conclusion of *Aurélia* leaves Gérard in a state of suspension, also, but one between light and dark, life and death, reality and dream, paradise and hell.

The causes of this unresolved dilemma lie in the very substance of Nerval's thought and experience, in what Georges Poulet calls the disaster that threatens his imagination. Nerval's constant tendency to absorb greater and greater areas in his imagination by a process of concentric expansion, Poulet notes, results in a vanishing: "For growing to great proportions is vanishing away . . . There is nothing more fascinating than this relation between *size* and *loss*." The two facets of Nerval's thought, according to Poulet, are described in this way: "The glorious facet: a truly divine movement whereby his creative thought develops farther and farther and more and more triumphantly into the nature that it absorbs; and the tragic movement, at the same time, since by absorbing everything that thought becomes no longer thinkable. It vanishes into its own largeness, leaving the inner universe in death and night."[26] This is essentially the thrust of "Artemis," reversing the upward dynamics of "El Desdichado": as the outer vision fades, the inner unity fades—the double is in control for good. On the cosmic level, this means that the syncretistic vision of the cosmos gives way once more to the very force that brought vision to being: the Gnostic conviction of the split between spirit and matter that needed to be repaired by magic and esoteric means. The Orphic vision of harmonizing the world, restoring its pristine unity, was one of the major ingredients of the syncretistic urge; but when the vision fades, all that is left is the derelict figure of Orpheus with a derelict Eurydice (it now no longer really matters whether he turns back to look at her at the risk of losing her), at the upper edge of the abyss.

In a sense, this marks the failure to realize an Orphic synthesis in the first part of the nineteenth century. Here is, as Poulet notes, the opposite pole of thought from Dante's: "Contrary to Dante's thought, Nerval's does not move from hell to paradise, but from paradise to hell . . . The spiritual history of Nerval is the history of a being who insisted on getting along without the world in order to bring *his own* world into existence."[27]

The intellectual and personal conflict that ultimately broke Nerval is the tension between the Christian view, which he wanted to adhere to, and the pagan-Gnostic view, which he did adhere to (though obviously with reservations). The magic circle of paganism constantly threatened to turn into the Ouroboros and consume his own substance. "Je me nourris de ma propre substance et ne me renouvelle pas"[28] (I feed on my own substance and do not renew myself). Nerval's last letter, written the night preceding his suicide, bears witness to the ultimate ambiguity of his position.

Quand j'aurai triomphé de tout . . . Ne m'attends pas ce soir car la nuit sera noire et blanche.[29]

When I have triumphed over everything . . . Do not wait for me tonight, for the night will be black and white.

IV

Mallarmé:
Orpheus and
the Néant

Although barely a decade separates Nerval's Orphic creations from Mallarmé's early poems and from the greatly significant "crisis years" 1864–1869, the conception of the Orphic poet in Mallarmé is so vastly different from that of Nerval that one must speak of a new phase. Both Novalis and Nerval transform the traditional conception of the Orphic concordance by placing new emphasis on the visionary and prophetic mission of the Romantic poet and by super-imposing thereon the tangled apparatus of mystical science, or scientific mys-tiques. The philosophical atmosphere remains that of the Neoplatonists and Swedenborgians, with some cross-ventilation from the German idealistic philos-ophers, particularly Fichte and Schelling.

With Mallarmé the ambience changes: the face of Orpheus appears in a new light, his lyre acquires a new intonation. At first glance much appears as it was before: the poet is still a visionary who possesses a certain key to the invisible world and accordingly speaks the language of correspondences. All this is pre-cisely formulated by Baudelaire without any specific recourse to the Orphic, but very obviously in tune with it, and is found again in such early work of Mallarmé as this note (1864) on Theodore de Banville:

C'est que cet homme représente en nos temps le poëte, l'éternel et le classique poëte, fidèle à la déesse, et vivant parmi la gloire oubliée des héros et des dieux. Sa parole est, sans fin, un chant d'enthousiasme, d'où s'élance la musique, et le cri de l'âme ivre de toute la gloire. Les vents sinistres qui parlent dans l'effarement de la nuit, les abîmes pittoresques de la nature, il ne les veut entendre ni ne doit les voir: il marche en roi à travers l'enchantement édenéen de l'âge d'or, célébrant à jamais la noblesse des rayons et la rougeur des roses, les cygnes et l'éclatante blancheur du lis enfant—la terre heureuse! Ainsi dut être celui qui le premier reçut des dieux la lyre et dit l'ode éblouie avant notre aïeul Orphée. Ainsi lui-même, Apollon.

Aussi j'ai institué dans mon rêve la cérémonie d'un triomphe que j'aime à évoquer aux heures de splendeur et de féerie, et je l'appelle la fête du poëte: l'élu est cet homme au nom prédestiné, harmonieux comme un poëme et charmant comme un décor.[1]

The fact is that this man represents the poet in our time, the eternal and classical poet, faithful to the goddess and living amid the forgotten glory of heroes and gods. His speech is, without end, a song of enthusiasm from which music takes its flight, and the cry of the soul intoxicated with all the glory. The sinister winds that speak in the dread of night, the picturesque abysses of nature—he does not wish to hear them, nor does he wish to see them: like a king he walks through the paradisaic enchantment of the golden age, forever celebrating the nobility of sunrays and the redness of roses, swans and doves, and the shining whiteness of the infant lily—earth in a state of happiness! This must have been the way of him who first received the lyre from the gods and spoke the dazzled ode before our ancestor Orpheus came. This was Apollo himself.

I too have instituted in my dream the ceremony of a triumph that I love to evoke in the hour of splendor and enchantment, and I call it the poet's feast: the elect is that man with the predestined name, harmonious as a poem and charming as scenery.

This passage with its overblown aestheticism obviously has less to do with Banville than with the ideal poet—with Mallarmé's own aspirations. The vocabulary of paradisaic enchantments, swans, white lilies, and particularly of the ceremony, triumph, and feast of the poet-elect is a harbinger of the Mallarmé-to-be. Significantly, the link between Orpheus and Apollo provides no tension yet. But at the very moment when this tribute to Banville was composed, Mallarmé was already entering upon a series of inner trials—five years of great despair and anguish, comparable to a prolonged Orphic descent, from which he emerged triumphant and transformed. Even though the experience is not specifically described by the author as Orphic, it has all the characteristics of the Orphic *katábasis*: the nocturnal setting, the plunge into the deepest recesses of the psyche, the encounter with death, and the recovery of song.

The well-known autobiographical letter to Paul Verlaine (November 16,

1885) in which Mallarmé speaks of his literary aspirations, projecting his "Grand Oeuvre," his "Livre," which is to be the Orphic explanation of the earth, contains the assertion that this book is the only poetic work that can ever exist.

J'ai toujours rêvé et tenté autre chose, avec une patience d'alchimiste, prêt à y sacrifier toute vanité et toute satisfaction, comme on brûlait jadis son mobilier et les poutres de son toit, pour alimenter le fourneau du Grand Oeuvre. Quoi? c'est difficile à dire: un livre, tout bonnement, en maints tomes, un livre qui soit un livre, architectural et prémédité, et non un recueil des inspirations de hasard fussent-elles merveilleuses . . . J'irai plus loin, je dirai: le Livre, persuadé qu'au fond il n'y en a qu'un, tenté à son insu par quiconque a écrit, même les Génies. L'explication orphique de la Terre, qui est le seul devoir du poëte et le jeu littéraire par excellence: car le rhythme même du livre, alors impersonnel et vivant, jusque dans sa pagination, se juxtapose aux équations de ce rêve, ou Ode. (662–663)

I have always dreamed of and attempted something else, with an alchemist's patience, ready to sacrifice to it every vanity and every satisfaction, as people once burned their furniture and the beams of their roofs to feed the fires of the Magnum Opus. What do I mean? Hard to say: a book, quite simply, in many volumes, a book that is really a book, architectural and premeditated, not merely a collection of random inspirations, however marvelous they might be . . . I'll go even further and say: the Book, since I am convinced that there is after all only one, striven for unknowingly by anyone who has ever written, even the Geniuses. The Orphic explanation of the Earth, which is the only duty of the poet and the literary game par excellence: for the very rhythm of the book, impersonal and yet alive, even its pagination, juxtaposes itself to the equations of this dream, of this Ode.

This is followed by the more subdued paragraph:

Voilà l'aveu de mon vice, mis à nu, cher ami, que mille fois j'ai rejeté, l'esprit meurtri ou las, mais cela me possède et je réussirai peut-être; non pas à faire cet ouvrage dans son ensemble (il faudrait être je ne sais qui pour cela!) mais à en montrer un fragment d'exécuté, à en faire scintiller par une place l'authenticité glorieuse, en indiquant le reste tout entier auquel ne suffit pas une vie. Prouver par les positions faites que ce livre existe, et que j'ai connu ce que je n'aurai pu accomplir. (663)

Here, then, is the confession of my vice laid bare, dear friend, which I have rejected a thousand times, when my mind was bruised or tired, but this thing has taken possession of me, and perhaps I'll succeed; not in accomplishing this work in its totality (who in the world *could* be that person!), but to show a fragment of it executed, to make the glorious authenticity of this book scintillate in one spot, so as to point up the entire rest for which one lifetime is not enough. To prove by the positions taken that this book exists, and that I have at least had knowledge of that which I will have been unable to achieve.

Outside of the two Banville essays, this is the only time I know of—other than in *Les Deuxi antiques*, a textbook on mythology compiled and translated from George W. Cox, the British comparative mythologist—that Mallarmé directly mentions the Orphic. In this particular case a crucial passage is being dealt with, namely, one regarding the nature of the Livre. That is to say, Mallarmé insists here that the Grand Oeuvre he has conceived, the one in which all poets have participated, is the Orphic explanation of the Earth: presumably an Orphic bible, a cosmology, or a set of Orphic hymns.

This statement occurs in 1885. Its possible antecedents can be traced by briefly reviewing the situation of Mallarmé as a poet and thinker between 1864 and 1869. The chronology of Mallarmé's works appears to me the only way of bringing order into research on such a difficult and forbidding topic. The poems of the young Mallarmé stand under the ban of Baudelaire, echoing the "Spleen-Idéal" tension of *Les Fleurs du mal*. They move toward the "blank page" and "Azur" poems such as "Les Fenêtres," "Brise marine," and "L'Azur" and culminate in the famous sonnet "Le Vierge, le vivace et le bel aujourd'hui" (though not published until 1885, on the evidence of its imagery it links this early group to the later poems[2]). The blank pages and bare spaces of these early poems are replaced later by the related, but intensified, vocabulary of nothingness—"rien," "aboli," "nul"; and, generally speaking, the auroral and matutinal settings are superseded by crepuscular or nocturnal décors. The 1864–1869 crisis years were marked by a desperate poetic and intellectual activity: poetry became a means of clinging to a vanishing reality. Certain works are of the utmost importance: "Hérodiade," "Monologue d'un faune," (the first draft of "L'Après-midi d'un faune"), and the sonnet "Sainte." The next cluster of poems is a group of sonnets, the most hermetic until that date, written during the later phase of Mallarmé's crisis; they have as their settings the "chambre vide." Triumphant assertions of the discovery of the Nothing, they constitute proof of Mallarmé's ascent from the depths, the record of which is found in the important and enigmatic fragment *Igitur*, dating from 1869.

Mallarmé's correspondence furnishes a number of clues as to the nature of his crisis. In January 1865 he writes: "J'ai le dégoût de moi: je recule devant les glaces, en voyant ma face dégradée et éteinte, et pleure quand je me sens vide et ne puis jeter un mot sur mon papier implacablement blanc."[3] (I am disgusted with myself: I recoil before mirrors, seeing my face degraded and extinguished, and weep at feeling myself empty and unable to put one word on my inexorably white piece of paper.) This still has the ring of the "Azur" poems—compare an earlier letter (1864) to Cazalis: "Mon pauvre cerveau est toujours fatigué. Après tout, tu sais que la seule occupation d'un homme qui se respecte est à mes yeux de regarder l'azur en mourant de faim."[4] (My poor brain is always fatigued. After all, you know that the only occupation for a man with self-respect is, in my opinion, to gaze upon the blue ideal while dying of hunger.)

Two important remarks occur in a letter to Henri Cazalis dated March 1866: Mallarmé speaks of having encountered "le Néant, auquel je suis arrivé sans connaître le Bouddhisme" (Nothingness, which I came to without knowing Buddhism), and of having realized that this Nothing is the truth that poetry must celebrate thenceforth:

Oui, *je le sais*, nous ne sommes que de vaines formes de la matière, mais bien sublimes pour avoir inventé Dieu et notre âme. Si sublimes, mon ami! que je veux me donner ce spectacle de la matière, ayant conscience d'être, et cependant, s'élançant forcenément dans le rêve qu'elle sait n'être pas, chantant l'Ame et toutes les divines impressions pareilles qui se sont amassées en nous depuis les premiers âges, et proclamant, devant le Rien qui est la vérité, ces glorieux mensonges!

Tel est le plan de mon volume lyrique, et tel sera peut-être son titre: *La Gloire du mensonge* ou *le Glorieux Mensonge*. Je le chanterai en désespéré![5]

Yes, *I know*, we are but vain forms of matter, but very sublime for having invented God and our soul. So sublime, my friend, that I want to offer myself this spectacle of matter, having consciousness of being and nevertheless, thrusting wildly into the dream which it knows as not-being, singing the Soul and all such divine impressions that have accumulated in us from the earliest epochs, and proclaiming, in the face of the Nothing which is the truth, all these glorious lies!

Such is the plan of my lyrical volume, and its title will probably be: *The Glory of the Lie* or *the Glorious Lie*. I shall sing it like a man in despair!

This marks the first turning point in which Mallarmé, having found clarification of his experience, hits upon a new resolve, albeit a desperate one. It is interesting to note that the first intimation of the Grand Oeuvre sketched out here already has overtones that, if not clearly Orphic, are at least cosmogonic. In July 1866 Mallarmé could exclaim, "après avoir trouvé le Néant, j'ai trouvé le Beau" (after finding Nothingness, I found the Beautiful); and, in the same month, "J'ai jeté les fondements d'une oeuvre magnifique . . . Je suis mort et ressuscité avec la clef des pierreries de ma dernière cassette spirituelle"[6] (I have laid the foundation of a magnificent work ... I have died and have been resurrected with the key to the jewelry of my last spiritual strongbox). At this point he speaks of "l'Oeuvre" as composed of five books—but this idea subsequently underwent several changes —and required twenty years of work.

I shall consider three important letters jointly, for the sake of brevity: one of September 24, 1866, to Villiers de l'Isle-Adam and two of May 1867, to Cazalis and Eugène Lefébure respectively. There were some remote cosmological allusions in earlier letters; but in these three it becomes increasingly evident that Mallarmé's descent into darkness and his encounter with Nothingness has the *shape* of the Orphic descent into Hades, with the important differences that there is no mention of a Eurydice figure and that Mallarmé has triumphantly returned with the Orphic knowledge of Beauty and the resolution to undertake what in his autobiographical letter of 1885 he called "the Orphic explanation of the Earth." At this point an immediate analogy suggests itself—Nerval's "descente aux enfers" described in *Aurélia* and his triumphant reascent in "El Desdichado": "Et j'ai deux fois vainqueur traversé l'Achéron: Modulant tour à tour sur ma lyre d'Orphée Les soupirs de la Sainte et les cris de la Fée." In *Aurélia* Nerval had specifically alluded to Beatrice and Eurydice as incarnations of his "Etoile morte"; in Mallarmé there is no Eurydice, or, rather, she is now an abstraction:

Je n'ai créé mon oeuvre que par élimination, et toute vérité acquise ne naissait que de la perte d'une impression qui, ayant étincelé, s'était consumée et me permettait, grâce à ses ténèbres dégagées, d'avancer plus profondément dans la sensation des Ténèbres Absolues. La Destruction fut ma Béatrice.[7]

I have created my work by mere elimination, and any truth I have acquired was born only of the loss of an impression that, after flashing, had been consumed and allowed me —thanks to the darkness supplanting it—to penetrate more deeply into the sensation of Absolute Darkness. Destruction was my Beatrice.

All descents into darkness require a process of self-destruction, self-abnegation, so that the new being can be born—this is the psychoanalytical, ontological, and theological meaning of the Orphic descent in modern times. It is also conjoined to the ultimate Narcissus gesture: the self-examination in which the beholder deliberately abolishes himself in order to go "beyond" (compare Cocteau's mirrors leading to the "other world"). Yet Mallarmé adds, in the same letter, a statement amounting to a demurrer—and a consolation. Here, once again, the considerable difference between Mallarmé and Nerval is noted: in Mallarmé's case the overcoming of Promethean aspirations, in Nerval self-destruction resulting from the Prometheus-Orpheus tension; in Mallarmé the discovery of impersonality, in Nerval the straining for an expanded personality. Thus, the scrupulous and patient Mallarmé succeeds precisely where the imprudent and impatient Nerval failed: in conquering and consecrating the darkness and extorting a particular illumination from it. The entire passage stands as a commentary and corrective to the "gates of horn and ivory" passages from *Aurélia* mentioned in Chapter III:

Mais je ne m'enorgueillis pas, mon ami, de ce résultat, et m'attriste plutôt. Car tout cela n'a pas été trouvé par le développement de mes facultés, mais par la voie pêcheresse et hâtive, satanique et *facile*, de la Destruction de moi, produisant non la force, mais une sensibilité qui, fatalement, m'a conduit là. Je n'ai, personnellement, aucun mérite, et c'est même pour éviter le remords (d'avoir désobéi à la lenteur des lois naturelles) que j'aime à me réfugier dans l'impersonnalité—qui me semble une consécration.

But, my friend, I cannot take any pride in this result; it rather saddens me. All this was not acquired through the normal development of my faculties, but by means of the sinful and hasty, satanic and *easy* road of Self-Destruction, and it did not produce the strength, but rather a sensibility that, fatally, brought me that far. I personally take no credit, and it is even for the sake of avoiding remorse (for having disobeyed the slow pace of natural laws) that I like to take refuge in impersonality—which seems like a consecration to me.

Mallarmé carried this process of depersonalization to its ultimate conclusion.

Ma pensée a été jusqu'à se penser elle-même et n'a plus la force d'évoquer en un néant unique le vide disséminé en sa porosité. J'avais, à la faveur d'une grande sensibilité, compris la correlation intime de la Poésie avec l'Univers.[8]

My thought has gone so far as to think itself, and it no longer has the strength to evoke in a unique nullity the void disseminated in its porousness. I had, thanks to a great sensibility, understood the intimate correlation of Poetry with the Universe.

The dizzying spectacle of thought thinking itself—the temptation that Valéry rejected in "Le Cimetière marin" but that haunted him throughout his entire life, from *Monsieur Teste* to *Mon Faust*—the serpent biting its tail, the pure intellectual process in which all the contingencies, matter, time, relations (including Chance), are abolished—this process of annihilation and nihilation comprises Mallarmé's categories. I believe they are *new* categories, applied to the idea of the Orphic descent that is now not so much an attempt to recover Eurydice as it is to recover a new sense of being, through which poetic vision and the power of song and the integrity of being are redeemed. This is the nature of Mallarmé's most important of these three letters, from which I shall quote several excerpts.

Je suis parfaitement mort, et la région la plus impure où mon Esprit puisse s'aventurer est l'Eternité, mon Esprit, ce solitaire habituel de sa propre pureté, que n'obscurcit plus même le reflet du Temps . . . Je suis maintenant impersonnel, et non plus Stéphane que tu as connu, mais une aptitude qu'a l'Univers Spirituel à se développer, à travers ce qui fut moi . . . J'ai fait une assez longue descente au Néant pour pourvoir parler avec exactitude. Il n'y a que la Beauté—et elle n'a qu'une expression parfaite: la Poésie. Tout le reste est mensonge . . . Pour moi, la Poésie me tient lieu de l'amour, parce qu'elle est éprise d'elle-même et que sa volupté d'elle retombe délicieusement en mon âme, mais j'avoue que la Science que j'ai acquise, ou retrouvée au fond de l'homme que je fus, ne me suffirait pas, et que ce ne serait pas sans un serrement de coeur réel que j'entrerais dans la Disparition suprême, si je n'avais pas fini mon oeuvre, qui est l'Oeuvre. Le Grand Oeuvre, comme disaient les alchimistes, nos ancêtres.[9]

I am perfectly dead, and the impurest region into which my Mind can venture is Eternity—my Mind, that hermit accustomed to its own purity, which is no longer even obscured by the reflection of Time . . . I am now impersonal and no longer the Stéphane that you have known, but an aptitude on the part of the Spiritual Universe to develop through that which once was myself . . . I have made a long enough descent into the Nothing to be able to speak with exactitude. There is only Beauty—and it has but one perfect expression: Poetry. All the rest is a lie . . . For me, Poetry takes the place of love because it is enamored of itself, and its voluptuousness drops deliciously into my soul; but I admit that the Knowledge I have acquired or rediscovered in the depths of the man I once was would not suffice me; and I would not take my final Departure without a real shrinking of the heart if I had not completed my work, which is The Work itself. The Magnum Opus, as the alchemists, our ancestors, used to say.

Not only is there in these letters a description of the Orphic descent and the explicit substitution of poetry for love, or the loved one, but also the result, formulated in two important ways. Mallarmé is now another—a depersonalized, Orphicized consciousness transmitting the vision of an abstract cosmos; secondly, there is the decision to undertake the great task, the *magnum opus alchemicum*. The vision is the new Orphic cosmogony of Beauty wrenched from the Nothing: "J'ai à revivre la vie de l'humanité depuis son enfance et prenant conscience d'elle-même"[10] (I must relive the life of mankind from its infancy onward and growing aware of itself).

In contrast to the journeys of Mallarmé's predecessors Novalis and Nerval, inspired by Orphic and illuministic doctrines which either absorb or collide with the Christian tradition, Mallarmé's "alchemy" or "kabbala" represents something radically new. It is difficult to say what Hegel's role was in all this, but it is evident from the preceding excerpts from correspondence that Mallarmé's experience is Hegelian.[11] Might the problem be resolved by saying that Mallarmé had, or was, an *anima naturaliter dialectica*? Of course Hegel's writings played some role in all this. Camille Mauclair, who knew Mallarmé, goes so far as to claim that Mallarmé's work constitutes a systematic application of Hegel's doctrine to literature. This is excessive, for in all likelihood the poet had only a partial acquaintance with Hegel's writings, to which he was probably introduced by his friend Lefébure, an Egyptologist, seconded by one of his other distinguished contemporaries, Villiers de l'Isle-Adam. Interestingly enough, Mallarmé's Hegelian moments coincide with the crisis years, particularly 1866–1867. There is no need to suppose that he read a great deal of Hegel, or to speculate whether it was the *Logic* or the *Phenomenology of Spirit*. The point is that he appears to have found some confirmation in Hegel's mode of thinking, inasmuch as it gave intellectual status to his own nocturnal experience: it provided some kind of framework to his "dark night of the soul"—a framework that accorded a place to nothingness and negation without being *merely* nihilistic, and one that could replace his residual Christianity without displacing his fundamentally mystical orientation. Just as Hegel's philosophy is constructed upon mystical ground, and along the way coincidentally echoes a number of Buddhistic tenets (note Mallarmé's remark quoted earlier, "Nothingness, which I came to without knowing Buddhism"), so Mallarmé develops out of the abortive Catholic mysticism of his adolescence into the negative-positive "mysticity" of his mature years. "The word 'nothingness' in Mallarmé means: the Universe from which God is absent," observes Adile Ayda.[12] After all—Mallarmé at the end of these crisis years did contemplate the idea of submitting a doctoral dissertation, "De Divinitate," a project which he appears to have rapidly abandoned but which in another sense he never abandoned at all. He very clearly saw his problem as theological, philosophical, and aesthetic at the same time; but, being primarily a poet, he saw its solution along the pathway of aesthetics, which after the Tournon-Avignon experience had superseded religion. "Il ne s'agit d'esthétique, mais de religiosité" (388) (It is not a question of aesthetics but of religiosity), he noted later.

Not religion, but religiosity. The statement does not really posit an either-or, but a coincidence: the problems of art are, or have become, questions of religiosity. Religiosity is the end, poetry the means; hence a completion of "De Divinitate" would have been unthinkable. The answer for Mallarmé came increasingly to be "de *poetae* divinitate," since he operates with the full consciousness of the poet as Creator—a theme implicit in Romantic poetry, here divested of its Promethean guilt but retaining, by way of compensation, an edge of Romantic irony. The cosmology of which Mallarmé's Grand Oeuvre was to be the exemplification and elucidation represented in its way a system as complete and comprehensive as Hegel's—an intellectual and poetic system that, in Kurt Wais's words, was to encompass "everything, from God to the ballerina, from absolute spirit to the poem."[13]

The letters quoted here delineate the progress from self-decomposition to self-integration; once the first wave of shocks had passed, Mallarmé increasingly relied on the terms "unity" and "impersonality" to dramatize his new-found integrity as a man, poet, and thinker:

Toute naissance est une destruction, et toute vie d'un moment l'agonie dans laquelle on ressuscite ce qu'on a perdu, pour le voir, on l'ignorait avant . . . Je crois pour être bien l'homme, la nature en pensant, il faut penser de tout son corps, ce qui donne une pensée pleine et à l'unisson comme ces cordes de violon vibrant immédiatement avec sa boîte de bois creux . . . Je suis véritablement décomposé, et dire qu'il faut cela pour avoir une vue très—une de l'Univers! Autrement, on ne sert d'autre unité que celle de sa vie.[14]

Every birth is a destruction, and the life of a moment is the agony in which something lost is resuscitated so that it can be seen, being unknown beforehand . . . I think that in order to be really a man, nature as thinking, one must think with his entire body, the result being thought full and in unison, like those violin strings vibrating immediately with its hollow sound box . . . I am truly decomposed; imagine all this being necessary in order to have a very *single* view of the Universe! Otherwise, one can't feel any other unity than that of one's life.

Some of these statements anticipate Rilke and bracket the second phase of the modern Orphic, Mallarmé-Rilke, in contradistinction with the first, Novalis-Nerval. But in a still wider sense, Mallarmé sounds the keynote of a distinctively modern literature that includes more than the specifically Orphic writers of recent decades and thus underscores the resonances and repercussions that the Orphic has had in the past seventy-five years: the aesthetics of transparency and, ultimately, of silence. The same letter concludes with what is tantamount to a prose poem about the cricket's song:

Hier seulement parmi les jeunes blés j'ai entendu cette voix sacré de la terre ingénue, moins décomposée déjà que celle de l'oiseau, fils des arbres parmi de la nuit solitaire, et qui a quelque chose des étoiles et de la lune, et un peu de mort; mais combien plus *une* surtout que celle d'une femme, qui marchait et chantait devant moi, et dont la voix semblait transparente de mille mots dans lesquels elle vibrait—et pénétrée de néant! Tant de bonheur qu'a la terre de ne pas être décomposée en matière et en esprit était dans ce son unique de grillon.[15]

Only yesterday amid the growing wheat I heard that sacred voice of the unspoiled earth, less decomposed than the voice of the bird, child of the trees in the midst of lonely night, which has something of the stars and the moon in it, and a little bit of death; but how much more *unified* this voice was, particularly when compared to the voice of a woman, who was walking and singing in front of me, transparent as it seemed with a thousand words through which it was vibrating—and how penetrated with nothingness! As much happiness as the earth can muster at not being decomposed into matter and spirit was present in this unique sound of the cricket.

A convenient and significant point of interaction between the early and later work of Mallarmé occurs in "Le Démon de l'analogie," written sometime in 1864 (*Oeuvres complètes*, 272–273). This confessional prose poem stands midway between "Azur" of January 1864 and "Sainte" of December 1865. Its obvious models are Poe's "Imp of the Perverse" and Baudelaire's adaptations of the same motif, as for example in "Le Mauvais Vitrier." Mallarmé, however, is more abstract than his predecessors. He begins: "Des paroles inconnues chantèrent-elles sur vos lèvres, lambeaux maudits d'une phrase absurde?" (Did unknown words, accursed tatters of an absurd phrase, sing on your lips?) The "phrase absurde" turns out to be an obsessive fragment of an unwritten poem,

La Pénultième

Est morte,

The Penultimate

Is dead,

devoid of significance and therefore tantalizing in its insistency, particularly because the syllable "nul" precipitates out as a quintessence. The occasion for the haunting phrase is the same as the situation basic to the poem "Sainte," in which a figure in a stained glass window—St. Cecilia—produces unheard melodies by touching the "harp" suggested by the shape of an angel's wing.

The persistent phrase of "Le Démon de l'analogie" is first associated with "la sensation propre d'une aile glissant sur les cordes d'un instrument" (the sensation suggesting a wing sliding across the strings of an instrument); subsequently,

Je . . . reconnus en le son *nul* la corde tendue de l'instrument de musique, qui était oublié et que le glorieux Souvenir certainement venait de visiter de son aile ou d'une palme et, le doigt sur l'artifice du mystère, je souris et implorai de voeux intellectuels une spéculation différente. La phrase revint, virtuelle, dégagée d'une chute antérieure de plume ou de rameau, dorénavant à travers la voix entendue, jusqu'à ce qu'enfin elle s'articula seule, vivant de sa personnalité.

I . . . recognized in the "null" sound the taut string of the musical instrument that had been forgotten and that the glorious Memory had certainly just visited with its wing or with a palm and, now that I had put my finger on the artifice of the mystery, I smiled and implored by means of intellectual vows a different speculation. The phrase returned, intact, freed from any anterior fall of feather or branch, henceforth through the voice heard, until finally it became articulated all by itself, living by its own personality.

This resembles, in a curious manner, the first stages of Proust's tenacious pursuit of the sensation that the petite madeleine had caused in him, a quest culminating eventually in the discovery of an analogy within the self and the metaphorical nature of art. There is, furthermore, a similarity in the way Mallarmé and Proust both bracket the experience by creating an empty space around it. But in Mallarmé the revelation does not come in this prose poem, as it does for Proust at the end of the episode. The interference in Mallarmé is caused by the persistence of the Azur, which mocks and frustrates him as it had in the poem "Azur":

> En vain! l'Azur triomphe, et je l'entends qui chante
> Dans les cloches . . .
> Il roule par la brume, ancien et traverse
> Ta native agonie ainsi qu'un glaive sûr

> In vain! the Azure triumphs, and I hear it singing
> In the bells . . .
> It throbs through the mist, age-old, and crosses
> Your inborn agony like a sturdy sword

or in "Renouveau":

> Cependant l'Azur rit sur la haie et l'éveil
> De tant d'oiseaux en fleur gazouillant au soleil.

> However the Azure laughs above the hedges and the awakening
> Of all those birds in bloom chirping in the sunlight.

The final paragraph of "Le Démon de l'analogie" registers this failure to discern the coordinates of analogy, to master the relation between the thing and its meaning:

Mais où s'installe l'irrécusable intervention du surnaturel, et le commencement de l'angoisse sous laquelle agonise mon esprit naguère seigneur c'est quand je vis, levant les yeux, dans la rue des antiquaires instinctivement suivie, que j'étais devant la boutique d'un luthier vendeur de vieux instruments pendus au mur, et à terre, des palmes jaunes et les ailes enfouies en l'ombre, d'oiseaux anciens. Je m'enfuis, bizarre, personne condamnée à porter probablement le deuil de l'inexplicable Pénultième.

But this is where the unimpeachable intervention of the supernatural makes itself felt, and the beginning of the anguish from which my mind, formerly in control, now lies dying, when, raising my eyes, I saw in the antiquarians' street that I was instinctively walking along, that I was in front of a lutemaker's shop, where old instruments were hung on the walls, and on the floor, yellow palms and wings of old birds, buried in the shadow. I ran off, bizarre, a man condemned to bear probably the affliction of the inexplicable Penultimate.

"Probablement," says Mallarmé, but the deathlike paralysis of the ending is only penultimate, so to speak. The hint was provided a little earlier, but not fully heeded or understood—another similarity with Proust. As the speaker stands in front of the lutenist's shop, he experiences the intimation of hearing the voice once again, this time in its original purity:

Je sentis que j'avais, ma main réfléchie par un vitrage de boutique y faisant le geste d'une caresse qui descend sur quelque chose, la voix même (la première, qui indubitablement avait été l'unique).

I felt that, with my hand reflected by a shop window in the process of outlining a caress as it settled on something, I had possession of that very voice (the first one, which undoubtedly had been the only one).

Mallarmé

The window of the shop is the potential convergence of what was ("le glorieux Souvenir") and what will be—were it not for the fact that the future is blocked by the agony of the Azur and the fact that the present is dominated by the torment of the falseness of the representation: "la sonorité même et l'air de mensonge assumé par la hâte de la facile affirmation étaient une cause de tourment" (the very sonority and the deceitful air assumed by an impatience for a facile affirmation were one cause of torment).

In effect, the blockage is identical with that outlined in "Les Fenêtres," written in 1863, which locates the dividing line between life ("triste hôpital") and the creative urge toward renascence ("la bouche, fiévreuse et d'azur bleu vorace") precisely in the transparent Narcissus-medium of a glass that separates and yet reveals the basic incompatibility of moribund life and renascent creation. The problem is presented with a touch of Baudelaire's Luciferism in terms of Icarus, who falls, and an angel, who soars:

> Je fuis et je m'accroche à toutes les croisées
> D'où l'on tourne l'épaule à la vie, et, béni,
> Dans leur verre, lavé d'éternelles rosées,
> Que dore le matin chaste de l'Infini

> Je me mire et me vois ange! et je meurs, et j'aime
> —Que la vitre soit l'art, soit la mysticité—
> A renaître, portant mon rêve en diadème,
> Au ciel antérieur où fleurit la Beauté!

> Mais, hélas! Ici-bas est maître: sa hantise
> Vient m'écoeurer parfois jusqu'en cet abri sûr,
> Et le vomissement impur de la Bêtise
> Me force à me boucher le nez devant l'azur.

> Est-il moyen, ô Moi qui connais l'amertume,
> D'enfoncer le cristal par le monstre insulté
> Et de m'enfuir, avec mes deux ailes sans plume
> —Au risque de tomber pendant l'éternité?

> I flee and cling to all the casements
> Where one turns one's back to life and, blessed,

94

In their glass, washed by eternal dews
Gilded by the chaste morning of the Infinite

I gaze at myself and see myself as an angel! and I die, and love
—Let the window be art, or mysticity—
To be reborn, bearing my dreams as a diadem,
In an anterior sky where Beauty flourishes!

But, alas! this world down here is in control: obsessively
It comes to dishearten me sometimes even in this secure shelter,
And the impure vomit of Stupidity
Forces me to stop up my nose before the azure.

Is there a way, o Self that knowest bitterness,
To strike through the crystal insulted by [the reflection of] the monster
and to take flight, with my two wings without plumage
—At the risk of falling during eternity?

The problem, clearly stated, is: How can I break through the glass? The episode in "Le Démon de l'analogie" suggests that a reflection in the glass—the Narcissus gesture—may be a way to surmount the contradiction of artistic existence. Finally, in "Sainte," the problem finds its resolution—not, however, in the potential rebellion of "Les Fenêtres" or in the possible double perspective of "Le Démon de l'analogie," but in the dialectic of negation and affirmation in which the musical instruments associated with St. Cecilia are invisible and the music arises from something not inherently a musical instrument but merely suggestive of one:

A ce vitrage d'ostensoir
Que frôle une harpe par l'Ange
Formée avec son vol du soir
Pour la délicate phalange

Du doigt que, sans le vieux santal
Ni le vieux livre, elle balance
Sur le plumage instrumental,
Musicienne du silence

At that monstrance-like stained glass
Brushed by the harp

Shaped out of the Angel's evening flight
For the [touch of] the delicate tip

Of the finger which, without the old sandalwood
Nor the old book, she holds poised
Upon the instrumental plumage,
[Like a] Musician of silence.

The music of silence *is* at the same time music and silence, therefore greater than either. The window, this time, has become the locus at which negation and affirmation coalesce: the "facile affirmation" of the "Démon de l'analogie" is no longer facile because it has been preceded by a negation. In this way the window of "Sainte" has become the site in which the mystery of analogy is enacted and revealed, the point at which the perverse demon of analogy transmutes itself into a benevolent daimon, an angel.

The well-known "Swan" sonnet was first published in 1885, yet its subject matter and imagery situate its conception and possibly its composition in the crisis years as an exemplar of Mallarméan self-examination and self-critique.

Le vierge, le vivace et le bel aujourd'hui
Va-t-il nous déchirer avec un coup d'aile ivre
Ce lac dur oublié que hante sous le givre
Le transparent glacier des vols qui n'ont pas fui!

Un cygne d'autrefois se souvient que c'est lui
Magnifique mais qui sans espoir se délivre
Pour n'avoir pas chanté la région où vivre
Quand du stérile hiver a resplendi l'ennui.

Tout son col secouera cette blanche agonie
Par l'espace infligée à l'oiseau qui le nie,
Mais non l'horreur du sol où le plumage est pris.

Fantôme qu'à ce lieu son pur éclat assigne,
Il s'immobilise au songe froid de mépris
Que vêt parmi l'exil inutile le Cygne.

The virgin, vivacious and beautiful new day
Will it tear open for us by means of a wild stroke of the wing

This hard forgotten lake haunted underneath the frost
By the transparent glacier of flights that did not take wing!

A swan of yesteryear remembers that it is himself
Magnificent, but giving himself up without hope
For not having sung the region where to live
When the tedium of sterile winter shone forth.

His whole neck will shake off that white agony
Inflicted by space upon the bird who negates it [space],
But [it can] not [shake off] the horror of the soil in which his plumage is caught.

[Turned] phantom assigned to this place by his pure brightness,
He immobilizes himself with a cold dream of scorn
That the Swan dons in the midst of useless exile.

This sonnet raises the question whether resurrection into the new day is possible
to the swan-poet; it focuses through the reply on the fallen, imprisoned condition of the poet but does so without a trace of romantic sentimentality, since the
"exil inutile" is the direct consequence of the swan's failure to elevate himself to
the "région où vivre." A passage from Ovid's *Metamorphoses* has relevance here.
Cygnus, lamenting the fall of Phaethon, his friend and relative, and the punishment visited upon Phaethon's sisters, was metamorphosed into a swan:

> And Cycnus was a new
> Thing called a swan, a creature who remembered
> Jove's burning thunderbolt, unjustly fired
> At falling Phaeton. Therefore he feared
> The higher heavens and sought out stagnant streams,
> Pools, quiet lakes, and since he hated fire,
> He took to shaded waters for his home.[16]

Besides the reference to the solar myth of Phaethon, one notes in this passage the
swan's retreat from Jupiter, and the fire-water antithesis. Mallarmé takes this
antithesis one step farther and freezes the swan; then he enlarges the mythological possibilities by extending a spatial axis from lake to sky in the final tercet. The
frozen lake is thus no more and no less than the window pane of "Les Fenêtres"
seen horizontally (both are "glaces"). The similarity with "Azur" is clear
enough; by the same reasoning, the present sonnet is also the antithesis of

"Sainte," in terms of the imagery of the paralyzed wing and plumage alone.

What is new in this poem is the time-structure of the sonnet and its significance. The fourteen lines make up a superbly coordinated whole, of which the traditional subdivisions are distinct but integrated entities. The first quatrain centers around the word "aujourd'hui"—the present moment in which the event must take place if it is to take place. The second focuses on "d'autrefois" in such a way that the expression can be taken to qualify "un cygne" or as an object of "se souvient" (the second way is, in my view, somewhat preferable). This quatrain establishes the *past* magnificence of the poet-swan as a haunting and imperative memory and links it to the present by "sans espoir se délivre"— the capitulation before the moment of decision. The pattern is similar for the first tercet, except that the projection is into the future and back to the present: only the swan's head and neck can be or will be free, but the body is inescapably clamped by the ice. The final tercet falls into the present, and in such a way that this present becomes, like the swan, immobilized and eternalized—a timeless present. The agony of the "i" rhymes and the shrill sonorities converges upon the "white" climax of "Il s'immobilise au songe frond de mépris / Que vêt parmi l'exil inutile le Cygne." The capitalization of the final word provides a problem. Is it a reaffirmation of the essence of the swan, the elevation of the swan to Platonic ideality? That is to say, is it the same as "Tel qu'en Lui-même l'éternité le change" in "Tombeau d'Edgar Poe"? The answer is ambiguous, and out of the attempt to resolve the ambiguity grows the Mallarméan quest and discovery of the crisis years.

Yes, the swan's immortality is affirmed here, but *only in a negative sense*:[17] Mallarmé's irony and paradox express the idea that the swan is most deeply himself because he has willed to negate himself—to commit metaphysical suicide. But in this will to self-annihilation, which occurs at the temporal moment of the poem—and this "now" is obsessively affirmed throughout the poem—the earth-bound "now" is transcended and virutally supplanted by a stellar "now," which is freed from the contingencies of existence and has absolute being in the beyond. The Cygne referred to at the end of the sonnet is also, as an ultimate meta-morphosis, the constellation Cycnus, emitting its white light in another exile that, too, is useless but nevertheless meaningful because it is eternal: Cycnus really is in the "région où vivre." The irony in this phrase has not been accorded sufficient comment by exegetes of the poem, except for Gardner Davies.[18] Mallarmé knew as well as everyone else that the swan sings only at the moment of death:

L'oiseau qu'on n'ouït jamais
Une autre fois en la vie
    ("Petit Air," II)

The bird that is never heard again
Another time in life.

The point is that the swan-poet must always die before he can sing; and the moment of the most intense vitality ("va-t-il nous déchirer d'un coup d'aile ivre") must also be the moment of the most intense fatality. The real theme of the sonnet is the paradox of poetic creation, not the description of poetic sterility. The theme of noncreativity has by now—in contrast to earlier poems, such as "L'Azur," "Renouveau," "Les Fenêtres," "Brise marine"—become a necessary ingredient of the Mallarméan metaphysical quest. The alternatives begin to assume clarity in the context of the creative anguish of Mallarmé's crisis years: either there will be a poetry of silence or a silence without poetry. The dilemma plagues Mallarmé in this sonnet, as it had in "Le Démon de l'analogie," but ironic hints of a breakthrough are already present. For instance, the possible vivacity of the first line deteriorates into useless shakes of neck and head and finally collapses into resignation that is equivalent to a phantasmagoric existence: "Fantôme qu'à ce lieu son pur éclat assigne."

But this "pur éclat" is really a reflection of the purest brilliance of the constellation: the relation of swan to constellation *seems* to end in a Platonic or Gnostic resolution, but this is not actually true—the swan remains caught in the death of terrestrial existence ("l'horreur du sol où le plumage est pris"), whereas Cycnus is fixed forever in a region without becoming, in a region without death ("la région où vivre"). The dualism of this perspective is only apparent and transient for Mallarmé, however, because it consigns the swan to death-in-life, noncreativity, silence—to nonbecoming, to be sure, but also to nonbeing. How can this negative photograph of the poet be changed into its positive? How can the fall of the swan be converted into the assumption of the swan and true renascence (the theme of the first quatrain) take place? The answer is that it can take place only in this place ("ce lieu") and at this moment. The present historical moment in the poem, as noted earlier, was supplanted by an eternal moment. The device by which Mallarmé accomplishes this is use of a spatial vocabulary ("il s'immobilise," not "il s'éternise"), not only to introduce the stellar reference, but to show that suspension of the moment in a point of space, by its identity, marks the point of departure from which poetry grows. This spatial imagery is provided in the axial line "Par l'espace infligée à l'oiseau qui le nie": space inflicts an agony of contingency upon the poet, whose task it is to negate space (and thus surmount the agony). The swan of the poem does not, in the long run, negate space but merely dons a mantle of contemptuous resignation: he remains impaled on the negative horn of his dilemma. The true resolution, only negatively sketched out here, would be to go beyond suicide into the affirmation of a constellated nonreality, as represented by Cycnus; this would render possible life-through-death, creativity, the poetry of silence.[19] In any case, the white swan in the wintry landscape remains the negative of the black sky, with one difference: the "éclat" of the terrestrial and the celestial swan become analogous.

The three fragments of *Herodiade*, "Ouverture ancienne," "Scène," and "Cantique de Saint-Jean," also reflect the radical self-examination and the new orientation of Mallarmé during the years 1864 and 1868. The "Ouverture" (1866) is the first poem to open on the new Mallarméan note of "aboli." Whereas the remarkable "Scène" is a dark, wintry, and original companion piece to the "Monologue d'un faune" and actually an elaborate projection of the Narcissistic temptations of the poet, the "Cantique" represents Mallarmé's victory over the temptation of sterility: in some way this would be the next episode in the life of the swan, who, as though his head had actually been severed, contemplates the glacial spectacle from beyond. The head in this case is that of John the Baptist, and the symbolic moment of day is that of sunset; the symbolic moment of the year is St. John's Eve and the summer solstice. These two aspects, though seemingly contradictory, merge into a unity. Valéry quotes Mallarmé as having said: "Le Cantique de Saint Jean, en sept strophes, est le saut de la tête coupée, volant du coup vers la lumière divine"[20]—the Canticle of St. John, in seven strophes, is the leap of the severed head, soaring straight toward the divine light. The interesting feature of this remarkable short work is that at the moment of the setting sun, which coincides with the head's severance from the body, the Gnostic duality is abolished and gives way to a clarity of vision and a new sense of election, another baptism and a special kind of resurrection:

> Le soleil que sa halte
> Surnaturelle exalte
> Aussitôt redescend
> Incandescent
>
> Je sens comme aux vertèbres
> S'éployer des ténèbres

Toutes dans un frisson
   A l'unisson

Et ma tête surgie
Solitaire vigie
Dans les vols triumphaux
   De cette faux

Comme rupture franche
Plutôt refoule ou tranche
Les anciens désaccords
   Avec le corps

Qu'elle de jeûnes ivre
S'opiniâtre à suivre
En quelque bond hagard
   Son pur regard

Là-haut où la froidure
Eternelle n'endure
Que vous le surpassiez
   Tous ô glaciers

Mais selon un baptême
Illuminée au même
Principe qui m'élut
   Penche un salut.

The sun, uplifted
To its supernatural halting place
Immediately goes down
   Incandescent

I feel as though in my bones [vertebrae]
Darkness unfolding
In a tremor
   In unison

And my head soaring aloft

> Like a solitary watchman
> In the triumphal flights
>   Of this scythe
>
> As an open rupture
> Rather driving back or severing
> The former disharmony
>   With the body
>
> May it mad from fasting
> Stubbornly follow
> In some haggard leap
>   Its pure glance
>
> Up there where cold
> Eternal endures
> But for you to overcome it
>   All, o glaciers
>
> But according to a baptism
> [My head] enlightened by the same
> Principle that elected me
>   There inclines a salvation [also health, salute].

The first stanza traces, in rapid strokes, the descent of the sun from the zenith to its vanishing point as contemplated by John the Baptist, who is about to be beheaded. The second, arresting the movement at the point of sunset and adroitly introducing the Baptist as the speaker, operates an analogy between the falling sun and the head that is about to fall; so "ténèbres" opens simultaneously to the darkness and to the Baptist's death and the "frisson" both to a kind of twilight sensation and to a death tremor. Thus the word "unisson" is also paradoxically the unison or coalescence of the opposing aspects of the moment, internally and externally, and explains why the head continues to speak during the rest of the canticle. Consequently, this conceit needs not only to be taken seriously, but it represents the triumphant survival of the Baptist in an "Assumption" that is completely Mallarméan. The head, severed by the curved sword (cette faux)—but also by the hemicycle of the sun—reascends the sky mentally by a reverse movement. The rupture of mind and body is a liberation because it removes the disharmony of mind and body; it flies up and occupies an icy zenith in which cold and hot, life and death are suspended and transcended. The final stanza fixes the *new* baptism, affirms the health and salvation, and salutes the regeneration: the illumination accorded to the severed head marks the Baptist one of the elect (*sicut erat in Principio*), a hero of a solar myth now converted into the myth of illuminated poetic genius.

This John the Baptist is also like the Orpheus after the *sparagmos* by the Maenads, whose head floats down the river Hebros singing. In other words, Mallarmé de-Christianizes the Baptist into a kind of Orpheus who has overcome the old matter-spirit discord in a new and pure way of beholding and has become the new elect, the bringer of a new life. The sunset is not merely decorative or symbolic in the "coucher de soleil-crépuscule" sense of the symbolists (particularly Baudelaire), but is functionally fixed in the poem because of Mallarmé's belief (following George W. Cox) that the myth of Orpheus is a solar myth. "Son nom est le même, Orpheus, que l'indien Ribhu, appellation qui paraît avoir été, à une époque très primitive, donnée au soleil" (His name is the same, Orpheus, as the Indian Ribhu, a name that appears to have been given to the sun in a very primitive epoch), writes Mallarmé in *Les Dieux antiques* (*Oeuvres complètes*, 1240). Arguing (so far as I know, mistakenly) that the name Eurydice denotes the bursting forth of dawn, he continues: "Le pèlerinage d'Orphée . . . représente le voyage que, pendant les heures de la nuit, le Soleil passait pour accomplir afin de ramener, au matin, l'Aurore, dont il cause la disparition par sa splendeur éblouissante" (Orpheus' pilgrimage . . . represents the journey which the Sun accomplished during the hours of the night to bring back the Dawn, whose disappearance it brings about as a result of its dazzling splendor). All these phenomena are deepened and metamorphosed by Mallarmé during his own "voyage aux ténèbres," with emphasis thenceforth on the nocturnal settings and the dazzling emergence of the hero or Idea.

Yet, the decapitation, the rupture of intellect and body, is also an act of depersonalization; and the important point that emerges in this poem is that the head continues to talk because it is now impersonal, as in the letter to Cazalis, quoted above ("Je suis maintenant impersonnel, et non plus Stéphane que tu as connu, mais une aptitude qu'a l'Univers Spirituel à se développer, à travers ce qui fut moi"). The dichotomy is not a deliverance of the individual psyche from matter, but a loss of the principle of individuation in favor of a principle of comic abstraction—an Orpheus that is no longer a poetic voice, but the voice of Poetry itself.

The same phenomenon is transposed into narrative in the fragment *Igitur*. The hero, in losing himself in the spirals of a descending staircase, becomes aware of his duality and identifies the sensation as evidence of his final persona attempting to abolish the double identity that has characterized Igitur so far. He is

un personnage dont la pensée n'a pas conscience de lui-même, de ma dernière figure, séparée de son personnage par une fraise arachnéenne et qui ne se connaît pas: aussi, maintenant que sa dualité est à jamais séparée, et que je n'ouïs même plus à travers lui le bruit de son progrès, je vais m'oublier à travers lui, et me dissoudre en moi. (439)

a personage whose mind is not conscious of himself, of my last face, separated from his personage by an arachnean ruff and who does not know himself: thus, now that his duality is forever divided and now that I no longer even hear through him the sound of his movements, I am going to forget myself through him and dissolve within myself.

Igitur, written about 1869 but not published until 1925, is Mallarmé's own Orphic descent, his experience of the critical years 1864–1869 transposed into narrative and left in fragmentary form. It is almost impossible to interpret this conte because it still has many characteristics of the *grimoire* (book of incantations or hieroglyphics) that serves Mallarmé as a starting point. Through the extant manuscript, with its variants, scholia, and marginal notes, one can form only a general idea of the pattern of the experience and the scheme of significance that Mallarmé gave to it; certain details must remain obscure. In any event, the persistently "autobiographical" aspects of Mallarmé's work are striking; hardly a single composition, poem or prose, during these crucial years is not a transposition of a personal experience, some sort of outgrowth of the "nuits de Tournon" anguish or its aftermath. On the subject of *Igitur*, Mallarmé wrote (without mentioning the title) to his friend Cazalis in November 1869:

C'est un conte, par lequel je veux terrasser le vieux monstre de l'Impuissance, son sujet du reste, afin de me cloîtrer dans mon grand labeur déjà réétudié. S'il est fait (le conte), je suis guéri; *simila similibus*.[21]

It's a narrative by means of which I want to overpower the old monster of Impotence, anyway that subject, so as to be able to cloister myself in my great labor already re-studied. If it gets done (the narrative), I am cured; *like cures like*.

Thus, by the end of 1869 Mallarmé was ready to work again.

It is not at all surprising that he chose the unexpected form of the prose narrative (with an additional request to the reader's intelligence to "set the stage" for the events of the story) for his most abstruse work. Here is a special kind of Orpheus—a Narcissus figure dressed in Hamlet's garb (*"le seigneur latent qui ne peut deviner*, juvenile ombre de tous, ainsi tenant du mythe," p. 300—*the latent lord who cannot become*, the youthful shadow of all, thus having something mythical about him) descending into the darkness in quest of a mystery, the mystery which will reveal to him his impersonal identity ("soi" instead of "moi") and thus release, liberate, the hymn out of the mystery itself.

The full title itself is enigmatic: *Igitur ou la folie d'Elbehnon*. Rolland de Rénéville has suggested[22] that "Igitur" comes from the Vulgate Genesis: "Igitur perfecti sunt coeli et terra et omnis ornatus eorum." The explanation is altogether satisfactory because it evokes a comparison with Creation itself, as a reminder that the poet's task is now understood as the attempt to rival Creation. "The long and mysterious labor of the poet of Igitur had no other objective than the power of the word," says Rolland de Rénéville.[23]

For at least an approximative idea of *Igitur*, the argument prefixed by Mallarmé to the narrative (*Oeuvres complètes*, 434) is of interest:

4 MORCEAUX:

1. *Le Minuit*
2. *L'escalier*
3. *Le coup de dés*
4. *Le sommeil sur les cendres, après la bougie soufflée.*

A peu près ce qui suit:

Minuit sonne—le Minuit où doivent être jetés les dés. Igitur descend les escaliers, de l'esprit humain, va au fond des choses: en "absolu" qu'il est. Tombeaux-cendres (pas sentiment, ni esprit) neutralité. Il récite la prédiction et fait le geste. Indifférence. Sifflements dans l'escalier. "Vous avez tort" nulle emotion. L'infini sort du hasard, que vous avez nié. Vous, mathématiciens expirâtes—moi projeté absolu. Devais finir en Infini. Simplement parole et geste. Quant à ce que je vous dis, pour expliquer ma vie. Rien ne restera de vous—L'infini enfin échappe à la famille, qui en a souffert—vieil espace—pas de hasard. Elle a eu raison de le nier—sa vie—pour qu'il ait été l'absolu. Ceci devait avoir lieu dans les combinaisons de l'Infini vis-à-vis de l'Absolu. Nécessaire—extrait l'Idée. Folie utile. Un des actes de l'univers vient d'être commis là. Plus rien, restait le souffle, fin de parole et geste unis—souffle la bougie de l'être, par quoi tout a été. Preuve.

(Creuser tout cela)

4 SECTIONS

1. Midnight
2. The staircase

3. The dice-throw
4. Sleep on the ashes, after the candle has been blown out.

More or less as follows:

Midnight strikes—the Midnight in which the dice must be cast. Igitur goes down the staircases, of the human mind, goes to the bottom of things: as the "absolute" that he is. Graves—ashes (not sentiment, nor mind) neutrality. He recites the prediction and makes the gesture. Indifference. Sound of whistling on the stairs. "You are wrong" no emotion. The infinite comes out of chance, which you have denied. You, the mathematicians, have expired—I projected as absolute. I was to wind up as Infinite. Simply word and gesture. As far as what I am saying to you, to explain my life. Nothing will remain of you—the infinite at last escapes from the family, who suffered from it—old space—no chance event. They were right to deny him—his life—so that he might have been the absolute one. This was to take place in the combinations of the Infinite with respect to the Absolute. Necessary—extracts the Idea. Useful folly. One of the acts of the universe has just been committed there. Nothing left, breath remained, end of speech and gesture united—blows out the candle of being, as a result of which all has been. Proof.

(Work all this out)

Despite the obscurities of this working outline, the intellectual structure of *Igitur* emerges in its broad features: The critical moment (Minuit) and place are established—down a winding staircase to the bottom of things, to death and ashes, to an absolute negativity. The problem is for Igitur not to retain the spatiotemporal self foisted on him by his ancestors, the Elbehnon family, but to acquire a neutral, impersonal, and absolute selfhood: "moi projeté absolu." This necessitates the supreme gesture required of him, the throw of the dice—the abolition of chance, which characterizes contingency and becoming—in order to establish pure Being, the infinite. This seems to be what his family has exacted of him, and it is their particular folly to have imposed the absurdity of the dice-throw upon their last descendant—as if to compel Igitur to "become" Hamlet, to *be* the myth of Hamlet. In executing the gesture Igitur, now impersonal and infinite, negates both the past (the ancestors) and the future (the ancestral expectations enjoined upon him), not because he can abolish chance, but because the absurd act he must accomplish releases the infinite, frees him from time and contingency, and, by a kind of Hegelian negation, opens the possibility of renovation and creation.

I pointed out earlier that Igitur's descent is an Orphic encounter with the sources of Eros-Thanatos in the human psyche, Eros in this case understood as the creative urge and Thanatos as the act of self-annihilation. But Mallarmé goes one important step beyond the earlier Orphics in that he wishes not only to regenerate Igitur individually, but, by a process of de-individualization, to conceive of the possibility of a regeneration of the entire cosmos: to remake the creation, intellectually (le Mystère) and poetically (l'Idée). In doing so, he reveals that he is more fundamentally Orphic than Novalis or Nerval because he understands more clearly the *impersonal* nature of ritual and priesthood. Moreover, after his loss of belief in God, Mallarmé was obliged to seek his particular solution in a completely negative ceremonial—a negative self-immolation, a symbolic suicide, rather than a crucifixion. It is as though Igitur had to take the burden of being and becoming on his own shoulders. The problem may be formulated thus: can becoming be annulled, so that what exists actually may *be*? Mallarmé conceives the problem in logical and mathematical terms. The "infinite" of the mathematician is made to be in some way commensurable with the finite: it provides a kind of limit, so that if, for example, all the infinite points could be joined to one another, the infinite line would result. This notion of the infinite, which can be called quantitative, is in radical opposition to the qualitative notion of the infinite of the poet or theologian. It asserts that the infinite is radically *other* than the finite—that the point is only an image, and the only *image*, but not a component of the infinite, usually designated as the absolute (because it is "cut loose") by Mallarmé. Igitur "se sépare du temps indéfini et il est" (p. 440)—separates himself from indefinite time, and he is. The infinite is the realm of becoming, made possible because it is not entirely predictable, because it contains chance within it. In order to fix this infinity, chance would have to be abolished by a throw of the dice: the supremacy of chance would thus be replaced by the supremacy of the Number, of the intellect. "Quant à l'Acte, il est parfaitement absurde sauf que mouvement (personnel) rendu à l'Infini: mais que l'Infini est enfin *fixé*" (442)—As for the Act, it is perfectly absurd save as a (personal) movement performed forever: but for the fact that the Infinite is at last *fixed*. Igitur arrives at this fixation of infinity through, and in spite of, the throw of the dice and thus achieves the new conditions of a pure creation: "Le Néant parti, reste le château de la pureté" (443)—With the Nothing gone, there remains the castle of purity.

Maurice Blanchot describes this unusual work as follows: "*Igitur* is then not merely an exploration but a purification of absence, an essay to make absence possible and to draw possibility out of it."[24] The fragment fixes the points of reference within which the Mallarméan metaphysical and poetic quest was being enacted and would continue to be enacted: indeed, *Igitur* is Mallarmé's metaphysical drama of suicide. The second drama, that of death, was projected in 1897 with *Un Coup de dés*, which prolongs and modifies the experience of Igitur.

What remains characteristic of Mallarmé's later poetry is the recurrent symbolism of the solar cycle, "le drame solaire," as Gardner Davies calls it. The fact that the poet regarded the Orpheus myth as primarily solar makes it possible to discern Orphic traits in Mallarmé's solar heroes and solar dramas without forcing specific Orphic interpretations upon each detail. This constitutes a remarkable instance of one of the first genuine examples of modern myth-making. The problem, seen in this perspective, is to discern the general direction of Mallarmé's poetic practice and to inquire whether it moves toward the "explication orphique de la Terre," how it does so, and what problems it encounters.

The triumphal sonnets written (or at least conceived) in 1868, notorious for their "obscurity," are the first signposts. Here is one of the most hermetic of the group, the famous sonnet in "yx":

> Ses purs ongles très haut dédiant leur onyx,
> L'Angoisse, ce minuit, soutient, lampadophore,
> Maint rêve vespéral brûlé par le Phénix
> Que ne recueille pas de cinéraire amphore
>
> Sur les crédences, au salon vide: nul ptyx,
> Aboli bibelot d'inanité sonore,
> (Car le Maître est allé puiser des pleurs au Styx
> Avec ce seul objet le Néant s'honore).
>
> Mais proche la croisée au nord vacante, un or
> Agonise selon peut-être le décor
> Des licornes ruant du feu contre une nixe,
>
> Elle, défunte nue en le miroir, encor
> Que, dans l'oubli fermé par le cadre, se fixe
> De scintillations sitôt le septuor.

> Her pure nails very high [in the sky] dedicating their onyx,
> Anguish, on this midnight, upholds, light-bearing

Many an evening dream burnt by the Phoenix [setting sun]
Not collected in any cinerary amphora

On the sideboards, in the empty room: [there is] no ptyx,
[That] abolished knick-knack of sonorous emptiness,
(For the Master has gone to dip tears from the Styx
With that only object by which the Nothing is honored).

But close by the casement open to the north, something golden
Lies dying, perhaps in keeping with the [mirror-frame] decoration
Of unicorns breathing fire against a water-nymph,

The latter, expiring naked in the mirror,
While, in that oblivion closed off by the frame [of the mirror] there becomes fixed
With its scintillations, straight away, the septet [Great Bear].

Another, probably earlier, version of this sonnet exists, bearing the revealing
title "Sonnet allégorique de lui-même." In a letter written in July 1868 to Cazalis,
Mallarmé gives a brief commentary but not an interpretation, of the sonnet: it
is "inverse, je veux dire que le sens s'il en a un (mais je me consolerais du contraire grâce à la dose de poésie qu'il renferme, ce me semble) est évoqué par un
mirage interne des mots mêmes. En se laissant aller à le murmurer plusieurs fois
on éprouve une sensation assez cabalistique"[25] (inverse, I mean that its meaning,
if any [yet I would on the contrary console myself thanks to the dose of poetry
contained in it—or so it seems to me] is evoked by an internal mirroring of the
words themselves. If you just let yourself murmur it a few times, you experience
quite a cabalistic sensation). This is almost exactly the way Nerval spoke about
Les Chimères. However, going beyond Nerval, Mallarmé's notion of the "dose
de poésie" is more precisely formulated in the lovely metaphor of the "mirage
interne," which carries the meaning of "reflection" and "unreality"; and his
cabalistic technique is more deliberate—and yet more original—than Nerval's.
This is a *trobar clus* in the best troubadour sense, a metaphysical poem full of
paradoxical "conceits." First of all, Mallarmé set himself a difficult task: to write
the octave in the impossible "ix" rhyme balanced off by the more natural "ore"
rhyme, then to transmute the procedure in the sestet by "inserting" the rhymes
to "ixe" and "or," thus providing, incidentally, the monotony that Baudelaire
regarded as essential to all lyric poetry and that Mallarmé perfected with a
subtlety that is probably unequalled in French verse. (I am tempted to speculate

that the original emblematic *verbe* underlying the poem may have been *elixir d'or*, an alchemical solution that turns dross into gold.)

Without attempting to go into all the complexities of the sonnet—and there is a good deal of critical disagreement here—one can begin by fixing its setting: a bare room, containing the mere hint of furniture, a sideboard [crédence], and a gilt-framed mirror, its glass surface dramatizing emptiness and absence—inhabited only by the reminder of the poet's anguish. Anguish is the mute nocturnal projection of the poet's frustration at seeing his expectations (rêve) burnt to ashes by the setting sun (Phénix), with no urn to receive the ashes and consequently no possibility of anything—Phoenix or rêve—rising out of them. Yet the Anguish, the threatened demise of the dream, of creating, upholds even in its darkest hour (ce minuit) the glimmers of light (lampadophore, light-bearing),[26] the stars, promise of resurrection. Meanwhile, the absent Master (he who experienced the anguish at twilight) has gone to the Nothingness of Hades; but in his "profoundest" absence a glimmer of light plays faintly upon the frame of a mirror, then vanishes, then the constellation of the Great Bear (le septuor) is reflected and inscribed on the surface of the mirror: the stamp of eternity is there—the Master has, emblematically, returned as the impersonal and constellated being that he has become.

The poem is about creative anguish, the descent into darkness, and the emergence of beauty, luminosity, resurrection out of Nothingness. As such it is both personal—an inside view of what has just been seen concerning Mallarmé's psychic crisis, the stages of which the sonnet alchemically transmutes—and, furthermore, a philosophical statement about the beauty that can be seen only at the terminus of the voyage into Nothingness. Looked at thus, the sonnet can be considered one of the *allégories somptueuses du néant* that Mallarmé had projected in his letter to Villiers de l'Isle-Adam in 1866. The specifically Orphic allusion is in the lines "Car le Maître est allé puiser des pleurs au Styx / Avec le seul objet dont le Néant s'honore."

Although this passage is usually taken to refer to the temptation of suicide, I see no reason why an Orphic interpretation would introduce any discrepancy. For Mallarmé the "descent" is made possible only by a spiritual suicide, by a destruction of the material self; this is, generally, the meaning for modern writers of the Orphic quest. But Mallarmé's treatment here of the Orphic theme seems more complex: there is a superimposition of part of the allegorical *Märchen* of Eros and Psyche. Psyche, the soul, persecuted by Venus for her beauty, is given the chore of going to the underworld to fetch a supply of beauty from Persephone—a task that tempted her to commit suicide by throwing herself from a tower. Like Orpheus, she grew impatient or curious and looked at the casket of beauty she had obtained; it contained a deathly sleep, not beauty, and she was finally liberated from this sleep by the intervention of Eros. Mallarmé introduces not only an ingenious superposition of myths but also a transposition: his Master, his Orpheus, is like the soul seeking beauty on the other side of life. The gift he brings back from Hades is not sleep, but Beauty itself—but only its reflection, its immateriality. Hence Mallarmé's Orpheus goes down empty-handed, so to speak, not with his lyre. He has taken with him the ptyx, the shell that is filled with a nothingness evocative of the myriad sounds of the sea: such is the intent of the conceit "aboli bibelot d'inanité sonore." The tears of the Styx reference may be to a passage in Pausanias, who speaks about the practice of pilgrims to Hades of collecting drops of water at the point where the Styx decreased to a trickle; these tears were thought to be "emanations of the Nothing" —a reference that Mallarmé, in all likelihood, found hard to resist.[27] The triumph-regeneration theme in the sestet is consequently heightened by the identification of the Big Bear's seven stars as a "septuor," with the musical connotation that may have been remembered by Proust in his *Septuor de Vinteuil*. The ptyx corresponds to the amphora, the urn, replacing the Orphic lyre, in which the Master retrieves his own being, his own poetic voice: it is like the "creux néant musicien" of the sonnet "Une dentelle s'abolit"—object of nothingness *and* of the reviving Phoenix. Emblematically, it is "le seul objet dont le Néant s'honore." This paradox is marvelously built into the language and forms the central conceit of the sonnet: le Néant s'honore = le Néant sonore— Nothingness is pregnant with a voice, with Beauty.

The verbal alchemy is heightened by another mythological metamorphosis: the nymph (nixe) is actually a prefiguration or annunciation of the Great Bear, as suggested by the myth of the nymph Callisto. Mallarmé's adaptation of George Cox's mythology (Cox's work appeared in French translation in 1867, the approximate time at which this sonnet was either conceived or composed; Mallarmé's adaptation did not appear until 1880) tells something about the poet's particular interest in the myth:

Callisto "la plus belle" est fille d'Arcas "le brillant"; mais la racine d'où vient Arcas est la même que la racine du mot Arctos, ours; et de là naquit l'histoire de Callisto, éveillant le courroux d'Artémis, et changée en ourse. La constellation connue à présent sous le nom latinisé d'Arctus ou d'Arcturus, a tiré ce nom de la racine qui veut dire: briller.

Mais pour la même raison que Callisto est changée en ourse, il se dit que ces étoile₁ étaient, elles, habitées par des ours: et c'est de là que viennent les noms de la Grande es de là Petite Ourse. (*Oeuvres complètes*, 1243)

Callisto "the most beautiful" is the daughter of Arcas "the shining"; but the root of Arcas is the same as that of the word Arctos, bear; and out of this grew the story of Callisto inviting the wrath of Artemis, and changed into a female bear. The constellation known now under the latinized form of Arctus or Arcturus drew its name from the root meaning: to shine. But for the same reason that Callisto is changed into a female bear, it is said that those stars were actually inhabited by bears; and from this come the names of the Ursa Major and Ursa Minor.

Thus, with the help of philology, Callisto is metamorphosed into Ursa Major, so to speak, although the change is no longer due to Artemis' wrath but to the Master's Orphic descent—more specifically, to the Master's Orphic absence.[28]

This poem already prefigures Mallarmé's later manner: the alchemy, the precision, the transpositions—the allegories of the personal into the universal by virtue of an abolition of material self and contingencies into universal transparencies. The transparencies are located in a particular *place*, where something *takes place*: a point of intersection in space and time, and involving the self, where by a dialectical reversal (very similar to Rilke's *Umkehr*) space and time are abolished by transmutation and the self becomes depersonalized. This basic scheme is to be found in all of Mallarmé's major late works; the coordinates for the "event" were already sketched out in "Le Vierge, le vivace," in "Sainte," and especially in *Igitur*. From a technical point of view, Mallarmé has in this sonnet elaborated the perfect formal equivalent of his dialectical vision: a series of multiple inner reflections to reinforce the larger pattern of affirmation-negation, presence-absence, death-resurrection, outside-inside. Thus, for example, the first two lines anticipate the final two; the Phoenix flame anticipates the unicorn fire; the trickling Stygian tears prefigure the "lake" of the polished mirror. The examples could be multiplied. Mallarmé has here made incandescent a formal design already noticeable in "Le Vierge, le vivace": a quadripartite division of the sonnet corresponding to its conventional division into two quatrains and two tercets. His favorite arrangement appears to be chiastic, X-shaped (and therefore ideally suited to the sonnet in "x"): quatrain I corresponds to tercet II, quatrain II to tercet I—without forgetting that the relations are tensional, that is, that there is progression and transformation within the correspondences. (The same pattern, applied to two sets of paired quatrains, was foreshadowed in "Sainte," where the fenêtre-vitrage combination had served as "lieu.") Madame Noulet gives a persuasive reminder that even the number fourteen is put to splendid use in "Ses purs ongles": "We must therefore be careful to visualize the setting well and to take hold of the constellation two times: as a simultaneous vision of fourteen stars. Twice the Septet = 14 = the number of lines that make up a sonnet. Fourteen lines that have been reflected in one another. That is why this sonnet is 'allegorical of himself.' That is a clue to the title and was therefore eliminated."[29]

Although Mallarmé did not designate any particular work as an "allégorie somptueuse du néant" (one of his titles for a number of works in progress), the preceding sonnet, as well as the one to be discussed next, could be placed in that category. "Quand l'Ombre menaça de la fatale loi," originally entitled "Cette Nuit," was written during this nocturnal crisis period (though published only in 1883) and stresses even more strongly than "Ses Purs Ongles" the positive achievement of the nihilistic experience: it is "la gloire du mensonge," with emphasis on "gloire." In this sense it extends the space of "Ses Purs Ongles" from the reflection of the constellation to the constellation itself. In a letter to Cazalis, Mallarmé had indicated that the bare room was linked to the world by negation: "la grande Ourse, qui relie au ciel seul ce logis abandonné du monde" —the Big Dipper, which links this lodging abandoned by the world to the heavens above. He continues:

J'ai pris ce sujet d'un sonnet nul se réfléchissant de toutes les façons; parce que mon oeuvre est à la fois si bien préparé et hiérarchisé, représentant comme il le peut l'Univers . . .[30]

I have taken this subject for a "null" sonnet, which mirrors itself in all sorts of ways, because my work is at the same time so well worked out and hierarchical, since it represents the Universe as well as it can . . .

This sonnet takes place in a room from which the world is absent, but this time the absence is offset by the triumphant presence of the poet. The reader of the poem witnesses the act of the genius transcending the world and death by negating them, then negating the cosmos by transcending it through the poetic act.

Quand l'ombre menaça de la fatale loi
Tel vieux Rêve, désir et mal de mes vertèbres,

Affligé de périr sous les plafonds funèbres
Il a ployé son aile indubitable en moi.

Luxe, ô salle d'ébène où, pour séduire un roi
Se tordent dans leur mort des guirlandes célèbres,
Vous n'êtes qu'un orgueil menti par les ténèbres
Aux yeux du solitaire ébloui de sa foi.

Oui, je sais qu'au lointain de cette nuit, la Terre
Jette d'un grand éclat l'insolite mystère,
Sous les siècles hideux qui l'obscurcissent moins.

L'espace à soi pareil qu'il s'accroisse ou se nie
Roule dans cet ennui des feux vils pour témoins
Que s'est d'un astre en fête allumé le génie.

When the shadow [darkness, death] threatened with its fatal law
An old Dream, the desire and malady of my bones [vertebrae],
Doomed to perish under deathlike ceilings
It [the Dream] folded its indubitable wing in me.

Luxury, oh ebony hall in which, to delight a king
Famous garlands writhe in their death,
You are but a pride belied by the darkness
In the eyes of the solitary man dazzled by his faith.

Yes, I know that at the far end of this night, the Earth
Casts forth with great brilliance the unaccustomed mystery
Under hideous worlds that obscure it less.

Space equal to itself, whether it increases or undoes itself,
Rolls on in that tedium having base fires for witnesses
That the genius of a rejoicing star [planet] has kindled for himself.

The rhymes are in themselves the bearers of emblematic significance: "loi" is superseded by "foi"; the "moi" becomes metamorphosed into "roi." The abstract sequence of the feminine rhymes (though they do not appear in this sequence in the poem) appears to be the chiasmus "vertèbres—ténèbres—funè-bres—célèbres," an order that grows directly out of the *Igitur* experience and remains absolutely fundamental for Mallarmé. Its most succinct formulation is the grouping "solitude, récif, étoile—solitude, reef, star" of the late poem "Salut," which simplifies the funèbres-ténèbres coupling and synthesizes the entire Mallarméan poetic experience to a triplet pattern (compare "solitaire" in line 8; "fatale loi," line 1; "astre en fête," line 14).

Taking the two quatrains together as the "solitude-récif" portion of the poem, it is of note that, as in the sonnet "Ses Purs Ongles," the coming of darkness (symbolically, death) forces a crisis in the poet, precipitated by the double awareness of impending disaster and the absolute exigency of the rêve, the poetic "thou shalt." In this sense, the word "indubitable," despite its unusual association with "aile," acquires the maximum force, a kind of Cartesian primacy[31] that leaves everything in doubt except the poet's duty. And with this awareness the poetic space, in danger of shrinking into nonexistence as expressed in the image of "plafonds funèbres" and in the symbol of the folded wing (as in "Le Vierge, le vivace"), expands marvelously into a celestial panorama that is now the poet's own creation, product of his solitude, his pride, his poetic faith. Though this "glorious lie" makes the empty room regal by equating its ceiling with the nocturnal sky, illuminated by the constellations ("guirlandes célèbres"), it nevertheless continues to reflect the mortality of the hermit's chamber (image of the constellations writhing in their death).

The sestet celebrates the glory of the poetic vision. Its two antithetical axes are the quasi-homonymous "cette nuit" (the original title of the poem) and "cet ennui," which stands in dialectical relation to each other. In a rather complex convergence of opposites, Mallarmé—introducing the sestet with an affirmation —now makes a spatial leap into that nocturnal sky projected by his own vision and contemplates the earth from afar, reaffirming its mystery and glory, but this time from the outside, beyond time and space, from the vantage point of the constellations. Key words such as "éclat" and "ébloui," the former more "objective" and the latter more "subjective," continue to set up inner resonances intensifying the dialectical antithesis basic to the poem. The final stance of the poet, and the supreme glory, is the total annulment of poetic space from the visionary point *beyond*, which corresponds both negatively and positively to the point of origin (the room, the solitary poet) beneath, so that even the constellations now become "feux vils" in comparison to the genius' grasp and possession of, and ultimately identity with, the earth "astre en fête"—very similar to Zarathustra's "dancing star." The sonnet is, as Robert Greer Cohn puts it, "a compact masterpiece of radiant darkness."[32]

Several things need to be remarked. The movement is a reverse Orphic progress, an *anábasis*, resembling and superseding the *katábasis*: upward into a night that is the counterpoise to the infernal night, but this night abolishes the *néant* and allows *beauté* to emerge. And the spatial movement from the point to the ever-widening circle to another point beyond this circle—a point no longer subject to the limitation of finitude—corresponds to the depersonalization of the poet, the progression from "vertèbres" and "en moi" to "roi" and "solitaire"; and again the movement, from "Oui, je sais" to "génie" is one continuous curve.

The depersonalization that Mallarmé had experienced in the crisis, and that led him to formulate the work of his lifetime as an impersonal "Livre," is superbly exemplified in these two sonnets. And since the Livre is, as noted earlier, understood in Orphic terms, the two poems mark a decisive dividing-line between earlier Orphic poets, Novalis and Nerval, and Mallarmé. In fact, the somewhat facile magic of Novalis and the anguished supernaturalism of Nerval are possible because symbols and personalities are piled on top of one another—the result being a sort of plenitude of confusion, a heap concealing a void. Mallarmé works in the opposite direction, discovering the void and emerging from his experience with sumptuous allegories of the void that transmute it into a glorious lie, but a lie that has more poetic reality than the void because it also has ontological reality. Jean-Pierre Richard sums up the climactic elements of the sonnet in this way: "And that glory, verified at last, sure of itself, can now burst out in the three terminal nouns of the poem: *astre fête, génie*. The feast is always for Mallarmé the moment when a flame is lit, spiritual or amorous, wherever an advent of being is celebrated. The star is the cosmic field of the feast. Genius in the mysterious inner power that, lighting itself in the most forsaken corner of our solitude, succeeds in populating it, animating it, conferring upon it a center and a meaning."[33]

Mallarmé's creative exaltation continued unabated—though the poems are few in number—for twelve to fifteen years after the crisis years. The vibrations of "une sonore, vaine et monotone ligne"—a sonorous, empty and monotonous line—of "L'Après-midi d'un faune" are prolonged, condensed, and elevated into the apotheosis poems "Toast funèbre" (1873), a funeral elegy, and "Prose pour des Esseintes" (1885), a hymn celebrating poetry. These two works, along with the related commemorative sonnets, constitute Mallarmé's major positive achievement prior to the final works (the sonnets written in the 1890's and *Un*

Coup de dés, and of course the final sonnets in the "tombeaux" series). Just as "L'Après-midi" had explored the poet-neophyte's relation to Eros, so the master poet in "Toast funèbre," now "magnifique, total et solitaire," expatiates upon the poet's relation to Thanatos—the poet is as mortal as all other mortals, but he is immortal by virtue of the creative act of naming things:

> Le Maître, par un oeil profond, a, sur ses pas,
> Apaisé de l'éden l'inquiète merveille
> Dont le frisson final, dans sa voix seule, éveille
> Pour la Rose et le Lys le mystère d'un nom.

> The Master, by means of a deep-searching eye, has, along the way
> Appeased the troubled miracle of Eden
> Whose terminal tremor, in his voice alone, awakens
> For Rose and Lily the mystery of a name.

The act of naming is the domain of man and continues to be his mission: the power conferred upon Adam in Paradise to name things is the perpetual task of the human creator, analogous to the accomplishment of the Creator. But within the context of modern poetry this formulation is seen in a new light. Hölderlin's mission, at the turn of the nineteenth century, was acceptance of a night situated between a departure of the gods and an awaited epiphany; in that night the naming of the gods became the ultimate assignment of the poet. With Mallarmé divine transcendence is abolished altogether and night accepted as the only reality in which an epiphany can occur. In this nocturnal state only the naming of things can create the epiphanies, not of the gods, but of immanent realities or an immanent Reality. Thus the mystery (merveille) inherent in the world causes things to vibrate with the unfulfilled desire to be "expressed," and it is the poet in which the vibrations finally come to rest and are transformed into a new mystery—that of language. Words capture not the thing itself, but the troubled and dim reality concealed in it. They abnegate the material object and incarnate its reality in the word; they make the mortal object immortal, they confer immortality upon the mortal poet—poetry is paradox, contradiction, hyperbole. This is the meaning of the frequently quoted passage from "Crise de vers":

A quoi bon la merveille de transposer un fait de nature en sa presque disparition vibratoire selon le jeu de la parole, cependant; si ce n'est pour qu'en émane, sans la gêne d'un proche ou concret rappel, la notion pure.
Je dis: une fleur! et, hors de l'oubli où ma voix relègue aucun contour, en tant que

quelque chose d'autre que les calices sus, musicalement se lève, idée même et suave, l'absente de tous bouquets.

Au contraire d'une fonction de numéraire facile et représentatif, comme le traite d'abord la foule, le dire, avant tout, rêve et chant, retrouve chez le Poëte, par nécessité constitutive d'un art consacré aux fictions, sa virtualité.

Le vers qui de plusieurs vocables refait un mot total, neuf, étranger à la langue et comme incantatoire, achève cet isolement de la parole: niant, d'un trait souverain, le hasard demeuré aux termes malgré l'artifice de leur retrempe alternée en le sens et la sonorité, et vous cause cette surprise de n'avoir ouï jamais tel fragment ordinaire d'élocution, en même temps que la réminiscence de l'objet nommé baigne dans une neuve atmosphère. (368)

What is the use of the marvel of transposing a fact of nature at the point of its virtual vibratory disappearance, in accordance with the game of language, nevertheless—unless it is for the sake of letting emanate from it, without being bothered by an immediate or concrete recall, the pure notion itself.

I say the word "flower!" and outside the oblivion to which my voice relegates any contour, insofar as this is anything other than the already familiar calyx, musically there rises, being itself the idea and also pleasantly agreeable, the very flower that is absent from all bouquets.

In contrast to fulfilling a facile and representative cash value function, as the masses would have it, speech, which is dream and song before anything else, recovers in the Poet's hands its virtuality, by the constituent necessity of an art devoted to fictions.

The line of poetry which out of several vocables reconstructs a total and brand new word, alien to the language and as if incantatory, accomplishes this isolation of the word: negating, with a sovereign stroke, chance arrested at the boundaries despite the artifice produced by their [the vocables'] alternate retempering in sense and sound; and it causes you that surprise feeling as if you had never heard this or that ordinary fragment of elocution, while at the same time the reminiscence of the object named bathes in a new atmosphere.

This aesthetics of presenting (not *re*presenting!) absence and of affirming negations is exemplified in the following lines, in which the Master stakes out his terrain (les jardins de cet astre) and measures his strength for the task of naming (je veux voir . . . survivre . . . une agitation solennelle par l'air de paroles):

> Moi, de votre désir soucieux, je veux voir,
> A qui s'évanouit, hier, dans le devoir
> Idéal que nous font les jardins de cet astre,

Survivre pour l'honneur du tranquille désastre
Une agitation solennelle par l'air
De paroles, pourpre ivre et grand calice clair,
Que, pluie et diamant, le regard diaphane
Resté là sur ces fleurs dont nulle ne se fane,
Isole parmi l'heure et le rayon du jour!

I, mindful of your desire, want to see,
In behalf of him who vanished only yesterday, in the
Ideal duty that the gardens of this planet impose on us,
[I want to see] survive for the honor of the quiet disaster
A solemn agitation in the air
Of words, wild purple and great bright flowercup,
Which, in the shape of rain and diamond, the diaphanous glance
As it has lingered there over these flowers, not one of which can wilt,
Isolates amid the hour of day and the ray of light!

This same imagery of gardens, flowers, contours, and survival leads directly into the poem in which the hyperbolic and resurrective power of poetry is apotheosized, the "Prose pour Des Esseintes" (1884).

This extremely difficult poem has caused almost as much bafflement as *Un Coup de dés* and has stimulated a host of divergent interpretations, excellently summarized by L. J. Austin,[34] whose own interpretation, along with Poulet's essay in *Les Métamorphoses du cercle*, is the best. What needs to be done is to place it in the general Orphic context of Mallarmé's creative development; in some ways this poem occupies the crest of the Orphic curve in Mallarmé. The perplexing title, "Prose" is to be understood in its liturgical meaning. (The fact that use of the term also constitutes a tribute to the protagonist of Huysmans' novel *A Rebours*, who had a special predilection for Church Latin—and for Mallarmé —is of no direct consequence here.) The ecclesiastical term "prosa" refers to a rhymed Latin hymn sung at Mass on solemn occasions before the reading of the Gospels. The ritual context and the hymnic nature of the "prosa" are the essential elements to consider in approaching the poem. "Prose pour des Esseintes" is Mallarmé's Orphic hymn to poetry—to poetry as hyperbole, to poetry as resurrection. The first two stanzas, by way of introduction, set up the cosmic dimensions of the hymn:

Hyperbole! de ma mémoire
Triomphalement ne sais-tu

Te lever, aujourd'hui grimoire
Dans un livre de fer vêtu:

Car j'installe, par la science
L'hymne des coeurs spirituels
En l'oeuvre de ma patience,
Atlas, herbiers et rituels.

Hyperbole! from my memory
Triumphantly can you not
Rise, [though] today you are an incantation
In a book with an iron clasp:

For I install, by science
The hymn of spiritual hearts
In the work of my patience:
Atlases, herbals, and rituals.

The "oeuvre de ma patience" is nothing more than the patient labor of creating the Grand Oeuvre, the Livre, that had been haunting Mallarmé since the late 1860's. In a sense, "Prose pour des Esseintes" is a progress report on Mallarmé and Le Livre—the poems of the preceding fifteen years were blueprints for the work to be done. Its importance lies in Mallarmé's more modest awareness of the limitations of his capacities—without a diminution, nevertheless, of the poetic ideal to be achieved. One of the best glosses on this mood of sobriety after Mallarmé had passed the midpoint of life (in the years between "Toast funèbre" and "Prose pour des Esseintes") is the autobiographical letter to Verlaine of 1885, which was quoted at the beginning of this chapter. There the point is affirmation of the Orphic stance, and the resolution that any one poet can create only a fragment of The Book, but a fragment that implies and invokes the existence of The Book. "Prose" (like the "poème" *Un Coup de dés* a decade later) is exactly such a minor microcosm within the major microcosm of Le Livre.

The poem is installed—established, placed, given a stall in the sanctuary of the poet's creation—as a central hymn in the general architecture of the magnum opus. It is to be noted that the hymn is the celebration issuing out of and for the "coeurs spirituels": it synthesizes the language of the heart and the mind. The hymn is to be the product of learned skill ("par la science"), and the learning is oriented toward three areas, which must be understood symbolically: the topography of the earth ("atlas"), everything that is in nature ("herbiers") and the comportment of men with relation to their surroundings ("rituels"). The hymn, then, is cosmological in intent, like the Orphic or Homeric hymns to which it thus obliquely alludes. The first stanza insists that this activity is "hyperbolic"— in all its possible meaning: it is a going or thrusting beyond (*huper-bouleúein*, to throw above), and its language will be that of exaggeration or hyperbole. The entire poem moves across the imagery of raising, lifting, uplifting, from the word "hyperbole" to "lever" through "s'exaltait" and "surgir" in the central eighth stanza, to "Anastase" and "le trop grand glaïeul" in the last two stanzas— a movement from surging to resurrection, in the Mallarméan sense. In many respects the language is the equivalent in meaning to Hegel's use of "aufheben": to uplift, to annul, to preserve. Nor is the interpretation of "hyperbole" as the mathematical figure of the hyperbole excluded—the figure that approaches its coordinates more and more as it approaches infinity is consistent with Mallarmé's view of the "impossibility" of poetry. Moreover, the task of poetry is once again seen in Orphic terms: to displace the indecipherable writing of the "grimoire" by hyperbolic elucidation.

The next ten stanzas delineate the geography of the *place*—the island ("dans une île que l'air charge / De vie et non de visions")—and the *moment* ("ce midi que notre double / Inconscience approfondit"), as well as the objects ("sol de cent iris"). From this initial point the hyperbole is to develop; the development takes place through a division of the self.

> Nous promenions notre visage
> (Nous fûmes deux, je le maintiens)
> Sur maints charmes de paysage
> O soeur, y comparant les tiens
>
> We were walking and beholding
> (There were two of us, I insist)
> Many a charm of the landscape,
> O sister, making comparison with yours [your charms]

A number of critics have taken the passage too literally—or even biographically, a practice that rarely hits the mark in Mallarmé exegesis. Mallarmé is never too far from the didactic (does not the Orphic *explanation* of the earth contain a didactic purpose?), and one progresses farther with the poem by taking the first two stanzas as propositions that raise the questions: what is the relation of the "hyperbole" to the "grimoire"; how can the "hymn" come into being and how did this one come into being? The poem begins with a promise of synthesis and transcendence, then proceeds to analysis and, in the final two stanzas, which balance the introductory stanzas, affirms ("triomphalement") the resurrection foreshadowed at the beginning. The architecture of *Prose* is perfectly symmetrical, especially if the ten-stanza middle section is divided into two equal parts: 2:5, 5:2. In fact, the poem could be called a sonnet-hymn, reproducing in a more extended way the X-shaped design of the sonnets examined previously. This would yield the following outline: annunciation (1–2) and seeing (3–7), followed by epiphany (8–12) and apotheosis (13–14). It should be noted that the time of the opening stanzas is "aujourd'hui," whereas the following ten stanzas are placed preponderantly in the past and the concluding two in an eternal moment. The result of Mallarmé's extended journey into the past in this poem seems to have licensed biographical digressions by interpreters. Such factors surely played a role in Mallarmé's creative method, but a literal adherence to known facts (devotion to his sister Maria, for instance) is misleading because of the allegorical and synthesizing nature of the poet's mind. What, then, is the real meaning of the parenthetical "Nous fûmes deux, je le maintiens"? The "soeur" mentioned is more like Baudelaire's "mon enfant, ma soeur" in "L'Invitation au voyage"—a mirror in which the poet can behold an aspect of himself. In a deeper sense, "Prose" has affinities with Baudelaire's prose poem "Le Thyrse," which projects a notion of artistic creation by means of a complementarity of male and female elements. The two persons on an ideal island, the two *promeneurs solitaires* in "Prose," compose an androgynous unit: they are both children, and they are both enjoying a sunny, Edenlike existence on a utopian isle. Outside their orbit of being is the "era of authority," ruled by the "spirit of strife," which insists that their utopia is literally a "no-place." But Mallarmé's objective is not to exalt merely the unity and ideality of the island against the divisions of the other world, but to render, metaphorically and symbolically, an account of the growth of the poet's soul. Thus, the perambulations of the poet's *animus* and *anima* culminate in the first cluster of affirmations, in stanzas 6 and 7.

> Oui, dans une île que l'air charge
> De vue et non de visions
> Toute fleur s'étalait plus large
> Sans que nous en devisions.

Telles, immenses, que chacune
Ordinairement se para
D'un lucide contour, lacune
Qui des jardins la sépara

Yes, in an island whose air is thick
With sight and not with visions
Every flower grew larger,
Without our making any comments about it.

So immense indeed that each **one**
Ordinarily decked itself out
With a lucid contour, a lacuna
That divided it off from the gardens

The first progress of the untutored soul in its dual *un*consciousness ("notre double inconscience") is toward *seeing* (vue), not imagining (visions). The distinction between seeing and envisioning is of great importance here. The prerational self sees clearly and distinctly; what seems present here is a Cartesianism of the eye—to see is to define, to distinguish, to separate from other objects of perception, to create a lucid space around an object. Up to this point the poet and his sister, the two selves, have been conjoined and virtually identical; now the rapport between them becomes reciprocal. The sister, the directly apprehending and unintellectual self, is satisfied with the *sight*; she continues to cast her glance horizontally over the landscape, and her response is a smile. The male component of the poet, now at the threshold of the epiphany, experiences the first surge of "vertical" exaltation and the first intimation of the "oeuvre de patience" that is to follow.

Gloire du long désir, Idées
Tout en moi s'exaltait de voir
La famille des iridées
Surgir à ce nouveau devoir,

Mais cette soeur sensée et tendre
Ne porta son regard plus loin
Que sourire et, comme à l'entendre
J'occupe mon antique soin.

Glory of long desire, Ideas
Everything in me became uplifted to see
The family of iridaceae
Rise to this new duty,

But that sensible and tender sister
Did not carry her glance any farther
Than to smile, and as if to understand her [or it]
I pursue my ancient concern.

The theme of triumph is not only announced, but also discreetly revealed by a learned metamorphosis from "des iridées" to "désir Idées," already the major hyperbole of the poem and thus the central mise-en-scène of the dominant metaphor of "Prose pour des Esseintes." Moreover, it is precisely in this stanza that the vertical concentration is at its greatest intensity, with "s'exaltait" and "surgir." The first person plural of the five preceding stanzas now shifts decisively to "moi" and then to "cette soeur," dramatizing the division of *animus* and *anima*, and the present tense appears briefly as a retrospective glance toward the opening stanzas and a prospective glimmer of the final ones.

What still remains now that time, place, object, and self are becoming "defined" (in the sense of delimited) is to assert that this experience, because it is hyperbolic, is more real than the reality that occasioned it—it exceeds and transcends it and thereby negates the real fact that the island does not actually exist. The poet has to his surprise discovered

. . . tout le ciel et la carte
Sans fin attestés sur mes pas,
Par le flot même qui s'écarte,
Que ce pays n'exista pas.

. . . the whole sky and the map
Ceaselessly attested by my steps,
By the very wave in the process of receding,
[and yet he knows] That this region did not exist.

There is on the one hand the negation, on the other the attestation. Between these two coordinates the possibility of poetry "arises" as the "gloire du mensonge." But there is still one obstacle, which calls for a mature resolution; it propels the poet beyond the unreflectiveness of his childhood (now that he has seen) into the dawn of *conscious* creation. The progression is from intuitive perception to learned art. The sister-*anima* now functions as a corrective or moderator (the smile is both enigmatic, like La Gioconda's, and humanizing, as in Dante, Botticelli, the pre-Raphaelites, and Rilke). The poet had noted in an earlier stanza that the lilies (actually, the irises) "grandissait trop pour nos raisons"—grew too much for our reasons—that is, the untutored mind is not ready to grasp the hyperbolic quality of the poetic experience. Thus the poet reaches the two concluding stanzas:

> L'enfant abdique son extase
> Et docte déjà par chemins
> Elle dit le mot: Anastase!
> Né pour d'éternels parchemins,
>
> Avant qu'un sépulcre ne rie
> Sous aucun climat, son aïeul,
> De porter ce nom: Pulchérie!
> Caché par le trop grand glaïeul.

> The child abdicates her ecstasy
> And tutored already by certain walks of life
> She says the word: Anastasius!
> [Which is] born [intended] for eternal parchments.
>
> Before a tomb may mock
> Under any clime, its ancestor,
> For bearing the name: Pulcheria!
> [The inscription being] hidden by the too large gladiolus.

These stanzas parallel, elucidate and complete the two opening stanzas: the hyperbole has been triumphantly evoked by reminiscence and the "hymn of the spiritual hearts" can now be installed, and will be in the future, by learned skill ("science"). The word "extase" in stanza 13 vibrates against "science" in stanza 2. But actually the resolution of the poem does not mean that the *poeta ecstaticus* must be repudiated in favor of the *poeta doctus*; Mallarmé is at pains to keep the references to the child in the final two stanzas feminine, referring to the sister-*anima*. That is, the balance of masculine to feminine undergoes a realignment in the poet's soul: the *anima* abdicates her ecstasy, which had been described as unreflective and muted ("sourire"), but she abdicates it (unsays it) in such a way that she can *say* the word "Anastasius"—or possibly *Anastasis*, referring to resurrection or a person resurrected. In this way, "Anastase!" is like a magic formula, an incantation, of resurrection; this idea is promptly strengthened by "*éternels* parchemins" and immediately offset by the temporal notions of "sépulcre" and "climat," which it supersedes and abolishes. The sequence Anastase-Pulchérie designates the triumphal resurrection of poetry (and the poet, as in "Toast funèbre" and the commemorative sonnets) into beauty, recapitulating and corroborating the experience of descent-suicide-resurrection of *Igitur* and the néant-beauté dialectic proposed in Mallarmé's letters. Moreover, it is a word that liberates the magic and a name that eternalizes it: the time structure of "becoming" utilized in this poem is now replaced by a new sense of being in which beauty and the poet achieve their fixity. The poetic *animus* has been "animated" by the sister; her ecstasy and learning have been abnegated so that they can rise again in the new being of the poet and be recorded by the poet working out patiently his skill and exaltation in the secret depths of his spirit. This resolution is Orphic, but in a new way: the ecstasy of the flesh is transmuted into the ecstasy of the spirit, flesh and spirit are united once again in an exultant celebration of the earth.

"Mallarmé bids us to heed this triumphal attempt at the hymn; a future hymn that will be a renascence of the old hymn and which, consequently, is introduced first in the form of a vision of the past," remarks Georges Poulet in his essay on "Prose."[35] The hymn that surges from this vision of the past is not, strictly speaking, a visionary poem. It would be more appropriate, in Mallarmé's case, to speak of a hypertrophy of the sight—a "hyperphany" rather than an epiphany. The epiphany is a moment of truth, whereas Mallarmé's hymn is a ritual installed beyond truth, a ritual retaining the form of the liturgical invocation, but emptied of the old content. Thus the final term in the inventory of the hymn, "Atlas, herbiers et rituels," is clarified; the nihilating process imposed upon place and object is ultimately paralleled in the ritual of Mallarméan creation. The implications of this act in the history of literature are far-reaching; Georges Poulet has seen the full impact of the phenomenon. "In contradiction to Church prose, the Mallarméan poem does not aim for an already existing transcendence, which poetic song evokes in order to make it come down to the immanent, but on the contrary it aims for a non-existent transcendence, which has to be made to exist by a process of aggrandizing oneself to make contact with it above the immanent; 'a mythical presence with which one wishes to become fused.' "[36]

The convergence of the opposites "transcendence" and "immanence" takes place by an impulsion from the reverse direction; Mallarmé's work provides a new conception of the Orphic, a reversal of the earlier Orphic vision of Novalis and Nerval. "*La divine transposition, pour l'accomplissement de quoi existe l'homme, ou du fait à l'idéal*" (*Oeuvres complètes*, 522)—*divine transposition*, for whose accomplishment man exists, *or from the fact to the ideal*.

"Prose pour Esseintes" marks the high-water mark of Mallarmé's Orphic creation, the moment in his career as a poet in which his new Orphic mission (as evidenced in the letter to Verlaine) was unequivocally articulated in theory and practice. I therefore take exception to L. J. Austin's statement that " 'orphic' means 'poetic,' quite simply; for Orpheus was for Mallarmé the first of poets";[37] I have tried to show that to Mallarmé the notion of the Orphic meant a great deal more. It should be noted, however, that the reference to Orpheus as "the first of poets" needs to be taken quite literally: not merely the foremost, but the first. Mallarmé asserted quite categorically that the direction of poetry had been altered by Homer, and that poetry since that time had been Homeric rather than Orphic. From the point of view of literary history this statement is intriguing: Homer's song is very close to the world of facts, Mallarmé wished to bring poetry back to the transcendent ideality of Orpheus and Pindar. In a sense, one might claim that this is the objective of all modern Orphic poets; Mallarmé, inspired by his predecessors Poe and Baudelaire, and probably Nerval, enunciated the purpose of the new poetry more clearly.

In the remaining years of Mallarmé's life, the Orphic ambition remained alive but underwent no further significant transformation or development. Nevertheless, a new accent is noticeable in the last creations centering around the enigmatic *Un Coup de dés jamais n'abolira le hasard* (1897) and the three sonnets "Salut" (1893, a "toast" that Mallarmé selected as the liminal poem of his collected poems), "A la Nue accablante tu" (1895), and "Au seul Souci de voyager" (1898). The four works reactivate a theme dear to Mallarmé in "Brise marine" of 1864 and closely related to the Icarus theme in "Les Fenêtres"—namely, the theme of shipwreck—giving it new cogency at the end of his own Orphic voyage. As a matter of fact, one can speak of a sequence of motifs spanning thirty-five years of his work in the following manner: (1) frustration, (2) glory, (3) patience, (4) shipwreck. Inasmuch as the latter has some bearing on Mallarmé's Orphic experience, it will be treated briefly here.

Two of the sonnets under discussion, "Salut" and "Au seul Souci de voyager," celebrate the pilot of the ship, the Master. "Salut" gives this self-assurance a particularly Orphic twist:

> Rien, cette écume, vierge vers
> A ne désigner que la coupe;
> Telle loin se noie une troupe
> De sirènes mainte à l'envers.

> [This] Nothing, this froth, virgin verse
> Merely to outline the cup;
> Thus far off drowns a troop
> Of sirens, many of whom [are] upside down.

Besides evoking echoes of the faun and his two nymphs, this charming poem brings to mind the Argonautic journey and the contest of Orpheus and the Sirens; in this instance Mallarmé makes the "shipwreck" of the Sirens the *occasion* of the poetry, the initiation into mastery, rather than the result of it. He compares the foam of the brimming cup, first of all, with the necessary contour-definition in which the object must be viewed, and secondly with the dematerialization of the object that renders it exempt from contingency and makes it suitable as a vehicle for the hyperbolic act. The vibratory evocation of the disappearing Sirens provides the moment and place for poetry; consequently, it does not really matter whether the Argonauts are ultimately shipwrecked or not, because Orpheus is triumphant so long as the Sirens' plunge takes place. In "A la Nue," below, the emphasis is squarely on the shipwreck motif; here, too, the Siren—or what is left of her—figures significantly.

> A la nue accablante tu
> Basse de basalte et de laves
> A même les échos esclaves
> Par une trompe sans vertu

> Quel sépulcral naufrage (tu
> Le sais, écume, mais y baves)
> Suprême une entre les épaves
> Abolit le mât dévêtu

> Ou cela que furibond faute
> De quelque perdition haute
> Tout l'abîme vain éployé

Dans le si blanc cheveu qui traîne
Avarement aura noyé
Le flanc enfant d'une sirène.

Kept silent from the overwhelming cloud,
Shoal [or bass] of basalt and lava
On the same level as the slavish echoes
By an ineffectual trumpet blast

What sepulchral shipwreck (you
Know about it, foam, but merely drool over it)
Topmost, just one of the pieces of flotsam,
Abolished the stripped mast?

Or kept hidden the fact that raging, for lack
Of some high perdition,
The whole empty abyss having opened up

In that so white strand of hair trailing along
Must have greedily drowned
The flank, child of a siren.

This bizarre and exasperatingly ambiguous sonnet nevertheless makes a declaration about the triumph of the poetic fragment—the nascent cosmological myth out of which the magnum opus will be shaped. The mise-en-scène is simple enough, despite the contorted, wreckage-like syntax: a forgotten corner of the ocean lapping against a reef, threatening overhanging clouds, and total silence. These constitute the Mallarméan place and moment, as in "Solitude, récif, étoile" of "Salut" or "Nuit, désespoir, et pierrerie" in "Au seul Souci de voyager," but with a new transmutation of the concept of stellar or jewel-like redemption. A shipwreck seems to have occurred in this place, as indicated perhaps by the disappearing pinnacle of a mast. Why did it occur, and who knows about it?—that is the implicit question. Wrath from on high, a storm? Wrath from below, the treacherous sea swallowing up the ship? All that remains in the form of testimony—virtually nothing—is a curved streak of white foam, suggesting perhaps the white mane of the pilot who went down with the ship (as in *Un Coup de dés*) or, a little more precisely, the flank of a Siren's offspring or perhaps of the child Siren herself, that "presque disparition vibratoire" of which all poetry should be made.

There is recognizable in this setting of maritime disaster something analogous to the Stygian descent of "Ses Purs Ongles." There the "nixe" (Callisto) vanished into the mirror-lake so that the constellation Ursa Major could take her place. The nymph had just been vanquished in some sort of erotic struggle, and her disappearance meant the symbolical elevation of the intellect over *eros*. The same problem had occupied Mallarmé in "L'Après-midi d'un faune," where the young faun's erotic escapades (real or imagined) were shown to be the unconscious foundations of his art of mastering the pipes of Pan. The Siren in this sonnet, like her cousins the nixe and the naiads, represents the necessity of the erotic as a precondition of artistic creation: a temptation to be overcome, but a necessity nevertheless. Another remote kinswoman of the watery semigoddesses is, curiously enough, the drowned Ophelia, "joyau intact sous le désastre" (*Oeuvres complètes*, 302)—jewel intact beneath the disaster. This phrase can be applied literally to the Siren of the poem; it thus links this particular Siren curve of the ocean waves to the "pierrerie" of "Au seul Souci de voyager," as contemplated by Mallarmé—Hamlet-Igitur-Master of the vessel of *Un Coup de dés*, and finally Orpheus.

Why Orpheus too? This goes back, of course, to the Argonautic journey, and it is altogether possible that the Argo has just suffered shipwreck along with the "drowned" Sirens. Obviously Mallarmé is playing havoc with his mythology, but that is precisely the point: he treats mythological tradition as an invitation to endless transformation; he outmetamorphoses Ovid. But that is the logical consequence of the ambition to remake all poetry, to return to Orphic beginnings in the modern world. As noted along the course of the present chapter, this is not the first time Mallarmé has remade mythology; this poem is simply a more extreme example of his radical practice.

But there is more to be said. How to resolve the ambiguity, or obscurity, of "flanc enfant"? Remembering the mythological and popular tradition of the "sirène" and Mallarmé's variations on the subject, there is a superimposition here (again ad libitum) of the myth of the birth of Dionysus. Semele, beloved of Zeus, had upon Hera's malicious advice requested of Zeus that he appear to her in all his radiance. Zeus complied by manifesting himself in the form of lightning and thunderbolts, with the result that Semele was burned to ashes. One tradition has it that Jupiter gathered up the ashes of the unborn child, placed them inside his own thigh, and eventually gave birth to Dionysus. Mallarmé's transposition allegorically suggests that, out of the shipwreck and ashes, the erotic principle is reborn by the godlike creator through the act of seeing and the transparency of the word. The mute shipwreck scene of the sonnet is silently contemplated by the Orphic poet: the Master has disappeared in a swirl of ocean foam, and so has the Siren. But out of all this wreckage there arises the impersonal Orpheus, receptive and responsive to the hint of the erotic myth, reborn and transformed out of the flank of what may have been a Siren. The place, the moment, the occasion—the epiphany, the apotheosis, the new Orpheus: the same pattern, in a somewhat different context.

Un Coup de dés jamais n'abolira le hasard is at the same time a sequel to *Igitur* and, like *Igitur*, an aesthetic experiment. The old notion that *Un Coup de dés* was Le Livre has been successfully dispelled, and there is general agreement that this perplexing and difficult poem is intended to be a major fragment of the Grand Oeuvre. But what sort of fragment is it, and where does it belong in the Orphic Book, as yet incomplete, to which all poets are contributors? As pointed out in the discussion of *Igitur*, *Un Coup de dés* is another personal-impersonal drama, a mise-en-scène whose subject is the death of the poet and the survival of poetry and whose occasion is again the dice-throw. The young Hamlet-Igitur is now the aged Orpheus-Maître *who does not cast the dice* and suffers shipwreck. But in a still broader sense, the poem is not only about poetry but about being: it is an ontological drama. The baroque-rococo curios and the spiral staircase and spider webs of *Igitur* have been discarded in favor of a completely stripped scene: the sea, a ship and pilot, the sky. The metaphysics of individual metamorphosis (midnight, clock, bare room) has become the metaphysics of the metamorphosis of Man in the cosmos: the drama of becoming and being is played in universal terms. The poem is ingeniously devised to deploy all the musical, plastic, lyrical, dramatic, and philosophical genius of the author: and this multiplicity is given the widest possible vibratory range by the blanks and typographical arrangements—not merely a calligram, but the Western equivalent of an expanded ideogram. Mallarmé states in his Preface:

Le papier intervient chaque fois qu'une image, d'elle-même, cesse ou rentre, acceptant la succession d'autres et, comme il ne s'agit pas, ainsi que toujours, de traits sonores réguliers ou vers—plutôt de subdivisions prismatiques de l'Idée, l'instant de paraître et que dure leur concours, dans quelque mise en scène spirituelle exacte, c'est à des places variables, près ou loin du fil conducteur latent, en raison de la vraisemblance, que s'impose le texte. (455)

The sheet of paper intervenes every time an image, of its own accord, stops or returns, accepting the succession of other images; and since here we are not concerned, as we normally would be, with regular sonorous features or with verse—but rather with prismatic subdivisions of the Idea, the moment of their appearance and the length of their performance, in the context of some exact spiritual setting; because of all this, the text gains its force at variable positionings, whether near or far from the connective thread, with respect to verisimilitude.

The principal strand is provided by the title of the work, which gives a skeleton guide: UN COUP DE DÉS . . . JAMAIS . . . N'ABOLIRA . . . LE HASARD. (—A DICE THROW WILL NEVER ABOLISH CHANCE.) Gramatically, the word "JAMAIS" is succeeded by a qualifying subordinate phrase

> QUAND BIEN MÊME LANCÉ DANS DES
> CIRCONSTANCES ÉTERNELLES
> DU FOND D'UN NAUFRAGE
>
> EVEN IF CAST IN
> ETERNAL CIRCUMSTANCES
> FROM THE DEPTHS OF A SHIPWRECK.

The subsequent appearance of "LE MAÎTRE" permits the witnessing of the prelude of the drama, in which the old master, piloting the foundering vessel, holds in his hands the dice—the possibility of "l'unique Nombre qui ne peut pas être un autre" (the one Number that cannot be another). The old man hesitates to execute the supreme act, sequel to the "absurd" gesture required of Igitur. The word "N'ABOLIRA," relegated alone to the bottom of a blank page, begins a series of "comme si" clauses, a set of Hamletic interrogations and hesitations (Hamlet is now "prince amer de l'écueil"— bitter prince of the reef), and converges on a series of verbs in contrary-to-fact subjunctives, all predicates of "le Nombre": existât-il (if the number existed), commençât-il et cessât-il (if it were a part of becoming), se chiffrât-il (if it were interpretable), . . illuminât-il (if it were to provide the answer). This number, if it did exist, would also be a product of chance: "*CE SERAIT / pire / non / davantage ni moins / indifféremment mais autant / LE HASARD*"—*IT WOULD BE / worse / no / more no less / indifferently but equally / CHANCE.* Paradoxically, then, the "illumination" expected of the Number is the counter-illumination that chance would *not* be abolished by the throw of the dice. Here is the insight of *Igitur* come to maturity in *Un Coup de dés*, just as the young "absolutist" has now become the old poet. At this point the ship and its pilot go down into the "neutralité identique du gouffre"—identical neutrality of the abyss.

The next page opens with the word "RIEN," which serves as the first link of the garlandlike phrase RIEN . . . N'AURA EU LIEU . . . QUE LE LIEU (NOTHING WILL HAVE TAKEN PLACE BUT THE PLACE) and is continued on the following page with EXCEPTÉ . . . PEUT-ÊTRE . . . UNE CONSTELLATION (EXCEPT PERHAPS A CONSTELLATION), the whole chain revealing itself as the emblem of a *constellation-guirlande* familiar from "Quand l'Ombre menaça" and "Ses Purs Ongles." As a matter of fact, the Great Bear is now specifically mentioned. Once more there is the affirmation of the Mallarméan axis abyss-sky, with the key expression "aussi loin qu'un endroit *fusionne* avec au delà"—as far as a spot [down here] *fuses* with the beyond (italics mine)—this time clearly insisting on the fusion of opposites. In a final apotheosis, the action of the pilot is recapitulated and suspended in analogy with the emergence and fixation of the constellation.

> veillant
> doutant
> roulant
> brillant et méditant
> avant de s'arrêter
> à quelque point dernier qui le sacre
> Toute Pensée émet un Coup de Dés

> keeping watch
> doubting
> rolling
> shining and meditating
> before coming to a halt
> at some last point that consecrates it
> Every Thought emits a Dice-Throw

The apotheosis of the *gesture* of the terrestrial dice-throw is the astral equivalent occupying its fixed position: the gesture itself is the ritual that consecrates, and is consecrated by, the Absolute. An identity has been established, and its meaning is that every human thought re-enacts the same ritual and attains—dialectically—the same consecration.

133

Un Coup de dés represents, along with the three "marine" sonnets, the final phase of Mallarmé's quest: the failure *and* triumph of the Orphic poet, the convergence of opposites of negation and affirmation, the installation of the hyperbolic poem of word and silence. The sketches recently published by Jacques Scherer entitled "Le Livre de Mallarmé," though interesting, do not supplement the understanding that can be extracted from the late poems and prose writings. In many ways, Scherer's "Livre" is a disappointment because it does not really reveal what one wants to know: how Mallarmé in his later years thought the Grand Oeuvre might be structured and what place his own fragmentary contributions might occupy within the overall scope. Taking a clue from the preface of *Un Coup de dés*, it can be said that each fragment would, ideally, be a "subdivision prismatique" of the Book, each component would incorporate potentially a segment of the Orphic explanation of the earth. The quantity of Mallarmé's "fragments" is impressive: the miniature "prisms" of the shorter poems and, more centrally, the unfinished conte *Igitur*, the prose hymn for "des Esseintes," the "poème" *Un Coup de dés*, the unfinished "mystère" *Les Noces d'Hérodiade*, and the sizable body of critical and theoretical reflections collected under the titles "Crayonné au théâtre" and particularly "Variations sur un sujet." Mallarmé insisted frequently that the task of producing Le Livre was, to a certain degree, a critical enterprise. Many of his major poems are critical in nature, and some of the best of these portions are not only about poetry but are poetic in themselves. Thus a more succinct idea of Le Livre can be formulated from some reflections in "Le Livre, instrument spirituel" of *Variations sur un sujet* (1895), from which the following three paragraphs are taken.

 . . . Tout, au monde, existe pour aboutir à un livre.

Les qualités, requises en cet ouvrage, à coup sûr le génie, m'épouvantent un parmi les dénués; ne l'y arrêter et, admis le volume ne comporter aucune signataire, quel est-il: l'hymne, harmonie et joie, comme pur ensemble groupé dans quelque circonstance fulgurante, des relations entre tout. L'homme chargé de voir divinement, en raison que le lien, à volonté, limpide, n'a d'expression qu'au parallélisme, devant son regard, de feuillets.

Le livre, expansion totale de la lettre, doit d'elle tirer, directement, une mobilité et spacieux, par correspondances, instituer un jeu, on ne sait, qui confirme la fiction. (*Oeuvres complètes*, 380)

 . . . Everything in the world exists in order to culminate in a book.

The qualities required for that work, certainly genius is one of them, frighten me, as one of those inadequately equipped; not to stop at anything and, in view of the fact that the volume is to have no signers, what sort of book is it: the hymn, harmony and joy, as a pure whole grouped in some fulgurating circumstance, of the relations between everything. Man entrusted with the task of seeing divinely, owing to the fact that the bond, limpid on purpose, can find no other expression than by means of the parallelism, before his eyes, of sheets of paper.

The book, as a totally expanded letter of the alphabet, must by itself draw, directly, a mobility and, spacious, by means of correspondences, institute a game, in some way or other, that confirms the fiction.

The first sentence reasserts the scriptural idea fundamental to Mallarmé's work; the second emphasizes the hymnic characteristic of the Book (as in "Prose pour des Esseintes") and hints at the typographical equivalences of the page (as in *Un Coup de dés*); the third focuses on the alchemical and artificial aspects of poetic creation.

How seriously does Mallarmé take the "jeu"? And how real or unreal is the fiction? How literally does he mean "la gloire du mensonge" or "le glorieux mensonge"? It is not only Mallarmé's poetry that is enigmatic; the enigma is in some way in the master himself. There is, on the one hand, the extraordinary asceticism, which Mallarmé raised to a level approaching saintliness: Mallarmé as St. John the Baptist. There is the whimsicality and preciousness: Mallarmé as the Faun, as editor of *La Dernière Mode*. And there is the irony, partly anguished, partly amused: Mallarmé as Hamlet, tragedian and clown. The *work*, however, remains serious and conscientious: "le jeu" was not merely a game, but the supreme intellectual and ontological struggle for lucidity and permanence. The glorious lie is just what it says, an affirmation and a negation—one could not exist without the other, as the "nuits de Tournon" proved. The ambiguity of Mallarmé's spirit is, in the final reckoning, the ambiguity of the modern spirit in the face of chaos and meaninglessness, but raised to the ultimate degree. In this respect, Mallarmé anticipates much of the twentieth century, perhaps in a recondite way, so that behind the crystalline or whimsical exterior we do not always recognize our affinity with him. We are still perhaps too prone to think in terms of sharply outlined Romantic contrasts, rather than in subtler gradations of contrary tensions. Speaking of Mallarmé's "angelism," Jean Starobinski observes astutely:

It is easy to see that Mallarmé's *angelism* constitutes the reverse face as well as one of the most intriguing metamorphoses of Romantic *satanism*, Baudelaire having served as the initiator. Angelism differs from satanism only in this: it opposes God not as a declared adversary but as a rival. It is Icarus' flight and not the Promethean revolt, but the important thing is still to seize divine power. Where the Romantic challenges and blasphemes, Mallarmé strives calmly to construct a poetry that would have the force of the demiurge's work and which can compete with the world of created things to the point of supplanting it in its totality. If Lucifer is an angel and desires purity, he is at the same time a demon and desires negation, in the very light that he brings.[38]

The enigma of Mallarmé the man appears to grow directly out of his profoundly *ironic* understanding of the nature of being and of creativity. Irony is by nature dualistic; the dialectic provides a means of overcoming this duality, but between irony and the convergence of opposites there lies a zone of obscurity, ambivalence, indecision, torment—and a special kind of humor, alternately grim and playful. This is no doubt what Mallarmé had in mind when he wrote to Guitry: "Tout écrivain complet aboutit à un humoriste"—Every complete writer ends by being a humorist.[39] It is possible that, in the widening perspective of the twentieth century, Mallarmé will come to appear more and more like the ancestor of that ontological comedian, Samuel Beckett. On this subject, Georges Poulet draws a valuable distinction between Nerval and Mallarmé: "The experience of the peripheral Nothing is for Mallarmé, as for Nerval, a catastrophe, but for Mallarmé it is a ludicrous catastrophe and consequently a return to reason . . . Whereas in Mallarmé's soul there is a part that most monstrously exalts the power of thought, there is also a part, no less lucid but gently skeptical, that in looking at this power of thought, never loses sight of its vanity."[40]

There is no reason why the modern Orphic poet should not be in some way a comic hero. If he goes to Hades convinced of the vanity of the world, the impossibility of art, the necessity of silence—can he not be considered heroic in his resolve, saintly in his obstination, pathetic in his suffering, ironic in his awareness? Mallarmé lives this ambiguity and frustration from "Le Guignon" to the shipwreck of *Un Coup de dés* and, in his own way, answers Hölderlin's "Wozu Dichter in dürftiger Zeit?" in the affirmative. The Mallarméan dilemma, as Poulet notes, leads in two opposing directions: "One of the propositions leads the mind infallibly toward affirmation, multiplication, aggrandizement, that is to say, toward hyperbole—and the hyperbole is a lie, a nothingness put into words; the other option carries the mind toward truth, construction, negation and consequently also toward silence. The irony is the act of negation whereby, everything being reduced to nothing, it appears clearly that there is no longer anything to say, that the poet can do no more than to be silent."[41]

The ironic struggle in Mallarmé is waged by two adversaries, the rational metaphysician and the mystic. Or, in another sense, the poet in Mallarmé, who must speak, is in conflict with the mystic in him, who must be silent. The philosopher is invoked to act as arbiter, but he tends to be somewhat capricious: as a skeptic he introduces irony into the combat, as a dialectician he conciliates the adversaries.

That Mallarmé set his goals too high for achievement has become a truism; but this craving for the absolute is the result of a remarkable lucidity concerning the condition of poetry in a devaluated universe that invites absurd and obstinate positions—Hölderlin, Baudelaire, Rimbaud, Mallarmé, Proust, Joyce, Rilke, Kafka, and Beckett are adequate proof of this state of affairs. What Mallarmé aimed for was no less than a discovery—an Orphic *recovery*—of the mysterious alchemical essence of poetry itself, not an insertion of alchemy into poetry from the outside, as in Novalis and Nerval, but revelation of poetry-as-magic. This is the reason why occultist writings had only marginal interest for him and why alchemistic interpretations of Mallarmé's work miss the mark. The great forge of the alchemists is extinct: the intelligence must do the work of magic, becoming cabalistic in itself:

Quelque déférence . . . envers le laboratoire éteint du grand oeuvre, consisterait à reprendre, sans fourneau, les manipulations, poisons, refroidis autrement qu'en pierreries, pour continuer par la simple intelligence. (*Oeuvres complètes*, 399)

A certain deference toward the exhausted laboratory of the magnum opus would be to resume, without forge, the manipulations, poisons, grown cold now except in the form of precious stones, in order to carry on by the strength of simple intelligence.

The poet, still artificer of the smithy, still alchemist, still *vates* but no longer directly linked to the alchemistic tradition (as Nerval had been) and now living in an "interregnum" (664), was to recreate poetic myths; because our time has "dissolved" myths by ratiocination they must now be remade (544–545). Literature, in re-establishing myths and mystery plays and conferring upon them again the sacrality they had once had (Mallarmé's own "Hérodiade'" appears to have been conceived as constituting ultimately such a *mystère—Les Noces d'Hérodiade*), by means of rigorous method was to invent a science of language open to and initiated in the magic properties of the *verbe*: "cette Littérature exactement dénommée les Lettres . . . implique sa doctrine propre, abstraite, ésotérique comme quelque théologie" (850)—that Literature exactly designated as Letters . . . implies its own doctrine, abstract and esoteric as some theology. This "théologie des Lettres" (856) would reinstitute and officiate over "une assimilation humaine à la tétralogie de l'An" (393)—a human assimilation to the tetralogy of the Year—that is to say, a seasonal and solar myth, such as the myth of Orpheus as Mallarmé understood it and the *drame solaire* studied by Gardner Davies, as well as the more far-fetched assimilations of classical mythology exemplified in Mallarmé's poetry that have been noted in the course of this chapter. The act of creation, for Mallarmé, always implies the obverse of being:

On n'écrit pas, lumineusement, sur champ obscur, l'alphabet des astres, seul, ainsi s'indique, ébauché ou interrompu; l'homme poursuit noir sur blanc. (370)

One does not write luminously on a dark background; the alphabet of the stars alone manifests itself like that, sketched out or interrupted; man must go on putting black on white.

Valéry's tribute to his master is somewhat in the same vein: "Il a essayé . . . d'élever enfin une page à la puissance du ciel étoilé"[42]—He has tried, after all, to raise one page to the power of the starry sky.

In a novel entitled *Le Soleil des morts*, written by Mallarmé's friend Camille Mauclair in 1897, there is, by Mauclair's admission, "un portrait tout intellectuel" of Mallarmé in the character of Calixte Armel. The name, but for one letter, contains anagramatically Mallarmé's name, and even the "ix" of the "Sonnet allégorique de lui-même." As a concluding, unscientific postscript, a quotation from Armel's discourses (is it not safe to assume that this discourse may be a transcription of sorts from one of Mallarmé's famous *mardis?*) seems appropriate:

[On peut se tromper] en religion . . . pas en art. Aussi est-ce une vocation terrible et exclusive, qui veut tout l'homme et ne permet pas l'erreur; il faut y entrer sans tourner la tête pour voir quelque joie secondaire, comme fit Orphée notre maître, qui perdit Eurydice, image de son âme, pour n'avoir pas eu la patience de ne la contempler qu'en pleine lumière. Notre lumière à nous, c'est la gloire. Et, si nous ne voulons pas qu'Eurydice meure et que la gloire soit, selon l'expression fatale, "le soleil des morts"—il nous faut fermer à jamais les yeux au soleil de la vie ordinaire . . . Le *credo* de l'artiste moderne, c'est le silence.[43]

You can make a mistake in religion . . . but not in art. Therefore it's a terrible and exclusive vocation, making demands on the whole man and allowing no error; you've got to go into it without turning your head to see some secondary joy, as did Orpheus our master; he lost Eurydice, the image of his soul, because he did not have the patience to contemplate her before he reached the light of day. Our own light is glory. And if we don't want Eurydice to die, and if we don't want our glory to be, as the fateful expression goes, "the sun of the dead"—then we must forever close our eyes to the sun of ordinary life . . . The credo of the modern artist is silence.

V

Rilke:
Orpheus and
the Double Realm

Rilke's work represents the confluence of the French and German Orphic currents; as Nerval was, in some respects, the logical successor to Novalis, so Rilke may be looked upon as the heir of Mallarmé. But this must be understood primarily in the sense of the Orphic convergence of opposites: the stylistic differences between Mallarmé and Rilke are of considerable importance. First, it is not altogether clear how intensely Rilke was interested in Mallarmé. He translated two of Mallarmé's poems, the "Eventail" for Mlle Mallarmé and the "Tombeau" sonnet for Verlaine; and it may be inferred that his personal contacts, particularly with Valéry and possibly with Rodin, may have enabled him to feel the afterglow of Mallarmé's magic presence. But the fact remains that references to Mallarmé in Rilke's correspondence are rare. If there is any debt to Mallarmé it is rather a general one, centered around the intransigent belief in the superiority of art and the self-discipline of the artist; it must be remembered, however, that precise information about Mallarmé's crisis years and his "descent" was not available to Rilke.

One looks in vain for the specific Rilkean tribute to Mallarmé's work, similar to his comments on Baudelaire's "La Charogne" in *Malte* or the exhilaration with which he greeted Valéry's *Charmes* and his two Socratic dialogues. If Rilke had fallen under the spell of Mallarmé, surely he would have done so during the years 1902–1914; as it turned out, his discovery of and personal friendship with Valéry after 1920 supplanted and in some way reformulated his potential interest in this great master of the symbolist period. It is worth noting that Rilke's French poems dating from 1924 to 1926 are closer stylistically to Verlaine—not even to Valéry, as might have been expected. The only affinity with Valéry that can be detected in these charming and sensitive brief poems are with Valéry's shorter poems in *Charmes*, such as "Les Pas," "L'Abeille," and "Le Sylphe."

But, it is precisely the unintentional similarities and differences between Rilke and Mallarmé that are of importance here. Both are Orphic poets, striving toward an integration of individual existence and the world under the aegis of poetry, and looking toward Orphic unification in the face of empirical diversity. For Mallarmé the goal was the Orphic explication of the earth; for Rilke the task is similar, except that the term "explication"—unfolding—describes Rilke's quest less satisfactorily than the word "implication"—infolding. If Rilke is—or rather, ultimately becomes—the poet of the *Weltinnenraum* (world space interiorized), then Mallarmé can be regarded as the poet of the *Weltaussenraum* (cosmic space exteriorized). The difference is not only suggestive, from the point of view of the transmutations of Orphic poetry in modern times, but it also accounts for a number of stylistic differences, and perhaps finally for the fact that Rilke did not respond to Mallarmé as vigorously as he did to Verlaine or Valéry. Verlaine is much more clearly the poet of nuances,

> Car nous voulons la Nuance encor,
> Pas la Couleur, rien que la nuance!
> Oh! la nuance seule fiance
> Le rêve au rêve et la flûte au cor!
>
> For we would have Nuance rather,
> Not Color, nothing but nuance!
> Oh! nuance alone affiances
> Dream with dream and flute with horn!
> ("Art poétique," *Jadis et naguère*)

and Valéry the poet of silence and waiting. The following lines from "Palme" were among Rilke's special favorites:

> Patience, patience,
> Patience dans l'azur!
> Chaque atome de silence
> Est la chance d'un fruit mûr!

> Patience, patience,
> Patience in the blue!
> Each atom of silence
> Is the chance of a ripe fruit!

Mallarmé, despite his *sorcellerie évocatoire*, is the poet of absence. The objects in his poetry are clearly defined, sharply contoured. The flower in the garden described in "Prose pour Des Esseintes" is set off by a lucid contour. The void surrounding the object vouchsafes that its presence and its absence do not merge; as in the didactic "cigar" sonnet, "Toute l'Âme résumée," the smoke

> Atteste quelque cigare
> Brûlant savamment pour peu
> Que la cendre se sépare
> De son clair baiser de feu

> Attests some cigar
> Burning knowingly so long
> As the ash separates
> From its bright kiss of fire

—that is to say, the precise details of the absent burning cigar are all attested by the presence of the smoke rings; the soul-body dialectic is maintained and reaffirmed. Mallarmé uses the metaphor hyperbolically: the image is outward-bound. In Rilke, on the other hand, everything moves toward fusion and metamorphosis and the image is inward-bound. The threshold between the visible and the invisible is, for Mallarmé, a space of definition. For Rilke it is the locus of redefinition, transformation; hence his insistence on *Bezug* (relationship), *Umkehr* (reversal), *Wandlung* (transmutation)—the convergence of opposites takes place in this sacred space, the space par excellence in which the Orphic metamorphosis of the earth becomes a reality here and now. The fourth Duino Elegy laments man's divorce from the world ("Wir sind nicht einig"—We are not at one):

> Uns aber, wo wir Eines meinen, ganz,
> ist schon des andern Aufwand fühlbar. Feindschaft
> ist uns das Nächste . . .
> . . . Wir kennen den Kontur
> des Fühlens nicht, nur was ihn formt von aussen. (ll. 9–18)

> But for us, the moment we aim at One thing, wholly,
> the pressure of the other thing already becomes perceptible. Opposition
> is what is closest to us . . .
> . . . We do not know the contour
> of feeling, only that which forms the contour from the outside.

Emphasis is on the *external* contour, which is too precise and therefore anti-thetical to inwardness; as the first Elegy asserts, we are not very much at home in the interpreted world. And, significantly enough, in the above quotation lovers, mediators between the open and closed worlds, are poised on the edge separating the two realms. In the seventh Elegy, the lamentation is abolished by the certitude of transformation:

> Nirgends, Geliebte, wird Welt sein, als innen. Unser
> Leben geht hin mit Verwandlung. Und immer geringer
> schwindet das Aussen. Wo einmal ein dauerndes Haus war,
> schlägt sich erdachtes Gebild vor, quer, zu Erdenklichem
> völlig gehörig, als ständ es noch ganz im Gehirne. (ll. 50–54)

> Nowhere, beloved, will world be except inside. Our
> life passes away with transformation. And ever more faintly
> the outside fades. Where once was a durable house,
> a mental image proposes itself, transversally,
> completely part of the imaginable, as if it still stood intact in the brain.

Like Rilke's lovers, the Orpheus of the *Sonnets* is forever poised between *Raum* (space) and *Innenraum* (inner space); in this *Zwischenraum* (intermediate space), which is also the abode of nuance, he becomes whole again, breathes, issues forth into song. For Eudo Mason, Rilke's world view is entirely governed by the sense of nuance:

Rilke is above all a poet of nuances . . . what is his idea about his own death if not a nuance reduced to a magic formula embracing everything that seems to argue *for* and everything that seems to argue *against* personal immortality? What is his idea of world interior space if not a nuance between all that constitutes the nature of philosophical subjectivism and of philosophical objectivism? What is his idea of unpossessive love if not a nuance between solitude and community and between asceticism raised to the most perilous level and sensuality raised to the most perilous level? What is his idea of reversal if not a nuance made absolute between affirmation and negation of life, between all varieties of optimism and pessimism, between heaven and hell, between infinity and nothingness? What is his notion of Being if not a nuance between time and eternity . . . What is the entire doctrine of the Elegies according to which all things are to be made invisible if not the assertion that nuance constitutes the one eternal component in everything that is transient? The world that his soul strives after is a world in which all beings would be related to one another only in terms of nuances, like mirror images to their originals.[1]

This somewhat severe but essentially valid analysis of Rilke's thought points to the conclusion that his handling of the *coincidentia oppositorum* is different from Mallarmé's and more deliberate. It may be said that Mallarmé's mind is truly a dialectical one, in this sense having certain affinities with that of Nicholas of Cusa and Hegel and, ultimately, Heraclitus, whereas Rilke with his "dialectic" *sensibility* is more Empedoclean in his predilection for the play of polarities and the quest of the exact center (*reine Mitte*) between extremes. This is why it is by no means startling, or inconsistent, for Rilke to treat the coincidence of opposites playfully, as he does in this charming late poem:

> Combien le pape au fond de son faste,
> sans être moins vénérable,
> par la sainte loi du contraste
> doit attirer le diable.

> Peut-être qu'on compte trop peu
> avec ce mouvant équilibre;
> il y a des courants dans le Tibre,
> tout jeu veut son contre-jeu.[2]

> How much the pope in all his ostentation,
> without being any the less venerable,
> by the holy law of contrast
> must attract the devil.

> Perhaps too little heed is paid
> to this moving equilibrium;
> there are currents within the Tiber,
> every game wants its counter-game.

This "holy law of contrast" is developed and refined in a magnificent manner in Rilke's late poetry, particularly the *Sonnets to Orpheus*.

Rilke's achievement as a poet presents a number of analogies to Beethoven. The early, derivative works from time to time show the mark of the individual creator to come; then a breakthrough occurs (in Beethoven's case, the *Eroica Symphony*), followed by works in which the mature profile of the artist becomes delineated; finally, there is an extraordinary harvest of ripe creations in the later years (for Beethoven the final quartets and sonatas, the Ninth Symphony, the *Missa Solemnis*). In Rilke's case the first breakthrough occurs with the *Stundenbuch* (1898–1902), reaches a kind of cul de sac with *Die Aufzeichnungen des Malte Laurids Brigge* (published in 1910), wavers uneasily during 1912–1922, becomes consolidated in February 1922, and continues vigorously until his death in December 1926. But even this analogy breaks down to some extent: the curve of Beethoven's career is smoother than Rilke's, and there are no major discontinuities. Beethoven's late works are full of conceptions and expressive devices that are but dimly foreshadowed by the earlier compositions and that make one wonder how this strange and moving language came into being. In Rilke the fulguration is even more startling. It is impossible to conclude that the *Duino Elegies*, much less than the *Sonnets to Orpheus*, are the necessary and logical consequence of the *Stundenbuch*, the *Buch der Bilder*, the *Neue Gedichte*, or *Malte*. The *Stundenbuch* is Rilke's first genuine achievement; after the derivative early poems, with their postsymbolist and fin de siècle atmosphere, he embarks on his own quest for God, a God who is at once a "neighbor" and at the same time always in the process of "becoming." In a sense, this work looks forward to *Malte* and to the Elegies more directly than the subsequent collections of poetry. It stands under the spell of Rilke's discovery of the Russian earth, whereas the poetry of the years 1904–1910, written almost exclusively in Paris, is the direct result of his contact with Rodin and with painting, especially that of Cézanne.

The title of the next collection, though in a way it prolongs the reminiscence of monastic illuminations and of the *Livre des très riches heures* implicit in the setting and content of *Das Stundenbuch*, is indicative of the new plasticity of Rilke's manner: *Buch der Bilder*. And this Book of Images (or Pictures) was followed by a considerably more original work, the *Neue Gedichte*, whose noncommittal title does not reveal that it might have been called "Buch der Dinge" (in this collection Rilke's attempt to penetrate the mystery of "things" results in the creation of a number of *Dinggedichte* that are quite unlike anything written before). But the period in which both of these collections were published was marked by sporadic activity on the prose work *Malte*, a document of Rilke's anguish and frustration during his Paris years. He was able subsequently to characterize it as a "watershed" (in a letter written on December 28, 1911[3]); in *Malte* he had not written out his anguish, he had merely come face to face with it. For some time he was undecided whether to try giving up poetry altogether, whether to subject himself to psychiatric analysis, whether to take up a different sort of vocation. Even the epiphany of the Angel at Duino in 1912 served only temporarily to reassure him: under the inspiration of this crucial experience he set out to write the first two Elegies and to draft the beginnings of a number of the others. But after 1913 the sense of artistic impotence returned and became aggravated by the war years. Only the third and gloomy fourth Elegies were written during 1914–1915, then—apparently—all activity stopped until that miraculous February of 1922. "Apparently" because Rilke quite evidently did not stop trying; the completed poems as well as the fragments of that period indicate work around the periphery of the Elegies and attempts to strike through to the center. In February 1922 he succeeded not only in completing the ten Elegies but harvested, gratis so to speak, some sixty-five sonnets, fifty-five of which became the *Sonnets to Orpheus*. This represents possibly the most extraordinary burst of poetic creation in the annals of literary history.

The second part of the *Neue Gedichte* opens with the famous sonnet "Archäischer Torso Apollos," in which hidden tension within the object—the torso of Apollo in the Vatican Museum—and, by implication, in the *Dinggedicht* is already manifest. The torso of Apollo is described in all its radiance, which, though contained within a plastic contour, is not only full of energy but also full of seeing:

> Wir kannten nicht sein unerhörtes Haupt,
> darin die Augenäpfel reiften. Aber
> sein Torso glüht noch wie ein Kandelaber,
> in dem sein Schauen, nur zurückgeschraubt,
>
> sich hält und glänzt.

> We did not know his unheard-of head
> in which the pupils [apples of the eye] ripened. But
> his torso still glows like a chandelier
> in which his beholding, merely twisted back,
>
> contains itself and shines.

The poem is all potential energy, despite its presumably calm and measured sculptural stoniness. The dynamic vocabulary ("reiften," "glüht," "zurück-geschraubt") twists against the static words, and the torsion is caught in the words "sich hält und glänzt." The sonnet goes on to record why and how this tension acts upon the spectator:

> Sonst könnte nicht der Bug
> der Brust dich blenden, und im leisen Drehen
> der Lenden könnte nicht ein Lächeln gehen
> zu jener Mitte, die die Zeugung trug.
>
> Sonst stünde dieser Stein entstellt und kurz
> unter der Schultern durchsichtigem Sturz
> und flimmerte nicht so wie Raubtierfelle;
>
> und bräche nicht aus allen seinen Rändern
> aus wie ein Stern: denn da ist keine Stelle,
> die dich nicht sieht. Du musst dein Leben ändern.

> Otherwise the flexing
> of the chest could not dazzle you, and in the quiet rotation
> of the loins a smile could not move
> toward that center that held the genitals.
>
> Otherwise this stone would be standing disfigured and curtailed
> beneath the transparent drop of the shoulders,
> nor could it glisten like the skins of savage beasts;
>
> nor could it burst out of all its bounds
> like a star: for there is not a single spot [on the surface]
> that does not see you. You must change your life.

All the tension and torsion of this Apollonian torso is charged with Dionysian energy ("Raubtierfelle" is most suggestive here), in order to scrutinize the spectator himself—it is he who is being contemplated by the statue; the work of art, though headless, beholds the beholder and demands unconditionally that he change his life. That is why Rilke can speak of the missing head as unheard-of. The message is so new, so radical; in a sense, as Rilke discovered later, this unheard-of head is like the decapitated Orpheus whom we must learn to hear again. The center of this torso, the generative center, is also the center of the last poem in the collection "Buddha in der Glorie":

> Mitte aller Mitten, Kern der Kerne,
> Mandel, die sich einschliesst und versüsst—
> dieses Alles bis an alle Sterne
> ist dein Fruchtfleisch: Sei gegrüsst.

> Center of all centers, core of cores,
> almond, which encloses and sweetens itself—
> this wholeness [reaching] to all the stars
> is your fruit pulp: Be saluted.

The quest for the center, in Rilke, lies in the realm of movement and energy situated between Apollo and the Buddha. The drama and triumph of the later poetry takes place within that realm.

Though many of the transformations in Rilke's mind and sensibility during the difficult years between 1912 and 1922 cannot be formulated in precise terms, two or three details may be observed. In many respects, the entire period corresponds to the Orphic descent already noted as a constant pattern in Novalis, Nerval, and Mallarmé, except that the experience seems more drawn out and perhaps less exacerbated at any single moment. In this phase, Rilke's nocturnal orientation becomes intensified; a number of the poems written in 1913 and 1914 belong to a cycle (never published as such) of "Gedichte an die Nacht," very much in the mood of Novalis and Hölderlin. It is particularly Rilke's reading of Hölderlin in 1914 that impressed him with the intransigence of a poet who had set for himself the noblest poetic task:

> Ach, was die Höchsten begehren, du legtest es wunschlos
> Baustein auf Baustein: es stand. Doch selber sein Umsturz
> irrte dich nicht . . .[4]

> Ah, what the highest crave for, you placed it without desire
> stone upon stone: it stood straight. But even its collapse
> did not mislead you . . .

Most significant for Rilke's poetry was his new interest in music. The earlier poetry, despite its "musical" sonority, was largely focused on the linear and plastic properties of objects and persons: Rilke tended to see things with the eyes of painters and fashion them with the hands of sculptors. About the time of the Duino epiphany, and shortly after, he evidences a new absorption with musical experience. This change is attributable to contact with friends such as Magda von Hattingberg ("Benvenuta") and others, to fascination with Fabre d'Olivet's discourse on music ("La musique expliquée"), or, to Rilke's long subconscious readiness for such a transformation (the entire period 1912–1922 is a succession of slow transmutations that crystallized in the creation of the Elegies and Sonnets that February). Interestingly enough, it is the silence behind (or within) music that begins to fascinate Rilke, just as one might say that in the "Archäischer Torso Apollos" (and in many other poems) it is the movement within the repose that engages his attention. A poem of 1918, "An die Musik," makes this connection between the visual and the auditory explicit:

> Musik: Atem der Statuen. Vielleicht:
> Stille der Bilder. Du Sprache wo Sprachen
> enden. Du Zeit,
> die senkrecht steht auf der Richtung vergehender Herzen.
>
> Gefühle zu wem? Oder der Gefühle
> Wandlung in was?— in hörbare Landschaft
> Du Fremde: Musik. Du uns entwachsener
> Herzraum. Innigstes unser,
> das, uns übersteigend, hinausdrängt—
> heiliger Abschied:
> da uns das Innre umsteht
> als geübteste Ferne, als andre
> Seite der Luft:
> rein,
> riesig,
> nicht mehr bewohnbar.[5]

> Music: breath of statues. Possibly:
> silence of pictures. Thou language where other languages
> end. Thou time
> standing vertically upon the direction of dissolving hearts.
>
> Feelings toward whom? Or the transformation
> of feelings into what?— into audible landscape.

> Thou alien one: music. Thou heart-space
> that has outgrown us. Most intimately ours,
> which, transcending us, strains outward—
> holy farewell:
> since what is inward surrounds us
> as a most practiced distance, as the other
> side of air:
> pure,
> immense,
> no longer habitable.

The "audible landscape" of this poem already looks forward to the landscape of Orpheus, and the words "heart-space that has outgrown us" define the nature of music in relation to the poetry of inwardness—music occupies that space which must be drawn into the heart. It is an effusion of inwardness that surrounds us with such grandeur, such purity that we cannot inhabit it: it can only inhabit us.

Rilke's entire impulse of the years following 1912 centers on the desire of the heart to dwell in a space of purity and immensity. This process requires a kind of alchemy—not quite the alchemy of nineteenth-century occultists, nor the intellectual sorcery of Mallarmé, but the alchemy of the sensibility effecting a series of metamorphoses upon the visible world. Two frequently cited poems reinforce more succinctly the sentiment expressed in "An die Musik." The first is "Wendung" (1914), characteristic even then for the idea of "turning" (later the more radical cognate words "Wandlung" and "Verwandlung" were used by Rilke) in its title. "Wendung" contains the following programmatic directive:

> Denn des Anschauns, siehe, ist eine Grenze.
> Und die geschautere Welt
> will in der Liebe gedeihen.
>
> Werk des Gesichts ist getan,
> tue nun Herz-Werk.[6]

> For there is, lo! a limit to beholding.
> And the more beheld world
> wants to prosper in love.

> The work of seeing is done,
> now do the work of the heart.

A poem written during the same year projects the method whereby the *Herz-Werk* is to be accomplished:

> Es winkt zu Fühlung fast aus allen Dingen,
> aus jeder Wendung weht es her: Gedenk!
> Ein Tag, an dem wir fremd vorübergingen,
> entschliesst im Künftigen sich zum Geschenk.
>
> Wer rechnet unseren Ertrag? Wer trennt
> uns von den alten, den vergangenen Jahren?
> Was haben wir seit Anbeginn erfahren,
> als dass sich eins im anderen erkennt?
>
> Als dass an uns Gleichgültiges erwarmt?
> O Haus, o Wiesenhang, o Abendlicht,
> auf einmal bringst du's beinah zum Gesicht
> und stehst an uns, umarmend und umarmt.

> Almost all things beckon toward feeling,
> every turning wafts: Remember!
> A day that we passed as a stranger
> discloses itself to be a gift in time to come.
>
> Who counts up our harvest? Who divides us
> from the old, past years?
> What have we learned since the beginning
> except that one thing recognizes itself in another?
>
> Except that what is indifferent grows warm next to us?
> O house, o meadow slope, o twilight,
> Suddenly you almost make it visible
> and stand next to us, embracing and embraced.

The poem is a call to mutuality, to recognition. Almost all things beckon to us, like Baudelaire's "forêt de symboles"; what was neutral and indifferent once becomes, later, familiar and intimate.

Durch alle Wesen reicht der *eine* Raum:
Weltinnenraum. Die Vögel fliegen still
durch uns hindurch. O der ich wachsen will,
ich seh hinaus, und *in* mir wächst der Baum.

Ich sorge mich, und in mir steht das Haus.
Ich hüte mich, und in mir ist die Hut.
Geliebter, der ich wurde: an mir ruht
der schönen Schöpfung Bild und weint sich aus.[7]

Through all beings extends the *one* space:
World-inner-space. The birds fly silently
through us. O, I who wish to grow,
I look outside, and *in* me grows the tree.

I am beset with care, and within me stands the house.
I ward things off, and within me is the ward.
Lover that I came to be: against me rests
the figure of lovely creation and cries its heart out.

The first three stanzas had been concerned with the way in which things offer themselves to us; the final two explain how this is possible—all beings share the world-inner-space. Once this is recognized, the most extraordinary things can happen. Rilke gives several examples, in which it becomes clear that the moment this receptivity to transformation exists within us the changes take place "naturally." The *Gesicht*, the face (or the power of seeing), becomes the place where the picture, the image of creation, finds its reflection and its resting place. The notion of the creation lamenting leads directly to the *Duino Elegies*.

The Elegies, prerequisite to a fuller understanding of the *Sonnets to Orpheus*, must be discussed at some length. They represent a monument of anguish, frustration, and hard (though intermittent) poetic labor over a ten-year period, in contrast to the Sonnets, which were "given" to Rilke within a few days. The Elegies expectably attempt more: they are Rilke's endeavor to encompass the problem of existence and creativity, destiny and poetry, death and affirmation. In view of this extraordinary ambitious design, and in keeping with Rilke's somewhat ambiguous and contradictory personality, the Elegies are at the same time luminous and obscure. In any case, they are difficult. Their principal relation to the Sonnets lies in the fact that, for one thing, their creation is continuous with those shorter poems; for another, there is a movement—not clearly continuous—that leads from lament to praise in the Elegies. It can therefore be said that the Sonnets give culminating expression to the theme of celebration toward which the Elegies move. A poem written on the eve of completion of the first Orpheus cycle and resumption of work on the Elegies—a poem which may be said to belong to the spasm of creativity that began on December 31, 1922, and ended on February 23—begins

> ... Wann wird, wann wird, wann wird es genügen
> das Klagen und Sagen? Waren nicht Meister im Fügen
> menschlicher Worte gekommen? Warum die neuen Versuche?[8]

> ... When, when, when will it suffice,
> This lamenting and speaking? Have there not been masters in the
>   art of composing
> human words? Why these new attempts?

"Klagen und Sagen" projects the movement of the Elegies from lamentation to "saying"; as a matter of fact, the question is precisely what is left to be said and how it is to be said. The answer that Rilke laboriously arrives at, in the ninth and tenth Elegies, is *praise*. The *Sonnets* celebrate this invitation to praise.

A number of passages in the *Duino Elegies* pave the way for the *Sonnets to Orpheus*.[9] The lowest note of lament is found in the "wintry" fourth Elegy. A key passage ("Uns aber, wo wir Eines meinen, ganz ...") was discussed earlier in this chapter as an example of man's distance from nature and his frustrated attempt to be at one with it. The setting for this Elegy is a stage performance with the poet looking on. He is repelled by the dancer because he sees the disguised bourgeois in him; he prefers the doll, the marionette, to the half-filled mask of the actor-dancer.

> Ich will nicht diese halbgefüllten Masken,
> lieber die Puppe. Die ist voll. Ich will
> den Balg aushalten und den Draht und ihr
> Gesicht aus Aussehn. (26–29)

> I do not want these half-filled masks,
> rather the doll. *That* one is filled. I want

to endure the stuffed body and the wire and its
face [made up] of looking.

The marionette has at least a subhuman existence; it is all mechanical; it is full of sawdust; it is, so to speak, complete in itself. To use a Rilkean paradox, it is full of emptiness, of a "zu-wenig" (too little). The actor—or at least the dancer who is being observed and who is certainly not *the* dancer par excellence but the bourgeois-turned-dancer—is half and half, a mixture of being and seeming, not a convergence of opposites (for Rilke art and the bourgeoisie cannot converge) but an unholy juxtaposition of contradictions that do not interact. What, then, is the fitting complement to the puppet: the superhuman existence that balances out with the will-lessness of the doll? The answer is the Angel.

> Wenn mir zumut ist,
> zu warten vor der Puppenbühne, nein,
> so völlig hinzuschaun, dass, um mein Schauen
> am Ende aufzuwiegen, dort als Spieler
> ein Engel hinmuss, der die Bälge hochreisst.
> Engel und Puppe: dann ist endlich Schauspiel.
> Dann kommt zusammen, was wir immerfort
> entzwein, indem wir da sind. Dann entsteht
> aus unsern Jahreszeiten erst der Umkreis
> des ganzen Wandelns. Über uns hinüber
> spielt dann der Engel. (52–62)

> When I am in the mood
> to wait in front of the marionette theater, no,
> to look at it so completely that, in order to balance off
> my looking at last, the actor
> would have to be an Angel, who can snatch up those stuffed dolls.
> Angel and doll: then can there be a spectacle at last.
> Then there is joined what we are constantly
> severing just by being here. Only then, there,
> can our seasons come to be the cycle
> of total transformation. Then the Angel
> will be playing past our heads.

The solution Rilke offers here is highly schematic and therefore somewhat more abstract than is customary with him. The purpose in positing the doll-angel antithesis is to make the polarities of dividedness as clear as possible. More will be said of the Angel later; for the time being it is important to grasp his presence as the absolute antithesis to the subhuman, mechanized puppet. That is, the Angel plays the role of the superhuman being whose will is completely centered, not dispersed or peripheral, as in the marionette. Only the conjunction of angel and doll completes the circle of nature ("seasons") and thereby of movement and transformation (both meanings are present in "Wandeln"). Yet this conjunction guarantees "spectacle"—not life, not existence: it is artificial, but at least it is a mirror that shows, in somewhat exaggerated form, what life is.

The fifth Elegy, the last to be written, translates the marionette problem from the abstract private theater (of the mind?) of the previous Elegy to a concrete public theater (of the senses). This is the famous commentary on Picasso's "Saltimbanques" in which Rilke uses that remarkable painting as a springboard for his own reminiscences of the circus and elaborates them into a meditation upon a form of human existence. A *form* of human existence: one must insist on that distinction. The acrobats of the poem provide a partial answer to the problem of the actor-dancer proposed in the fourth Elegy. They exist by virtue of their own skill, but not by their own will. The poem opens

> Wer aber *sind* sie, sag mir, die Fahrenden, diese ein wenig
> Flüchtigern noch als wir selbst, die dringend von früh an
> wringt ein wem—wem zuliebe
> niemals zufriedener Wille? Sondern er wringt sie,
> biegt sie, schlingt sie und schwingt sie,
> wirft sie und fängt sie zurück; wie aus geölter
> glatterer Luft kommen sie nieder
> auf dem verzehrten, von ihrem ewigen
> Aufsprung dünneren Teppich, diesem verlorenen
> Teppich im Weltall. (ll. 1–10)

> But who *are* they, tell me, those migratory persons, who are slightly
> more fleeting still than we ourselves, whom urgently from early in the morning
> wrings a—for whose satisfaction?—
> never satisfied will? Yet it wrings them,
> bends them, slings them and swings them,
> casts them up and catches them again; as if out of an oiled
> more slippery air they come down
> on the frayed rug, by their perpetual
> impact worn thin, this forlorn
> rug in the universe.

This superb opening, with its assonances and swirling rhythms, shows perhaps more clearly than the meaning of the words themselves that the tumbling acrobats are in the grip of an exterior force. In this respect they illustrate a heightened form of man's existence. If they are not artists, at least they are *artistes*, technicians: they accept their destiny in the world and deploy their skill in the enactment of it. For this reason Rilke describes them as "more fleeting than ourselves" and less fixed, constantly on the move ("die Fahrenden"). They exist where their carpet happens to be laid—anywhere in the wide world—and their human existence is bound to the same, only more threadbare from continuous effort, fabric as our own. But this existence is a kind of unconscious boredom ("Unlust"), a result of living in a world of appearances—the result of their effort is a false fruit ("Scheinfrucht"), a sham. Their salvation, trademark or profession, is the smile at the foot of the human pyramid, the *subrisio saltatoris*, as Rilke indicates.

An equilibrium achieved, as the saying goes, in defiance of the laws of nature, is still a collaboration with nature and a submission to it. The acrobat's skill and endurance is, in the final reckoning, a mastery of the mechanics of gravitation and therefore not really free. It is an accomplishment, a kind of levitation, that brings the tumblers close to genuine existence and entitles them to the smile, but it is not enough in itself. Where is the place of inwardness, the poet muses, where the skill of the acrobats is of no account, where a more difficult equilibrium has to be achieved—in brief, how does one attain the pyramid of inwardness?

> Und plötzlich in diesem mühsamen Nirgends, plötzlich
> die unsägliche Stelle, wo sich das reine Zuwenig
> unbegreiflich verwandelt—umspringt
> in jenes leere Zuviel.
> Wo die vielstellige Rechnung
> zahlenlos aufgeht. (ll. 83–86)

> And suddenly in this effortful Nowhere, suddenly
> that unsayable spot where the pure too-little
> incomprehensibly transforms itself—whirls around
> into that empty too-much.
> Where the multidigit calculation
> is resolved into zero.

This place ("ich trag ihn im Herzen"—I bear it in my heart) is the mysterious spot where, suddenly, the "pure too-little" capsizes "into that empty too-much," where the minuses and pluses of existence cancel each other out (the metaphor of an equation would have carried this idea more forcefully than that of a sum). The too-little of the marionette in the fourth Elegy and the too-much of the Angel have thus been incarnated in the acrobats, who are at the same time heavy and fleeting, self-directed and "other-directed"—who offer us an exteriorized image of human existence. This exteriority, if it can be transposed by means of a reversal-conversion into interiority (where external skill is fruitless), will vouchsafe genuine being.

In the last section of the poem the Angel is invoked and with him the lovers, who also attempt to do the impossible, but inwardly:

> Engel: as wäre ein Platz, den wir nicht wissen, und dorten,
> auf unsäglichem Teppich, zeigten die Liebenden, die's hier
> bis zum Können nie bringen, ihre kühnen
> hohen Figuren des Herzschwungs,
> ihre Türme aus Lust, ihre
> längst, wo Boden nie war, nur aneinander
> lehnenden Leitern, bebend—und *könntens*,
> vor den Zuschauern rings, unzähligen lautlosen Toten:
> Würfen die dann ihre letzten, immer ersparten,
> immer verborgenen, die wir nicht kennen, ewig
> gültigen Münzen des Glücks vor das endlich
> wahrhaft lächelnde Paar auf gestilltem
> Teppich? (ll. 96–108)

> Angel: there might exist a place, unknown to us, where
> upon an unsayable rug, lovers might show us, since here on earth
> they never reach the point of achievement, their bold
> high figures of the heart's soaring,
> their pyramids of sheer delight, their
> ladders that have so long been leaning against each other
> where there was never any ground [to support them], swaying—and
>   if they *could* achieve it,
> before the circle of spectators, the numberless silent dead:
> Would *they* then throw their last, ever saved,
> ever hidden, unfamiliar to us, ever
> valid coins of bliss in front of the at last
> truly smiling couple on the satisfied [still]
> rug?

This is the mythical transformation that takes place beyond life, in which the lovers show us how, in which they accomplish the deed and achieve the bliss that would unify the divided realms of the finite and the infinite. In the poem this transformation is vividly suggested by the "Türme aus Lust" which cancels out the earlier attitude of "Unlust"; the *subrisio saltatoris* becomes the "truly smiling couple"; the carpet, originally lost in the cosmos, is now described as "unsayable" and finally as "satisfied."

The fullest development of the theme of dividedness and its counter-theme of the about-turn occurs in the eighth Elegy, where Rilke contrasts the "natural" existence of the "creature" with the denatured (or disnatured) existence of the human being.

> Mit allen Augen sieht die Kreatur
> das Offene. Nur unsre Augen sind
> wie umgekehrt und ganz um sie gestellt
> als Fallen, rings um ihren freien Ausgang. (ll. 1–4)

> With all its eyes the creature sees
> Openness. Only our eyes are
> as if reversed and placed all around it
> like traps, around its free passage.

The creature (the allusion seems to be to a fly, or some other insect, with "many" eyes) sees only that which is open, a kind of free cosmic space in which it can, presumably, move unhampered. By contrast, human eyes are as if turned backward (away from "the open") and surround the natural creature like a trap. The difference is not a natural one: we are, in a sense, as creaturely as the creature, but somewhere along our path of development we were "turned around." We deprive the child—and here Rilke implies that our social habits are to blame—of the contact with the open:

> Was draussen *ist*, wir wissens aus des Tiers
> Antlitz allein; denn schon das frühe Kind
> wenden wir um und zwingens, dass es rückwärts
> Gestaltung sehe, nicht das Offene, das
> im Tiergesicht so tief ist. Frei von Tod.
> *Ihn* sehen wir allein; das freie Tier
> hat seinen Untergang stets hinter sich
> und vor sich Gott, und wenn es geht, so gehts
> in Ewigkeit, so wie die Brunnen gehen. (ll. 5–13)

Whatever *is* outside we know from the animal's
face alone; even when the child is young
we turn it around and force it to look backward at
configuration, not at the Openness which
is so deep in the animal's face. Free of death.
It [death] we see only; the free animal
has its demise always behind itself
and God in front, and when it goes, it goes
in eternity, as fountains go.

A diagram shows the difference between the creature's orientation and man's:

CREATURE: Death→ Animal→ "Open" $\left\{ \begin{array}{l} \text{(God)} \\ \text{(Pure Space)} \end{array} \right.$

HUMAN BEING: Death←Man→ World / Open

The creature, which has not lost its nature, its essence, always has death *behind* it: it has no consciousness of death, yet death is always nearby. Consequently the animal's face is always turned toward the open (and we human beings can see it mirrored there), that is, toward God. This is one of the few references in the Elegies to God and in the context of the Elegies must not be given a narrow Christian interpretation (if such a thing is possible). Here God is equated with "open," "free," and "infinite"—something to *go* toward. The entire passage is an ingenious variation on composites of "gehen" and "Gang": the eighth Elegy describes what is "gone" and where we must "go" to retrieve it. The human being, as a result of this forcible reversal that occurred in his childhood, is death-conscious and alienated from the infinite. What has replaced the open in this turning away from it is simply "the world."

Wir haben nie, nicht einen einzigen Tag,
den reinen Raum vor uns, in den die Blumen
unendlich aufgehn. Immer ist es Welt
und niemals Nirgends ohne Nicht:
Das Reine, Unüberwachte, das man atmet und
unendlich weiss und nicht begehrt . . .
Der Schöpfung immer zugewendet, sehn
wir nur auf ihr die Spiegelung des Frein,
von uns verdunkelt. Oder dass ein Tier,
ein stummes, aufschaut, ruhig durch uns durch.

Dieses heisst Schicksal: gegenüber sein
und nichts als das und immer gegenüber. (ll. 14–19, 29–34)

We have never, not for a single day,
pure space before us, into which flowers
open infinitely. Always we have the world
and never Nowhere without No:
that which is pure, unguarded, that which we breathe and
know infinitely and yet do not crave for . . .
Always turned toward the creation, we see
on its surface but the reflection of what is free,
but obscured by us. Except that an animal,
mute, may look up and quickly look through us.
This is what destiny means: to be opposite
and nothing but that and always opposite.

This passage discloses more clearly the contrasting concepts in the poem. The "pure space" that the animal faces is infinite, or, in Rilke's strangely compelling formulation, "never Nowhere without No"—internal space that is not contradictory (to the idea of space). Its antithesis is the finite space of the "world." Joseph Steiner's comment is helpful: "Pure space cannot be grasped from the point of view of the World, because in this way it would be self-explanatory. The Nowhere without No, however, exists as an inner place; thus it is a Nowhere, because it is not merely exempt from time, but also situated outside of the category of space."[10] The cleavage is not absolute: we still breathe pure space (this idea will be elaborated in discussing the *Sonnets to Orpheus*); we have never lost the knowledge of it, though we have stopped desiring it. And finally, the image of openness is mirrored by the created world but blurred and obscured by our presence.

Modifying the diagram slightly

Death
←Man→ Creation
"Open"

it is clear that the two extremes of "death" and "open" are similar, if not identical. Hence the human experience of death, if properly lived and understood, prepares one again for "the open."

> Denn nah am Tod sieht man den Tod nicht mehr
> und starrt *hinaus*, vielleicht mit grossem Tierblick. (ll. 22–23)
>
> For when one is near death one no longer sees death
> And stares *outward*, perhaps with a great animal stare.

This brings Rilke to his grim definition of destiny: being divided from something, being vis-à-vis and no more. The conclusion is that unless we recover this lost nature of ours we will always remain vis-à-vis, spectators.

> Und wir: Zuschauer, immer, überall,
> dem allen zugewandt und nie hinaus!
> Uns überfüllts. Wir ordnens wieder und zerfallen selbst. (ll. 66–69)
>
> And we: spectators, always, everywhere,
> turned toward all this and yet never outward!
> It saturates us. We arrange it. It disintegrates.
> We rearrange it and disintegrate ourselves.

These lines are succinct, and harsh in their succinctness. Any attempt at creating order in terms of this false, perverted existence is doomed to failure and finally wrecks our existence altogether. The problem is how to metamorphose being face to face with the world into being in the world.

The human being is divided in a divided world. Rilke's first concern in the Elegies is to demonstrate this (in the fourth, fifth, and eighth Elegies), then to develop the attitude that will make a radical reversal possible and significant. In his absolute demand for conversion he speaks like a religious reformer; but in actuality the conversion he is after is aesthetic and ontological, rather than religious. At best one might say that the poet retains some elements of saintliness; but strictly speaking, this is only an analogy—the saint is primarily a doer, not a sayer. With Rilke the obverse is true. The "we" of the *Duino Elegies* is in part misleading: it is a sort of tentative "we," reflecting Rilke's own deep and lonely experience. It touches and persuades us in many points, but it remains, in the long run, an intensely private experience capped by a unique solution (or attempted solution) very much like Proust's. The visionary of transformation and the celebrant of this new life remains the poet, specifically the poet Rilke: the transformation of the world is primarily aesthetic and metaphysical (contemplative), rather than religious or moral (active). In this respect, it is faithful to the Orphic tradition. But before Orpheus' impact can be felt, the presence of

Rilke

Rilke's Angel, who ushers in the first two Elegies, serves as a standard of reference in the fourth and fifth, and becomes the impetus for transformation in the seventh and ninth, must be understood.

In the first Elegy the Angel is characterized as terrifying: his being is more powerful than ours.

> Wer, wenn ich schriee, hörte mich denn aus der Engel
> Ordnungen? und gesetzt selbst, es nähme
> einer mich plötzlich ans Herz: ich verginge von seinem
> stärkeren Dasein. Denn das Schöne ist nichts
> als des Schrecklichen Anfang, den wir noch gerade ertragen,
> und wir bewundern es so, weil es gelassen verschmäht,
> uns zu zerstören. Ein jeder Engel ist schrecklich. (ll. 1–7)

> Who, if I were to shout, would hear me from among the angelic
> orders? and even assuming one of them
> suddenly pressed me to his heart: I would dissolve from his
> stronger existence. For the beautiful is nothing more
> than the beginning of the dreadful, something we can just barely endure,
> and we admire it so much because it cooly deigns
> not to destroy us. Every angel is dreadful.

The second Elegy reiterates and develops the last statement and states the question "Wer seid ihr?" (Who are you?) which is answered not so much by a definition as by a series of equivalent images.

> Frühe Geglückte, ihr Verwöhnten der Schöpfung,
> Höhenzüge, morgenrötliche Grate
> aller Erschaffung—Pollen der blühenden Gottheit,
> Gelenke des Lichtes, Gänge, Treppen, Throne,
> Räume aus Wesen, Schilde aus Wonne, Tumulte
> stürmisch entzückten Gefühls und plötzlich, einzeln,
> Spiegel: die die entströmte eigne Schönheit
> wiederschöpfen zurück in das eigene Antlitz. (ll. 10–17)

> Early successes, spoiled darlings of Creation,
> mountain ranges, dawn-flecked ridges
> of all that has been created—pollen of the blossoming divinity,
> hinges of light, corridors, stairways, thrones,
> spaces made of being, shields made of joy, tumults
> of tempestuously ecstatic feelings and suddenly, one by one,

mirrors: that draw their own escaped beauty
back into their own countenance.

The profusion of images can be simplified into four major groupings: the angels are the summit, or favorite, of created beings—the very substance and seed of divinity. They are in themselves "world-inner-space," they are intense feelings, and, singly, they achieve totally the gesture that Narcissus could not complete. Because of their transcendency, their other, more powerful existence, they are in a secret way continuous with us: in the sense that they are infinite and eternal they are profoundly in touch with us wherever we have gone beyond the confines of time and space, that is, in our inwardness. But the contact is not direct; we cannot woo the angel (seventh Elegy) nor can we use him (first Elegy):

> Ach, wen vermögen
> wir denn zu brauchen? Engel nicht, Menschen nicht,
> und die findigen Tiere merken es schon,
> dass wir nicht sehr verlässlich zu Haus sind
> in der gedeuteten Welt. (ll. 9–13)

> Alas, whom are we capable
> of making use of? Not angels, not men,
> and the resourceful animals sense easily
> that we are not very reliably at home
> in the interpreted world.

The interpreted world is the numbered, labeled world without mystery, without inwardness, without infinity. Animals, the eighth Elegy stated, are still at home in nature; the Angel is the summit of the creation and consubstantial with it. Men are "alienated" from this real world and therefore not "usable." Here the difficulty of Rilke's use of the first person plural is evident: he is speaking of the situation of all men, but in asking "whom are we capable of using" he is already editorializing the "we" to indicate himself as poet, or someone like himself in whom the mandate—the *Auftrag*—of transformation is already operative. The interpreted world is the world of nothing but contour, the contour of knowledge and explication; the transformed world registers the contour of feeling, of inwardness.

The seventh Elegy addresses the Angel but rejects the tone of solicitation in favor of the poet's decision to go toward him: the pilgrimage of the *Stundenbuch* is now an *anábasis* toward "the open."

Glaub *nicht*, dass ich werbe.
Engel, und würb ich dich auch! Du kommst nicht. Denn mein
Anruf ist immer voll Hinweg; wider so starke
Strömung kannst du nicht schreiten. Wie ein gestreckter
Arm ist mein Rufen. Und seine zum Greifen
oben offene Hand bleibt vor dir
offen, wie Abwehr und Warnung,
Unfasslicher, weitauf. (ll. 86–93)

Do *not* think that I am courting.
Angel, and even if I did court you! You do not come. My
appeal is always full of going-there; against so strong
a current you cannot advance. Like an outstretched
arm is my appeal. And, as if for the purpose of grasping,
its hand held upward and open remains
open before you, as defense and warning,
o, you ungraspable being, wide open.

Clearly, the Angel's immobility and inaccessibility is the occasion and impulsion of human effort: the Angel is what we must move toward. The way from man to Angel is through the "open." Once the journey is begun, a strong current sweeps man along, but never to grasp the Angel, the Ungraspable. But in the seventh Elegy the human being has acquired such purposefulness, such resolution, that, thenceforth, the entire human situation is affirmed and lamentation converted into jubilation:

O staune, Engel, denn *wir* sinds,
Wir, o du Grosser, erzähls, dass wir solches vermochten, mein Atem
reicht für die Rühmung nicht aus. (ll. 75–77)

O be astonished, Angel, that *we* are the ones,
We, o you grand one; make it known that we are capable of such things,
    my own breath
Is not sufficient for such praise.

In the ninth Elegy the theme of affirmation of existence and affirmation of poetry reaches its climax. It is difficult to resist quoting the Elegy in its entirety, because all the yea-saying consolidates here and is raised to its highest point of intensity. The tenth Elegy, a magnificent coda, reiterates the theme of celebration despite and through lamentation, fusing the earlier Elegies with the later ones and projecting the allegory of the City of Lament; but for our purposes a few key passages (most of which are well known) of the ninth will suffice.

> Aber weil Hiersein viel ist, und weil uns scheinbar
> alles das Hiesige braucht, dieses Schwindende, das
> seltsam uns angeht. Uns, die Schwindendsten. *Einmal*
> jedes, nur *einmal*. *Einmal* und nichtmehr. Und wir auch
> *einmal*. Nie wieder. Aber dieses
> *einmal* gewesen zu sein, wenn auch nur *einmal*:
> *irdisch* gewesen zu sein, scheint nicht widerrufbar. (ll. 11–17)

> But because being here is a great deal, because apparently
> all that is down here needs us, all that is fleeting, which
> so strangely concerns us. Us, the most fleeting of all. *One* time
> everything, only *one* time. *One* time and no more. And we, too,
> *one* time. Never again. But this fact
> of having been *one* time, even if just *one* time:
> to have been *earthly*, that seems irrevocable.

This passage is constructed entirely around the note of absolute, irrevocable certainty. "Hiersein ist herrlich"—being here (on this earth) is splendid—the seventh Elegy asserted categorically. Even though we are evanescent (compare the initial description of the acrobats in the fifth Elegy), the earth *needs* us (the theme of "using" stated initially in the first Elegy), so that we can be truly earthly, just once at least.

> Sind wir vielleicht *hier*, um zu sagen: Haus,
> Brücke, Brunnen, Tor, Krug, Obstbaum, Fenster—
> höchstens: Säule, Turm . . . aber zu *sagen*, verstehs,
> oh zu sagen *so*, wie selber die Dinge niemals
> innig meinten zu sein. (ll. 32–36)

> Are we perhaps *here* in order to say: house,
> bridge, fountain, gate, pitcher, fruit tree, window—
> at the most: column, tower . . . but to *say* (mark me well)
> oh to say *so* as things themselves never
> intimately thought to be.

Our hereness consists, most deeply, in giving voice—our voice—to things: in saying them more intensely than their own mute language can utter. We are here to praise the common, the familiar, objects around us—not because they are the most universal, but because they are the most intimate.

> Hier ist des *Säglichen* Zeit, hier seine Heimat.
> Sprich und bekenn.
>
> . . .
>
> Preise den Engel die Welt, nicht die unsägliche, ihm
> kannst du nicht grosstun mit herrlich Erfühltem; im Weltall,
> wo er fühlender fühlt, bist du ein Neuling. Drum zeig
> ihm das Einfache, das, von Geschlecht zu Geschlechtern gestaltet,
> als ein Unsriges lebt neben der Hand und im Blick.
> Sag ihm die Dinge. (ll. 43–44, 53–58)
>
> Here is the time of the *sayable*, here its home.
> Speak and confess.
>
> . . .
>
> Praise the world to the Angel, not the unsayable world, him
> you cannot impress with magnificent feelings; in the universe,
> where he feels more feelingly, you are a neophyte. Therefore show
> him simple things which, shaped from one generation to the next,
> live on as being our own, beside our hands and in our eyes.
> Tell him the *things*.

This is our task with respect to the Angel: to praise the world of the sayable, to consecrate the familiar and the intimate. And out of this process of interiorization, and the power of "saying" that restores and reincarnates the outer world of things in an epiphanic metamorphosis, Rilke distills his most daring alchemy and endows it with his most radical affirmation. At the same time he demands of us the will to transmute:

> Erde, ist es nicht dies, was du willst: *unsichtbar*
> in uns erstehn?—Ist es dein Traum nicht,
> einmal unsichtbar zu sein?—Erde! unsichtbar!
> Was, wenn Verwandlung nicht, ist dein drängender Auftrag?
> Erde, du liebe, ich will. (ll. 68–72)
>
> Earth, is not this what you want: *invisibly*
> to arise in us?—Is it not your dream
> to be invisible just once?—Earth! invisible!
> What is your urgent demand, if not transmutation?
> Earth, beloved earth, I want to.

Aside from the fact that the two cycles of Orpheus sonnets surround the completion of the *Duino Elegies*, the relation of their Angel to Orpheus must be clarified. The principal relevant document is Rilke's famous letter to Witold Hulewicz, his Polish translator, dated November 13, 1925. (Though Rilke is prone toward extravagant and pontifical statements in his correspondence, many of his letters are enlightening but must be used cautiously; frequently they document the apprenticeship of his sensibility and the progress of his opinions.)

In den Elegien wird . . . das Leben wieder möglich, ja es erfährt hier diejenige end-gültige *Bejahung*, zu der es der junge Malte, obwohl auf dem richtigen schweren Wege "des longues études," es noch nicht führen konnte. *Lebens- und Todesbejahung erweist sich als Eines in den "Elegien."* Das eine zuzugeben ohne das andere, sei, so wird hier erfahren und gefeiert, eine schliesslich alles Unendliche ausschliessende Einschränkung. Der Tod ist die uns abgekehrte, von uns unbeschienene *Seite des Lebens*: wir müssen versuchen, das grösseste Bewusstsein unseres Daseins zu leisten, das in *beiden unabgegrenzten Bereichen* zu Hause ist, *aus beiden unerschöpflich genährt* . . . Die wahre Lebensgestalt reicht durch *beide* Gebiete, das Blut des grössesten Kreislaufs treibt durch beide: *es gibt weder ein Diesseits noch Jenseits, sondern die grosse Einheit,* in der die uns übertreffenden Wesen, die "Engel," zu Hause sind.[11]

In the Elegies life becomes possible once more, as a matter of fact it is given precisely that ultimate *affirmation* that young Malte could not attain, though he had embarked upon the right and difficult way of protracted study. *The affirmation of life and death proves to be one and the same thing in the "Elegies."* To admit the one without the other is, and that is the lesson and the celebration of the Elegies, shown ultimately to be a limitation that excludes all that is infinite. Death is that *side of life* which is turned away from us and not illuminated by us: we must make the effort to muster the greatest consciousness of our being which is at home in *both of these undifferentiated domains* and *nourished inexhaustibly by both* . . . Life's true form extends through *both* domains, the blood of the greatest circulation courses through both: *there is neither a Here nor a Beyond, but only the great Unity,* in which those beings superior to us, the "Angels," dwell.

The Angel is terrifying, inaccessible, frigid—as observed in the above discussions of the Elegies—because he represents, he *is*, the realm of undivided unity. The Orpheus sonnets, Rilke continues, are filled "with the same essence"; they hadn't been in his original plan, but they "imposed themselves tempestuously." The impetus for both sequences comes from the human alienation from time. The task of transforming the visible into the invisible, as proclaimed in the ninth Elegy, is therefore a direct result of the modern anguish of temporal existence

deprived of the reference point of transcendence; it is therefore the radical assertion of an immanence that, like Nietzsche's Eternal Recurrence, affirms temporal, terrestrial experience in *all* its aspects.

Unsere Aufgabe ist es, diese vorläufige, hinfällige Erde uns so tief, so leidend und
leidenschaftlich einzuprägen, dass ihr Wesen in uns "unsichtbar" wieder aufersteht.
*Wir sind die Bienen des Unsichtbaren. Nous butinons éperdument le miel du visible, pour
l'accumuler dans la grande ruche d'or de l'Invisible* . . . Die Erde hat keine andere Ausflucht,
als unsichtbar zu werden: *in* uns, die wir mit einem Teile unseres Wesens am Unsichtbaren beteiligt sind . . . Die *Elegien* stellen diese Norm des Daseins auf: sie versichern, sie
feiern dieses Bewusstsein . . . Der Engel der *Elegien* ist dasjenige Geschöpf, in dem die
Verwandlung des Sichtbaren in Unsichtbares, die wir leisten, schon vollzogen erscheint
. . . Der Engel der Elegien ist dasjenige Wesen, das dafür einsteht, im Unsichtbaren
einen höheren Rang der Realität zu erkennen . . . *Wir sind,* noch einmal sei's betont, *im
Sinne der Elegien, sind wir diese Verwandler der Erde, unser ganzes Dasein, die Flüge und
Stürze unserer Liebe, alles befähigt uns zu dieser Aufgabe* (neben der keine andere, wesent-
lich, besteht). (Die Sonette zeigen Einzelheiten aus dieser Tätigkeit . . .) Elegien und
Sonette unterstützen einander beständig—und ich sehe eine unendliche Gnade darin,
dass ich, mit dem gleichen Atem, diese beiden Segel füllen dürfte: das kleine rostfarbene
Segel der Sonette und der Elegien riesiges weisses Segel-Tuch.[12]

It is our task to imprint this transitory and perishable earth so deeply, sufferingly, and
passionately in ourselves that its being will "invisibly" become resurrected within us.
*We are the bees of the Invisible. We frantically gather in the honey of the visible in order to
store it up in the great golden hive of the invisible* . . . The earth has no recourse but to become invisible: *in* us, since a part of our being participates in the invisible . . . The
Elegies set up this norm of being: they guarantee, they celebrate this consciousness . . .
The Angel of the Elegies is that being which enables us to recognize a higher level of
reality in the invisible . . . *We are,* let me emphasize it once more, *in the sense of the
Elegies, we are those transformers of the earth our entire existence, the rise and fall of our love,
everything equips us for that task* (beside which there is, essentially, no other). (The Sonnets
give details of that activity . . .) The Elegies and the Sonnets constantly supplement each
other—and I see an infinite grace in the fact that I was permitted to fill both these sails
with the same breath: the little rust-colored sail of the Sonnets and the immense white
sail of the Elegies.

The Sonnets, then, supplement, rather than complement, the Elegies: they
are not two sides of the same coin, nor opposites that converge, but reinforce-
ments of certain aspects of the Elegies that are not fully elaborated in the larger
poems. The intersection between inter-related modes of poetic expression—la-

ment and praise—is implicit in the very arrangement of the Elegies, particularly in the last four, in which seven and nine are the jubilant outbursts, eight the lamentation, and ten the allegory of lament culminating in the affirmation, *malgré tout*, of existence.

> Und wir, die an *steigendes* Glück
> denken, empfänden die Rührung,
> die uns beinah bestürzt,
> wenn ein Glückliches *fällt*. (ll. 111–114)

> And we who think of bliss as *rising*
> would experience the emotion
> that almost strikes us down
> when something blissful [be]*falls* [us].

Constructed entirely upon the Orphic antinomy of ascent-descent, this is one of the most eloquent examples of the Rilkean *coincidentia oppositorum*. The eighth sonnet of the first Orpheus cycle expounds the distinction between jubilation and lamentation:

> Nur im Raum der Rühmung darf die Klage
> gehn, die Nymphe des geweinten Quells,
> wachend über unserm Niederschlage,
> dass er klar sei an demselben Fels,

> der die Tore trägt und die Altäre—
> Sieh, um ihre stillen Schultern früht
> das Gefühl, dass sie die jüngste wäre
> unter den Geschwistern im Gemüt.

> Jubel *weiss*, und Sehnsucht ist geständig—
> nur die Klage lernt noch; mädchenhändig
> zählt sie nächtelang das alte Schlimme.

> Aber plötzlich, schräg und ungeübt,
> hält sie doch ein Sternbild unsrer Stimme
> in den Himmel, den ihr Hauch nicht trübt.

> Only in the space of Praise may Lamentation
> move, that nymph of the source made by tears,

standing guard over our precipitation,
so that it may be clear at the same rock,

which holds the portals and the altars—
See, about her still shoulders dawns
the feeling that she might be the youngest
of the sisters of sentiment.

Jubilation *knows*, and Longing is confessional—
only Lamentation is still learning; with maiden hands
she counts up old evils through the night.

But suddenly, awkward and unpracticed,
she yet holds a constellation of our voice
into a sky not dimmed by her breath.

This poem is consistent with the general mythical tendency of the Orpheus sonnets (and therefore different from the *Märchen* allegory of the tenth Elegy). Lament is represented as a young girl, a nymph of the source "made by tears," the youngest of three sisters. The eldest is evidently Praise, who already *knows*; Longing, the middle one, is "confessional"—she knows a number of things but not with full assurance or independence; Lament is still learning. But in her untutored way, says Rilke, she converts the voice of lamentation into a pure constellation, something that partakes of and enters into the supreme domain of Praise. Here again are Rilke's favorite themes of patient growth and transmutation.

But the finest transition from the threnody of the Elegies to the panegyric of the Sonnets is to be found at the end of the first Elegy, in the reference to the myth of Linos:

Ist die Sage umsonst, dass einst in der Klage um Linos
wagende erste Musik dürre Erstarrung durchdrang,
dass erst im erschrockenen Raum, dem ein beinah göttlicher Jüngling
plötzlich für immer enttrat, das Leere in jene
Schwingung geriet, die uns jetzt hinreisst und tröstet und hilft. (ll. 91–95)

Is it a vain legend which tells us that once, during the lament for Linos
audacious first-heard music penetrated dry numbness,
that first in startled space that was suddenly bereft

of a nearly divine youth forever, the emptiness fell into that
vibration, which now enraptures and consoles and helps us.

Although Rilke, in composing this Elegy in 1912, may not have been consciously aware of the mythological kinship between Linos and Orpheus (some
accounts call them both sons of Apollo, and in late antiquity both were regarded
as apocryphal authors), he certainly sensed the resemblance. Linos, a beautiful
youth, was loved by all; his untimely death brought a barren numbness to
everyone who had known him. The legend in which Hercules is responsible for
killing Linos with his own lyre is surely irrelevant in this instance—the point is
that a space emptied of a singing presence begins to vibrate again with threnodic
song, and this song represents an absence of song and its effect upon the hearer is
one of rapture and consolation.

Another way to formulate the relation of the Elegies to the Sonnets is with
reference to the Angel and to Orpheus. Rilke's Angel is that being in whom the
task of transformation has been accomplished: he is perfect and unified. The
human task, however, devolves upon Orpheus—or, perhaps more accurately,
on the Orphic poet, the poet-as-Orpheus. His task is to will the transformation
and to perform its accomplishment. Thus he stands between the ordinary
human being and the Angel, partaking, as humans do, of the double realm, but
having experienced the identity of the two realms and being thus at home in
both. He knows the unity of life and death, since he has been in the underworld;
he has experienced the identity of descent and ascent. Yet his deepest meaning is
to be found in his dismemberment by the Maenads and in the perpetuity of song
that issues from his lips even after the *sparagmós*: he is divided and yet he is one,
and so he guarantees the possibility of reassembling the shattered fragments.

The voluntaristic side of Rilke's Orpheus is important. The Angel is being,
Orpheus is the will to be. Erich Heller, in a memorable phrase, calls Rilke the
"St. Francis of the Will to Power" and draws an analogy between Rilke's
Orpheus and Nietzsche's Dionysus.[13] Reflecting on the loss of transcendence in
the modern, disinherited world, Heller says: "The imaginations of both
Nietzsche and Rilke have given birth to symbolic creatures moving with perfect
grace and ease in a sphere to which man can attain only in the utmost realization
of his spiritual powers. These creatures of immanence, transcending immanence
in the achievement of a yet profounder immanence, are Nietzsche's Superman
and Rilke's Angel . . . The Superman is for Nietzsche what Orpheus is for Rilke:
the transfigurer of unredeemable existence, with the 'mystery of its unending

repetition issuing from superhuman delight.' "[14] But the Angel and Orpheus serve different purposes. The correlation is, rather: Dionysus is to the Angel as the Superman-Zarathustra is to Orpheus. Both Nietzsche and Rilke perform the task that Dionysus and the Angel demand and whose validity they vouchsafe.

The realization and performance of this Orphic task came slowly to Rilke. The Orpheus myth appears only once in Rilke's work prior to 1922, in the poem "Orpheus. Eurydike. Hermes," of 1904, included in the *Neue Gedichte*. Probably occasioned by a bas-relief that Rilke saw in Naples, the poem depicts the return of Eurydice to the upper world: Orpheus leads the way, the god Hermes, as *psychopompos*, leads Eurydice by the hand. Even though this treatment is reminiscent of traditional versions of the return, Rilke is unique in focussing his attention on Eurydice and her suspension between life and death.

The atmosphere is nocturnal; Hades is described as the "wondrous mineshaft of souls." The first of the trio to be described is Orpheus, and he is characterized by impatience and the anxiety that prompts him to ascertain whether the other two are really following. Then there is Hermes, with his traditional attributes, and finally Eurydice, whose death had brought a "world of lamentation" into being. She is already absorbed in her new existence-in-death and has become unmindful of the world, and of Orpheus:

> Sie war in sich, wie Eine hoher Hoffnung,
> und dachte nicht des Mannes, der voranging,
> und nicht des Weges, der ins Leben aufstieg.
> Sie war in sich. Und ihr Gestorbensein
> erfüllte sie wie Fülle.
> Wie eine Frucht von Süssigkeit und Dunkel,
> so war sie voll von ihrem grossen Tode,
> der also neu war, dass sie nichts begriff.[15]

> She was self-contained, like one harboring high hopes,
> and gave no heed to the man who preceded,
> nor to the road leading up to life.
> She was self-contained. And having died
> filled her like fullness.
> As a fruit [is full] of sweetness and darkness,
> she was full of her great death,
> which was so new that she comprehended nothing.

The emphasis is on Eurydice's otherness, on the disproportion between her being and that of Orpheus: she has entered the other realm, whereas Orpheus is still, effectively, in this world. Consequently, she no longer belongs to Orpheus, but to herself and death:

> Sie war schon aufgelöst wie langes Haar
> und hingegeben wie gefallner Regen
> und ausgeteilt wie hundertfacher Vorrat.
>
> Sie war schon Wurzel.[16]

> She was already unloosed, like long hair
> and given out, like fallen rain
> and distributed, like hundredfold supply.
>
> She was already root.

The sequence of three verbs—aufgelöst, hingegeben, ausgeteilt—document a progressive metamorphosis of dissolution-distribution, return to a yielding passivity that ultimately becomes part of the earth, part of its strength, and breaks the agreement with the infernal powers. Eurydice remains completely unmindful of what has happened:

> Und als plötzlich jäh
> der Gott sie anhielt und mit Schmerz im Ausruf
> die Worte aprach: Er hat sich umgewendet—
> begriff sie nichts und sagte leise: *Wer?*

> And when suddenly, abruptly,
> the god stopped her and with grief in his voice
> spoke the words: He has turned around—
> she understood nothing and said softly: *Who?*

She allows Orpheus, whom she no longer recognizes, to return to the upper world, while she gently and patiently turns back to the dead.

This poem, similar to "Alkestis" (written at approximately the same time and dealing with the same theme), is part of Rilke's familiar mythology of maidens or women, prematurely dead, who find their highest fulfillment in nonfulfillment, in unrequited love and a kind of inviolate chastity. One of the less felicitous inventions of Rilke, the theme persists in his verse until the very end and has a significant role in the vision of the Elegies. The point worth noting in this particular instance is that, at this juncture of Rilke's development (1904), the discrepancy between the death experience of Eurydice and Orpheus' lack of knowledge is all-important and explains why Eurydice finally *had* to go back, almost regardless of whether Orpheus broke his pledge or not. The eighteen years that separate this Orpheus from the Orpheus of the Sonnets are crucial: whereas Eurydice remains the same, Orpheus had to learn precisely what Eurydice knew and more. He had to learn to encounter death, accept it, and transcend it by becoming the mediator between its realm and that of life, not by remaining rooted in death, but by drawing his very strength from this source so that it could be converted into the mediating power of song. This becomes apparent in the poem "Gegen-Strophen," begun in 1912 and completed on February 9, 1922, which Rilke originally intended as the fifth Elegy. Only five days later he removed it from the Elegies and replaced it with the new "Saltimbanque" Elegy, the present fifth. The "Gegen-Strophen" were undoubtedly intended to be the dramatic counterpart of the third Elegy, which dealt with the psychology of the male; even so, their antistrophic form would have been rather unusual in the context of the other Elegies (though Rilke probably did not remove the poem for merely asethetic reasons alone). The contrast is achieved by a series of stanzas celebrating the female, alternating with antithetical laments directed toward the male. Nevertheless, had this poem been retained as one of the Elegies, there would have been at least one overt connection between the Elegies and the Sonnets by way of the reference to Eurydice. This stanza is a reminiscence of "Orpheus. Eurydike. Hermes," enlarged and applied. All women are designated as "sisters of Eurydice," and their effect upon the martial, restless male is that of calm and protectiveness.

> Blumen des tieferen Erdreichs,
> von allen Wurzeln geliebte,
> ihr, der Eurydike Schwestern,
> immer voll heiliger Umkehr
> hinter dem steigenden Mann.

> Wir, von uns selber gekränkt,
> Kränkende gern und gern
> Wiedergekränkte aus Not.
> Wir, wie Waffen, dem Zorn
> neben den Schlaf gelegt.

Ihr, die ihr beinah Schutz seid, wo niemand
schützt. Wie ein schattiger Schlafbaum
ist der Gedanke an euch
für die Schwärme des Einsamen.[17]

Flowers of a deeper soil,
beloved of all roots,
you, the sisters of Eurydice,
always full of holy turning
behind the climbing man.

> We, self-insulted,
> glad to insult and glad
> in turn to be insulted out of need.
> We, like weapons, placed
> beside sleeping wrath.

You, who are almost protection, where no one
protects. Like a shady slumber-tree
is the thought of you
for the swarms [assailing] the solitary man.

By the end of January 1922, the Orpheus theme had asserted itself insistently and triumphantly. Rilke had seen a reproduction of Cima da Conegliano's *Orpheus* in a shop window and procured a copy, which he kept within view of his work table. The earliest poetic evidence of this entry of Orpheus into Muzot is the charming triptych of January 31 entitled "Kleiner Gedichtkreis mit der Vignette: in Laub ausschlagende Leyer" (Short poetic cycle with the vignette: lyre breaking into foliage).[18] The first begins with an expectant silence in a mythological setting (Narcissus, Artemis, Acis and Galatea, Polyphemus) and the expectancy of "hearing," the principal motif that would introduce the Orpheus Sonnets:

> Aber ein Mund, ein Mund—
> einer, der singt und spricht . . .

> But a mouth, a mouth—
> one that sings and speaks . . .

The second vignette is dominated by the shape of the lyre as it appeared in Cima da Conegliano's etching: its frame is compared to the horns of a gazelle, with the head missing—in other words, it is a reference to the decapitated Orpheus and his lyre:

> Gab ihr die Hörnergestalt,
> wie der Gazelle geraubt;
> trat dann allein aus dem Wald—
> wo ist das Haupt?

> Gave it the shape of horns,
> as if stolen from the gazelle;
> then stepped out of the forest alone—
> where is the head?

The third and most interesting deals with Orphic creation, with the metamorphosis of idea into act, design into object. The central figure is the traditional potter at his wheel, shaping a well-wrought urn the general form of which is reminiscent of the horns of the lyre:

> Töpfer, nur tröste, treib
> treib deiner Scheibe Lauf!
> Mir gehts in Hauchen auf,
> du formst den Leib.

> Wär ich wie Du! Ich spür
> wie ich da säss . . .
> *Was* ist sie? . . . Zeichnung für
> . . . ein . . . Gefäss?

> Diese? die Leyer?—So
> dreh mir den Trug;
> wenn auch aus Schleier, oh!
> wird's doch ein Krug.

> Potter, give solace, urge,
> urge in the spin of your wheel,
> for me it dissolves into air,
> you mold the shape [body].

> Would I were like you! I can feel
> myself sitting in your place . . .

What is it? . . . sketch for
. . . a . . . vessel?

This [sketch]? the lyre?—thus
turn the illusion for me;
even if it's [shaped] out of a haze, oh!
it will still turn out to be a pitcher.

This charming little poem, so rich in its inner harmonies, so delicate, so hesitant, is the final hushed note preceding the Orphic crescendo.

The *Sonnets to Orpheus* were written in two remarkably rapid bursts of creativity, the first cycle of twenty-six (with three exceptions) written down between February 2 and 5, the second cycle of twenty-nine between February 15 and 23, 1922. The fifty-five sonnets surround, extend, and deepen the *Duino Elegies*, which were revised and completed between February 5 and 15. In this month of February 1922, Rilke's mensis mirabilis, the creation of eight supplementary sonnets, a number of fragments, and a few scattered poems took place. It is best for our purposes to think of an Orphic ambience of sixty-three sonnets, fifty-five of which belong to the two cycles proper. Exclusion of the remaining eight resulted from a number of decisions on Rilke's part, the reasons for which are not altogether clear. Some of them are distinctly superior to the ones he chose to retain, others are not. In any case, they belong together.

There is no predetermined order within, nor calculated correspondence between the two individual cycles. There are some structural relationships, however. In the first cycle, sonnet 1 corresponds to sonnet 26 and 2 to 25. The latter two are specifically addressed to Wera Ouckama Knoop, the eighteen-year old daughter of a friend of Rilke's, a girl Rilke had known only slightly but admired for her skill as a dancer and, more apropos, for the simple fact that she was a young girl who could be included in his gallery of jeunes filles. Her sudden death from an unexplained disease, her mother's grief, and Rilke's poetic imagination combined to set off a chain reaction in him that gave all the uncoordinated Orphic material in his mind a new focus. It should be remembered that some of Rilke's finest poetic outbursts in earlier years had been occasioned by the death of friends and acquaintances, and the Orpheus sonnets are conceived as a requiem or *tombeau* for Wera. Similarly, in the second cycle sonnet 1 corresponds again to 29 and 2 (though less ostensibly) to 28, providing the "Wera" thread again. These two sets of sonnet-pairs bracket the more loosely grouped intervening sonnets, a number of which, in the first cycle, deal with the nature of the Orphic myth as Rilke understood it; others are concerned with problems arising out of the Orphic vision; others still are illustrations of this vision and therefore poems of celebration (of the earth, fruit, objects); and a small group is critical or polemical in orientation, setting the modern world and its machinery in sharp contrast with the Orphic world view. The same thing is true of the second cycle, with the emphasis somewhat altered. The very looseness, the seeming arbitrariness of the sonnet sequences has its charm, and the deeper meaning of this lack of tight cohesion lies in the fact that Rilke is inviting the reader to understand the Orphic vision and to participate in it. Because the vision is cosmic in its intent, he attempts to include as many of the essentials as possible.

It is the Orphic *vision* that matters here, not merely the myth of Orpheus. The figure of the Greek singer-god is used merely to consolidate Rilke's own myth, to give it archetypal foundation. Orpheus is mentioned only a few times, Eurydice only once, but the entire set is impregnated with the spirit of song so that the title *Sonnets to Orpheus* is absolutely correct. But there is an important distinction between the first cycle and the second that constitutes a kind of dramatic progression from the discovery of Orpheus to the call to transformation (which closes the series). Johanna von Freydorf, in her study of the Sonnets, characterizes this distinction as follows: "The first part of the Sonnets was included in the Orpheus legend properly speaking: the nature of the god and the nature of his singing stood at the center. Principal theme of Part I: What is singing? Principal theme of Part II: Our manner of singing. How does nature sing, and how do we sing? Strengths, inhibitions, possibilities and limits of our singing. Our nature against and with Orpheus. Disadvantages and advantages of our human consciousness by comparison with the other way of being."[19] The leitmotif of the first part is "listening"; the countermotif is Orpheus' singing. Before the dismembered world, and we with it, can be made whole again, we must once again learn to listen to the Orphic lyre. The sonnets of this cycle demonstrate and illustrate the lyre's powers. The second part is introduced by the leitmotif of "breathing"; the countermotif is again that of singing, but this time it is *our* (Orphic) singing and the metamorphosis that we must undergo to achieve it. The sonnets of this cycle demonstrate and illustrate the possibilities of Orphic regeneration. Hans-Egon Holthusen has described the second part with concision:

The second part differs from the first by its greater independence of the Orphic legend.

The singer, by virtue of Orphic wisdom, takes the measure of the dimension of felt existence. The situation of man, and his transformation are at stake. This part too contains a sonnet to Wera in the parallel next-to-last position, but this sonnet does not, this time, lead directly to Orpheus but to "a friend of Wera," to whom the word about transformation is spoken. This sequence too is bridged by a great arch joining the first and last sonnets by means of the theme of breathing, which signifies the interchange of man and space: the first sonnet designates our situation as a rhythmic event, the final sonnet issues the command of transformation, the will to rhythm.[20]

The first cycle. The first sonnet is what Holthusen calls an *Offenbarungssonett*: Orpheus is revealed, and the power of his song. The first two lines are as magnificent as they are daring:

> Da stieg ein Baum. O reine Übersteigung!
> O Orpheus singt! O hoher Baum im Ohr!

> There rose a tree. O pure surpassing!
> O Orpheus sings! O tall tree in the ear!

Three matrix images are stated here: the ascending tree, the tree that is apprehended by the hearing, the motif of "climbing beyond"—rising ("da stieg") and rising beyond ("Übersteigung"). The power of Orphic song is manifested in the ear of man, which can be attuned to the energy, the power of transformation in nature. The precondition for this perception is silence:

> Und alles schwieg. Doch selbst in der Verschweigung
> ging neuer Anfang, Wink und Wandlung vor.

> And all was silent. And yet in the silence
> new beginning, sign, and transformation were taking place.

The acoustical parallels stieg-schwieg, Übersteigung-Verschweigung are intentional and functional. For the Orphic miracle to be apprehensible there must first be an Orphic silence, a receptivity. It is this hush in nature that ushers in the new era. Similarly the alliteration Wink-Wandlung is functional and progressive: first the beckoning, then the motion—or, since the meanings are somewhat flexible, first the sign, then the transformation. Now Rilke turns from the acoustical to the pictorial:

> Tiere aus Stille drangen aus dem klaren
> gelösten Wald von Lager und Genist;
> und da ergab sich, dass sie nicht aus List
> und nicht aus Angst in sich so leise waren,
>
> sondern aus Hören. Brüllen, Schrei, Geröhr
> schien klein in ihren Herzen.

> Animals, all silent, flocked out of the clear
> forest, having left their lairs and nests;
> and it happened that neither from ruse
> nor from fear they were so silent within,
>
> but from hearing. All howling, screeching, roaring
> seemed petty in their hearts.

The rest of the sonnet is somewhat more difficult for the interpreter, because the demonstratives and pronouns are not completely clear in their grammatical reference.

> Und wo eben
> kaum eine Hütte war, dies zu empfangen,
> ein Unterschlupf aus dunkelstem Verlangen
> mit einem Zugang, dessen Pfosten beben—
> da schufst du ihnen Tempel im Gehör.

> And where
> there was barely a [human] hut to receive all this,
> some shelter of darkest desire
> with an entrance whose posts quake—
> there you created for them [us] temples in the ear.

The problems follow. There is no clear antecedent for "dies," but the context establishes that the reference is to "all this" (silence and the revelation of the Orphic song); "du" has no grammatical antecedent, since Orpheus is referred to in the third person, but clearly the reference is to him; "ihnen" seems to refer to the animals, but I think this would be a misinterpretation. The "Hütte" is a human habitation and stands in contrast to "Lager und Genist"; consequently, Rilke proceeds from the "harkening" of the animals, a natural response to the Orphic voice, to the potential receptivity of human beings, heightening the significance of the Orphic song by assigning to it a sacred place, a sanctuary in the hearing.

This metaphor of "listening" dominates the entire first cycle and is appropriately affirmed in the last sonnet (26), which can be regarded as mythologically "prior" to the first. These two sonnets establish the pillars, the arch, and the passageway within which the Orphic voice reverberates. In the final sonnet Orpheus' dismemberment is described as the precondition to the Orphic survival-resurrection, with which the first sonnet had opened (recall the imagery of ascension noted above):

> Du aber, Göttlicher, du, bis zuletzt noch Ertöner,
> da ihn der Schwarm der verschmähten Mänaden befiel,
> hast ihr Geschrei übertönt mit Ordnung, du Schöner,
> aus den Zerstörenden stieg dein erbauendes Spiel.

> But you, o divine one, singing out till the very end,
> When the swarm of scorned Maenads fell on him,
> You outsang their shouts with order, o fair one,
> out of those destroyers arose your edifying music.

The imagery of line 4 echoes the beginning of the opening sonnet, now serving as a conjunction of opposites: out of the destroying Maenads arose Orpheus' constructive, edifying activity, described as "play" (playing the lyre), rather than "work"; moreover, it is the ordered play-activity of art. On this subject, Herbert Marcuse's observations are immediately relevant: "Orpheus and Narcissus (like Dionysus to whom they are akin: the antagonist of the god who sanctions the logic of domination, the realm of reason) . . . have not become the culture-heroes of the Western world: theirs is the image of joy and fulfillment; the voice which does not command but sings; the gesture which offers and receives; the deed which is peace and ends the labor of conquest; the liberation from the time which unites man with god, man with nature."[21] The final tercet is an apostrophe to the dying god and a mandate to man: Orpheus has been dismembered and nature fragmented, and it has become the task of mankind to assemble the *disjecta membra* and restore the lost unity:

> O du verlorener Gott! Du unendliche Spur!
> Nur weil dich reissend zuletzt die Feindschaft verteilte,
> sind wir die Hörenden jetzt und ein Mund der Natur.

Rilke

O you lost god! Infinite trace!
Only because at last enmity tore you to pieces and scattered you,
We are now [entrusted with] hearing, [we are now] nature's mouthpiece.

The arch within the greater span of the liminal sonnets, namely sonnets 2 and 25, inscribe the death theme (Wera) into the first cycle.

Und fast ein Mädchen wars und ging hervor
aus diesem einigen Glück von Sang und Leier
und glänzte klar durch ihre Frühlingsschleier
und machte sich ein Bett in meinem Ohr.

Und schlief in mir. Und alles war ihr Schlaf.
Die Bäume, die ich je bewundert, diese
fühlbare Ferne, die gefühlte Wiese
und jedes Staunen, das mich selbst betraf.

Sie schlief die Welt. Singender Gott, wie hast
du sie vollendet, dass sie nicht begehrte,
erst wach zu sein? Sieh, sie erstand und schlief.

Wo ist ihr Tod? O, wirst du dies Motiv
erfinden noch, eh sich dein Lied verzehrte?—
Wo sinkt sie hin aus mir? . . . Ein Mädchen fast . . .

And she was a girl almost and stepped forward
out of this unanimous bliss of song and lyre
and shone brightly through her spring veil
and made herself a bed in my ear.

And slept in me. And everything was her sleep.
Those trees I had ever cherished, that
distance open to feeling, that meadow already felt,
and each astonishment that ever struck me.

She slept the universe. Singing god, how
did you complete her, so that she did not desire
first to be awake? Look, she arose and slept.

Where is her death? O, will you still invent
this motif, before your song might consume itself?—
Whither will she sink, after me? . . . A girl almost . . .

The description of the "sleeping" Wera leads to a series of interrogations; the
neutral, predominantly third-person arrangement of the first sonnet gives way
to the first person here. The inquiry is really into the Orphic potential of the
poet: how to convert feeling into song. The poet knew how to listen to this
message, which transfigured all of his experience so that it became all feeling and
wonderment. Thus the world became "inward" in her, and reposeful, as in
sleep, and death had no real dominion over her. The analogy with the rapt and
detached Eurydice of "Orpheus. Eurydike. Hermes" is evident here, but it
would be wrong to identify Wera with Eurydice. Rilke, as the Orphic poet, is
not trying to redeem Eurydice from the dead; his mandate is to know what
Eurydice knows, to understand it, and to transpose it into song. And that is, in
effect, the subject of the Wera sonnet.

The third sonnet prolongs the interrogation and offers the first approximate
and tentative answers.

Ein Gott vermags. Wie aber, sag mir, soll
ein Mann ihm folgen durch die schmale Leier?
Sein Sinn ist Zwiespalt. An der Kreuzung zweier
Herzwege steht kein Tempel für Apoll.

A god can do it. But how, tell me, is
a man to follow him through the narrow lyre?
His [man's] meaning [characteristic] is discord. At the crossing of two
heartways there stands no temple for Apollo.

The poet's familiar tone toward the god persists in this sonnet. "A god can do it"
—burst into song—but what can man do, divided as he is? This inner division is
beautifully dramatized as the crossing of two paths of heart, and the image of the
temple of Apollo not only recalls the image of the temple of Orpheus in sonnet
1, but also serves to invoke the collaboration of the god of beauty and establish
his place within the Orphic-Dionysian framework of Rilke's thought. The
mediation is prolonged into the second quatrain and reformulated as a question
of being, not merely singing: the Orphic power is not merely dependent on a
new way of creation, but it presupposes a new way of being.

Gesang, wie du ihn lehrst, ist nicht Begehr,
nicht Werbung um ein endlich noch Erreichtes;
Gesang ist Dasein. Für den Gott ein Leichtes.
Wann aber *sind* wir? Une wann wendet er

an unser Sein die Erde und die Sterne?

Song, as you teach it, is not desire
not courtship for something finally attained;
Song is being-here. An easy matter for the god.
But when *are* we? And when does he turn

the earth and the stars toward our being?

This portion of the sonnet is a miniature companion-piece to the seventh Elegy, in which solicitation of the Angel is renounced and repudiated; thus the word "endlich," by virtue of its rhythmic position in the line, needs the interpretation of "finite" (along with "final"). And then comes one of the key phrases of the entire Orpheus cycle and, indeed, of all of Rilke's mature work: song is being-here, easy for the god but difficult for man. What, then, is the standard for this new Orphic ontology, the poet asks—when is nature turned toward man's being? One of the ambiguities of the sentence revolves around the referent of "er": the antecedent could be the god or the song. But this is only an apparent ambiguity, as god and song are identical. In any case, the question posed is: How can Orphic song convert the world in such a way that its being and our being are in tune? This is, again, the problem of the eighth and ninth Elegies, and the answer given there is, in brief: reversal-conversion of self, conversion of world into self, internalization of world-space. That same answer is briefly and tentatively adumbrated in the remaining lines:

Dies *ists* nicht, Jüngling, dass du liebst, wenn auch
die Stimme dann den Mund dir aufstösst—lerne

vergessen, dass du aufsangst. Das verrinnt.
In Wahrheit singen, ist ein andrer Hauch.
Ein Hauch um nichts. Ein Wehn im Gott. Ein Wind.

It is not the fact, o young man, that you are in love, even if
your voice then bursts from your mouth—learn

to forget that you began singing. That trickles away.
To sing in truth is another kind of breath.
A breath surrounding nothing. A wafting in the god. A wind.

The answer to the problem is *not* inspiration drawn from love. True song is another kind of respiration altogether—a breath surrounding nothing, therefore equated to a breeze arising in the god. This last image, very Mallarméan, contains the kind of paradox that both Rilke and Mallarmé attempted to resolve in their poetry by the device of a convergence of opposites. The whole Orphic union of contraries is essentially sketched out here, and subsequent examples serve primarily as exemplifications and amplifications of the same idea. Moreover, the entire first triad of sonnets in the first cycle, embracing the radical themes of song-hearing-death-being-breath, anticipates the opening of the second cycle.

The next group of sonnets, 5 through 9, proceeds to greater and greater certitude; the questions are now superseded by declarations, sometimes even imperatives. The fifth speaks of the perpetuity and ambiguity of Orpheus, his "metamorphosis in this and that," and declares categorically

> Ein für alle Male
> ists Orpheus, wenn es singt.

> Once and for all
> it is Orpheus, whenever there is song.

The poem is about the fleetingness of existence and Orphic resurrection, and it is a comment on the transcension motif of the opening sonnet.

> Indem sein Wort das Hiersein übertrifft,
>
> ist er schon dort, wohin ihrs nicht begleitet.
> Der Leier Gitter zwängt ihm nicht die Hände.
> Und er gehorcht, indem er überschreitet.

> Since this word surpasses being-here,
>
> he is already there where you cannot accompany it.
> The lyre's cage does not constrain his hands.
> And he obeys by transgressing.

The last line is particularly effective because it makes literal use of the meaning of "transgress"; Orpheus obeys by going beyond the here and now, not by by-passing it, but by surpassing it—in the manner of Zarathustra.

The sixth sonnet supplies the foundation for the previous argument:

> Ist er ein Hiesiger? Nein, aus beiden
> Reichen erwuchs seine weite Natur.
>
> Does he belong down here? No, out of both
> Domains his broad nature grew.

This is the doctrine of the double realm, life and death. Orpheus, as a result both of his descent and his dismemberment, is perfectly at home in both realms and unites them. Thus he abolishes the Orpheus of the 1904 poem, surpassing Eurydice at the same time. His being-here and being-beyond are coextensive because the thread joining them has been restored. Everything now becomes explicable under the category of "der klarste Bezug"—the clearest connections —an important idea in subsequent sonnets. The ninth sonnet illustrates the duality, with only a passing reference to the Orphic lyre. Only he who is at home in both realms can know the relation of change to permanence and can preserve that which is really lasting: "Wisse das Bild"—have knowledge of the image. This attractive small poem deserves quotation in full:

> Nur wer die Leier schon hob
> auch unter Schatten,
> darf das unendliche Lob
> ahnend erstatten.
>
> Nur wer mit Toten vom Mohn
> ass, von dem ihren,
> wird nicht den leisesten Ton
> wieder verlieren.
>
> Mag auch die Spieglung im Teich
> oft uns verschwimmen:
> Wisse das Bild.
>
> Erst in dem Doppelbereich
> werden die Stimmen
> ewig und mild.

Only he who has already raised the lyre
even among the shades [the dead],
may, foreboding,
dispense infinite praise.

Only he who with the dead
has shared poppies, their own,
will no longer lose
even the faintest note.

Even if the reflection in the pond
may often become blurred:
Know the image.

Only in the double realm
the voices become
eternal and mild.

Sonnets 7 and 8 proceed to the theme of praise. The eighth, discussed earlier, projects an allegorical relation between lament, longing, and praise; the seventh begins with the exclamation "Rühmen, das ists" (Praising, that is it)! and leaves no doubt that Orpheus stands for panegyric song. The first version of this sonnet, subsequently eliminated from the series, represents an interesting variant on the journey to the dead. In this "sarcophagus" poem Orpheus descends into the tombs of worm-eaten and rotting corpses.

Er zerrang den Gestank und pries
Tägiges täglich und Nächtiges nächtlich,

denn wer erkennt die verwandten Gnaden?
Knieend aus dem Markte der Maden
hob er das heile Goldene Vliess.[22]

He dispelled the stench and praised
By day what was the day's and by night what was the night's,

for who recognizes related favors?
Kneeling, out of the teeming of maggots
he lifted intact the Golden Fleece.

Here Rilke makes new use of the Golden Fleece saga, to which the Orpheus legend becomes attached in later Greek mythology, with the ingenious transposition of Orpheus, not Jason, capturing the Fleece, and in the realm of the dead.

The power of Orpheus having been outlined and illustrated in the first nine sonnets, Rilke proceeds to a number of illustrations and finally a number of attacks on the modern world. Only some of the poems are relevant here. Among them the fruit and flower poems (12–15), in which the Orphic dispensation finds its most exquisite and persuasive application, are outstanding. Sonnet 12 ends with the assertion "Die Erde schenkt"—the earth gives gifts; 13 attempts to express in words what delight the taste of a fruit provides:

> Wird euch langsam namenlos im Munde?
> Wo sonst Worte waren, fliessen Funde,
> aus dem Fruchtfleisch überrascht befreit.
>
> Wagt zu sagen, was ihr Apfel nennt.
> Diese Süsse, die sich erst verdichtet,
> um, im Schmecken leise aufgerichtet,
>
> klar zu werden, wach und transparent,
> doppeldeutig, sonnig, erdig, hiesig—
> O Erfahrung, Fühlung, Freude—riesig!

> Do you note that unnamed feeling in your mouth?
> Where there were words before, discoveries are flowing,
> surprised at being liberated from the pulp.
>
> Dare to say what you call "apple."
> That sweetness which condenses,
> quietly established in the tasting,
>
> before it becomes clear, awake and transparent,
> ambiguous, sunny, earthy, belonging here—
> O experience, feeling, joy—immense!

Sonnet 15 converts the taste of the fruit into rhythm. The opening is particularly beautiful, with its first rhythmically hesitant tetrameters that give way to dance pulsations:

Wartet . . . das schmeckt . . . Schon ists auf der Flucht.
. . . Wenig Musik nur, ein Stampfen, ein Summen—
Mädchen, ihr warmen, Mädchen, ihr stummen,
tanzt den Geschmack der erfahrenen Frucht!

Tanzt die Orange.

Wait . . . that taste . . . it's already gone.
. . . Just a touch of music, a stamping of the feet, a hum—
Girls, you who are warm, you who are mute,
dance the taste of the fruit experienced!

Dance the orange.

Rilke's attacks on the modern world, especially on the machine, are an important aspect of the new Orphism; but most of the poems (22–24) are not among his best. A fourth one, originally the twenty-first, was eliminated and published separately, probably to reduce the cluster of machine poems. It was replaced by a poem celebrating spring. The rejected sonnet is superior to the ones retained, and it is quoted here to illustrate Rilke's hostility to the industrial world:

O das Neue, Freunde, ist nicht dies,
dass Maschinen uns die Hand verdrängen.
Lasst euch nicht beirren von Übergängen,
bald wird schweigen, wer das "Neue" pries.

O the New, friends, is not this:
machines displacing our hands.
Do not be misled by transitions,
Soon all those who praised the "New" will cease talking.

This is somewhat more sober than most of Rilke's attacks. The present, the "modern," is, after all, but a transition, not an end in itself. What needs to be celebrated is not the modern world but the total world.

Denn das Ganze ist unendlich neuer,
als ein Kabel und ein hohes Haus.
Seht, die Sterne sind ein altes Feuer,
und die neuen Feuer löschen aus.

> Glaubt nicht, dass die längsten Transmissionen
> schon des Künftigen Räder drehn.
> Denn Aeonen reden mit Aeonen.

> For the Whole is infinitely newer
> than a cable and a skyscraper.
> Look, the stars are an ancient fire,
> and the new fires die out.

> Do not believe that the longest transmissions
> are already turning the wheels of the future.
> For aeons communicate with aeons.

The totality of things is always newer than the "latest," and the gears of today do not turn the gears of tomorrow: only aeons are in communication with other aeons because they stand outside of time and space. I do not think it is extravagant to say that Orpheus and the Angel of the Elegies are meant to usher in a new aeon, that aeon of inwardness.

> Mehr, als wir erfuhren, ist geschehn.
> Und die Zukunft fasst das Allerfernste
> rein in eins mit unserm innern Ernste.[23]

> More has happened than we know about.
> And the future grasps what is utterly remote
> and combines it into a pure unit with our inner seriousness.

The second cycle. The overall pattern of the second cycle, as noted before, is similar to the first. Here again some of the best sonnets are the "applied" sonnets, free from the pontification and didacticism which, though they constitute an integral part of Rilke's call to conversion, do not always release the best of his extraordinary lyrical powers. The "dance" poem (18) of the second part corresponds to the "orange" poem (15) of the first, and both may be regarded as tributes to Wera.

> Tänzerin, o du Verlegung
> alles Vergehens in Gang: wie brachtest du's dar.
> Und der Wirbel am Schluss, dieser Baum aus Bewegung,
> nahm er nicht ganz in Besitz das erschwungene Jahr?

Dancer, a transposition
of all that is transient into motion: how did you accomplish it.
And that whirl at the end, that tree made of movement,
did it not totally take possession of the attainable year?

It is tempting to say that even within the two weeks separating composition of the cycles Rilke had grown: poetic images recur now with the greatest of ease, the utmost subtlety. The sonnet form, too, handled with astonishing flexibility throughout the Orpheus series, becomes in the poet's hand an instrument of supreme refinement. The "dance" poem is a good example—and it is one of many—of the rhythmic pliability of Rilke's art even when he worked within as tradition-bound a form as the sonnet. The prevailing line is a pentameter, with striking syncopations, and *raccourcis* (tetrameters and trimeters) that are in themselves linear syncopations, abbreviated gestures. The initial trimeter serves, so to speak, as the leitmotif or definition. The dancer is a translator who changes what is transitory into a pattern of motion. And Rilke's precision with words (especially with verbs, usually gerunds) as substantives parallels the idea by grammatical transposition. The verb "gehen" is infused with new dynamics: "Vergehen" (going into dissolution, disappearance) becomes "Gang" (going, motion, activity). With similar effortlessness the final whirl of the dancer becomes a tree of motion, surely the twin of the Orphic tree of hearing, thus the reference to the tree and its seasons ushers in the imagery of spring and summer.

Blühte nicht, dass ihn dein Schwingen von vorhin umschwärme,
plötzlich sein Wipfel von Stille? Und über ihr,
war sie nicht Sonne, war sie nicht Sommer, die Wärme,
diese unzählige Wärme aus dir?

Did not its top, so that your swirls just a moment ago might swarm about it,
suddenly bloom, this top of tranquillity? And above this silence,
was there not the sun, the summer, warmth,
that infinite warmth coming from you?

The entire conception of the poem stands under the spell of Valéry, whose *L'Ame et la danse* Rilke had read in 1921. In that dialogue, Socrates summarizes the dance of Athikte in language that appears to have left a deep imprint on Rilke's sensibility, putting into clear perspective what may still have been blurred:

Rilke

Socrate: Ne sentez-vous pas qu'elle est l'acte pur des métamorphoses? . . . Elle tourne, et tout ce qui est visible, se détache de son âme; toute la vase de son âme se sépare enfin du plus pur; les hommes et les choses vont former autour d'elle une lie informe et circulaire . . .[24]

Socrates: Do you not feel that she is the act of metamorphosis in its pure form? . . . She whirls, and whatever is visible becomes detached from her soul; all the slime in her soul at last separates off from what is purest; human beings and things around her become shaped into formless and circular dregs . . .

Rilke has made these perceptions his own. The rest of the sonnet introduces some of his favorite image-objects (compare the ninth Elegy) and utilizes a marvelous *jeu de mots* in the final line that fixes forever the metamorphic relation of change and form in art. "Wandung"—partition, lining—and "Wendung"—turning—echo Rilke's favorite word, "Wandlung"—transformation.

> Aber er trug auch, er trug, dein Baum der Ekstase.
> Sind sie nicht seine ruhigen Früchte: der Krug,
> reifend gestreift, und die gereiftere Vase?
>
> Und in den Bildern: ist nicht die Zeichnung geblieben,
> die deiner Braue dunkler Zug
> rasch an die Wandung der eigenen Wendung geschrieben?

> But it also bore fruit, your ecstasy tree bore fruit.
> Are these not its tranquil fruits: the pitcher,
> brushed at [or, striped] in its ripening, and the even riper vase?
>
> And in the figures [you created]: did not the drawing remain
> inscribed by the dark curve of your brow
> rapidly upon the lining of your own rotation?

Equally remarkable is the "fountain" sonnet (15), the *monologue intérieur*, and yet also *extérieur*, of the earth. As in the sonnet just discussed, the very mention of Rilke's favorite objects is the seal of authentic being:

> O Brunnen-Mund, du gebender, du Mund,
> der unerschöpflich Eines, Reines, spricht—
> du, vor des Wassers fliessendem Gesicht,
> marmorne Maske.

O fountain-mouth, offering gifts, o mouth
saying inexhaustibly Unity, Purity—
o marble mask, placed in front of the water's
flowing face.

The central image, the mouth of the fountain, the water-giving spout (it is
helpful to visualize a spout in the shape of a face, as is common in Europe), is
developed into the mask-face antithesis. Here, as elsewhere in Rilke, the very
juxtapositions and echoes have poetic and intellectual significance. Eines, Reines
—they not only have identical sounds but identical meanings in Rilke's context.

Und im Hintergrund
der Aquädukte Herkunft. Weither an Gräbern
vorbei, vom Hang des Apennins
tragen sie dir dein Sagen zu, das dann
am schwarzen Altern deines Kinns

vorüberfällt in das Gefäss davor.

And behind you
the descent from aqueducts. From far away, past graveyards,
from the slopes of the Apennines
they bring you your speech, which then
past the black marks of age upon your chin,

drops into the vessel held in front of you.

The image is expanded spatially and temporally: the waters of the Roman
fountain come from or are reminiscent of aqueducts, they acquire wisdom by
passing by the tombs, and their mature "speech"—superbly condensed in the
simple gerund "Sagen," as in the ninth Elegy—flows through and beyond the
aging fountain mouth to fill the human pitcher. Now the image shifts from
saying to hearing by focusing on the hollowed-out basin into which the water
flows; the basin becomes the "ear" that receives the water's saying.

Dies ist das schlafend hingelegte Ohr,
das Marmor-Ohr, in das du immer sprichst.

Ein Ohr der Erde. Nur mit sich allein
redet sie also. Schiebt ein Krug sich ein,
so scheint es ihr, dass du sie unterbrichst.

This is your ear, lying asleep before you,
the marble ear into which you are always speaking.

An ear upon the earth. Thus the earth
converses with herself alone. If a pitcher is interposed,
it seems to her that you are interrupting.

The approach of a human hand and a pitcher appear to be an interruption of the earth's dialogue with itself. But because the human intrusion is necessary, inasmuch as both fountain-mouth and fountain-ear are manmade, the poem does not constitute a rejection of the human; the last line is cautiously worded. From the Elegies and from the other sonnets, we know that if man learns once again to listen, to become like the fountain basin, he will learn once again how to speak. Seen in this way, the sonnets become a capsule-statement of the entire Orpheus sequence.

The following sonnet (16), complementing this Orphic image of "speaking," is linked to its predecessor by the metaphor of the "heard" spring.

Immer wieder von uns aufgerissen,
ist der Gott die Stelle, welche heilt.
Wir sind Scharfe, denn wir wollen wissen,
aber er ist heiter und verteilt.

Again and again torn open by us
the god is the spot that heals.
We are sharp, because we want to know,
but he is gay and parceled out.

The imagery is reminiscent of the third Elegy and of "Gegen-Strophen," in which Rilke characterizes the male as sharp-edged, like a stone chipped off a mountainside. For Rilke, the very "smartness" of the male is what makes him smart with pain, and the world with him. By contrast, Orpheus (but also the Orphicized Apollo) is the healer who closes the gashes made by our chipped, jagged personalities.

Nur der Tote trinkt
aus der hier von uns *gehörten* Quelle,
wenn der Gott ihm schweigend winkt, dem Toten.

Uns wird nur das Lärmen angeboten.

Only the dead man drinks
from the source that is *heard* by us here,
when the god silently beckons to him, the dead man.

To *us* only tumult is offered.

The wellspring whose message we hear but dimly in this world is fully apprehended by the dead when Hermes beckons him. The spring beckons in the same way, and its silent meaning can be apprehended if man learns to live his death here and now; otherwise he can perceive only the noise and chaos of the earth.

The climax of the second Orpheus cycle comes in the "imperative" sonnets 12 through 14, of which the first two are of supreme importance. Here, near the center of the second part, all the questions of the first part have crystallized in the "thou shalt" of certainty; they correspond to the more subdued affirmation of the twelfth sonnet of the first cycle.

Heil dem Geist, der uns verbinden mag;
denn wir leben wahrhaft in Figuren.
Und mit kleinen Schritten gehn die Uhren
Neben unserm eigentlichen Tag.

Ohne unsern wahren Platz zu kennen,
handeln wir aus wirklichem Bezug . . .
Reine Spannung. O Musik der Kräfte!

Hail to the spirit that may conjoin us;
for we truly live in figures.
And the clocks, with their small steps,
walk alongside our real day.

Without knowing our true place
We act from genuine relatedness . . .
Pure tension. O music of energies!

Pure tension and true relatedness—these are the subjects of the two key sonnets, capped by an imperative to human action, namely, transformation. Both sonnets are difficult because of their abstractedness and didactic import. Rilke regarded the thirteenth as "das überhaupt gültigste der Sonette" (generally the most valid of the sonnets):

> Sei allem Abschied voran, als wäre er hinter
> dir, wie der Winter, der eben geht.
> Denn unter Wintern ist einer so endlos Winter,
> dass, überwinternd, dein Herz überhaupt übersteht.
>
> Sei immer tot in Eurydike—singender steige,
> preisender steige zurück in den reinen Bezug.
> Hier, unter Schwindenden, sei, im Reiche der Neige,
> sei ein klingendes Glas, das sich im Klang schon zerschlug.
>
> Sei—und wisse zugleich des Nicht-Seins Bedingung,
> den unendlichen Grund deiner innigen Schwingung,
> dass du sie völlig vollziehst dieses einzige Mal.
>
> Zu dem gebrauchten sowohl, wie zum dumpfen und stummen
> Vorrat der vollen Natur, den unsäglichen Summen,
> zähle dich jubelnd hinzu und vernichte die Zahl.

> Be ahead of all parting, as if it were behind you
> like the winter that is now going.
> For among winters one [winter] is so endlessly winter
> that, hibernating, your heart endures at all.
>
> Be ever dead in Eurydice—ascend more singing,
> more praising climb back into pure relatedness.
> Here, among the vanishing be, in the realm of decline,
> be a sounding glass that shattered in its sound.
>
> Be—and know at the same time the condition of nonbeing,
> the infinite ground of your intimate vibration,
> so that you can accomplish it completely this one time.
>
> To the used as well as to the dull and mute

store of full nature, to the uncountable sums,
add yourself jubilantly and annul the amount.

The axial contrasts in this poem revolve around the images of "Neige" (decline, diminution, decrease) that dominate the sonnet's octave and "Vorrat" (supply, store) the sestet. The contrast is really between void and plenitude, and in line 9 this opposition is understood as a tension between nonbeing and being. Supplementary images in the first section are those of parting: winter, death, and vanishing. In the second part there is the antithetical idea of fullness, applied both to nature and to arithmetical sums. Another pair of correspondences are the words "endlos" in line 3 and "unendlich" in line 10. They are at the same time synonyms and antonyms; it is as if one were to take the mathematical term "infinite series" and place the accent alternately on "series" (the forward movement, the process) and then on "infinite" (the limit, the resting point). This ambivalence represents one way in which Rilke achieves the reconciliation of opposites in the poem. But the sonnet is more subtly organized than that. The opening phrase, "be ahead of all parting," ushers in a hyperbolic statement: it is, in a way, a contradiction. The subsequent insistence on the word "winter," four times repeated, is no less effective than the triple use of composites beginning with the prefix "über." Thus there is in the first quatrain a seasonal mise en scène of nature's decline (winter), nature's farewell, surpassed and transcended —the idea of the self hibernating, outlasting winter. Lines 5 and 6 invoke death in Eurydice and thereby the Orphic ontology, the death that must be understood and experienced as the other side of life, this fusion of death and life achieving its fullest being in pure relatedness—the midpoint at which opposites merge. This idea is enlarged in line 7 and transposed into the key image of the sonnet in line 8: here, in this world of decline and evanescence—the world of nature and creature—be like the glass that in order to give off its *own* vibration must be shattered.

The sestet begins with the recapitulating imperative "Sei" and expands it into a call for knowledge: "Wisse." True being is conditioned by nonbeing: nonbeing is the "infinite ground," the impulse governing one's most inward vibration (and the word "Schwingung," because its resonance with the word "Schwindenden" in line 7 again reiterates—as if to call attention simultaneously to intensified and damped oscillations—the dialectical movement of the poem) so that it can be totally accomplished once and for all. The voluntaristic side of Rilke is in evidence here. This dialectic of opposites, a Nietzschean act accomplished on Cusanian (or Hegelian) ground, is accomplished by the will. The last tercet sums up the world of supply, of possessions—the world of "having"— the things that are useful and the things that are not, all those bank deposits of nature whose total can be calculated. And the final line completes and supersedes line 8: to this arithmetical figure of having, this endless amount that is not calculable, add your own figure of being and number itself (the sum) is abolished. Number, the integer, disappears in the new integrity and joy of "supernumerous" existence in pure relation. The dialectical movement of the poem is from the ground of nonbeing through the world understood as having number, and from there to the annihilation of this countable, accountable, interpreted world, then finally to the metamorphosis of the self here and now as being in pure relatedness.

The coincidence of opposites for Rilke takes place as a metamorphosis in the context of the human will to transform the here and now into the infinite, without losing its *hic et nunc* aspects. Thus, the mythological Daphne who is pursued by Apollo and metamorphosed into a laurel tree is still Daphne, and the breeze caressing her is still Apollo. But Daphne and Apollo are now invisible. Precisely this metamorphosis, with its echoes of Ovid and its reminiscences of the plastic arts, forms the nucleus of sonnet 12.

Wolle die Wandlung. O sei für die Flamme begeistert,
drin sich ein Ding dir entzieht, das mit Verwandlungen prunkt;
jener entwerfende Geist, welcher das Irdische meistert,
liebt in dem Schwung der Figur nichts wie den wendenden Punkt.

Was sich ins Bleiben verschliesst, schon *ists* das Erstarrte;
wähnt es sich sicher im Schutz des unscheinbaren Grau's?
Warte, ein Härtestes warnt aus der Ferne das Harte.
Wehe—abwesender Hammer holt aus!

Wer sich als Quelle ergiesst, den erkennt die Erkennung;
und sie führt ihn entzückt durch das heiter Geschaffne,
das mit Anfang oft schliesst und mit Ende beginnt.

Jeder glückliche Raum ist Kind oder Enkel von Trennung,
den sie staunend durchgehn. Und die verwandelte Daphne
will, seit sie lorbeern fühlt, dass du dich wandelst in Wind.

Will the transformation. O be enthusiastic about the flame
in which a thing withdraws from you that boasts of transmutations;
that spirit of design which masters earthly things,
likes in the curve of a figure nothing but the pivotal point.

Whatever encloses itself in staying, in an instant it *is* already congealed;
does it delude itself into being safe in the plainness of gray?
Wait: something extremely solid from a distance sends warning to something solid.
Woe: an absent hammer is poised for its downward stroke!

Whoever pours forth as a source, him recognition recognizes;
and it leads him enraptured through the joyous Creation
which often ends with beginning and begins with the end.

Every blissful space is parting's progeny,
and they [the parted lovers] traverse it astonished. And Daphne metamorphosed,
wishes—since she now feels as a laurel does—that you change into wind.

This superbly structured sonnet is, with the thirteenth, cosmic in scope; each of
its four subdivisions center on one of the four elements, and internal correspondences are established between fire (quatrain I) and air (tercet II), and
between matter (quatrain II) and water (tercet I). Each subdivision tends toward
absence or invisibility.

The initial imperative is, once again, the core of the didactic import of the
sonnet—no longer, as in the "Archäischer Torso Apollos," the exhortation,
"You must change your life"; but now the particular command, "Will the
transformation." The first quatrain is very like Valéry: the flame is the emblem
of perpetual change, in which the object is continually receding. Yet here again,
in Valéry's formulation, the mastery of design and outline originates from an
initial pleasure produced by the (turning point in the) curve. Rilke uses the
word "entwerfend" also in its root meaning of "casting forth, projecting," and
alludes indirectly to the trajectory (an important image in his late poetry) made
by a thrown object.

The second quatrain is all solidity and rigidity and changelessness; the security
that matter arrogates to itself is illusory. For any hard substance there is always a
harder substance, always an abstract hammer poised to crush it. By contrast, the
first tercet is all fluidity and circularity; the image of the spring, familiar through
other sonnets discussed here, is the channel of reciprocal recognition (man

and world). The acoustical parallelism of lines 5 and 9 is deliberate for its
contrasting meanings: "Was sich ins Bleiben verschliesst . . . / Wer sich als
Quelle ergiesst . . ."

The final tercet begins with a reference to "blissful space," here rather oddly
concrete-abstract by equation with a descendant of parting. The language is
somewhat elliptical and obscure, but the meaning appears to be that parted
lovers give birth to an aura of bliss in which they move in astonishment. This
somewhat precious idea leads to the superb climax of Apollo and Daphne
(involving all the other parted lovers, including Orpheus and Eurydice), symbols of the metamorphosis. Daphne, who already feels like a laurel, wants
Apollo to make himself invisible, too, as the wind that caresses the tree. The
last line echoes and completes the first line even to the point of alliteration; flame
and wind complement each other. The ending of the sonnet is a perfect exemplification of the pledge, uttered at the end of the ninth Elegy, to make the earth
invisible.

One of the later sonnets (21) celebrates such gardens "unknown to the heart"
as those of Isfahan or Shiraz. This Persian theme leads to the lovely sestet containing the image of the tapestry of being:

> Meide den Irrtum, dass es Entbehrungen gebe
> für den geschehnen Entschluss, diesen: zu sein!
> Seidener Faden, kamst du hinein ins Gewebe.
>
> Welchem der Bilder du auch im Innern geeint bist
> (sei es selbst ein Moment aus dem Leben der Pein),
> fühl, dass der ganze, der rühmliche Teppich gemeint ist.

> Avoid the error that there are renunciations
> of the decision, once it is taken, namely: to be!
> Silken thread, [thus] you entered the fabric.
>
> Whatever the figure inside [the carpet] you may be part of
> (even if it is a moment in the life of pain),
> feel [certain] that the meaning is in the whole praiseworthy carpet.

The same problem, the problem of being, informs sonnet 26, which focuses on
children's play, their shouts, and the cries of birds and develops one of Rilke's
favorite distinctions between disordered shouting (*Lärm*, noise) and the Orphic
ordered outburst like that in sonnet 26 of the first cycle.

Wie ergreift uns der Vogelschrei . . .
Irgend einmal erschaffenes Schreien.
Aber die Kinder schon, spielend im Freien,
schreien an wirklichen Schreien vorbei.

Schreien den Zufall. In Zwischenräume
dieses, des Weltraums, (in welchen der heile
Vogelschrei eingeht, wie Menschen in Träume—)
treiben sie ihre, des Kreischens, Keile.

Wehe, wo sind wir? Immer noch freier,
wie die losgerissenen Drachen
jagen wir halbhoch, mit Rändern von Lachen,

windig zerfetzten—Ordne die Schreier,
singender Gott! dass sie rauschend erwachen,
tragend als Strömung das Haupt und die Leier.

How the cry of birds moves us . . .
A cry created once upon a time.
But already children playing outdoors
cry past the true cry.

They cry what is accidental. Into the interstices
of this world-space, (into which the healthy
bird-cry enters, like men into dreams—)
they drive their wedges of screaming.

Woe, where are we? Freer even
than kites torn loose
we knock about halfway [between earth and sky] with edges of laughter

ragged from the wind—Make order among the screamers,
O singing god! so that they may waken [like a] rushing [stream],
bearing as a current head and lyre.

Much of this sonnet is related to the eighth and ninth Elegies, yet the concentration of imagery is altogether characteristic of the admirable density of the Orpheus sonnets. The four central images, bird-cry, space, kite, Orpheus, are handled in an antithetical interlocking symmetry. The first quatrain contrasts the bird-cry, which is real, with the shouting of children, already falsified (compare the idea of turning the child backward in the eighth Elegy). All false cries are in the category of "chance," by which Rilke means rather transiency than indeterminacy. The conceptual difference between Rilke and Mallarmé on the subject of *le hasard* is of major importance because it pinpoints the checkmate of Mallarmé (particularly in *Un coup de dés*) against the "transgression" of Rilke. Mallarmé insists on staying within the game by executing the dice-throw in spite of the certainty of defeat; Rilke tries to abolish, or invert, the game itself by going out of bounds. The image in Rilke correlative to Mallarmé's throw of the dice is the throw of a ball into cosmic space. In this sonnet the image is related but also contrasted. The loose kites (wedge-shaped, no doubt) are only seemingly free; they are in mid-air, buffeted by the wind, and tattered. The second quatrain posits the image of interstices of space ("Zwischenräume") poignantly between the metaphors of playground diversion. The play of abstractions and concretions is worked out to the extent of arranging the rhymes themselves in pairs of contraries: the interstices of space are like little wedges driven into real, cosmic, space, which is sane and whole. "Heile" is in tension with "Keile" and "Zwischenräume" with "Träume," equated with real human inner existence. Thus the implied third element in this spatial triad is "Innenräume," interior spaces. The diagram that results from this arrangement is, in effect, the counterpart of the diagram extracted from the eighth Elegy.

	Zwischenraum	
Weltraum	(interstice)	Innenraum
(cosmic interior space)	∧	(interior space)

There the interstice prevents the translation of exterior into interior space, creating a kind of negative mid-space that acts like a void wedged in between the two aspects of real space. Elimination of this hostile and divisive void is Orpheus' accomplishment and glory.

The relationship between the first and second Orpheus cycles can now be formulated differently. The first group, from the first sonnet on, embraces the revelation of Orphic space, simultaneously exterior and interior, and the revelation of the efficacy of Orpheus within it, within ourselves. This first part is dominated by the metaphors of silence and the attentive ear; true Orphic space is silent space, and Orphic song is but the celebration of this silence of inwardness. The second group is the call to action that follows the revelation. It is concerned with the changes—with the exchanges—that need to be effected so that mankind, too, can sing with the Orphic voice. The dominant metaphor is that of speech and the praising mouth. More basic still is the concept of breath, seen not merely as the animation of poetic speech, but as the very element with which the exchange between world-space and world-inner-space needs negotiation. The first sonnet of the second part marks this new, and final, stage of the Orphic regeneration:

> Atmen, du unsichtbares Gedicht!
> Immerfort um das eigne
> Sein rein eingetauschter Weltraum. Gegengewicht,
> in dem ich mich rhythmisch ereigne.
>
> Einzige Welle, deren
> allmähliches Meer ich bin;
> sparsamstes du von allen möglichen Meeren—
> Raumgewinn.

> Breathing, o invisible poem!
> Perpetually for its own
> being purely exchanged world-space. Counterweight,
> in which I discover my own self rhythmically.
>
> Single wave, whose
> gradual sea I am;
> thriftiest of all the possible seas—
> gain of space.

The very asymmetry of this human poet's exclamation is in marked contrast to the symmetry of sonnet I in the first part, which revealed the perfected presence of the divine poet. The tentativeness, the breathlessness of this poem, with its irregular lines and rhythms, is an exact equivalent of the inchoateness of the Orphic inspiration that has now devolved upon the human poet. The very first line encapsulates the resolution to "say" by making invisible, which had crowned the vision of the ninth Elegy. Breathing is the pure exchange of world-space for one's own being; or, it is the counteraction which ontologically—and rhythmically—creates an authentic self and gives it existential meaning (*ereigne*, to take place, but basically to come into one's own). The image of the sea, which begins with a wave and becomes the whole ocean, an abundant treasure—(note the supplementary imagery of the bank transaction!)—completes this notion of total "intake": *Raumgewinn*, gain of space, space-"income."

The excitement before the struggle, in the preceding sonnet, is superseded by the measured and calm assurance of the final sonnet of the series. According to Rilke's note accompanying the text, it is addressed to a friend of Wera's, by which he evidently meant himself. Here most of the major themes of the second cycle are *verdichtet*, condensed into poetic statement; just as the act of breathing, "inspiration," condenses world-space into inner-space by making it "more," or greater.

> Stiller Freund der vielen Fernen, fühle,
> wie dein Atem noch den Raum vermehrt.
> Im Gebälk der finstern Glockenstühle
> lass dich läuten.

> Silent friend of the many distances, feel
> how your breath augments space.
> Among the timbers of the dark bell-lofts
> Let yourself ring.

The alliterations in "f" of line 1 prepare the greater space of line 2. Subsequently breath becomes wind, singing becomes ringing.

> Das, was an dir zehrt,
>
> wird ein Starkes über dieser Nahrung.
> Geh in der Verwandlung aus und ein.
> Was ist deine leidendste Erfahrung?
> Ist dir Trinken bitter, werde Wein.

> Sei in dieser Nacht aus Übermass
> Zauberkraft am Kreuzweg deiner Sinne,
> ihrer seltsamen Begegnung Sinn.

> That which consumes you
>
> Will grow strong from this food.
> Go back and forth in metamorphosis.
> What is your most painful experience?
> If drinking is bitter for you, become wine.

> Be in this night of abundance
> a magic power at the crossroads of your senses,
> the very sense of their strange encounter.

As is frequently the case, Rilke places his pivotal line somewhere near the center of the poem and lets his play of contraries oscillate about this pure center. "Geh in der Verwandlung aus und ein" denotes a familiarity with transformation, so that the act of metamorphosis becomes habitual. Suffering is converted into strength, variety magically transmuted into convergence. The reference to the "crossroads of your senses" supplies the jubilant answer to the lament of sonnet 3 in the first part: "At the crossing of two heart-ways there stands no temple for Apollo."

> Und wenn dich das Irdische vergass,
> zu der stillen Erde sag: Ich rinne.
> Zu dem raschen Wasser sprich: Ich bin.
>
> And whenever what is earthly forgot you,
> to the silent earth say: I flow.
> To the rapid water say: I am.

Being and becoming, earth and water merge into a final unity, the unity of the earthly made invisible, the flesh made word again but without being annulled in the process. And so the *Sonnets to Orpheus* end quietly and nobly with the assertion of the *unitas oppositorum*.

Two months after completing the Elegies and the Sonnets, Rilke wrote to Countess Sizzo:

Wer nicht der Fürchterlichkeit des Lebens irgandwann, mit einem endgültigen Entschlusse, zustimmt, ja ihr zujubelt, der nimmt die unsäglichen Vollmächte unseres Daseins nie in Besitz, der geht am Rande hin, der wird, wenn einaml die Entscheidung fällt, weder ein Lebendiger noch ein Toter gewesen sein. Die *Identität* von Furchtbarkeit und Seligkeit zu erweisen, dieser zwei Gesichter an demselben göttlichen Haupte, ja dieses einen *einzigen* Gesichts, das sich uns so oder so darstellt, je nach der Entfernung aus der, oder der Verfassung, in der wir es wahrnehmen . . . dies ist der wesentliche Sinn und Begriff meiner beiden Bücher . . .[25]

Whoever does not at some time make the ultimate decision of consenting to the awfulness of life, even to the point of rejoicing in it, never takes possession of the unutterable powers of our existence; he leads a marginal existence, and when the sentence is pronounced, he will have been neither alive nor dead. To demonstrate the *identity* of awfulness and blessedness, those two faces of the same divine head, indeed of that one *single* face, which is manifest to us in the one aspect or the other, depending upon the distance or the attitude of our perception . . . that is the essential meaning and conception of my two books.

The final reference is, of course, to the *Duino Elegies* and the *Sonnets to Orpheus*. The preceding pages have shown that this identity motif characterizes the vision of the Elegies and the revelation of the Sonnets; it is virtually always implied in the second cycle of the Sonnets and appears with great frequency and much ingenuity in Rilke's late poems, sometimes handled with solemnity, sometimes playfulness. A number of brief examples suffice here. One of the rejected sonnets of the second Orpheus series has the lovely ending

> Hier- und Dortsein, dich ergreife beides
> seltsam ohne Unterschied. Du trennst
> sonst das Weisssein von dem Weiss des Kleides[26]

> Being here and being there, let both take hold of you
> strangely without difference. Else you separate
> the whiteness of the garment from the white itself

with its warning not to separate object from concept. Another charming sonnet of the same group offers a playful comment on "moving eternity":

> Wir hören seit lange die Brunnen mit.
> Sie klingen uns beinah wie Zeit.
> Aber sie halten viel eher Schritt
> mit der wandelnden Ewigkeit.

> Das Wasser ist fremd und das Wasser ist dein,
> von hier und *doch* nicht von hier.
> Eine Weile bist du der Brunnenstein
> und es spiegelt die Dinge in dir.

> Wie ist das alles entfernt und verwandt
> und lange enträtselt und unerkannt,
> sinnlos und wieder voll Sinn . . .[27]

For a long while we have been hearing [along with] the fountains.
They sound to us almost like time.
But they are much rather in step
with moving eternity.

The water is strange and the water is yours,
belonging here and *yet* not belonging here.
For a while you are the stone of the fountain,
and it mirrors things in you.

How all this is remote and familiar
and long deciphered and unrecognized,
senseless and again full of sense . . .

In another vein, the echo of Maurice de Guérin's "Le Centaure," which Rilke had translated, is converted into a tribute to Guérin and uses one of the archetypes of the *coincidentia oppositorum*, the androgyne.

C'est le Centaure qui a raison
qui traverse par bonds les saisons
d'un monde à peine commencé
qu'il a de sa force comblé.

Ce n'est que l'Hermaphrodite
qui est complet dans son gîte.
Nous cherchons en tous les lieux
la moitié perdue de ces demi-Dieux.[28]

The Centaur is right
to traverse by leaps the seasons
of a world barely begun
which he has overwhelmed by his strength.

Only the Hermaphrodite
is complete in his lair.
We seek in all places
the lost half of those demigods.

As the cortège of Orpheus has been steadily enlarging—Apollo, Daphne, Wera, the poet himself, the Centaur—now Eros himself reclaims his place of honor:

> Ce n'est pas la justice qui tient la balance précise,
> c'est toi, ô Dieu à l'envie indivise,
> qui pèses nos torts,
> et qui de deux coeurs qu'il meurtrit et triture
> fais un immense coeur plus grand que nature,
> qui voudrait encor
>
>   grandir . . . Toi, qui indifférent et superbe,
> humilies la bouche et exaltes le verbe
> vers un ciel ignorant . . .
> Toi qui mutiles les êtres en les ajoutant
> à l'ultime absence dont ils sont des fragments.[29]

> It is not justice that holds the exact scales,
> it is rather thyself, o God of undivided desire,
> who weighest our wrongs
> and who, from two hearts that he bruises and shatters,
> makest an immense heart larger than nature,
> one which would like to grow even
>
>   larger . . . Thou who, indifferent and superb,
> dost humiliate the mouth and exalt the word
> toward an ignorant heaven . . .
> Thou who dost mutilate beings by adding to them
> to the ultimate absence whose fragments they are.

In the same series of four Eros poems, the god is introduced by

> Ô toi! centre du jeu
> où l'on perd quand on gagne[30]

> O thou! center of the game
> in which to lose is to win

so that Eros may be said to occupy the center of the arena of opposing tensions along with Orpheus. This center is for Rilke the space in which the *Umschlag* (reversal) of the transformation occurs, where the exchange of outer for inner takes place.

Rilke's late poetry can be described, therefore, as a search for the center—*à la recherche de l'espace perdu.* Sonnet 28 of the second cycle elevates Wera into a sort of Orphic messenger-angel:

> Denn die [die Natur] regte
> sich völlig hörend nur, da Orpheus sang.
> Du warst noch die von damals her Bewegte
> und leicht befremdet, wenn ein Baum sich lang
>
> besann, mit dir nach dem Gehör zu gehn.
> Du wusstest noch die Stelle, wo die Leier
> sich tönend hob—die unerhörte Mitte.

> For [Nature] stirred
> to total hearing only when Orpheus sang.
> You were the one who, moved from that moment on
> and quick to feel disturbed when a tree took a long time
>
> to decide to accompany you according to [or, after] hearing.
> You still know the place where the lyre
> raised itself in sound—the unheard-of center.

Here again the poet "translates" the Orphic tree into dance movement and heard music. The unheard-of center, progeny of Apollo's unheard-of head, is the place where the Orphic lyre sounds.

The theme of circle and center assumed a new importance for Rilke, as might have been expected, during composition of the Elegies and Sonnets. Georges Poulet, in a brief study, calls Rilke a centrifugal poet: "Rilke is perhaps the only poet for whom the expansion of thought in space seems to be due to a phenomenon not so much of tensed energies but of a release from the bonds of being. It is as if in the Rilkean cosmos, since the centripetal force is altogether nonexistent, as a result things, abandoned from the outset to nothing but the impetus of centripetal force, flew off spontaneously in all directions, far from their point of departure."[31] This statement is simply not correct. It is valid only with the proviso that it applies to Rilke's earlier poetry or, better yet, to the state of disintegration or nonbeing that the Angel and Orpheus are called to annul. The quest for the pure center is the "rhythmic counterweight" to offset the centrifugality of untransformed existence.

A number of poems written in the years 1922–1926 bear witness to this quest. Virtually all of them are structured around the image of the trajectory of a

Rilke

missile or the image of an arch. One of the best was written on January 31, 1922:

Solang du Selbstageworfnes fängst, ist alles
Geschicklichkeit und lässlicher Gewinn—
erst wenn du plötzlich Fänger wirst des Balles,
den eine ewige Mit-Spielerin
dir zuwarf, deiner Mitte, in genau
gekonntem Schwung, in einem jener Bögen
aus Gottes grossem Brücken-Bau:
erst dann ist Fangen-Können ein Vermögen—
nicht deines, einer Welt. Und wenn du gar
zurückzuwerfen Kraft und Mut besässest,
nein, wunderbarer: Mut und Kraft vergässest
und schon geworfen *hättest* . . . (wie das Jahr
die Vögel wirft, die Wandervogelschwärme,
die eine ältre einer jungen Wärme
hinüberschleudert über Meere—) erst
in diesem Wagnis spielst du gültig mit.
Erleichterst dir den Wurf nicht mehr; erschwerst
dir ihn nicht mehr. Aus deinen Händen tritt
das Meteor und rast in seine Räume.[32]

So long as you catch things thrown by yourself, everything
is a matter of agility and [therefore] of venial gain—
only when you suddenly become the catcher of the ball
that a girl, an eternal partner,
threw to you, to your center, with a precisely
achieved curve, in one of those arcs
that make up God's grand bridge-design:
only then is being-able-to-catch a real property—
not your own, but the world's. And if indeed you
had the strength and courage to return the throw,
nay, even more wonderful: if you forgot courage and strength
and *had* already thrown . . . (as the year
throws the birds, those swarms of migratory birds,
hurled by an older toward a young
warmth across the seas—) only
in this bold venture are you validly a partner.
No longer can you facilitate the throw; no longer
aggravate it. Out of your hands flies
a meteor and speeds through space.

Three modes of existence are delineated here. First, sufficiency of the self—the Narcissus gesture—the self throwing and catching. This is dependent on skill and offers negligible rewards. Second, dependence on some other person, presumably someone beloved who already "knows how"; here the self catches the ball thrown by a more accomplished "playmate." The third stage is the most complex. The self actually surpasses itself by virtue of having become self-less. This is the ultimate phase of "daring," in which weight becomes nonexistent, in which matter becomes aerial and the ball becomes a meteor. But the point here is that the hub of the action is the center, the self transformed.

A poem written in 1924 elaborates the theme of gravity.

> Mitte, wie du aus allen
> dich ziehst, auch noch aus Fliegenden dich
> wiedergewinnst, Mitte, du Stärkste.
>
> Stehender: wie ein Trank den Durst
> durchstürzt ihn die Schwerkraft.
>
> Doch aus dem Schlafenden fällt,
> wie aus lagernder Wolke,
> reichlicher Regen der Schwere.[33]

> Center, drawing yourself
> out of all things, even regaining yourself
> out of flying things, center, o strongest of all.
>
> [One] Standing upright: as a drink cascades through thirst,
> so gravity cascades through him.
>
> Yet out of a sleeping man falls,
> as if out of a hovering cloud,
> abundant rain of heaviness.

The sequence of verbs and nouns summarizes the pull of the poem's gravity—Fliegender, Stehender, Schlafender; ziehen, durchstürzen, fallen—with the heaviest element in the middle. But the word "ziehen" is reinforced by "widergewinnen," and this in turn is reinforced by the apposition of "du Stärkste." This strength, however, is the strength of pure forces.

Rilke

Heidegger, who has a particular predilection for this poem, into which he reads a confirmation of his own philosophy of being ("die Mitte des Seienden im Ganzen"—the center of that which is within the whole), remarks astutely:

Das Wort "der ganze Bezug" ist gar nicht denkbar, wenn man Bezug als blosse Relation vorstellt. Die Schwerkraft der reinen Kräfte, die unerhörte Mitte, der reine Bezug, der ganze Bezug, die volle Natur, das Leben, das Wagnis sind das Selbe.[34]

The expression "total relatedness" is not even imaginable if relatedness is taken to be mere relation. The gravity of pure forces, the unheard-of center, pure relatedness, total relatedness, nature's plenitude, life, the bold venture—they all mean the same thing.

Accordingly, it may be advantageous to think of "pure relatedness" as a tension of forces, opposing forces, around a center. Rilke wrote in 1924:

> Nicht um-stossen, was steht!
> Aber das Stehende stehender,
> aber das Wehende wehender
> zuzugeben—gedreht
>
> zu der Mitte des Schauenden,
> der es im Schauen preist,
> dass es sich am Vertrauenden
> jener Schwere entreisst,
>
> drin die Dinge, verlorener
> und gebundener, fliehn—
> bis sie, durch uns, geborener,
> sich in die Spannung beziehn.[35]

> Do not overturn what is standing!
> But to admit that which is standing as more standing,
> that which is fleeting as more fleeting,
> to admit this—turned
>
> toward the center of the beholder,
> who in beholding praises it,
> so that in the trustful man
> it strips itself of that gravity,

212

within which things, more lost
and more bound, escape—
until they, thanks to us, more born,
relate themselves into the tension.

The whole process, gramatically expressed by means of the five comparatives, is that of heightening and intensifying: to live *more*. (The superlatives are reserved for the Angel.) In a similar vein:

Über dem Nirgendsein   spannt sich das Überall!
Ach der geworfene,   ach der gewagte Ball,
füllt er die Hände nicht   anders mit Wiederkehr:
rein um sein Heimgewicht   ist er mehr.[36]

Above the Nowhere   stretches the Everywhere!
Ah, the thrown ball,   ah, the ventured ball,
does it not fill the hands   differently when it returns:
in its sheer homecoming weight   it is more [precious].

A poem written in 1924 summarizes movingly and concisely a number of these images by fitting them into the arch of an unheard-of bridge:

Da dich das geflügelte Entzücken
über manchen frühen Abgrund trug,
baue jetzt der unerhörten Brücken
kühn berechenbaren Bug.

Wunder ist nicht nur im unerklärten
Überstehen der Gefahr:
erst in einer klaren reingewährten
Leistung wird das Wunder wunderbar.

Mitzuwirken ist nicht Überhebung
an dem unbeschreiblichen Bezug,
immer inniger wird die Verwebung,
nur Getragensein ist nicht genug.

Deine ausgeübten Kräfte spanne,
bis sie reichen, zwischen zwein
Widersprüchen . . . Denn im Manne
will der Gott beraten sein.[37]

Since winged ecstasy
carried you over many an early abyss,
now build the boldly calculated arch
of unheard-of bridges.

Miracles do not lie merely in the unexplained
surmounting of danger;
only in a clear and neatly done
achievement the miracle becomes miraculous.

To participate is not arrogance
toward the indescribable relatedness,
involvement becomes ever more intimate,
simply letting yourself be carried along is not enough.

Stretch your practiced energies,
until they suffice, between two
contradictions . . . For in a man
god wishes to find his counselor.

The last stanza particularly is bold in its assertion that the god wants to be complemented by man, specifically by a man who has mastered the art of relationship, one who has built bridges—in brief, by Orphic man. The use of the verb "reichen" carries the meanings of both "reaching, spanning," and "sufficing." The arch of the bridge connects and resolves two contradictions; thus pure relatedness is equal to pure contradiction.

The ultimate symbol of this perfect reconciliation of opposites for Rilke is the rose. In a letter of January 4, 1923, he wrote from Muzot:

Tous les jours en contemplant ces admirables roses blanches, je me demande si elles ne sont pas l'image la plus parfaite de cette unité, je dirais même de cette identité d'absence et de présence qui, peut-être, constitue l'équation fondamentale de notre vie?[38]

Every day, while contemplating those admirable white roses, I wonder if they are not the most perfect image of that unity, I would go so far as to say that identity, of absence and presence that perhaps makes up the fundamental equation of our life?

In the French cycle "Les Roses," of 1924, there are these lines:

Rose, toi, ô chose par excellence complète
qui se contient infiniment
et qui infiniment se répand, ô tête
d'un corps par trop de douceur absent.[39]

Rose, o thing of excellence complete
containing itself infinitely
and infinitely spreading itself, o head
of a body absent because of too much sweetness.

And Rilke's epitaph for himself is the well-known apostrophe to the rose:

Rose, oh reiner Widerspruch, Lust
Niemandes Schlaf zu sein unter soviel
Lidern.

Rose, o pure contradiction, delight
at being no one's sleep beneath so many
eyelids.

Not only the imagery, but also the thought of these late rose poems moves close to the climate of Mallarmé. But for Mallarmé the reconciliation of opposites is not effected by nuance, nor by the search for the pure center. Rilke moves toward an interiorization, a contraction of space, Mallarmé toward a rarefaction of space, a void *defining* a space contour around itself, not (as in Rilke) a void entering into mutual transactions with space. Moreover, a major difference between the two poets involves the conception of chance. For Mallarmé, chance cannot, after all, be abolished; for Rilke it *must* be abolished. Note this very un-Mallarméan stanza from Rilke's "La Fenêtre":

Tous les hasards sont abolis. L'être
se tient au milieu de l'amour,
avec ce peu d'espace autour
dont on est maître.[40]

All chance is abolished. The [human] being
remains upright in the midst of love,
with that small portion of surrounding space
of which one is master.

One of Mallarmé's key words during his later years was *nier* (to deny, negate), always to be superseded by some kind of poetic glory or victory no matter how slight: a vigorous nay-saying, followed by an even more resolute yea-saying. One of Rilke's favorite expressions in his final years was *consentir* (possibly taken over from Valéry), used in its full etymological force meaning "to feel with."

> Tendre nature, nature heureuse, où tant
> de désirs se recherchent et s'entrecroisent,
> indifférente, et pourtant base
> des consentements[41]

> Tender nature, happy nature, where so many
> desires seek one another and intersect,
> indifferent [nature], and yet basis
> of consents

and then finally:

> C'est qu'il nous faut consentir
> à toutes les forces extrêmes;
> l'audace est notre problème
> malgré le grand repentir.

> Et puis, il arrive souvent
> que ce qu'on affronte, change:
> le calme devient ouragan,
> l'abîme le moule d'un ange.

> Ne craignons pas le détour.
> Il faut que les Orgues grondent,
> pour que la musique abonde
> de toutes les notes de l'amour.[42]

> We must indeed consent
> to all extreme forces:
> boldness is our problem
> despite the great repentance.

And so it happens often
that what is affronted changes:
calm turns into hurricane,
the abyss into an angel's mold.

Let us not fear the roundabout way.
The Organs must necessarily rumble
so that music may abound
in all the notes of love.

VI

After Rilke:
Orpheus, Paradigm
or Paradox?

The preceding five chapters have dealt with what might be called the meta-morphoses of the Orphic from 1800 to 1925. The general development traced by way of Novalis, Nerval, Mallarmé, and Rilke has been a series of trans-mutations in the understanding of the Orphic: the attempt to conquer a meta-physical dualism in the name of Orpheus, reconciliator of opposites and harmo-nizer of man and nature, poetry and the cosmos. These four poets are links in a sequence representing an evolving consciousness concerning the function as-signed to itself by Orphic poetry—or better, poetry in general—in a world increasingly fragmented and devalued. The Orphic dispensation in Novalis provided the signal and frame of reference for the new poetic sensibility: the reconciliation of fact and fantasy, the Christian and the pagan, the visible and the occult. Nerval began by traversing the same ground, but with a more intense consciousness of the demise of transcendent reality, so that toward the end of his brief career he reached an impasse that could no longer be overcome by a simple union of opposites, as in Novalis. Nerval's realization in his later writings that the opposites are truly, not merely apparently, contraries would have required a dialectic moving toward a new and radically different reconciliation; this task was performed by Mallarmé and Rilke. The Orphic resolution contained in their poetry calls for a vision of the creative act centered from then on in the poet's inwardness, a process sanctioned and sanctified by an immanentization of spiritual reality. In this respect, the Orphic consciousness of the nineteenth and early twentieth centuries can be said to have evolved from a Gnostic to an immanentistic view of the world.

From this vantage point it becomes evident that the new Orphic sensibility can serve as a series of milestones in understanding poetry and the poet in modern times. The history of the Orphic in the modern world is an abbreviated version of the history of modern poetry in general. In all fairness, it must be added that the Orphic itself remains in continuous tension with the Promethean attitude (conforming to the distinction made in the first chapter, in accordance with Herbert Marcuse's analysis), and a comprehensive study of poetry in the one hundred twenty-five year period covered thus far would also document an intermittent conflict between these two mythic orientations. The fact remains that the lyric poet's principal impulse is always toward self-transformation, but that the vicissitudes of modern history have impelled him more insistently than ever to convert his poetic vision into an activist doctrine. In such cases the poet is likely to forsake lyrical utterance for a more public rhetoric the normal outlets of which are drama, a modified version of the epic, or prose fiction. Romantic poetry contained the germs of both mythic orientations; this study has done no more than to trace the transmutation of one, in my opinion the principal, current.

The literary situation after 1925 presents once more the old Orphic-Promethean conflict, plus a new problem. This chapter is intended to deal with the conflict somewhat summarily; I shall try to outline the new problem, but in such a way as to leave the question of the Orphic in the twentieth century necessarily ambiguous and open-ended, since it seems impossible to arrive at any satisfactory conclusion at this point.

To begin with, there is the continuation of the nineteenth-century Orphic, elements of which can be observed in poets like Valéry, Yeats, Trakl, Supervielle, Eluard, Cocteau, Pierre-Jean Jouve, Pierre Emmanuel, Hermann Broch, and, finally, Perse. Despite their considerable divergences, these poets either invoke the myth of Orpheus or speak the language of Orphic reconciliation. There are others who, as the result of their conviction that individual change is not sufficient, espouse a prophetic attitude that embodies strong Promethean energies. This line runs from Blake through Shelley, Hugo, and Rimbaud to the surrealists; it attempts to alter the world by poetic assault rather than by tranquil persuasion. Rimbaud's experience is of particular interest in this context because he moves, without ever specifically mentioning Orpheus, from a Promethean-prophetic position to a more subdued Dionysiac-Orphic posture in *Les Illumina-tions*, only to attempt to transcend it in *Une Saison en enfer*. Accordingly, the problem of Rimbaud's Orphism can serve to foreshadow the dilemma of litera-ture in the twentieth century.

A recent work on the Orpheus theme by Gwendolyn Bays[1] treats Rimbaud as a culminating figure in the Orphic tradition in France. Bays' notion of the Orphic, however, is no more than an identification of illuminism and Orphism —in effect, the book is an interesting sequel to Auguste Viatte's *Les Sources occultes du romantisme*[2] and consequently demonstrates no more than Rimbaud's proclivity and reliance on occultistic texts and speculations. (As usual with all such illuministic readings of Rimbaud, there is considerable Procrustean stretch-ing and straining to fit him into cabalistic patterns—a method that has been widely perpetrated upon Nerval's poetry, though with more productive re-sults.) I have already argued that Orphism and illuminism do indeed overlap, but that the Orphic dispensation is a good deal more munificent and flexible than the cabalistic cannibalism of the Romantics. However, and this is the main point, Rimbaud at least for a brief moment approaches what we call the Orphic vision and then abandons it.

The central text is of course *Une Saison en enfer*. Like *Aurélia*, it is a spiritual autobiography, closer to prose poetry even than Nerval's work and more radical than Nerval in its uncompromising urge toward a personal myth. Both works are descents into the hell of the unconscious; but Rimbaud's hell is broader and more complex than Nerval's, having a more precise historical reference to the world in which Rimbaud lived (the West in its declining phase) and a greater degree of psychological presence: "Je me crois en enfer, donc j'y suis"—I believe myself to be in hell, therefore that's where I am. This means, moreover, that Rimbaud's hell has the characteristics of a newer and more radical theology. It is more a state of ontological than ethical punishment—although it must be said that Rimbaud uneasily shuttles back and forth between feelings of damna-tion that betray their Christian basis of sin and pride, and a kind of will to power that frantically strives to invert the plunge into hell into a redemptive experi-ence and a new dawn.[3]

For Nerval as well as for Baudelaire, the descent into the depths had ulti-mately revealed itself as a "way out"— "Au fond de l'inconnu, pour trouver du *nouveau*" (At the bottom of the unknown, to find something *new*)—thus defin-ing the limits of profundity for the nineteenth-century sensibility. Rimbaud is the heir of this sensibility, but he differs essentially from his two precursors (and thereby resembles Mallarmé) in exerting a more determined ascensional energy to counterbalance and indeed overbalance the downward pull. Consequently, the word "profundity" as applied to Rimbaud's season in hell is not altogether valid: like all other Rimbaldian sallies and escapades, this one is a raid on the dark absolute, in contrast to the Promethean stance in the famous "Lettre du voyant" of May 15, 1871: "Donc le poëte est vraiment voleur de feu," hence the poet is truly a fire-stealer. "Le Bateau ivre" defines this Promethean rhythm: the liberating descent of the ship from the normal into the magic visionary experience of the abnormal, accompanied by immersion and merger of the *voyant* with a cosmic "enormity"—then a (momentary) collapse of the self, and a lapse back into the norm. The vision of the celestial magic cosmos open to the already fatigued (surfeited?) voyager calls for new, superhuman energy and promises infinities beyond the already perceived infinity, a kind of psychedelic escalation:

> J'ai vu des archipels sidéraux! et des îles
> Dont les cieux délirants sont ouverts au vogueur:
> —Est-ce en ces nuits sans fond que tu dors et t'exiles,
> Millions d'oiseaux d'or, ô future Vigueur?—

> I've seen starry archipelagoes! and islands
> Whose frenzied skies are open to the sailor:
> —Are you asleep and exiled in those depthless nights,
> Millions of golden birds, o future Energy?—

Une Saison en enfer reverses the upward quest of "Le Bateau ivre" into a downward movement without sacrificing the basic rhythmic pattern of the Promethean aspiration. Is this still Promethean or is it Orphic, or is it something else?

The problem is as intricate poetically as it is psychologically and theologically because it involves the question of chronology and of the relative weight given *Une Saison en enfer* over *Les Illuminations*—in brief, the issues central to all Rimbaud criticism: how and why did the poet turn into a globe-trotter, adventurer, and gun-trader, and what bearing did his ambiguous attitude toward Christianity have upon his repudiation of literature? On all of these subjects our factual information is woefully deficient.

It is clear, nonetheless, that *Une Saison en enfer* marks a precarious transition from one stage to another. The general pattern of the work is relatively simple: a prologue is followed by an extensive series of liquidations of the past. "Mauvais

Sang" serves as a backward movement, Rimbaud's return to a pagan atavism; "Nuit de l'enfer" marks the critical recognition of malediction and infernality; "Délires I and II" are rejections of the eroticism and the poetics of the recent past. The next two sections, "L'Impossible" and "L'Eclair," are despite their brevity the pivotal points of the work, statements of the poet's predicament, a sort of *misère et grandeur* of the new Rimbaud. The concluding sections, with their virtually self-evident titles "Matin" and "Adieu," usher the regenerated poet into a future of new resolves and new projects for action; but this future is clearly not a literary quest and probably no longer a theological quest, at least not in the ordinary sense of the term.

The principal scheme of *Une Saison* is that of a progressive stripping of the self, a *dénuement* which, theologically considered, is tantamount to the act of self-emptying or *kénosis*. Even the opening sentences denote the dynamism of emptying plenitude of its content:

Jadis, je me souviens bien, ma vie était un festin où s'ouvraient tous les coeurs, où tous les vins coulaient.

Un soir, j'ai assis la Beauté sur mes genoux. Et je l'ai trouvée amère. Et je l'ai injuriée.

Je me suis armé contre la justice.

Je me suis enfui. Ô sorcières, ô misère, ô haine, c'est à vous que mon trésor a été confié!

Je parvins à faire s'évanouir dans mon esprit toute l'espérance humaine. Sur toute joie pour l'étrangler j'ai fait le bond sourd de la bête féroce.

J'ai appelé les bourreaux pour, en périssant, mordre la crosse de leurs fusils. J'ai appelé les fléaux, pour m'étouffer avec le sable, le sang. Le malheur a été mon dieu. Je me suis allongé dans la boue. Je me suis séché à l'air du crime. Et j'ai joué de bons tours à la folie.

Et le printemps m'a apporté l'affreux rire de l'idiot.[4]

Once upon a time, I remember it well, my life was a feast in which all hearts opened, in which all wines flowed.

One evening I sat Beauty down on my knees. And I found her bitter. And I insulted her.

I took up arms against justice.

I ran away. O sorceresses, a wretchedness, o hatred, my treasure was entrusted to you!

I succeeded in making all human hope vanish from my mind. I pounced noiselessly like a wild beast upon every joy, in order to strangle it.

I called upon the executioners so that, perishing, I might sink my teeth into their rifle butts. I called upon the scourges so that they might smother me in sand, in blood.

Misfortune was my god. I stretched out in the mud. I dried myself in the air of crime. And I played some good tricks on folly.

And spring brought me the frightful laughter of the idiot.

This represents one side of Rimbaud's dialectic: the rejection of hope, joy, and beauty that had amply characterized virtually all his poetry from the time of the "Lettres du voyant" (May 1871) to the time of *Une Saison* (April–August 1873), and along with it the magical presuppositions of his visionary and illuministic poetics. The other half of the dialectic is more specifically the demonism growing out of his inhibited and, in part, inverted Christianity. The note of abjectness, folly, and criminality—Baudelaire's legacy—leads directly into the second half of the prologue, in which the striving for charity is obviated by the sense of personal damnation:

> Or, tout dernièrement m'étant trouvé sur le point de faire le dernier *couac*! j'ai songé à rechercher la clef du festin ancien, où je reprendrais peut-être appétit.
>
> La charité est cette clef. Cette inspiration prouve que j'ai rêvé!
>
> "Tu resteras hyène, etc. . . ." se récrie le démon qui me couronna de si aimables pavots. "Gagne la mort avec tous tes appétits, et ton égoïsme et tous les péchés capitaux."
>
> Ah! j'en ai trop pris: Mais cher Satan, je vous en conjure, une prunelle moins irritée! et en attendant les quelques petites lâchetés en retard, vous qui aimez dans l'écrivain l'absence des facultés descriptives ou instructives, je vous détache ces quelques hideux feuillets de mon carnet de damné. (219)

> However, having quite recently found myself on the point of doing my last *squawk*! I thought of retrieving the key of the former feast, so that I might perhaps regain my appetite.
>
> Charity is that key. This inspiration proves that I've been dreaming!
>
> "You'll always be a hyena, etc. . . ." protests the demon that crowned me with such nice poppies. "Win death with all your appetites, with your egotism and all the mortal sins."
>
> Oh! I let him give me too much: But, dear Satan, I beg of you, let's not have that irritated look in your eye! and while waiting for all those little belated cowardly deeds, you who like in a writer the lack of descriptive or instructive faculties, I offer you these hideous loose leaves from my notebooks of a damned soul.

The tone of mockery masks frustration and despair. Rimbaud sees his former existence as a magician and immoralist as a nullity, suggests that charity has been missing, and immediately withdraws into his pride, but now with the acute consciousness of sin. His first reaction is to return to the sources of his being, which he identifies as pagan, accursed, "nègre." The retreat into heathenism is offset, however, by a quest for God, but no longer the Christian God:

> Le sang païen revient! L'Esprit est proche, pourquoi Christ ne m'aide-t-il pas, en donnant à mon âme noblesse et liberté. Hélas! l'Evangile a passé! l'Evangile! l'Evangile.
> J'attends Dieu avec gourmandise. Je suis de race inférieure de toute éternité. (221)
>
> . . .
>
> Je ne suis pas prisonnier de ma raison. J'ai dit: Dieu. Je veux la liberté dans le salut: comment la poursuivre? (225)

> Pagan blood returns! The Spirit is near, why doesn't Christ help me by giving my soul nobility and liberty. Alas! the Gospel has passed by! the Gospel! the Gospel.
> I await God gluttonously. I belong to an inferior race for all eternity.
>
> . . .
>
> I am not the captive of my reason. I have said: God. I want liberty in salvation: how to go after it?

Here is the central question of *Une Saison*: this God, so gluttonously awaited, would constitute freedom—Rimbaud surely means unfettered freedom—within the possibility of salvation. It is entirely characteristic of Rimbaud to want to *pursue* this chimera. His dilemma is also that of impatience; a number of poems written prior to *Une Saison* had celebrated the "feasts of patience," yet in their immediate apprehension of a moment of eternity these poems exalted patience only in a vision of time dissolved. Their time-bound counterparts are Rimbaud's poems of hunger, thirst, and restlessness—of impatience.

This conflict of psychological and theological polarities prompts Rimbaud's fierce plunge into his own hell and a wholesale repudiation of his former self. The action necessitates a break with his poetic practice, his *voyance*, which he now dismisses contemptuously as "l'histoire d'une de mes folies" (232)—the story of one of my follies—which had brought him to the point of sanctifying this folly ("Je finis par trouver sacré le désordre de mon esprit" [234], I wound up by finding the disorder of my mind sacred). The draft of *Une Saison* contains the following revelatory sentences not incorporated into the final version:

> Je hais maintenant les élans mystiques et les bizarreries de style.
> Maintenant je puis dire que l'art est une sottise. (251)

I now hate mystic flights and oddities of style.
Now I can say that art is foolishness.

Although Rimbaud in this section ("Délires II—alchimie du verbe") quotes only a number of poems now categorized as "Derniers Vers" and dating from 1872, he dismisses his entire activity as an alchemistic, hallucinatory poet. This inevitably raises the problem of *Les Illuminations* and their chronological and psychological rapport with *Une Saison en enfer*.

Les Illuminations represents the logical step beyond Rimbaud's experiment in prosody following "Le Bateau ivre" and "Voyelles." After the deliberate, and highly overdue, repudiation of the time-honored rules of French versification (operative from the Pléïade to Rimbaud's time) in such poems as "Larme," "Mémoire," and "La Comédie de la soif" and after the gemlike concision of the mystical visions of "Chanson de la plus haute tour," "L'Eternité," "Age d'or," and "O Saisons, ô châteaux"—after these extraordinary achievements, Rimbaud, apparently mindful of the problem of expression ("Trouver une langue" [271], to find a language) hinted at in his Letter to Démeny, moved on to the more pliable technique of the *poème en prose* (and the invention of *vers libre* in two instances) of *Les Illuminations*. These poems, deliberately reminiscent of illuminated manuscripts and of tinted etchings Occidental and Oriental, free in form and yet disciplined in the manipulation of their phantasmagoric materials, alternating and juxtaposing and superimposing familiar scenes and visions, are the summit of Rimbaud's poetic *alchimie du verbe*. And even though in *Une Saison* he makes no specific reference to the poems, his self-critical and mocking repudiation of the visionary technique clearly includes, or at least implies, a dismissal of *Les Illuminations* also. This does not necessarily mean that *all* the prose poems were written before the summer of 1873, but that in effect Rimbaud was ready to break with hallucinatory poetics: whether the final break came in 1873 or 1874 (surely no later, despite Bouillane de Lacoste's lucubrations on the subject[5]) does not matter essentially and will probably never be clarified. Rimbaud had a way—as the "Lettres du voyant" demonstrate—of projecting his poetic ideas and then trying them out, but always in the context of his own unstable and restless temperament and his variegated experiences. Consequently, *Une Saison* marks a new and *final* stage in Rimbaud's poetic, psychological, and religious development even though the final line of his poetry came somewhat later.

But the main interest of *Les Illuminations* has to do with the fact that here, as

well as in the "poems of eternity and bliss," Rimbaud comes as close to the
Orphic as he ever would. The Promethean attitudes of "Le Bateau ivre" and the
Lettres du voyant are metamorphosed into a Dionysiac-Orphic rapture in which
the spectacle of human endeavor and experience is transmuted into the most
exquisite and poignant kind of identity of poet and world—a total pantheism, a
special kind of Orphism in which the phenomena of nature need no longer be
tamed because they are already in tune with the poet-adolescent, as for example
in "Aube":

> Rien ne bougeait encore au front des palais. L'eau était morte. Les camps d'ombres ne
> quittaient pas la route du bois. J'ai marché, réveillant les haleines vives et tièdes, et les
> pierreries regardèrent, et les ailes se levèrent sans bruit.
>
> La première entreprise fut, dans le sentier déjà empli de frais et blêmes éclats, une
> fleur qui me dit son nom. (194)

> Nothing stirred as yet on the façade of the palaces. The water was dead. The encamp-
> ments of shadow did not move from the forest path. I walked along, waking the live
> and lukewarm breaths, and the stones started to look up, and wings noiselessly began to
> take flight.
>
> The first undertaking was, in the path already filled with fresh and pale brightness,
> a flower that told me its name.

The patron saint of this total immersion in the rhythms and energies of nature
would appear to be that lyre-playing son of Pan conjured up in "Antique," an
androgynous reconciliation of opposites:

> Gracieux fils de Pan! Autour de ton front couronné de fleurettes et de baies tes yeux, des
> boules précieuses, remuent. Tachées de lies brunes, tes joues se creusent. Tes crocs
> luisent. Ta poitrine ressemble à une cithare, des tintements circulent dans tes bras blonds.
> Ton coeur bat dans ce ventre où dort le double sexe. Promène-toi, la nuit, en mouvant
> doucement cette cuisse, cette seconde cuisse et cette jambe de gauche. (180)

> Gracious son of Pan! Around your forehead crowned with small flowers and bay
> leaves your eyes roll, like precious balls. Stained with brown dregs, your cheeks grow
> hollow. Your fangs glisten. Your chest resembles a cithara, tinkling sounds circulate in
> your blond arms. Your heart beats in that belly in which the double genitals are asleep.
> Walk about during the night, gently moving that thigh, that second thigh and that
> left leg.

As a complement to the mythical abolition of polarities, the prose poem

"Conte" projects a personal synthesis of contrasting psychic forces. A bored prince fails to satisfy his desires by means of random carnage, until one day he meets his other, idealized self in the form of a genie:

> Un soir il galopait fièrement. Un Génie apparut d'une beauté ineffable, inavouable même. De sa physionomie et de son maintien ressortait la promesse d'un amour multiple et complexe! d'un bonheur indicible, insupportable même! Le Prince et le Génie s'anéantirent probablement dans la santé essentielle. Comment n'auraient-ils pas pu en mourir? Ensemble donc ils moururent.
>
> Mais ce Prince décéda, dans son palais, à un âge ordinaire. Le prince était le Génie. Le Génie était le Prince.
>
> La musique savante manque à notre désir. (179)

> One evening he was galloping along proudly. There appeared a Genie of ineffable beauty, even unavowable. His physiognomy and his bearing breathed forth the promise of a multiple and complex love! an unspeakable, even unbearable happiness! The Prince and the Genie annihilated each other probably in essential health. How could they not have died of it? So, together they died.
>
> Yet this prince passed away, in his palace, at a normal age. The prince was the Genie. The Genie was the Prince.
>
> Learned music falls short of our desire.

Desire unsatisfied and desire ideally satisfied annihilate each other and produce a new being. But is not Rimbaud also saying, in that final gnomic statement, that art never succeeds in fully knowing human desire, that something in the creative process falls short of life's truth? One final example: the cosmic correlative to this Orphic Pan is in the verse poem "L'Eternité," where Rimbaud's image for eternity is the fusion of radiance with mobile matter (the "aurum potabile" of the alchemists, according to Enid Starkie):

> Elle est retrouvée!
> Quoi? l'éternité.
> C'est la mer mêlée
>   Au soleil. (236)

> It has been recovered!
> What? eternity.
> It is the sea mingled
>   With the sun.

(Another version of the same poem has "C'est la mer allée / Avec le soleil" [133].) Here the moment of total illumination is grasped as an intuition of eternity, and the liberation from temporal and human limitations is consummated:

> Donc tu te dégages
> Des humaines suffrages,
> Des communs élans!
> Tu voles selon . . . (237)

> Thus you cut loose
> From human opinions,
> From common strivings!
> And then you fly . . .

And this deliverance prepares the way for the invasion of happiness and the irresistible capitulation to its power in "Ô Saisons, ô châteaux!"

> Ah! Je n'aurais plus d'envie:
> Il [le bonheur] s'est chargé de ma vie.

> Ce charme a pris âme et corps
> Et dispersé les efforts. (238)

> Ah! I would be free from desire:
> [Happiness] has taken charge of my life.

> This charm has laid hold of soul and body
> And dispersed all effort.

In these songs of experience and innocence, Rimbaud did indeed achieve his own marriage of heaven and earth, self and nature. "Enfin, ô bonheur, ô raison, j'écartais du ciel l'azur, qui est du noir, et je vécus, étincelle d'or de la lumière *nature*" (236)—at last, o happiness, I drew aside the sky's azure, which is of a black hue, and I lived, a golden spark of *natural* light. But this is from *Une Saison en enfer*, which turns out to be not Rimbaud's marriage of heaven and hell, but of earth and hell.

The reasons for this volte-face are also in *Les Illuminations*. The examples above lie within the orbit of the Orphic, but the pull seems centrifugal; the ambivalences of the poems are proof of this. Music—poetry—does not really know or embrace our desire. Moreover, a large number of the poems in *Les Illuminations* are, in contrast to "Aube," nonparticipating visions; in them prince and genie remain distinct. In "Mystique," for instance, a miniature fresco depicting juxtaposed images of whirling angels, human beings in combat, and disastrous noises—and beyond them a "line of progress"—remains essentially detached from the observer, who is visited by a tranquillity that remains all his own to savor:

> Et, tandis que la bande en haut du tableau est formée de la rumeur tournante et bondissante des conques des mers et des nuits humaines,
>   La douceur fleurie des étoiles et du ciel et du reste descend en face du talus, comme un panier—contre notre face, et fait l'abîme fleurant et bleu là-dessous. (193)

> And, whereas the upper strip of the picture is made up of the whirling and leaping rumor of seashells and of human nights,
>   The flowering mildness of stars and sky and of all the rest comes down in front of the slope, like a basket—against our face, and makes the abyss flowering and blue beneath.

This is the same syndrome as that found in the eternity and happiness *yantras*—the feeling of being no longer of this world. In *Les Illuminations* the temptation of visionary detachment is most notable in Rimbaud's pervasive tendency to treat the world as a spectacle, a fairy-tale. Hence the key phrase of the work may be "J'ai seul le clé de cette parade sauvage" (180) (I alone have the clue to this savage parade)—the world offers itself as panorama and nourishment to the appetite of the beholder. That seems to be the meaning of the final section of the (surely autobiographical) poem "Jeunesse":

> Tu en es encore à la tentation d'Antoine. L'ébat du zèle écourté, les tics d'orgueil puéril, l'affaiblissement et l'effroi. Mais tu te mettras à ce travail: toutes les possibilités harmoniques et architecturales s'émouvront autour de ton siège. Des êtres parfaits, imprévus, s'offriront à tes expériences. Dans tes environs affluera rêveusement la curiosité d'anciennes foules et de luxes oisifs. Ta mémoire et tes sens ne seront que la nourriture de ton impulsion créatrice. Quant au monde, quand tu sortiras, que sera-t-il devenu? En tout cas, rien des apparences actuelles. (208)

> You are still no further along than the temptation of Anthony. The frolic of zeal curtailed, the twitchings of boyish pride, growing weak and frightened. But you will start doing this: all harmonic and architectural possibilities will begin stirring about your chair. Perfect, unexpected beings will volunteer for your experiments. The curiosity of old crowds and of idle luxuries will dreamily flow within your reach. Your memory

and your senses will merely be food for your creative impulse. As for the world, when you leave it, what will have become of it? In any case, nothing like present appearances.

But Rimbaud-St. Anthony does not overcome the demons; or, rather, he shifts his ground and storms hell directly in *Une Saison en enfer*. His quest is no longer for an innocence recovered ("l'éternité retrouvée"), but for a new kind of purity. And it appears from the Prologue to *Une Saison* that Rimbaud wishes to consider his past failures primarily as a springboard for a new celebration whose key will be charity—that is to say, an energy that will free him from his solipsism and restore him in some way to his "peasant" origins. After renouncing his former poetic alchemy, he exclaims disdainfully: "Cela s'est passé. Je sais aujourd'hui saluer la beauté" (All that is over now. Today I know how to salute beauty)—that same beauty, presumably, that in the Prologue he had taken upon his knees and insulted. The attitude is now different: he is no longer bound to her, but free to greet her—and possibly pass her by. It is not altogether clear from this statement whether Rimbaud wants to repudiate beauty or simply keep a respectful distance—this may account for his hesitation to break with poetry completely at the time of completing *Une Saison*.

Nevertheless, a new vision has already begun to sweep the old one aside. A few pages later, in the section prophetically and aptly entitled "L'Impossible," he exclaims

Ô pureté! pureté!
C'est cette minute d'éveil qui m'a donné la vision de la pureté!—Par l'esprit
    on va à Dieu!
Déchirante infortune! (240–241)

O purity! purity!
This minute of awakening has given me the vision of purity!—The way
    to God is through the spirit!
Lacerating misfortune!

With this, the old hell ("celui dont le fils de l'homme ouvrit les portes" (242)—the one whose gates the son of man opened) begins to fade away. The final resolve as sketched in the concluding sections of the work, "Matin" and "Adieu," envisages a new nativity that will dispense (presumably) the new charity: "Quand irons-nous, par delà les grèves et les monts, saluer la naissance du travail nouveau, la sagesse nouvelle, la fuite des tyrans et des démons, la fin de la superstition, adorer—les premiers!—Noël sur la terre!" (242)—When shall we go, past shores and mountains, to salute the birth of a new kind of work, a new kind of wisdom, the flight of tyrants and demons, the end of superstition, and adore—we the first ones—Christmas upon the earth! And the final conviction is "il me sera loisible de *posséder la vérité dans une âme et un corps*"—I shall be entitled to *possess truth in one soul and one body.*

But this no longer necessarily has anything to do with artistic creation. The quest for truth has displaced the pursuit of beauty; in fact, beauty and truth are no longer really compatible—or at least this is what Rimbaud decides subsequently.

J'ai créé toutes les fêtes, tous les triomphes, tous les drames. J'ai essayé d'inventer de nouvelles fleurs, de nouveaux astres, de nouvelles chairs, de nouvelles langues. J'ai cru acquérir des pouvoirs surnaturels. Eh bien! je dois enterrer mon imagination et mes souvenirs! Une belle gloire d'artiste et de conteur emportée! . . . Enfin, je demanderai pardon pour m'être nourri de mensonge. Et allons. (243)

I have created all feast, all triumphs, all dramas. I have tried to invent new flowers, new stars, new flesh, new tongues. I thought I had acquired supernatural powers. Very well! I must now bury my imagination and my memories. Such a splendid reputation of an artist and teller of tales gone with the wind! . . . So now I shall ask pardon for having fed on lies. Let's go.

This, then, is the final chapter of the Promethean and the Orphic Rimbaud. The only mythological resemblance with other poets of the symbolist epoch remains the Icarus figure, which both Baudelaire and Mallarmé cherished as emblems of the modern poet. But Rimbaud does not want to be the fallen Icarus as poet, but the Icarus who has hurtled back to earth and deliberately forgets his poetic astronautics. Without passing judgment on the remainder of his life, what remains is an incredible poetic journey through the regions of Prometheus and Orpheus into the realm of silence. In one of his prose poems ("Enfance") he wrote "Je suis maître du silence" (178)—I am a master of silence. That is not altogether so; he is more accurately describable as a master of the impossible. The real master of silence, Mallarmé, perfected his own calculus of linguistic impossibility (to borrow and alter a phrase of George Steiner) and remained profoundly Orphic, because in devising his own *alchimie du verbe* he reaffirmed the Orphic nobility of poetry in a new way. Rimbaud, on the other hand, aspired above all to project himself into a future of his own visionary devising at the expense of annihilating his past. His motto is, indeed, this startling phrase near the end of *Une Saison en enfer*: "Il faut être absolument moderne" (243)— being modern is absolutely necessary. Orpheus, reconciler of past and present, hell and heaven, body and soul, action and meditation, is no longer the guide here. The demons of action, creations of the modern psyche, have become too impatient; and the Mallarméan and Rilkean angels are in danger of being relegated to the periphery during the course of the twentieth century.

The historical and political conditions of the world between 1925 and 1945 tended to emphasize the public commitment of writers; but the past twenty years have been marked by a withdrawal inward once again. What this actually means is that the prevalent tendency in modern literature toward that "progressive colonization of inwardness," as Erich Heller calls it, is continuing, after a series of brief but significant forays into the outside world. One would expect the Orphic to reassert its hegemony successfully at this point. But such is not entirely the case.

The germs of the problem are embedded in Mallarmé. When, after his "nuits de Tournon" crisis, Mallarmé found *his* reconciliation of opposites in his negation of the *néant* and called it *le Beau*, he paved the way toward an aesthetic of structure that he himself was the first to explore and that all twentieth-century art, in its various ways, has followed. What seems to be missing in Mallarmé is a belief in the empirical validity of the Beautiful. There remains, even in the mystical Mallarmé, a strong substratum of the skepticism that had to some extent triggered the original crisis. The point here is not to raise the question of whether a notion of the Beautiful is valid if it is rooted in phenomenal experience, or whether the Beautiful can be predicated only in the noumenal experience, but whether our notion of the Orphic can still hold in the face of the Mallarméan vision. In Rilke, for instance, this problem does not arise: Rilke believed in the possibility of poetically reordering the universe and of reassembling the *disjecta membra*. For him, the world could be regenerated inwardly by the poetic afflatus. In this sense, Rilke is the *pure* Orphic poet of the modern epoch. But in Mallarmé, either as the result of a residual positivism or, better, an endemic Cartesianism, the new vision remains predominantly intellectual and aesthetically fertile, a kind of glorious schizophrenia. His countervailing sanity is due to a capacity to regard his work with a certain amount of irony and skepticism; this *côté Beckett de Mallarmé*, to use a Proustian formula, is perhaps the most elusive part of Mallarmé, more elusive even than his most difficult poems.

The monumentality of Mallarmé's difficulties becomes clear only with an understanding that in his poetry the problems raised by Hölderlin, Keats, and Baudelaire come to a head for the first time because for the first time they really collide in a spiritual void: the mind, now fully divested of its accumulated heritage, as in the experience of Igitur, attempts to project into the Nothingness its own theater of exquisite sensibilities. But this enterprise requires a new framework of language—a language that expresses silences and thereby remains caught in a paradox. For Hölderlin the "naming" of the gods still served a positive function, to keep alive the memory of the departed gods and to invest the night with its own plenitude. For Mallarmé, in contrast to Rilke, there is no interregnum: the nights at Tournon threatened for a while to become permanent. But whereas for the symbolists, as well as for Rilke, the problem of poetic discourse was still the attempt to find a workable set of linguistic correspondences for man and nature, in Mallarmé the emphasis shifts solely toward the integrity of language itself. The problem of the symbolic reference of language becomes the problem of language in a dialectical relationship with its opposite, silence. Mallarmé's solution of this dilemma is brilliant and heroic, but it leaves us with the question of whether the Orphic can be defined from his time onward as the reconciliation of man with language, rather than the reconciliation of man and world.

This problem embarrasses contemporary literature, whether one chooses to deal with it in terms of the Orphic tradition or not. With Mallarmé something subversive has crept into literature, a kind of suspicion—not quite in Nathalie Sarraute's sense, but related to it: can we trust literature? Can we trust language itself? This distrust is perhaps more apparent in some works of twentieth-century fiction than poetry: it is central to the work of both Kafka and Beckett. The two, because of their vision of a hopelessly fragmented and absurd universe, would surely render the Orphic obsolete were it not for the attempts of Maurice Blanchot to resurrect the Orphic attitude of the writer by reinterpreting it in light of a new understanding of literature in our time. Blanchot's studies take into account, centrally, the experience of Hölderlin, Mallarmé, Rilke, and Kafka and reassert the fundamentally *Orphic* quality of the act of (modern) writing itself.

Thus, the Orphic situation in the twentieth century is full of paradoxes; as observed earlier, this is characteristic of modern literature in general, and within the modern Orphic tradition from Nerval on. In the opening chapter of this book I divided the Orphic myth into three convenient moments: Orpheus the singer and harmonizer, the power of poetry; the descent into Hades coupled with the Eurydice motif, the *katábasis*; the emergence from Hades followed by the dismemberment, the *sparagmós*. The Eurydice motif was diminished by Mallarmé and Rilke in favor of the descent theme and this shift in interpretation accompanied by a new emphasis on the emerging *impersonal* voice of Orpheus. In order to discern the Orphic features of contemporary literature at all, one must seek them in the new quest for impersonal utterance. Here again, the Rimbaud of *Les Illuminations* and the poetry of Perse are of particular interest, along with the radically different development analyzed by Barthes in *Le Degré zéro de l'écriture*, which argues that there is in modern fiction a crisis marked by the exploration of this vanishing point in writing. Barthes[6] is aware of the Orphic qualities of the quest for neutral utterance in fiction—of Camus in *L'Etranger*, of Blanchot and Robbe-Grillet—and although this study has been exclusively concerned with poetry, its closing chapter must touch, albeit briefly, on this point.

As in the Renaissance, Orpheus appears to have reconquered a secure place in modern art and literature. He seems here to stay, though it is a little difficult to say in what guise or for what purpose; this study has noted a number of slightly varying roles he has played in poetry since 1800, and several further alterations will be commented on in this chapter. It seems safe to say that, as far as the poetry of the Romantic and symbolist periods is concerned, Orpheus occupied the place of a patron saint, as Ideal Bard and Great Unifier; and the history of that overwhelming segment of modern literature that grows out of the Romantic quest for unity and the symbolist thirst for correspondences—the literature of the "hedgehogs," to use Sir Isaiah Berlin's well-known distinction—can be said to be either directly or indirectly Orphic. In music, Orpheus left the operatic stage temporarily for the more frivolous and irreverent musical comedy atmosphere of Offenbach's *Orphée aux enfers*, only to regain a new dignity in Stravinsky's superb ballet *Orpheus* in 1946. Recent dramatic versions are Cocteau's *Orphée* (1925), Anouilh's *Eurydice* (1943), and Tennessee Williams' *Orpheus Descending* (1958); the last two are modernizations of the legend and of no particular interest here,[7] whereas Cocteau's streamlining of the theme represents at least a serious attempt to state the situation of the contemporary poet. Cocteau's play and his two films, *Orphée* (1950) and *Le Testament d'Orphée* (1963), focus on the poet's dilemma (nonsense versus sense, the temptation of the supernatural versus everyday reality) and on the necessity of the descent, followed by an apotheosis; they summarize the myth's outline without modifying our comprehension of the materials. Other modernizations of the legend, such as Marcel Camus's film *Orfeu negro* (1958), in which realistic elements are blended with popular folklore, are likely to set the pace for future theatrical and cinematic versions of the theme.

To return to the lyric poets after Mallarmé and Rilke: Valéry, Mallarmé's foremost disciple, might have been expected to carry on the Orphic ambitions of his master, but it turns out that he is not really concerned with an *explication orphique de la Terre*, but with the complex inter-relationships within the layers of consciousness. To put it succinctly, Valéry's exemplary heroes are Monsieur Teste, and his own Faust, not the Mallarméan Orphic-solar hero whether in the guise of faun, swan, clown, or master of shipwreck. The only real point of thematic intersection between Mallarmé and Valéry involves the figure of Narcissus, highly important in Valéry's development. But it should be added that Valéry's self-contemplators—Narcissus, "La Jeune Parque," the first-person speaker of "Le Cimetière marin," Monsieur Teste, and Faust—are fascinated by the encounter of the mind with the phenomenal world, whereas the Mallarméan Narcissus figure (who actually appears only up to "Hérodiade" and "L'Après-midi d'un faune") is frustrated by the glass partition separating illusion from reality.

The theme of Orpheus does occur in Valéry's early poetry, but only as an "architectural" Orpheus, that is, as Amphion. An early essay (1891) entitled "Paradoxe sur l'architecte" begins "Autrefois, aux siècles orphiques, l'esprit soufflait sur le marbre"[8]—long ago, in the Orphic ages, the spirit breathed upon marble—and concludes with an apostrophe to Orpheus. Despite the typographical prose arrangement it is really a sonnet written in alexandrines, and the following quotations comprise the concluding sestet:

Il chante! assis au bord du ciel splendide, Orphée! Son oeuvre se revêt d'un vespéral trophée, et sa lyre divine enchante les porphyres, car le temple érigé par ce *musicien* unit la sûreté des rythmes anciens à l'âme immense du grand hymne sur la lyre![9]

He sings! seated at the rim of the splendid sky, Orpheus! His work clothes itself in an evening trophy, and his divine lyre enchants the porphyry, for the temple erected by this *musician* unites the steadiness of the old rhythms to the immense soul of the great hymn on the lyre!

This earlier version provides the basis for the more accomplished sonnet "Orphée" in the *Album de vers anciens*; note that in this later version the specific

term "musician" has been eliminated, though the vision of Orpheus the builder
has in no way been altered:

> . . . Je compose en esprit, sous les myrtes, Orphée
> L'Admirable! . . . Le feu, des cirques purs descend;
> Il change le mont chauve en auguste trophée
> D'où s'exhale d'un dieu l'acte retentissant.
>
> Si le dieu chante, il rompt le site tout-pouissant;
> Le soleil voit l'horreur du mouvement des pierres;
> Une plainte inouïe appelle éblouissants
> Les hauts murs d'or harmonieux d'un sanctuaire.
>
> Il chante, assis au bord du ciel splendide, Orphée!
> Le roc marche, et trébuche; et chaque pierre fée
> Se sent un poids nouveau qui vers l'azur délire!
>
> D'un temple à demi nu le soir baigne l'essor,
> Et soi-même il s'assemble et s'ordonne dans l'or
> A l'âme immense du grand hymne sur la lyre![10]

> . . . I compose in my mind, under the myrtles, Orpheus
> The Admirable! . . . The fire comes down from amphitheaters;
> It changes the bare mountain into an august trophy
> Breathing forth the resounding deed of a god.
>
> If the god sings, he breaks site all-powerful;
> The sun sees horrified the motion of stones;
> An unheard-of lament summons dazzling
> The high harmonious golden walls of a sanctuary.
>
> He sings, seated at the rim of the splendid sky, Orpheus!
> The rock moves and stumbles; and each stone, fairy-like,
> Feels itself a new weight madly aspiring toward the blue!
>
> The evening bathes the upward thrust of a half-naked temple,
> And all by itself it falls into place and takes form in the golden glow
> For the immense soul of the great hymn on the lyre!

The mood of the sonnet is obviously closer to *Eupalinos* than to the more Mallarméan *L'Ame et la danse*.

Valéry wrote a "mélodrame" entitled *Amphion* (with a score by Honegger) for Ida Rubenstein that was performed in 1931. This short work is primarily a scenic arrangement of the Orphic awakening of nature and its arrangement into temple and citadel; Valéry's *Amphion* is a servant of Apollo.

> Apollon me possède, il sonne dans ma voix,
> Il vient soi-même édifier son Temple,
> Et la Cité qui doit paraître aux yeux des hommes
> Est déjà toute conçue étincelante
> Dans les Hautes Demeures des Immortels![11]

> I am possessed by Apollo, he sounds in my voice,
> He comes himself to edify his Temple,
> And the city which is to appear to men's eyes
> Is already conceived scintillating
> In the High Dwellings of the Immortals!

But on the whole, *Amphion* is disappointing, all the more so because Valéry surely had a great deal more to say on the subject of Orpheus-Amphion. A letter to Debussy written in 1900 only serves to whet one's appetite concerning a plan of collaboration never realized: "J'avais songé incidemment au Mythe d'Orphée, c'est-à-dire l'animation de toute chose par un esprit—la fable même de la mobilité et de l'arrangement"[12]—I had thought incidentally of the Myth of Orpheus, that is to say the animation of everything by a spirit—the very fable of mobility and arrangement. A much later notebook jotting reminds one that Valéry, even as late as 1920, still stood in a particular relationship to Orpheus, a relationship he never elaborated: "Orphée. O divinité familière. A chaque ennui, je me tourne vers toi. Sans retard. [Songe que dans cet esprit si libre, tu tiens la place d'une idole.]"[13] (Orpheus. O familiar deity. In every troubled moment, I turn toward you. Without delay. [Imagine that in a mind so free, you occupy the place of an idol.]) Valéry's free mind seduced by the idol of Orpheus! But Valéry, like Lord Bacon, preferred to avoid idols; and one might say that his Orphic impulses were channeled and subdued finally into the twin dialogues *Eupalinos* and *L'Ame et la danse*, of 1923–1924:—the celebration of architectonic form and of the *acte pur des metamorphoses*, the *pure* act, not the metamorphosis itself.

The nineteenth and early twentieth centuries may be characterized as having in one way created an Orphic atmosphere on the Continent, particularly in France and Germany. This accounts for the fact that "Orpheus" and "Orphic" have become convenient and often useful bywords for poets who wish to re-generate poetry in a world of materialism and technology, or for those eager to narrow the gap between poetry and science or religion and science. These more or less traditional features of modern Orphism are by now familiar from the survey conducted in the previous chapters. Apollinaire's early poem sequence *Cortège d'Orphée*, and a number of references scattered throughout his poems to Orpheus or Orphic themes, are the result of his immersion in occultist readings and his general familiarity with the illuministic tradition. Moreover, by virtue of his lively interest in painting and his activities as a promoter of innovations in art, Apollinaire had intimate contacts with Robert Delaunay's Orphicism in painting and Henri Barzun's Orphic movement initiated in 1913. Similarly, Jules Supervielle, possibly as a result of his friendship with Rilke, manifested an occasional interest in the Orpheus theme.[14] Outside of France, George Trakl and Hermann Broch have written poems celebrating Orpheus;[15] and in Italy, Dino Campana's *Canti orfici* (1914) bridges the gap between the neoclassical and impressionist poetry of Carducci and D'Annunzio, on the one hand, and the more intimate and compressed poetic experiments of Ungaretti, Montale, and Quasimodo, on the other.

The most striking treatment of the Orpheus theme in France toward the end of the thirties and the early forties is to be found in Pierre-Jean Jouve's *Matière céleste* (1937) and in the cycle of poems entitled *Tombeau d'Orphée* (1941) by Jouve's foremost disciple Pierre Emmanuel. Both poets are descendants of Baudelaire: they share his religious anguish, their fiercely erotic disposition comes into full conflict with the Pascalian dimension of their temperaments, and, somewhat in contrast to Baudelaire, they are intensely involved in the historical and political torments of their time. For both the Orphic descent constitutes a crucial but transitional experience; and it is evident that the Orphic interpreta-tion of this experience owes a great deal to the disclosure of the Orphic context and content of Romantic literature, particularly of German Romanticism as revealed by Albert Béguin's *L'Ame romantique et le rêve*. Consequently, Jouve and Emmanuel really prolong and modify the Orphism of Novalis and Nerval, rather than that of Mallarmé and Rilke. This is not to say, however, that Jouve and Emmanuel represent a resurgence of Romanticism. Jouve's criticism of Nerval is astute:

Notre rêve diffère de celui qui inspira les Romantiques. Le rêve romantique brode, autour de la masse crépusculaire, des mythes et des spéculations philosophiques. Nerval écrit "Ne pas offenser la pudeur des divinités du songe"—Nerval déclare alors censurer le principal surgissement, qui est l'érotique.[16]

Our dream differs from the one that inspired the Romantics. The romantic dream weaves myths and philosophical speculations around crepuscular materials. Nerval writes "Do not offend the modesty of the dream deities"—in this way he purports to censure their major drive, which is eroticism.

This represents an understanding of the Romantic dream of life elucidated and at the same time exacerbated by a knowledge of modern depth psychology.

The Orphic experience in Jouve gains strength on the battlefield of Eros and Thanatos, a battlefield located within the confines of Hell and Nothingness. The tripartite division of *Matière céleste*—"Hélène," Nada," and "Matière céleste"— represents a personal erotic experience, a pilgrim's progress, and the *via dolorosa* of the poet: Faust, St. John of the Cross, and Orpheus combined. All of the poet's erotic yearnings for his dead mistress Hélène[17] are recapitulated, merged with the theme of Nothingness ("Le thème Nada, ou de l'Absence, m'a profondément hanté et poursuivi"[18]—the Nada theme, the theme of Absence, has deeply haunted and pursued me), and finally transmuted into an Orphic apotheosis in which Hélène becomes Eurydice. This final transmutation constitutes the *matière céleste* toward which the various poems in the collection had been tending. In a wider sense, the Orphic poems at the end of the section denote a new and higher stage in Jouve's evolution as a poet, sketched out as early as 1928 in his preface to *Les Noces*, in which the note of renewal echoes both Dante and Nerval:

Cet ouvrage porte l'épigraphe "Vita nuova" parce qu'il témoigne d'un conversion à l'idée religieuse la plus inconnue, la plus haute et la plus humble et tremblante, celle que nous pouvons à peine concevoir en ce temps-ci, mais hors laquelle notre vie n'a point d'existence.[19]

This work bears the epigraph "Vita nuova" because it testifies to a conversion to the most unknown, the highest and the humblest and most fearsome religious idea, one which we can hardly conceive of in our time, but outside of which our life has no existence at all.

This note of affirmation in a devaluated world gives the Orpheus poems in the collection their special poignancy; the Orphic lyre is no longer intact.

Une harpe ayant plusieurs cordes brisées
Mais résistante de douleur et d'or sur le fond bleu
Acharnée, et des mains suspendues des mains coupées
Touchent en pleurant les accords,
Il se fait parfois des sons si expirants
Il s'ouvre en cet instant des volcans si terribles
Et tant de mâle ciel est architectural
Avec le calme et l'éternelle nudité,
Que c'est la voie l'ineffable voie la voie trouvée.[20]

A harp having several broken strings
But resistant with grief and with gold on the blue background
Intent, and hands suspended hands cut
Strike weeping the chords,
Sometimes sounds so expiring are made
At that moment volcanoes so terrifying are opened
And so much male sky is architectural
With the calm and the eternal nakedness
That it is the way the ineffable way the way found.

In keeping with the mood of dejection, the Maenads come to resemble more and more the sinister and destructive forces that characterize Europe of the late thirties:

Ménades retentissantes organisées
Vous qui occupez les sommets des crêtes
De ce monde inhumain qui n'aime plus l'amour
Estuaires de guerre aux cuisses écartées
Ménades de sommeil qui hurlez à la mort
Du chanteur, furies d'or et d'autorité
Mes soeurs soyez armées soyez nues soyez ivres
Dévorez ce que mon coeur vous a créé.[21]

Resounding organized Maenads
You who dwell on the summits of the crests
Of this inhuman world that no longer loves love
Estuaries of war with your thighs spread apart
Maenads of sleep who clamor for the death
Of the singer, furies of gold and authority
My sisters be armed be naked be drunk
Devour what my heart has created for you.

Emmanuel's mythical self-awareness is more intense than Jouve's; in an early essay, "Le Poete et le mythe," he gives a Mallarméan definition of the poet's mission but repudiates Mallarméan nihilism:

Le poète, d'instinct, abolit l'objet, et rend la chose à son silence, qui est l'antique respiration du tout. Il rétablit ainsi dans le monde une innocence et un néant: innocence, puisque le monde se retrouve antérieur à la parole, et néant, puisque la parole (ne fût-ce que temporairement) en est exclue. Ce faisant, le poète abîme, avec une hardiesse étonnante le fossé qui séparait l'homme du monde. Homme, il ne peut inverser le sens du temps; et de la contradiction entre l'acte originel, l'acte *seul* qu'il vient d'accomplir, en rendant la matière aux eaux primordiales, et sa nature coupable, limitée, accablée d'histoire, naît l'orgueilleuse nostalgie du pur néant, volonté d'être le Dieu créateur, qui sur les eaux retient le Verbe prêt à fondre . . .[22]

The poet instinctively abolishes the object and returns the thing to its silence, which is the ancient respiration of the whole. Thus he re-establishes in the world an innocence and a nothingness: an innocence, because the world recovers itself anterior to speech; and a nothingness, because speech (even if temporarily) is excluded. In doing this, the poet swallows up with an astounding audacity the gulf that separated man from the world. As a man, he cannot invert the sense of time; and from the contradiction between the original act, the *sole* act that he has just accomplished by returning matter to its primordial waters, and the guilty, limited, and history-dominated nature of the act, there arises the sovereign nostalgia for pure nothingness, the will to be God the creator, who holds the Word poised in readiness over the waters . . .

The poet is defined as beginning with "things"; here again, despite Emmanuel's demonstrable admiration for Rilke, the definition of "things" is not immanent-istic, as in the *Duino Elegies*, but transcendental. "La chose en effet n'est le monde que dans l'absolue vision de Dieu, non dans celle contingente de l'homme"— Things in effect are the world only in God's absolute vision, not in man's contingent vision; and "Le poète part de la chose, ou plus exactement de l'angoisse qu'il éprouve devant elle: angoisse qui révèle la présence du mystère, sans parvenir à la cerner"[23]—The poet begins with things, or rather with the anguish he experiences in the face of things: an anguish revealing the presence of the mystery, without being able to encompass it. Myth is, for Emmanuel, the attempt to close the gap between human limitation and divine absolute. Thus the poet readily assumes the stance of the mythical hero: "le *mythe* résume, avec une concision admirable, l'expérience ténébreuse du genre humain"[24]—myth is an admirably concise résumé of the shadowy experience of mankind. Thus each one of us tends to transform certain key events of his life into myth. The examples Emmanuel cites are, not unexpectedly, Novalis and Nerval: "il est possible d'avancer que le mythe d'Orphée a été consommé, consciemment ou non, et sous des dehors différents, par Novalis et Nerval"[25]—it is possible to maintain that the myth of Orpheus was consummated, consciously or unconsciously, and under different guises, by Novalis and Nerval.

Quinconque a du mythe quelqu'il soit une expérience religieuse, reconnaît en lui le climat naturel—quoique défendu—de l'homme: dans l'énergie de la parole primitive, toutes choses, réintégrées dans leur ordre, deviennent les signes tangibles de la création en marche. Ainsi, organisant le monde suivant le plan de sa propre destinée, et réarticulant toute chose dans son être et son devenir, le poète peut prétendre à une vision très nouvelle et très ancienne, celle sans doute sous-jacente à tout accroissement possible de sa pensée.[26]

Whoever has a religious experience of any myth whatsoever recognizes in it the natural —though forbidden—climate of man in it: in the energy of primitive speech all things, reintegrated into their order, become tangible signs of creation moving on. Thus, organizing the world according to the plan of his own destiny, and rearticulating everything in its being and its becoming, the poet may claim a very new and a very old vision, no doubt that vision that underlies any possible growth of his mind.

In Emmanuel's own case, the Orphic myth is the substratum of his own poetic development—a quest for a religious, moral, and poetic unity ("le goût de l'Un," to use his later phrase), which links him to the Orphic tradition of Novalis, Nerval, and Jouve (rather than that of Mallarmé and Rilke), reinforced by the powerful poetic imaginations of Hölderlin and Claudel. In Emmanuel's instance, as in Jouve's, the religious and ethical conflict precipitated by a sense of the incompatibility of flesh and spirit is aggravated by a prolonged struggle with Manicheanism, particularly via Pascal and Baudelaire. And here too, as in Jouve's experience, a lost love shades off inexorably into a Eurydice figure and stands at the turning point of a personal and spiritual crisis.[27] But Emmanuel's treatment of the Orpheus myth, though deeply indebted to Jouve and sharing with his mentor's poetry an almost frantic preoccupation with the erotic, is more intricate inasmuch as it involves a number of complex psychological and religious elements. In an essay entitled "Erotique et poésie" Emmanuel admits the presence of an Oedipal drama within his work and a preoccupation with resolving the problem of duality by way of the androgyne.[28]

L'autre sexe est le médiateur vers un être autre, analogue non pas de tout autre, mais du *Tout Autre* en lequel, et avec lequel, parachever l'Identité. Tout rapport érotique est une relation à trois où l'absolu est l'un des partenaires. Relation ambivalente—donc poétique —par excellence, qui fait de l'érotique et du religieux la source et la fin de la poésie.[29]

The other sex is the mediator toward another kind of being, analogous not to any other but to the *Wholly Other*, in which and with which to achieve Identity. Every erotic relationship is a three-way relation in which the absolute is one of the partners. It is the ambivalent—and thus poetic—relation par excellence which makes the erotic and the religious the source and the end of poetry.

This mystique, drawn from the medieval mystics and filtered through Karl Barth, is further complicated by an ingenious and highly ambiguous correlation-substitution of Eurydice and Christ. The author himself has tried[30] to elucidate this unusual mythical intuition:

Ma poésie part de deux images-mères, surgies ensemble vers ma vingt-deuxième année . . .
   La première image est celle du Christ au tombeau, entre le Vendredi Saint et Pâques. Image de chute où l'être se défait, ni mort ni vivant, livré à l'angoisse. Soudain le Verbe se concentre en lui, le crie hors du chaos intérieur et de la tombe. En même temps, ses plaies se remettent à saigner. La deuxième image—également de chute—est celle d'Orphée aux enfers. Il tombe et descend: à la fois de gré et de force. Il croit saisir Eurydice, et tout au fond c'est le Christ qu'il saisit, qui le saisit. Avec et dans le Christ, Orphée meurt et ressuscite: résurrection qui lui coûte Eurydice, abandonée par amour aux bras du Christ. Cette image, surgie quelques mois après la première, en présente une version plus complexe, sexualisée, donc contradictoire et obscure, qui annonce et aussitôt dérobe une rivalité en triangle, à la fois érotique et sacrée.[31]

My poetry has its starting point in two matrix images, which came into being together when I was about twenty-two . . .
   The first image is that of Christ in the tomb, between Good Friday and Easter. It is the image of a fall in which being disintegrates, neither alive nor dead, delivered up to anguish. Suddenly the Word becomes concentrated in him, proclaims him out of the inner chaos and out of the tomb. At the same time, his wounds begin to bleed again. The second image—also of a fall—is that of Orpheus in hell. He falls and descends: simultaneously of his own will and under compulsion. He thinks he takes hold of Eurydice, and in actuality it is Christ whom he takes hold of, who takes hold of him. With and in Christ, Orpheus dies and is reborn: resurrection which costs him Eurydice, abandoned by love into the arms of Christ. That image, which came into being several months after the first one, offers a more complex and sexual version of the former one,

and consequently a more contradictory and more obscure one which announces and immediately withdraws a triangular rivalry that is both erotic and sacred.

Actually, this amounts to a compounding of the Orphic descent theme and the Harrowing of Hell: the Christian theme provides a setting of total occlusion, of a real death of God, within the context of the Easter Story and thus enlarges the psychic and erotic meaning of the Orphic quest for Eurydice. The fusion of Orpheus and Christ is already foreshadowed in the poem "La Pierre du sépulcre" of *Le Poète et son Christ* (1938).

> Pour l'amant
> reste le seuil béant et la nocturne aurore
> reste le cri de la naissance informulé
> reste la charité de l'Enfer à ses pieds
> car le sépulcre ouvert j'avance entre ses roches
> puisqu'il est le chemin unique dit Orphée.[32]

> For the lover
> there remains the gaping threshold and the nocturnal dawn
> there remains the unformulated birth-cry
> there remains the Charity of hell at his feet
> the sepulcher now that it is open, I move forward between its stones
> since it is the one and only way says Orpheus.

The cycle of poems *Le Tombeau d'Orphée* constitutes a psychodrama enacted by Orpheus, Eurydice, and Christ along the mythical lines of force discussed above. Eva Kushner characterizes it as "a long poetic development based on the spiritual experience of the myth" and "a continued revery at the frontiers of the unconscious life, where life and myth are one and the same thing."[33] A certain prolixity and diffuseness blur the outlines of the mythical pattern, but a number of key moments can be isolated. First, here are the juxtaposition of Eurydice and Christ and Orpheus' transfer of Eurydice to Christ:

> Mais la Femme cachée derrière son dieu mort
> Orphée souffre la mort de dieu par pur blasphème.
>
> . . .
>
> Alors
> Orphée avec fureur pénètre au corps de dieu
> il traverse la Faute, et sent la mort du Christ

roidir ses membres,
mais va et chante

. . .

Mais son chant

maintenant tient la bien-aimée ô jeu ancien.
Qu'importe: elle perdue toujours, elle adorable
absence! il l'a livrée au ténébreux époux
pour le sang noir d'une journée d'amour: Orphée la couche
entre les bras du jeune Christ—et vus d'en-haut
il les aime, et jouit de sa mort qui les crée
il jouit! de les voir noués et ruisselants
d'infamie et de gloire, et morts la bien-aimée
qui n'est plus sienne, en son amant d'ivoire.[34]

But Woman hidden behind her dead god
Orpheus suffers the death of god by pure blasphemy.

. . .

Then
Orpheus with fury penetrates to the body of god
he passes across Sin, and feels the death of Christ
stiffening his limbs
but goes and sings

. . .

But his song

now holds the beloved, oh play as of old.
What does it matter: she, lost forever, she, adorable
absence! he has given her up to the shadowy bridegroom
for the black blood of a day's love: Orpheus lays her down
between the arms of the young Christ, and seen from above
he loves them and rejoices in his death which creates them
he rejoices! to see them entwined and moist
with infamy and glory, and dead! the beloved one
who is no longer his, and her ivory lover.

The scene marks the peripeteia of the sacred drama of Orpheus from negation to affirmation: blasphemy into glorification, *eros* into *agápe*, death into resurrection, silence into song. The androgyny theme obtrudes itself at this moment:

O abîme je suis et non sexe!

ma chair

se bat avec les armes folles du désir
dans le passé mué en femme où je suis nu
et dans l'Orphée futur où la femme est renée,[35]

Oh abyss I am and not sexual power!

                                                    my flesh
fights with the mad weapons of desire
in the past transmuted into woman, in which I am naked
and into the future Orpheus in whom the woman is reborn,

and

Un double enchantement liait en un seul corps
deux contraires violences, deux sciences
science d'enfantement et de soumission
enseignée inlassablement par les montagnes
et, signifiée par le couteau d'un sexe mâle
science de mort ou criminelle adoration.[36]

A double enchantment bound into a single body
two contrary violences, two ways of knowing
the knowledge of giving birth and of submission
taught untiringly by the mountains
and, signified by the blade of a male sex
knowledge of death or criminal adoration.

Emmanuel is fully aware of the psychoanalytical ramifications of his particular version of the Orpheus myth and regards his particular treatment as an inevitable phenomenon of adolescent sexuality. "Le mythe d'Orphée, avec son érotique et sa spiritualité juvéniles, est secrètement androgyne et souvent homosexuel. L'inhibition qui frappe le rapport unitaire avec l'Autre—cette rivale de Dieu *par définition*—est tournée par la rêverie homosexuelle, le Même s'identifiant à un Autre-Même pour se pénétrer et se saturer d'identité."[37] (The myth of Orpheus, with its juvenile eroticism and spirituality, is secretly androgynous and often homosexual. The inhibition that strikes the unitary relation with the Other—that rival of God *by definition*—is inverted by homosexual revery, the Same identifying himself with Another-Same in order to penetrate and saturate himself with identity.) Accordingly, the Orphic theme retreats into the background after *Tombeau d'Orphée* and a number of subsidiary poems in *Orphiques* (1942); its principal function in Emmanuel's poetic development was to master a crisis of youth, to effect a *rite de purification*. Similarly, it represents a major stage on life's way for Emmanuel: a transition from the Catharist religion of his earlier years toward the more resolutely incarnational position of his later poems. The Catharistic obstacles in *Tombeau d'Orphée* are so powerful that Emmanuel is compelled to renounce his Eurydice more resolutely than another Christian poet, Paul Claudel, is forced in *Partage de midi* to have his hero Mesa reject Ysé. Mrs. Kushner observes astutely that "Orpheus' tomb is the Female."[38] The final triumph of Emmanuel's Orpheus is the triumph over youth, a total regeneration and possession of *la Parole*.

> Le pur poète
> né du Christ et de l'aimée
> dans la fruition d'une aube effroyable,
> franchit le seuil de la durée incorruptible sans
> voir abolir, sous le tonnerre de ses pas
> foulant la gloire! la tombe antique et le seigneur
> qu'il incarna trois jours dans la matrice vierge
> de celle qui jamais ne fut.
>   . . .
> Lui, rejetant le lin des morts gravit l'aurore
> et marche vers la Chair promise à l'Orient,
> enfance grave! un seul jet d'eau troublant le cours
> de son destin
> aux déchirants déserts de la jeunesse
> ranime le secret.[39]

> The pure poet
> born of Christ and the loved one
> in the fruition of a frightful dawn,
> crosses the threshold of incorruptible duration without
> seeing abolished, under the thunder of his steps
> trampling on glory! the ancient tomb and the lord
> which it incarnated for three days in the virgin womb
> of her who never was.
>   . . .
> He, throwing off the linen cloth of the dead climbs the dawn
> and strides toward the promised Flesh in the East,

> heavy childhood! a single jet of water dimming the course
> of his destiny
> in the lacerating deserts of youth
> reawakens the secret.

The poetry of Jouve and Emmanuel bears witness to the continuing vitality of the Orphic theme in the most troubled years of this century. It has been remarked that both poets attempt to transcend the narrower limitations of the theme by striving for an integration with the harrowing responsibilities of life beset by warfare and mendacity, on the outside, and confusion and anguish on the inside. Perhaps it is significant that for neither one does the Orpheus theme supply a full-scale program of regeneration; it is therefore relegated to the more modest task of preparing the way out of self-division into unification. The same problem has evidently troubled other major writers of the epoch; for a while, in the thirties and early forties, it seemed that writers such as Malraux and Sartre on one hand and the surrealists on the other were more attracted to Promethean attitudes. Certainly Sartre's *Les Mouches* (1943) suggests the necessity of de-throning a tyrannical Jupiter in order to enable man to forge his own destiny. More apropos, Camus' early writings (*Les Noces*, *L'Envers et l'endroit*) are born out of passionate desire to celebrate a harmony between nature and man, which collides face to face with death and absurdity and thus brings on a shift from an abortive pantheism to an existentialistic dualism—an Orphic impulse perverted, or converted, into an attitude of rebellion that seeks to regenerate the "fallen" Prometheus.[40]

An even more drastic rejection of Orpheus can be found in Nikos Kazantza-kis' *Odyssey: A Modern Sequel* (1938), which reaches back to the theme of Orpheus' participation in the Argonautic voyage, albeit in modified form, and places him once more in the company of Odysseus. The quest is not for the Golden Fleece, but for a total integration of all the contraries—matter and spirit, life and death, intellect and intuition, being and becoming. One would expect Orpheus to be the hero of such an enterprise, but Kazantzakis assigns all the superhuman potential to his Odysseus, who is both sensualist and ascetic and a follower of both Bergson and Buddha. Orpheus, by contrast, is reduced to the role of an accompanying musician and aesthete, contemptuously referred to as "the piper," who is sooner or later left behind as misguided and irrelevant. As a matter of fact, from the very beginning he is characterized as a comic figure:

> . . . one with a lean cricket's shape and pointed head,
> his reed pipe stuck under his arm. . . .   (I, 951–952)

and

> the piper sighed, then wedged his flute between his lips,
> trilled twice or thrice in air, summoned his wandering mind
> till his small cross-eyes were with distant rapture glazed.
>   (III, 80–82)

In one of the epic's central episodes Orpheus is assigned the task of carving out an idol which he is to offer to a tribe of African Negroes in recompense for food needed by Odysseus and his crew. Orpheus poses so successfully as a witch doctor that he is hypnotized by his own priestliness and ecstatically worships the wooden image he has fabricated. He remains with the tribe, a false priest in a benighted community, while his companions move on.

In addition to the repudiation of Orpheus there is his negation, implied by the work of those writers in whom silence becomes a kind of end product of the literary process. The Orphic silence is something else: it is the poetic voice that temporarily ceases singing in the face of Nothingness, only to embrace a new gamut that will henceforward "echo" this silence, but *in song*. In other words, the Orphic, no matter what its particular shape in the hands of different poets, *presupposes the possibility of song and the relevance of poetry* to the life of the individual soul and the community. The new kind of silence, proceeding on one hand out of Rimbaud's refusal to write and, on the other, out of Mallarmé's systematic effort to reduce poetry to sheer suggestivity and immateriality, is caught up in the paradox of a literature no longer able to believe in itself fully, much less to affirm itself. This paradoxical situation, the most striking expressions of which are to be found in the work of Kafka and Beckett (and in a lesser way in Robbe-Grillet), marks a total discrepancy between the written word and the realities that written words traditionally have referred to. In Kafka the divorce is not as yet total; but Kafka's works are enigmatic precisely because they seem to refer to a world of familiar realities that are alienated from us (and we from them), but actually because the phenomenal world constitutes a monstrous screen that prevents us from apprehending the reality concealed behind it and within ourselves. In Beckett the process is carried still farther, since the apprehending self (which in Kafka still represents a unifying element, or at least the quest for an integral understanding) is fragmented into disembodied units to the point of atomization. Here then, language is no longer an instrument approximating silence; it has become a deafening and tedious, yet poignant, equivalent of the silence itself.

Of the various crises of language that writers and critics have commented upon, this is surely the most radical and central. It is not per se an abdication from literature altogether—in a contradictory sort of way, it represents an *à rebours* tribute to the art of writing—but a seemingly inevitable phase that contemporary literature must pass through if it is to survive. In this sense, the crisis is analogous to the crises of music and painting in our time, for it could be said that the arts in the twentieth century have been embarked upon an intensive exploration of origins as well as limits. In a way, this new quest for redefinition of the nature and purpose of the creative process has certain elements in common with the Orphic quest; one might go so far as to call it, in part, the final outcome of a number of problems brought to the surface by nineteenth- and twentieth-century Orphism. A number of critics, many of them apologists for contemporary nihilistic styles, have addressed themselves to this problem recently. Roland Barthes, who formulates the problem in terms of a "zero point of writing" and links it to the deterioration of bourgeois culture, writes:

Partie d'un néant où la pensée semblait s'élever sur le décor des mots, l'écriture a ainsi traversé tous les états d'une solidification progressive: d'abord objet d'un regard, puis d'un faire, et enfin d'un meurtre, elle atteint aujourd'hui un dernier avatar, l'absence: dans ces écritures neutres, appelés ici "le degré zéro de l'écriture," on peut facilement désarmer le mouvement même d'une négation, et l'impuissance à accomplir dans une durée, comme si la Littérature, tendant depuis un siècle à transmuer sa surface dans une forme sans hérédité, ne trouvait plus de pureté que dans l'absence de tout signe, proposant enfin l'accomplissement de ce rêve orphéen: un écrivain sans Littérature. L'écriture blanche, celle de Camus, celle de Blanchot ou de Cayrol, par exemple, ou l'écriture parlée de Queneau, c'est le dernier épisode d'une Passion de l'écriture, qui suit pas à pas le déchirement de la conscience bourgeoise.[41]

Proceeding out of a nothingness from which thought seemed to rise above the ornament of words, writing has thus gone through all the stages of a progressive solidification: first as the object of contemplation, then of action, and finally of murder, and today it has reached its final avatar, absence: in these neuter writings called here the "zero degree of writing," the very movement of negation may be easily disarmed as well as the impotence to accomplish within a space of time, as if Literature, after striving for a century to transmute its surface into a form without heredity, could no longer find purity except in the absence of any sign whatsoever, thus proposing at last the accomplishment of that Orphic dream: a writer without Literature. Blank writing, that of Camus, that of Blanchot or of Cayrol, for example, or the speech-oriented writing of Queneau, are the final episode in the Passion of writing as it follows on the heels of the collapse of the bourgeois consciousness.

This statement, deeply indebted to the reflections of Maurice Blanchot, leads to the heart of the contemporary problem of Orpheus.

The most original transformation of the Orpheus theme in the twentieth century occurs in the thought of Maurice Blanchot. Blanchot, generally classified as a critic, is actually an independent thinker whose primary concern is with the ontological situation of the work of literature in our time: he is haunted by the *being* of the work of art and its ambiguous relation to the artist and to the reader. Blanchot's inquiry begins with "Comment la litterature est-elle possible?" —a long essay written in 1942 and reprinted in *Faux Pas*—and he proposes a series of answers in subsequent critical-philosophical writings (*L'Espace littéraire*, 1955, and *Le Livre à venir*, 1959). In close but somewhat uneasy conjunction with Blanchot the essayist there is Blanchot the artist, who has been writing fiction since the end of the thirties, novels and, most recently, *récits*. Among the most inaccessible of contemporary fictional works, they are at the same time remarkably original: abstract narratives of great precision and purity, projections of certain states of mind investigated discursively in Blanchot's essays. In many ways, Blanchot continues the tradition of the French *récit* from Madame de Lafayette and Constant's *Adolphe* into the present, but by transforming the *récit* along lines foreshadowed by Mallarmé's ontological autobiography, *Igitur*.

Blanchot's beginnings as a writer of fiction go back to the early thirties (the first version of *Thomas l'obscur* was begun in 1932, though the novel was not published until 1941). There is, at first glance, a superficial affinity with the surrealistic novel of that epoch in what appears as his concern with states of fantasy; and a number of readers have noted an affinity with Kafka, especially in the longer early novels *Aminadab* (1942) and *Le Très-Haut* (1948).[42] But these early assimilations of surrealism and Kafka are merely parts of a much larger intellectual culture. Blanchot's literary masters are Hölderlin, Mallarmé, Kafka, and Rilke; his philosophical antecedents are Hegel, Nietzsche, and Heidegger (particularly the latter, whose impact has been dominant in determining the course of his ontological inquiry about existence and art).

With this parallel formation, Blanchot is superbly equipped to raise the problem of Orpheus in our time. He is thoroughly familiar with the new Orphic tradition from Novalis on; and the context of his thought is the anguish of the world depleted of the sacred (Hölderlin, Mallarmé, Kafka), coupled with the resolution to restructure being and, along with it, the creative act as a measure and warranty of being (Nietzsche, Heidegger, Rilke). There is in Blanchot, just as there has been throughout the present examination of the Orphic poet-thinkers from Novalis to Rilke, a quest for a new center. Or, better: for Blanchot this quest turns into an "approach" toward an ambiguous center, and it is precisely at this point that he converts the Orphic myth into the myth of the contemporary writer.

Blanchot focuses on the moment when Orpheus, violating his promise, looks at Eurydice—a kind of betrayal. This conception obviously owes a great deal to Rilke, and in a more remote way, to Mallarmé.

Quand Rilke exalte Orphée, quand il exalte le chant qui est être, ce n'est pas le chant tel qu'il peut s'accomplir à partir de l'homme qui le prononce, ni même la plénitude du chant, mais le chant comme origine et l'origine du chant. Il y a, à la vérité, une ambiguïté essentielle dans la figure d'Orphée, cette ambiguïté appartient au mythe qui est la réserve de cette figure, mais elle tient aussi à l'incertitude des pensées de Rilke, à la manière dont il a peu à peu dissous, au cours de l'expérience, la substance et la réalité de la mort. Orphée n'est pas comme l'Ange en qui la transformation est accomplie, qui en ignore les risques, mais en ignore aussi la faveur et la signification. Orphée est l'acte des métamorphoses, non pas l'Orphée qui a vaincu la mort, mais celui qui toujours meurt, qui est l'exigence de la disparition, qui disparaît dans l'angoisse de cette disparition, angoisse qui se fait chant, parole qui est le pur mouvement de mourir.[43]

When Rilke exalts Orpheus, when he exalts song as being, this does not mean song as it may be achieved by the man who pronounces it, nor even the plenitude of song, but it means the song as beginning and the beginning of song. In truth, there is an essential ambiguity in the figure of Orpheus, and this ambiguity belongs to the myth which is the preserve of that figure, but it also has something to do with the uncertainty of Rilke's thinking, with the way he dissolved gradually, in the course of experience, the substance and reality of death. Orpheus is not like the Angel in whom the transformation is accomplished and who does not know its hazards, but who also does not know its privilege and significance. Orpheus is the act of metamorphoses, not the Orpheus who vanquished death, but the Orpheus who is forever dying, who is himself the exigency of disappearance, who disappears in the anguish of that disappearance—an anguish that turns into song, speech that is the pure movement of dying.

Blanchot begins with the Rilkean declaration "Gesang ist Dasein," and his

Orpheus, like Rilke's and like Mallarmé himself, is in search of the sources of poetry. But here Blanchot shows himself to be the disciple of Mallarmé rather than Rilke. For Rilke, as noted earlier, Orpheus is (as Blanchot says) the "act of metamorphosis"—and here we are also reminded of Valéry's *L'Ame et la danse*—but he is also beyond death because he unites the fragmented creation. In Blanchot the emphasis is not on this Rilkean countermovement, but on a Mallarméan total negation (as in *Igitur*, much more radical than Rilke's), "l'exigence de la disparition . . . le pur mouvement de mourir." Rilke's dialectic of death has been displaced by the Mallarméan dialectic of suicide. Blanchot is perfectly aware of the difference between his two great predecessors:

Rilke, comme Mallarmé, fait de la poésie un rapport avec l'absence, mais combien cependant les expériences de ces deux poètes, apparemment si proches, sont différentes, comme au sein de la même expérience ils sont occupés par des exigences différentes. Alors que, pour Mallarmé, l'absence reste la *force* du négatif, ce qui écarte "la réalité des choses," ce qui nous délivre de leur poids, pour Rilke l'absence est aussi la présence des choses, l'intimité de l'être-chose où se rassemble le désir de tomber vers le centre par une chute silencieuse, immobile et sans fin. (164)

Rilke, like Mallarmé, makes poetry into a relation with absence, and yet how different is the experience of those two apparently so similar poets, how at the center of the same experience they are concerned with different exigencies. Whereas for Mallarmé absence remains the *force* of the negative, the thing that keeps the "reality of things" at bay, that which frees us from their weight, for Rilke absence is also the presence of things, the intimacy of being and thing, in which the desire of falling toward the center by a silent, immobile and endless fall is gathered up again.

The difference is that of the coincidence of opposites (in Rilke) and the identity of opposites (in Mallarmé). Blanchot then elaborates the difference between Mallarmé and Rilke into an analysis of time and space apprehension:

L'absence se lie, chez Mallarmé, à la soudaineté de l'*instant*. Un instant, brille la pureté de l'être au moment où tout retombe au néant. Un instant, l'absence universelle se fait pure présence et quand tout diaparaît, la disparition apparaît, est la pure clarté apparente, le point unique où il y a lumière de par l'obscur et jour de nuit. L'absence, chez Rilke, se lie à l'*espace* qui lui-même est peut-être libre du temps, mais qui cependant, par la lente transmutation qui le consacre, est aussi comme un *autre* temps, une manière de s'approcher d'un temps qui serait le temps même de mourir ou l'essence de la mort, temps bien différent de l'affairement impatient et violent qui est le nôtre, aussi différent que l'est de l'action efficace l'action sans efficacité de la poésie. (165)

Absence in Mallarmé is linked to the suddenness of the instant. For an instant, the purity of being shines at the moment when everything collapses into the nothing. For an instant, universal absence becomes pure presence and when everything disappears, disappearance appears and is pure apparent clarity, the unique point where there is light by virtue of the dark and nocturnal light. Absence in Rilke is linked to *space* which in itself is perhaps free from time but which nevertheless, through the slow transmutation that consecrates it, is also like an *other* time, a way of approaching time that would be the very time of dying or the essence of death, a very different time from the impatient and violent busy-ness that is ours, as different as the action without efficacity of poetry is from efficacious action.

In a way, Blanchot's fusion of these two "moments" constitutes his particular version of the Orphic: the Rilkean transmutation of space, filtered through the Mallarméan moment, becomes the exigency of modern writing in its approach to the work to be accomplished.

Quand Orphée descend vers Eurydice, l'art est la puissance vers laquelle s'ouvre la nuit. La nuit, par sa force de l'art, l'accueille, devient l'intimité accueillante, l'entente et l'accord de la première nuit. Mais c'est vers Eurydice qu'Orphée est descendu: Eurydice est, pour lui, l'extrême que l'art puisse atteindre, elle est, sous un nom qui la dissimule et sous un voile qui la couvre, le point profondément obscur vers lequel l'art, le désir, la mort, la nuit semblent tendre. Elle est l'instant où l'essence de la nuit s'approche comme l'*autre* nuit. (179)

When Orpheus descends toward Eurydice, art is the power toward which the night opens. Night, through its force of art, welcomes him, becomes a welcoming intimacy, agreement and accord of the first night. But Orpheus has descended toward Eurydice: Eurydice is for him the extreme that art can reach, she is, under a name which dissimulates her and under a veil which covers her, the profoundly obscure point toward which art, desire, death, the night seem to strive. She is the instant in which the essence of the night approaches as the *other* night.

In this reading of the myth Eurydice becomes the center of polar attraction to which the modern Orpheus, in quest of being and in quest of creation, is drawn. But this "point" is paradoxical and ambiguous: it cannot be possessed, it can only be contemplated, and even that glance constitutes a venture into the ambiguous—a confrontation with pure absence—and is therefore a transgression. It is this confrontation that remains central to Blanchot's myth:

Ce "point," l'oeuvre d'Orphée ne consiste pas cependant à en assurer l'approche en descendant vers la profondeur. Son *oeuvre*, c'est de le ramener au jour et de lui donner, dans le jour, forme, figure et réalité. Orphée peut tout, sauf regarder ce "point" en face, sauf regarder le centre de la nuit dans la nuit. Il peut descendre vers lui, il peut, pouvoir encore plus fort, l'attirer à soi et, avec soi, l'attirer vers le haut, mais en s'en détournant. Ce détour est le seul moyen de s'en approcher: tel est le sens de la dissimulation qui se révèle dans la nuit. (179)

The work of Orpheus, however, does not consist of insuring the approach to this "point" by descending toward the depth. His *work* is to bring it back to daylight and to confer upon it, in daylight, form, figure and reality. Orpheus can do everything but look this "point" in the face, everything but behold the center of the night in the night. He can descend toward it, he can by an even greater power attract it to himself and draw it along and upward, but only so long as he turns away from it. This turning aside is the only way to approach it: such is the meaning of the dissimulation revealing itself in the night.

At the same time, Orpheus' mission involves the possibility of an omission, a kind of transgression:

Mais Orphée, dans le mouvement de sa migration, oublie l'oeuvre qu'il doit accomplir, et il l'oublie necessairement, parce que l'exigence ultime de son mouvement, ce n'est pas qu'il y ait oeuvre, mais que quelqu'un se tienne en face de ce "point," en saisisse l'essence, là où cette essence apparaît, où elle est essentielle et essentiellement apparence: au coeur de la nuit. (179)

But Orpheus in the process of his migration forgets the work he is to accomplish, and forgets it necessarily, because the ultimate exigency of his progress is not that there should be the work, but that someone should place himself opposite that "point," grasp its essence where that essence appears, where it is essential and essentially appearance: at the midpoint of the night.

Blanchot's Orpheus clearly is not in search of poetry for its own sake, but of an existential authenticity which guarantees the authenticity of the work to be created: not the inclination to descend for the sake of the descent (this may have been Nerval's error), but for the sake of the return. Blanchot understands that the experience of descent into the night is a going beyond the bounds, whereas the work to be created must be placed within bounds. In a way, it is a restatement of the Dionysiac-Apollonian antithesis and another form of resolving the tension inherent in it.

Eurydice ne représente rien d'autre que cette dépendance magique qui hors du chant fait de lui une ombre et ne le rend libre, vivant et souverain que dans l'espace de la mesure orphique. Oui, cela est vrai: dans le chant seulement, Orphée a pouvoir sur Eurydice, mais, dans le chant aussi, Eurydice est déjà perdue et Orphée lui-même est l'Orphée dispersé, l'"infiniment mort" que la force du chant fait dès maintenant de lui. Il perd Eurydice, parce qu'il la désire par delà les limites mesurées du chant, et il se perd lui-même, mais ce désir et Eurydice perdue et Orphée dispersé sont nécessaires au chant, comme est nécessaire à l'oeuvre l'épreuve du désoeuvrement éternel . . . Mais si l'inspiration dit l'échec d'Orphée et Eurydice deux fois perdue, dit l'insignificance et le vide de la nuit, l'inspiration, vers cet échec et vers cette insignificance, tourne et force Orphée par un mouvement irrésistible, comme si renoncer à échouer était beaucoup plus grave que renoncer à réussir, comme si ce que nous appelons l'insignifiant, l'inessentiel, l'erreur, pouvait, à celui qui en accepte le risque et s'y livre sans retenue, se révéler comme la source de toute authenticité. (181–182)

Eurydice represents nothing else but that magic dependence which over and beyond the power of song makes song into a shadow and gives it freedom, life and dominion only in the space of the Orphic measure. Yes, this is true: in the song only Orpheus has power over Eurydice, but also in the song Eurydice is already lost and Orpheus himself is Orpheus scattered, that "infinitely dead" being which the power of song now makes of him. He loses Eurydice because he desires her beyond the measured limits of the song, and thus he loses himself, but that desire and Eurydice lost and Orpheus scattered are necessary to the song, as the work needs the proof of the eternal idleness . . . But if inspiration means Orpheus' failure and Eurydice twice lost, if it means the insignificance and the emptiness of night, inspiration turns and compels Orpheus by an irresistible movement toward that failure and toward that insignificance, as if to renounce failure were much more serious than to renounce success, as if what we call insignificance, inessentiality, error could reveal itself as the source of all authenticity to anyone who accepts their risk and delivers himself to them without reserve.

Blanchot's Orpheus is more precariously poised than Mallarmé's Orphic "descendant" of a hieratic line. He is an Igitur in an empty corridor, without the emblems of the past, a bard in quest of the mystery of his power of song. Eurydice is this power, the truth residing in this power. The poet's most secret desire is to know the truth of his mysterious gift, and in his anxiety to learn the truth, Orpheus turns back, renouncing, betraying his mission: he wants to *see*, not to sing. This act of renunciation—like the Rilkean "Wagnis"—annihilates literature momentarily, but it lays the foundation of the authenticity of the work to be done, though the price is the second loss of Eurydice. The act is like the lifting of the veil at Saïs; it is as paradoxical as Mallarmé's discovery of the *néant*, like Rilke's *Umkehr*—a transgression that is necessary to assure continuity, no matter how ambiguous, between art and reality. It is not difficult to understand why Blanchot thinks of this event as taking place in a *lieu sacré*, in a sacred zone of darkness in which the Orphic writer confronts the darkest nucleus of darkness. And Blanchot enables us to see, perhaps more clearly than the other Orphic poets, that the new dispensation of Orpheus in our time has been the quest for a nocturnal center—a dark radiance at the center of the labyrinth: "la recherche d'un centre imaginaire."[44]

But what is specifically contemporary in Blanchot is not merely this attraction toward a "null" center, a tendency sufficiently clear in the poets already discussed, but the sense of radical discrepancy between art and life, foreshadowed by the *rêve-réalité* antagonism in Nerval and aggravated by Mallarmé's *glorieux mensonge*. Here again Blanchot is the heir of Mallarmé, as well as the disciple of Kafka (who had questioned perhaps more sharply than any of his contemporaries the capacity of literature to relate itself to truth or reality).

Qui affirme la littérature en elle-même, n'affirme rien. Qui la cherche, ne cherche que ce qui se dérobe; qui la trouve, ne trouve que ce qui est en deçà ou, chose pire, au delà de la littérature. C'est pourquoi, finalement, c'est la non-littérature que chaque livre poursuit comme l'essence de ce qu'il aime et voudrait passionnément découvrir.[45]

Whoever affirms literature in itself affirms nothing. Whoever seeks to find it seeks only what eludes him; whoever finds it finds only what is this side of or, worse still, on the other side of literature. That is why, in the final reckoning, each book pursues non-literature as the essence of what it loves and wants passionately to discover.

So, for Blanchot, the Orphic experience of the writer passes through an encounter with nothingness and silence into a reversal endowed with speech, but with anonymous speech: the dismembered Orpheus from then on sings impersonally.

Blanchot's fiction transposes this experience into imaginative terms: "L'oeuvre attire celui qui s'y consacre vers le point où elle est à l'épreuve de l'impossibilité"[46]—The work attracts him who dedicates himself to it toward the point where the work is impossibility-proof. The pattern of the shorter and more characteristic works (*récits*) is generally a protagonist's encounter with death or nothingness in the guise of a Eurydice-figure, a negation of the experience ("arrêt de mort")—suspension of time and death—and the protagonist's return to life, transformed and depersonalized. Blanchot rejects the term "allegories" for his novels, and rightly so, because allegories stand in some relation to a received truth. Nor are these fictions parables, like the writings of Kafka and Camus. They are, rather, symbolic projections of mental events, with a fictional form necessitated by the fact that the words we use more readily embrace fictions than verities. "Si j'ai écrit des romans," says the narrator of *L'Arrêt de mort*, "les romans sont nés au moment où les mots ont commencé de reculer devant la vérité . . . Il serait extrêmement utile à la vérité de ne pas se découvrir"[47]—If I have written novels, they were born at the moment when words began to recoil before the truth . . . It would be extremely useful to the truth not to let itself be discovered.

The three short novels of 1948–1951, *L'Arrêt de mort*, the revised and shortened version of *Thomas l'obscur* (1950), and *Au Moment voulu* (1951) gravitate around the Eurydice encounter. The most remarkable is *Thomas l'obscur*,[48] Blanchot's closest approach to *Igitur*, constituting a transposition of the Orphic event into narrative form. The epithet "l'obscur" alone suggests the remoteness and anonymity of the protagonist and the conditions of his experience: the novel depicts the dark night of the intellect. There are, in effect, only three major episodes in the work, each representing a transformation. First, Thomas departs from an accustomed mode of existence—in contrast to Kafka's novels or Sartre's *La Nausée*, which revolve around lapses from one form of existential consciousness to another, Blanchot's hero is ready to choose the new direction: "Mais aujourd'hui il avait choisi un itinéraire nouveau" (p. 10)—But today he had chosen a new itinerary. Thomas, seen in this episode as a swimmer (like Conrad's "Secret Sharer"), achieves a new kind of liberty in the attainment of this *lieu intime* or *lieu sacré*, at which all of Blanchot's thinking originates:

Il chercha à se glisser dans une région vague et pourtant infiniment précise, quelque chose comme un lieu sacré, à lui-même si bien approprié qu'il lui suffisait d'être là pour être; c'était comme un creux imaginaire où il s'enfonçait parce qu'avant qu'il y fût, son empreinte y était déjà marquée. Il fit donc un dernier effort pour s'engager totalement. Cela fut facile, il ne recontrait aucun obstacle, il se rejoignait, il se confondait avec soi en s'installant dans ce lieu où nul autre ne pouvait pénétrer. (p. 13)

He tried to slip into a vague and yet infinitely precise region, something like a sacred spot so greatly appropriate to him that it would be enough for him to be in it in order to be; it was like an imaginary void into which he thrust himself because before he was there his imprint had already been stamped upon it. Consequently, he made a last effort to plunge into it totally. That was easy, he did not encounter any obstacle, he caught up with himself, he confused himself with himself by installing himself in this place where no one else could penetrate.

This is the preliminary transformation with which the novel opens. Jean Starobinski, who has analyzed the first chapter of *Thomas l'obscur* with remarkable perspicacity, notes that installation in this new position makes possible a correlation between Blanchot the novelist and Blanchot the critic.

Blanchot the novelist is Thomas moving away from the shore, penetrating in solitude the "sacred place"; Blanchot the critic is Thomas, who, by virtue of having passed through absolute removal but also by virtue of having attained solitary coincidence, then discovers his power of observing closely from the shore the motions of the distant swimmer, with the feeling of the greatest intimacy. Thus the *removal-distance* (which leads to the place "where no one else can penetrate") becomes the very condition of the increased *relationship* with someone else, whose possibility Thomas discovers upon his return to the shore: the "novelistic" experience of solitude becomes the source of a "critical" presence across the distance.[49]

Perhaps the word "contemplative" would be more appropriate than "critical" here. The validity in Starobinski's observation lies in the fact that it defines the change in perspective provoked by Blanchot's thought—between the imaginative and the reflective, between the quest for a fiction and the quest for the truth and their necessary interconnections. As the imagination *projects* the thinker toward the truth, so Blanchot's novels can be said to be projects that reinforce the meditative activity of the mind bent on authenticity.

The second and major episode of the novel takes shape from this newly gained installation. It is in effect the encounter, loss, and second loss of Eurydice (here called Anne). The encounter is introduced by a quasi-Orphic reference to Lazarus. At the end of Chapter V Blanchot writes:

[Thomas] marchait, seul Lazare véritable dont la mort même était ressuscitée. Il avançait, passant par-dessus les dernières ombres de la nuit, sans rien perdre de sa gloire, couvert d'herbes et de terre, allant, sous la chute des étoiles, d'un pas égal, du même pas qui, pour les hommes qui ne sont pas enveloppés d'un suaire, marque l'ascension vers le point le plus précieux de la vie. (pp. 52–53)

[Thomas] was walking, like the only true Lazarus whose very death had been resuscitated. He went forward, passing above the last shadows of night, without losing anything of his glory, covered with grass and earth, moving, under the fall of the stars, with the same step which for men not wrapped in a shroud marks their ascension toward the most precious point of life.

Chapter VI opens immediately thereafter with "Anne le vit s'approcher sans

surprise, cet être inévitable en qui elle reconnaissait celui qu'elle aurait vainement
cherché à fuir, qu'elle rencontrerait tous les jours" (p. 54)—Anne saw him
approach without surprise, that inevitable being in whom she recognized him
whom she would have vainly tried to flee, whom she would meet every day.
But Anne-Eurydice represents the negation of Thomas-Lazarus' state. This becomes evident if one considers the polarity "opaque-transparent" that accom-
panies Thomas' leap into darkness. Before the involvement with Anne, Thomas
is described as follows: "Son corps, après tant du luttes, devint entièrement
opaque et, à ceux qui le regardaient, il donnait l'impression reposante du sommeil, bien qu'il n'êut cessé d'être éveillé" (p. 41)—His body, after so many
struggles, became entirely opaque and gave those who looked at it the restful
impression of sleep, even though he never stopped being awake. This is a kind
of death-in-life not very different from the description of Lazarus mentioned
earlier. During the "descent" episode with Anne, Thomas begins the process of
transmutation:

C'est comme l'homme le moins obscur qu'il sortait de la nuit, baigné dans la transparence par le privilege d'être au-dessus de toute interrogation, personnage transfiguré
mais falot, d'où les problèmes maintenant s'écartaient, de la même manière qu'elle aussi
se voyait détournée de lui par ce spectacle dramatiquement nul . . ." (p. 97)

He went out of the night like the least obscure man, bathed in transparence by the
privilege of being above all interrogation, a transfigured but quaint person, from whom
problems now took their distance, in the same way in which she too saw herself averted
from him by this dramatically null spectacle . . ."

Anne's true function in the encounter is delineated in the passage that marks
her first disappearance and in a reflection that ensues:

Au coeur du néant, elle fit intrusion comme une présence triomphante et elle s'y jeta,
cadavre, néant assimilable, Anne qui existait encore et qui n'existait plus, suprême
moquerie à la pensée de Thomas. (89)

At the center of the nothing, she intruded like a triumphant presence and threw herself
into it, a cadaver, an assimilable nothingness, this Anne who still existed and who no
longer existed, a supreme mockery for Thomas' mind.

And then:

Elle existait comme un problème capable de donner la mort, non pas à la manière du sphinx, par la difficulté de l'énigme, mais par la tentation qu'elle apportait de résoudre le problème dans la mort. (94)

She existed as a problem capable of giving death, not like the sphinx with the difficulty of its riddle, but by the temptation inherent in her to resolve the problem in death.

As observed earlier, Eurydice represents for Blanchot the vanishing point, the pull toward death and nothingness that must be countenanced and overcome by Orpheus. After Anne's final disappearance, Thomas in his solitude meditates upon her death in a long monologue that begins with an analytical meditation on the event that has just occurred and terminates in a lyrical recognition and a burst of joy: "Moi-même, je me suis fait créateur contre l'acte de créer" (p. 164) —I have made myself a creator against the act of creating—a Mallarméan-Heideggerian resolution to a new "creatio *in* nihilo." The concluding chapter of the novel stands in direct contrast to the earlier opaque agonies of Thomas' return to the world of man; the setting is springtime; the language is traditionally Orphic: "Comme un berger, [Thomas] conduisait le troupeau des constellations, la marée des hommes—étoiles vers la première nuit." (172) (Like a shepherd, Thomas led the flock of constellations, the tide of men—stars toward the first night.) The Orphic elements in the new Thomas are, to be sure, somewhat attenuated and ambiguous, primarily because his experience in solitude has radically dissociated him from the "flock"; but the Orphic mission is affirmed nevertheless.

Geoffrey Hartman observes that Blanchot's novels "create a void rather than a world, an *espace littéraire* as ontologically equivocal as mind itself, and which neither reader, author, nor characters can cross to reach Being . . . His novels evoke a curious middle-world, or rather middle-void."[50] And yet this strange, ambiguous and yet pure creation ("oeuvre de pure imagination," says Georges Poulet) may very well be one of the most original ventures into a new kind of fiction in our time. Poulet observes that "Blanchot's novel is no longer even a fiction, it is the record of the fictive character of what it narrates. Like a Mallarmé poem, it is the reverse replica of an absence."[51] In synthesizing the Orphic components of Mallarmé and Rilke and subjecting them to a radically nihilistic dialectic, Blanchot has proposed a contemporary understanding of the Orphic that celebrates only the sheer transmutation of death into the creative act.

But is it enough? Is the Orphic writer henceforth no longer the reconciler of life and death, the outer and the inner, reality and poetry? Blanchot's ontological passion and his celebration of the writer's anguish are admirable. But it is also possible to see in his position a *reduction* of the Orphic—a reduction, in fact, that has parallels in all of contemporary literature, art, and music, and indeed in modern philosophy and science: partial perspectives admirably focused on intensity and profundity, implying but not encompassing the larger cosmic horizons or even the mute and limitless hunger of the human heart. In the final reckoning, is the culmination of the Orphic experience not the return and celebration of the defeated and dismembered Orpheus, who continues to sing *nevertheless*? Is it not the transmutation of silence into song? Of the dark center into radiance?

At certain moments the Orpheus story shades off into one of its variants, the myth of Amphion or Linus. This happens at the end of Rilke's first Elegy and, by implication, in certain of the Orpheus sonnets, and it explains Valéry's peripheral interest in the Orpheus theme. In a way, the difference between Rilke's Orphism and that of Mallarmé and Blanchot can be characterized as a difference of direction: Mallarmé and Blanchot accept the shipwreck (*naufrage* is one of their favorite terms) of the modern situation and attempt to shore up a few precious belongings against perdition—and that is what they celebrate as Orphics. Rilke wants to rebuild the entire earth, to construct the Orphic citadel of inwardness.

Saint-John Perse is a poet who, without being Orphic in a strict or narrow sense—and who nowhere in his work makes specific reference to the Orphic theme—is nevertheless the poet of reconciliation in our time. (His great predecessor, Paul Claudel, should be mentioned as the Catholic Orpheus of the twentieth century, despite the fact that the term "Catholic" and "Orpheus" in the context of this study appear inconsistent.) In the case of Perse, we have no idea and probably never shall about the inner experience that finally led to the ultimate glorification of the things of this world and the place of man in it; we can only note and praise the great festive hymn that has become, for us, Perse's voice: the very anonymity of his pen entitles us to refer to a "voice," and it is unmistakably Orphic.

Another remarkable feature of Perse's achievement is that the hymn of celebration has its renewal in exile, after a seventeen-year silence following the two great earlier panegyrics, *Eloges* and *Anabase*. Significantly, this poetry-in-exile opens upon the theme of nothingness. A very modern beginning, but one which leads somewhere: from "Exil" to "Pluies" and "Neiges," then to *Vents* and culminating in *Amers*.

Perse's poetry is a poetry of forward movement, of biological and spiritual growth: *une poésie en marche.* The movement is inexorable and increases in momentum at every point; Poulet is correct in referring to its "snowball" effect.[52] Its perspective is threefold: the world of elements and natural forces (the Greek *phúsis*, in its original meaning); the community of men animated by passion, desire, and ceremony; and the endless reservoir of human speech. It is this third component that links the first two and inspires the poet. In the beginning there is a definition of a physical location and the delineation of a human action in that particular place. As the poem progresses, the space enlarges and becomes more and more cosmic, and human activity increasingly fills out that space with deeds and passions. And the spatial and dynamic extension turns out to be correlative with a heightening of articulation, a linguistic crescendo that embraces ever-expanding areas of man's participation in the world's processes. The texture of man's aspiration becomes the text of the poet's inspiration.

In the opening lines of "Exil" (1941),[53] the poet, homeless now and in an alien land, chooses "un lieu flagrant et nul comme l'ossuaire des saisons" (vol. I, p. 167)—a flagrant and null place like the boneheap of the seasons—in order to recapture a new poetic voice.

... pour assembler aux syrtes de l'exil un grand poème né de rien, un grand poème fait de rien ... (vol. I, p. 168)

... to assemble on the Syrtis-shores of exile a great poem born of nothing, a great poem made of nothing ...

The nullity of the beginning has nothing to do with the *néant* of Mallarmé or Blanchot; Perse's *néant* is a point of pure inception and conception, pregnant with possibility and needing only the insemination and fructification that the elements and man can and will provide. And its very magnetism lies in its capacity for revitalization; unlike Mallarmé's and Blanchot's *néant*, Perse's is the antithesis of death and obliteration. And so Perse's "pure amorce de ce chant"— pure enticement of this song—contains within it the promise of plenitude and ecstasy. The Dionysiac outburst that follows offers the guarantee that splendor, grandeur, and poetic fury are within reach of lips and soul:

... Toujours il y eut cette clameur, toujours il y eut cette splendeur,
Et comme un haut fait d'armes en marche par le monde, comme un dénombrement de peuples en exode, comme une fondation d'empires par tumulte prétorien, ha! comme un gonflement de lèvres sur la naissance des grands Livres,
Cette grande chose sourde par le monde et qui s'accroît soudain comme une ébriété.

... Toujours il y eut cette clameur, toujours il y eut cette grandeur,
 Cette chose errante par le monde, cette haute transe par le monde, et sur toutes
grèves de ce monde, du même souffle proférée, la même vague proférant
 Une seule et longue phrase sans césure à jamais inintelligible . . .

... Toujours il y eut cette clameur, toujours il y eut cette fureur,
 Et ce très haut ressac au comble de l'accès, toujours, au faîte du désir, la même mouette
sur son aile, la même mouette sur son aire, à tire-d'aile ralliant les stances de l'exil, et sur
toutes grèves de ce monde, du même souffle proférée, la même plainte sans mesure
 A la poursuite, sur les sables, de mon âme numide . . . (I, 171–172)

... Always there has been that clamor, always there has been that splendor,
 And like a great feat of arms in motion in the world, like a numeration of peoples in
exodus, like a foundation of empires by pretorian tumult, ha! like the puffing-up of lips
over the birth of great Books,
 That great deaf thing in the world which increases suddenly like an ebriety.

... Always there has been that clamor, always there has been that grandeur,
 That thing erring through the world, that high trance through the world, and on all
shores of this world, by the same breath proffered, the same wave proffering
 A single and long phrase without caesura forever unintelligible . . .

... Always there has been that clamor, always there has been that furor,
 And those very high breakers at the peak of access, always, at the crest of desire, the
same seagull on its wing, the same seagull on its flight, swift-soaringly rallying the
stances of exile, and on all shores of this world, by the same beat proffered, the same
lament without measure
 In pursuit over the sands of my Numidian soul . . .

 This short passage, a superb example of Perse's art, is a microcosm of his entire
work: forward-moving poetry, full of incremental repetitions, inner harmonies
(generally metaphrastic), and achieving without any apparent difficulty the
fusion of the personal and impersonal voices of the poet, as well as the conjunction of man, nature, and the poetic, in this instance at the point of genesis.
Curiously enough, exodus and numbers are alluded to; but the animating force
of the passage is that of genesis. The closest parallel to this passage of Perse is
Claudel's ode "L'Esprit et l'eau," an extended meditation upon the first chapter
of Genesis.

The poet in exile, having recovered the capacity for song, proceeds to define and refine his own relations to the world of men and the uses of language. His language is still "un pur language sans office" (I, 176): it is functionless until he has taken his bearing. At this point Perse proclaims the soul to be the homeland of the exiled poet:

Me voici restitué à ma rive natale . . . Il n'est d'histoire que de l'âme, il n'est d'aisance que l'âme. (I, 177)

Here I am restored to my native shore . . . There is no history but the soul's history, there is no ease but the soul's ease.

This newly acquired domicile—" 'J'habiterai mon nom' fut ta réponse aux questionnaires du port" (I, 185), "I shall inhabit my name" was your answer to the questionnaires of the port authority—demands a reordering of the self, of an anonymous self that has in no way lost the power of its personal voice nor become alienated from men through proscription. On the contrary, by being joined to them once more through the bonds of the soul and the condition of human existence—"L'exil n'est point d'hier! l'exil n'est point d'hier!" (I, 170) Exile is not yesterday's matter!—the poet resolves to integrate himself anew and take his place among men.

Et c'est l'heure, ô Poète, de décliner ton nom, ta naissance, et ta race . . . (I, 188)

And now is the moment, O Poet, to decline your name, birth and race . . .

Alain Bosquet characterizes "Exil" as a poem that points up "the eternal relationship of poet and society, of poet and his time. Speaking henceforth in the name of all grieved men and all poets . . . Saint-John Perse draws up in 'Exil' a veritable 'declaration of the rights of the poet.' "[54]

The subsequent "Pluies," "Neiges," *Vents*, and *Amers* initiate and complete the cycle of elemental odes that grow directly out of the regeneration experience celebrated in "Exil." The triple-aspect perspective is equally valid for these majestic works, which must be classified as odes but which grow to epic proportions. Actually, *Vents* and *Amers* are giant epinician odes in the spirit of Pindar, with elements of hymnic poetry drawn from Greek hymns and particularly from the Psalms. The "elemental" design of the four draws attention to the primacy of the arena of Nature in which the lyric drama of human experience has its setting. The forward movement of this hymn-in-motion begins with the fertilizing agency of the rain, momentarily rests in silent and exquisite contemplation over cosmic expanses of snow, then proceeds under the animating and inspiriting efficacy of wind. In the culminating poem *Amers*, the world of the elements and the society of men are brought together in a juxtaposition of opposites: sea and land, change and fixity, male and female. The entire poem is a nuptial hymn in honor of the contiguity and conjunction of these polarities. Poulet points out that *discordia concors* could never be Perse's motto: "Never in any poet has the universal harmony been found to be so naturally just; never has it depended less on some initial discord."[55]

There is not in Perse an identity of opposites, but a coexistence and cohabitation of opposites, within the framework of which certain ritual enactments designate the possibility of the conjunction noted above, as if to show that the very reciprocity of these vital and animating tensions insures the continuing dynamics of the human quest—Empedocles driven by Bergson. This pagan-Dionysiac energy, with its magnificently spiritualized sensuality, makes possible a view of *Amers* as a hierogamic celebration and procession in whose ritual center stands the sea itself as altar and nuptial couch. The central section of the poem is, as a matter of fact, an extended Song of Songs, an ecstatic rhapsody of the alliance of male and female, sea and land, man and the cosmos;

Une même vague par le monde, une même vague parmi nous, haussant, roulant l'hydre amoureuse de sa force . . . Et du talon divin, cette pulsation très forte, et qui tout gagne . . . Amour et mer de même lit, amour et mer au même lit . . . (II, 276)

One same wave throughout the world, one same wave among us, raising, rolling the loving hydra of its strength . . . And from the divine heel, that very strong pulsation, which invades everything . . . Love and sea of the same bed, love and sea in the same bed . . .

Conjointly with man's nuptials with the woman and with the cosmos, there is in *Amers*, perhaps more decisively and powerfully than in the preceding works, the marriage of language and things. The final metamorphic power of man resides in his ability to transform speech into song and thereby to register transformations within the elemental structures of nature and within the inward spirit of man himself. Thus this triple entente of world, man, and language seals the greatest achievement of the diplomat-poet Léger-Perse, exiled yet at home in the world, anonymous yet personal, Orphic architect of reintegration:

C'est l'intégrité même de l'homme—et de l'homme de tout temps, physique et moral, sous sa vocation de puissance et son goût du divin—que j'ai voulu dresser sur le seuil le plus nu, face à la nuit splendide de son destin en cours . . . Ainsi ai-je voulu mener à la limite de l'expression humaine cette vocation secrète de l'homme, au sein même de l'action, pour ce qui dépasse en lui l'ordre temporel. Reprise de la grande phrase humaine, à son plus haut mouvement de mer, pour une réintégration totale de l'homme sur ses deux plans complémentaires . . .[56]

The integrity of man—man at any time, physical and moral man, in his vocation of energy and his desire for the divine—that is what I wanted to set up on the barest threshold, confronting the splendid night of his moving destiny . . . Thus I wanted to bring to the limit of human expression that secret vocation of man, at the very heart of action, for whatever in him surpasses the temporal order. To reiterate the great human phrase, at its highest sea-swell, for the sake of a total reintegration of man on his two complementary levels . . .

Would it be presumptuous to call Perse the poet of complementarity? It is true that scientific categories can be used only as approximations, at best as analogies, for poetic creation. But Perse is himself concerned with a rapprochement between what has come to be known as "the two cultures." In his Nobel Prize acceptance speech he insisted on the parallel quests of modern science and modern poetry. Only the manner of inquiry differs, he says, but:

Le mystère est commun. Et la grande aventure de l'esprit poétique ne le cède en rien aux ouvertures dramatiques de la science moderne. Des astronomes ont pu s'affoler d'une théorie de l'univers en expansion; il n'est pas moins d'expansion dans l'infini moral de l'homme—cet univers. Aussi loin que la science recule ses frontières, on entendra courir encore la meute chasseresse du poète. Car si la poésie n'est pas, comme on l'a dit, "le réel absolu," elle en est bien la plus proche convoitise et la plus proche appréhension, à cette limite extrême de complicité où le réel dans le poème semble s'informer lui-même.[57]

All that matters is the mystery in which they both share. The high spiritual adventure of poetry need yield nothing in drama to the new vistas of modern science. Astronomers may have faced with panic the idea of an expanding universe: is not a similar expansion taking place in the moral infinite of that other universe, the universe of man? As far as the frontiers of science extend and along their whole stretched arc, we can still hear the hounds of the poet in full cry. For, if poetry is not itself, as some have claimed, "absolute reality," it is poetry which shows the strongest passion for and the keenest apprehension of it, to that extreme limit of complicity where reality seems to shape itself within the poem.

And so, using diplomatic terminology again, Perse defines the poet as a sort of *agent de liaison*: "Par son adhésion totale à ce qui est, le poète tient pour nous liaison avec le permanence et l'unité de l'Etre"[58]—By his absolute adhesion to what exists, the poet keeps us in touch with the permanence and unity of Being. Not the creation of establishment of unity we have observed in the Orphic poets, but a continuing ambassadorship-at-large with unity and totality. In another context, Perse returns to the contemporary scientific world picture by saying: "Si j'étais physicien, je serais avec Einstein pour l'Unité et la Continuité contre la philosophie 'quantique' du hasard et du discontinu. Si j'étais métaphysicien, j'accepterais allègrement l'illustration du mythe de Shiva..."[59] (If I were a physicist, I would side with Einstein for Unity and Continuity against the quantum philosophy of chance and discontinuity. If I were a metaphysician, I would gladly accept the illustration of the myth of Shiva...) Perse's adherence to an Einsteinian rather than a Heisenbergian universe is perfectly consistent with what he celebrates in his poetry; yet ought not the name of Niels Bohr have been mentioned in this discussion as a "mediator?"[60] The metaphysical evocation of Shiva, the destroyer-god of Brahman mythology and complement of Vishnu the preserver-god, attests to a world view the essence of which lies in reciprocal interaction of the polarities of change and stability. The realm of temporality is likened by Perse to that all-encompassing dance of Shiva itself:

"Ne crains pas," dit l'Histoire, levant un jour son masque de violence—et de sa main levée elle fait ce geste conciliant de la Divinité asiatique au plus fort de sa danse destructrice. "Ne crains pas, ni ne doute—car le doute est stérile et la crainte est servile. Ecoute plutôt le battement rythmique que ma main haute imprime, novatrice, à la grande phrase humaine en voie toujours de création . . ."[61]

"Fear not," says History, taking off her mask of violence—and raising her hand in the conciliatory gesture of the Asiatic Divinity at the climax of her dance of destruction. "Fear not, neither doubt—for doubt is impotent and fear servile. Listen, rather, to the rhythm that I, the renewer of all things, impose upon the great theme which mankind is forever engaged in composing . . ."

The three concepts devised to explain the contemporary world of physics—continuity, discontinuity, and complementarity—invite a retrospective glance over the metamorphosis of Orpheus during the nineteenth and twentieth centuries. The new Orphism can in this way be located in a context of intellectual history and its present dilemma be articulated. The modern Orpheus, as observed in this study, was born within the compass of the Romantic quest for reunification of the cosmos. This quest took the form of a creative urge to reassemble the fragments of the intellect and soul under the protectorate of a new Orphic dispensation that was to transform the outer world by first transforming the inner self of man. The beginnings of the undertaking were clouded by Gnostic escapes into a purer, spiritual reality at the expense of the outer, empirical reality, which the poets regarded as chaotic or evil. Novalis and Nerval followed that path, but without finding a satisfactory liberation from Gnostic duality. In the second phase of this study, Mallarmé and Rilke found a way of transcending the duality by rediscovering, each in his own way, a dialectical scheme enabling him to make opposites coincide and to recapture the sense of a poetic unity that the Orphics so fervently desire. Only Rilke can be said to have actually succeeded in this enterprise; Mallarmé's solution remains unstable because tinged with remnants of materialism, Gnosticism, and, particularly in its latest form, nihilism.

In the mid-twentieth century, the tension within the Orphic sensibility has taken two directions. On the one hand there have been poets steadfastly persisting in the quest for continuity and unity (Apollinaire, Emmanuel); and, there have been the descendants of Mallarmé, mostly prose writers, who have created a literature of negation and discontinuity. Most of the latter have abandoned the Orphic ideal altogether—Kafka, Beckett, Robbe-Grillet are authors for whom it is utterly meaningless—or else, like Blanchot, they have attempted to give the Orpheus myth a restricted and predominantly negative interpretation.

Considering once more the three principal "moments" of the Orphic myth— (a) the harmonizing, reconciling, civilizing Orpheus, (b) Orpheus descending into Hades, and (c) the returning Orpheus, dismembered but still singing—it can be remarked that the modern epoch has significantly emphasized the experience of the descent and the subsequent return, as if to declare that Orpheus is not really Orpheus until he has been tested and tempered by the underworld experience. The highlighting of the *katábasis* differentiates modern from Renaissance Orphism. The traditional versions of the myth place their accent on the unifying power of Orpheus' song and on the reassertion, even the heightening, of this power after the double loss of Eurydice and in Orpheus' own death. Accordingly, the Hades episode is generally treated—particularly in the operatic versions of the myth by Monteverdi, Gluck, and Haydn—as a dramatic exemplification of the omnipotence of poetry and song. In Orphic poetry after the eighteenth century, the power of song is generally taken for granted; now it is the plunge into darkness, inwardness, and death that engages the interest of the poets, somewhat at the expense of the "outer" movements of the Orphic myth. An imbalance has been introduced into the myth itself, a fascinating and brilliant shift of emphasis has taken place; yet it is not true to say that this "displacement" of Orphic forces is also an index of the dislocations characteristic of all aspects of modern life?

Here let us turn back again to Goethe, a model of a different, and older, Orphic sensibility from that of his contemporaries and successors. Charles Du Bos, in his study of Goethe's Orphic poetry, makes a perceptive comparison between Goethe and Nerval; the difference is, for Du Bos, one between sanity and delirium, between poetry that remains self-contained and poetry that involves itself in philosophical and theological doctrines.

While Goethe in his poetry opens that "most secret chamber" of his genius, there is never properly speaking any delirium, nor does the spiritual matter informed by his Orphic poetry ever leave the *pure* poetic plane, it neither jostles or even approaches the sphere of philosophical or doctrinal poetry. Not only is glimpsing (*l'entrevision*) the very act of Goethe's Orphic poetry, but because he is neither this side or the other side of this glimpsing, because he remains so faithful to it, Orphic poetry here institutes a quality and something like a category which Goethe alone, by virtue of his entire nature, was able to institute: *balance* in the midst of the *act of glimpsing*.[62]

It has been observed above that in the Orphic poets after Nerval, particularly Mallarmé and Rilke, a pure poetry is envisaged and realized but always at the risk of a distorted perspective, with the institution of a world view that is partial and private. There was, possibly, no alternative: poetry, deprived and dispossessed, strove to recover and chart its own cosmos—not necessarily the cosmos that the human intellect had laboriously constructed as a form of mediation between outer and inner experience, in which poetry had been able to function as the balance between fact and feeling.

In brief, the revival of Orpheus in modern literature gives evidence perhaps more cogently than any other motif of what Erich Heller calls the "progressive colonization of inwardness" in modern poetry. Camus once observed that myths exist so that the mind of men can animate them. But the modern sensibility has been drawn particularly to those myths that lend themselves in one way or another to "internalization"—Orpheus, Don Juan, Faust, Oedipus. This is true even of the Prometheus myth, despite its characteristics as an anti-Orphic theme, which has tended to focus more and more on the inner life of the great humanistic rebel-figure. One is prompted to conclude that the myths of the past are a gigantic mine-deposit from which that ore must be extracted which can best be utilized for our currency—and the past itself is an endless hall of mirrors in which we try to recognize and rediscover ourselves. For this reason, the image of Orpheus observed from Novalis onward has been a consistently distorted one in which the "original" Orpheus (if one can even speak of such a phenomenon) has become somewhat unrecognizable, as if the likeness were that of a photographic negative or an X-ray.

This is perhaps the reason why today, two-thirds of the way through the twentieth century, the new Orphism has reached a point of no return. Saint-John Perse may very well be, as intimated, the only great "balanced" Orphic poet of our time. Passing in silence over the encounter with darkness or nothingness, he has made us vibrate once again with the intoxicating and at the same time sobering power of song. In that sense, he does not altogether fit the Orphic pattern whose design has been traced in this study. And yet, free from the Gnostic and nihilistic seductions of the modern world, he reminds us that if opposites do not quite manage to coincide, they can at least complement each other like the Taoist Yin and Yang; and if we cannot create unity, we can at least try to embrace totality.

"Et c'est assez, pour le poète, d'être la mauvaise conscience de son temps"— And it is enough for the poet to be the guilty conscience of his time—were the final words of Perse's Stockholm address. All the Orphic writers have been the uneasy consciences of their times, to a greater or lesser extent; all modern literature has demonstrated its "agenbite of inwit," its share of guilt. But the sense of purpose and direction that links the vision of literature with the destiny of men has not always been as clearly in evidence as the sense of anguish. In an early work by Martin Buber called *Daniel* and subtitled *Dialogues on Realization*, a work that marks one of the great contemporary prophet's early attempts to break away from anguish and solitude into the "dialogue" of his later thought, the name of Orpheus occurs, surprisingly, in the first page of the dialogue "On Direction":

DANIEL: Concerning Dionysus-Zagreus the legend reports the Titans had enticed him by means of a game and torn him to pieces and devoured him. This is the fate of him who yields to ecstasy with his soul undirected. The forces of chaos take hold of him, the demonism of the Unformed shatters his soul and swallows it. For me, the antithesis is the figure of Orpheus, who descends into Hades lyre in hand, not in order to regain the realm of Dionysus, who is Hades, thus accomplishing the act of renewal in which that rhythm of breathing and sleeping is transfigured into sacrament. But what is archetypal in Orpheus is the fact that with his lyre he meets ecstatic death. Not enticed: resolved, and with his lyre.

Music is the pure word of the directed soul. It is no longer the place where polarities are fettered into an artistic framework into which experiences are inserted and forcibly made to fit, and the amorphous mixture and its dispersion is banished from this domain. Here the directed soul reigns supreme. It projects its innate direction, it projects the melody into the abyss, and the forces of the deep gather around it like the "wild creatures" around Orpheus playing . . . You cannot arrive at the Mother otherwise than through the Son.

WOMAN: This means that direction is inner song?

DANIEL: The soul, resolute, which descends and returns renewed, the soul dying and becoming possesses the magic of its song, which makes it inviolable and immortal to all death—that is the work of its direction. Indeed, direction is itself nothing but magic.[63]

In this capacity of Orpheus to reconcile Apollo and Dionysus, direction and magic, lies his power over men, and this power will continue to assert itself so long as man is willing to be tamed by song.

Notes
Index of Names

Notes

CHAPTER I. INTRODUCTION:
THE METAMORPHOSIS OF ORPHEUS

1. *The Complete Works of Horace*, ed. Casper J. Craemer, Jr. (New York: Modern Library, 1936), p. 410.

2. André Boulanger, *Orphée: rapports de l'orphisme et du christianisme* (Paris: F. Rieder, 1925); F. M. Cornford, *From Religion to Philosophy* (London: E. Arnold, 1912); W. K. C. Guthrie, *Orpheus and Greek Religion* (London: Methuen, 1935); Jane Harrison, *Prolegomena to the Study of Greek Religion*, 3rd ed. (Cambridge, Eng.: Cambridge University Press, 1922); Vittorio D. Macchioro, *From Orpheus to Paul: A History of Orphism* (New York: Henry Holt & Company, 1930); Ivan M. Linforth, *The Arts of Orpheus* (Berkeley and Los Angeles: University of California Press, 1941); Louis Moulinier, *Orphée et l'orphisme à l'époque classique* (Paris: Les Belles Lettres, 1955); Joseph Ronald Watmough, *Orphism* (Cambridge, Eng.: Cambridge University Press, 1934).

3. Elizabeth Sewell, *The Orphic Voice: Poetry and Natural History* (New Haven: Yale University Press, 1960).

4. Walter Rehm, *Orpheus: der Dichter und die Toten* (Düsseldorf: L. Schwann, 1950); Eva Kushner, *Le Mythe d'Orphée dans la littérature français contemporaine* (Paris: Nizet, 1961); Gwendolyn M. Bays, *The Orphic Vision: Seer Poets from Novalis to Rimbaud* (Lincoln: University of Nebraska Press, 1964); Georges Cattaui, *Orphisme et prophétie chez les poètes français 1850–1950* (Paris: Plon, 1965).

5. Mircea Eliade, *Images et symboles* (Paris: Gallimard, 1952), p. 20.

6. *Ibid.*, p. 12.

7. See Erich Heller, *The Hazard of Modern Poetry* (Cambridge, Eng.: Bowes & Bowes, 1953).

8. E. R. Dodds, *The Greeks and the Irrational* (Berkeley: University of California Press, 1951), p. 148.

9. Harrison, *Prolegomena*, p. 455.

10. Kushner, *Le Mythe d'Orphée*, p. 55.

11. Cornford, *From Religion to Philosophy*, p. 195.

12. See Karl Kérenyi, *Pythagoras und Orpheus* (Zürich: Rhein-Verlag, 1950).

13. Gertrude Rachel Levy, *The Gate of Horn* (London: Faber & Faber, 1948), p. 287.

14. Mircea Eliade, *Patterns in Comparative Religion*, trans. Rosemary Sheed (New York: Sheed & Ward, 1958), p. 415.

15. This is the crux of my disagreement with Miss Sewell's book: the Orphic orientation in the nineteenth century becomes *twofold* by the middle of the century—Miss Sewell opts for Goethe over Mallarmé.

16. M. H. Abrams, *The Mirror and the Lamp* (New York: Oxford University Press, 1953), p. 282.

17. Herbert Marcuse, *Eros and Civilization: A Philosophical Inquiry into Freud* (Boston: Beacon Press, 1955), pp. 162, 171.

18. See Jean Seznec, *The Survival of the Pagan Gods* (New York: Pantheon, 1953), *passim*, esp. p. 213.

19. All quotations from the pre-Socratic philosophers are taken from Kathleen Freeman, *An Ancilla to the Pre-Socratic Philosophers* (Cambridge, Mass.: Harvard University Press, 1957). See also the same author's *The Pre-Socratic Philosophers* (Oxford: Blackwell, 1949), and Eduard Zeller, *A History of Greek Philosophy from the Earliest Period to the Time of Socrates* (London: Longmans, Green and Company, 1881).

20. See Rudolf Otto, *Mysticism East and West* (New York: Macmillan, 1932).

21. Ernst Cassirer, *Individuum und Kosmos in der Philosophie der Renaissance* (Darmstadt: Wissenschaftliche Buchgesellschaft, 1962), p. 15.

22. *Ibid.*, p. 24.

23. Pointed out by Hans Jonas, "Gnosticism and Modern Nihilism," *Social Research*, 19 (1952), 430–452.

24. *The Selected Poetry and Prose of Samuel Taylor Coleridge*, ed. Donald A. Stauffer (New York: Modern Library, 1951), p. 269.

25. Abrams, *The Mirror and the Lamp*, p. 314.

26. J. J. Bachofen, *Der Mythus von Orient und Occident* (Munich: C. H. Beck, 1956), pp. 396–397.

27. Kérenyi, *Pythagoras und Orpheus*, p. 38.

28. Erich Heller, *The Disinherited Mind: Essays in Modern German Literature and Thought* (Cambridge, Eng.: Bowes & Bowes, 1952), p. 109.

CHAPTER II. NOVALIS: ORPHEUS THE MAGICIAN

1. *Athenäum* (Berlin, 1798–1800), III, 18, 96. (All translations are my own.)

2. Johann Wolfgang Goethe, *Gedenkausgabe der Werke, Briefe und Gespräche* (Zürich: Artemis-Verlag, 1953), II, 616.

3. *Ibid.*, p. 617.

4. Elizabeth Sewell, *The Orphic Voice*, (New Haven: Yale University Press, 1960), p. 274.

5. Erich Heller, *The Disinherited Mind*, (Cambridge: Bowes & Bowes, 1952), pp. 29–49.

6. See Walter A. Strauss, "New Life, Tree of Life: The *Vita Nuova* and Nerval's *Aurélia*," *Books Abroad*, Special Issue: A Homage to Dante (May 1965), 144–150.

7. Charles S. Singleton, *An Essay on the Vita Nuova* (Cambridge, Mass.: Harvard University Press, 1949).

8. Novalis, *Schriften*, ed. P. Kluckhohn and R. Samuel (Stuttgart: W. Kohlhammer, 1960), I, 552–553.

9. *Ibid.*, pp. 547–551.

10. Novalis, *Werke und Briefe*, ed. A. Kellerat (Munich: Winkler-Verlag, 1962), p. 612.

11. *Ibid.*, pp. 614, 616, 617, 622, 625, 627.

12. *Ibid.*, p. 389.

13. *Ibid.*, p. 391.

14. *Ibid.*, p. 398.

15. *Ibid.*, p. 406.

16. Mircea Eliade, *Méphistophélès et l'Androgyne* (Paris: Gallimard, 1962), p. 152.

17. Novalis, *Werke und Briefe*, p. 470.

18. *Ibid.*, p. 113 ("Die Lehrlinge von Sais").

19. See Eugène Susini, *Franz von Baader et le romantisme mystique*, vol. II: *La Philosophie de Franz von Baader* (Paris: Vrin, 1942), p. 24.

20. Novalis, *Werke, Briefe, Dokumente*, vol. 2: *Fragmente I*, ed. E. Wasmuth (Heidelberg: L. Schneider, 1957), p. 12.

21. Theodor Haering, *Novalis als Philosoph* (Stuttgart: Kohlhammer, 1954), p. 12.

22. Novalis, *Werke und Briefe*, p. 472.

23. *Ibid.*, p. 410.

24. Michael Hamburger, *Reason and Energy: Studies in German Literature* (New York: Grove Press, 1957) p. 83.

25. Novalis, *Werke und Briefe*, pp. 466, 467.

26. *Ibid.*, pp. 502–503.

27. *Ibid.*, pp. 161–162.

28. *Ibid.*, p. 274.

29. *Ibid.*, p. 280.

30. *Ibid.*, p. 291.

31. *Ibid.*, p. 292.

32. *Ibid.*, pp. 303 (Tieck), 317 (Novalis).

33. *Ibid.*, p. 315.

34. *Ibid.*, p. 304.

35. *Ibid.*, p. 349.

36. *Ibid.*, p. 299.

37. Hamburger, *Reason and Energy*, p. 72.

CHAPTER III.   THE SEASONING OF HELL: NERVAL

1. Novalis, *Werke und Briefe*, ed. A. Kellerat (Munich: Winkler-Verlag, 1962), p. 283. Gérard de Nerval, *Oeuvres*, ed. Henri Lemaitre (Paris: Garnier, 1958), I, 758.

2. Nerval, *Oeuvres*, ed. Lemaitre, I, 656.

3. *Ibid.*, pp. 334, 336.

4. Jean Richer, *Gérard de Nerval et les doctrines ésotériques* (Paris: Editions du Griffon d'Or, 1947), p. 177.

5. Nerval, *Oeuvres*, ed. Lemaitre, I, 862.

6. Gérard de Nerval, *Oeuvres*, ed. A. Béguin and J. Richer (Paris: Editions de la Pléïade, 1960), I, 429.

7. The occult sources of Nerval's work have been studied by Jean Richer, *Gérard de Nerval et les doctrines ésotériques*. See also Richer's *Nerval: expérience et création* (Paris: Hachette, 1963) and articles by Georges Le Breton and François Constans listed in James Villas, *Gérard de Nerval: A Critical Bibliography 1900 to 1967* (Columbia: University of Missouri Press, 1968), pp. 50–53, 75–76.

8. Nerval, *Oeuvres*, ed. Lemaitre, I, 659.

9. See Walter A. Strauss, "New Life, Tree of Life: The *Vita Nuova* and Nerval's *Aurélia*," *Books Abroad*, Special Issue: *A Homage to Dante* (May 1965), 144–150.

10. Nerval, *Oeuvres*, ed. Lemaitre, I, 753. Subsequent references from *Aurélia* will refer to this edition.

11. Jean Richer, "Nerval et ses fantômes," *Mercure de France*, no. 312 (June 1, 1951), 291–292.

12. Georges Poulet, *Trois essais de mythologie romantique* (Paris: Corti, 1966), p. 79.

13. Charles S. Singleton, *An Essay on the Vita Nuova* (Cambridge, Mass.: Harvard University Press, 1949).

14. Nerval, *Oeuvres*, ed. Lemaitre, I, 503. Subsequent page references to *Les Chimères* are from this edition.

15. Georges Le Breton, "La Clé des *Chimères*: l'alchimie," *Fontaine*, no. 44 (1945), 441–460; Richer, *Gérard de Nerval et les doctrines ésotériques* and *Nerval: expérience et création*; Janine Moulin, *Les Chimères. Exégèses* (Geneva: Droz, 1949).

16. Nerval, *Oeuvres*, ed. Lemaitre, II, 798 ("Carnet du Voyage en Orient").

17. Georges Poulet, *Les Metamorphoses du cercle* (Paris: Plon, 1961), pp. 244–268.

18. *Oeuvres complémentaires de Gérard de Nerval*, ed. Jean Richer, vol. I: *La Vie des lettres* (Paris: Minard, 1959), p. 19.

19. Nerval, *Oeuvres*, ed. Lemaitre, II, 251–252.

20. Gérard de Nerval, *Poésies*, ed. Albert Béguin (Lausanne: Mermod, 1947), pp. 10–11.

21. Richer, *Nerval: expérience et création*, p. 446.

22. Nerval, *Oeuvres*, ed. Lemaitre, I, 743.

23. *Ibid.*, pp. 745–746.

24. Richer, *Nerval: expérience et création*, p. 572.

25. Nerval, *Oeuvres*, ed. de la Pléïade, I, 1158 (to Antony Deschamps, Oct. 24, 1854).

26. Poulet, *Les Métamorphoses du cercle*, pp. 258, 259.

27. *Ibid.*, pp. 262, 263.

28. Nerval, *Oeuvres*, ed. de la Pléiade, I, 1091 (to George Bell, Dec. 4, 1853).

29. *Ibid.*, p. 1169 (Jan. 24, 1955).

CHAPTER IV. MALLARMÉ: ORPHEUS AND THE "NÉANT"

1. Stéphane Mallarmé, "Symphonie littéraire," *Oeuvres complètes* (Paris: Editions de la Pléiade, 1945), pp. 264–265. All references in the text will be to this edition. See, in the same ed. (p. 521), a later, modified version (1892) of the same passage.

2. E. Noulet thinks similarly, but there appears to be no concrete evidence. See her *Vingt poèmes de Stéphane Mallarmé* (Geneva: Droz, 1967), p. 131.

3. Stéphane Mallarmé, *Correspondance 1862–1871*, (Paris: Gallimard, 1959), p. 150.

4. *Ibid.*, p. 118.

5. *Ibid.*, pp. 207–208.

6. *Ibid.*, pp. 220, 222.

7. *Ibid.*, pp. 245–246 (to Eugène Lefébure, May 17, 1867).

8. *Ibid.*, p. 259 (to Villiers de l'Isle-Adam, Sept. 24, 1867).

9. *Ibid.*, pp. 240–244 (to Henry Cazalis, May 14, 1867).

10. *Ibid.*, p. 301 (to Henry Cazalis, Feb. 18, 1869).

11. See Jean-Pierre Richard, *L'Univers imaginaire de Mallarmé* (Paris: Editions du Seuil, 1961), pp. 231–233, for a convenient summary.

12. Adile Ayda, *Le Drame intérieur de Mallarmé* (Istanbul: Editions "La Turquie Moderne" 1955), p. 243.

13. Kurt Wais, Mallarmé (Munich: Beck-Verlag, 1952), p. 25.

14. Mallarmé, *Correspondance 1862–1871*, p. 249 (to Eugène Lefébure, May 17, 1867).

15. *Ibid.*, p. 250.

16. Ovid, *The Metamorphoses*, trans. Horace Gregory (New York: Viking Press, 1958), p. 42.

17. Robert Greer Cohn speaks of the "negative capability" of art in this connection: *Toward the Poems of Mallarmé* (Berkeley and Los Angeles: University of California Press, 1965), p. 126.

18. Gardner Davies, *Vers Une Explication rationelle du "Coup de dés"* (Paris: Corti, 1953), p. 30.

19. Could it perhaps be that the swan has been arrested (immobilized) in his Orphic journey? The Orpheus-swan analogy is suggested by a sentence from the "Myth of Er" in Plato's *Republic* (Book X, 620a): "There he saw the soul which had once been Orpheus choosing the life of a swan out of enmity to the race of women, hating to be born of a woman because they had been his murderers." Recalling that Mallarmé tends to substitute "poetry" for "the woman," the second half of the sentence can be applied to Mallarmé's swan as well, provided one remembers that a "fallen" swan is under consideration.

20. Quoted in Pierre-Olivier Walzer, *Essai sur Stéphane Mallarmé* (Paris[?]: Pierre Seghers, 1963), p. 125.

21. Mallarmé, *Correspondance 1862–1871*, p. 313.

22. André Rolland de Renéville, *L'Expérience poétique* (Paris: Gallimard, 1938), p. 99. Rolland de Renéville's explanation for the subtitle, however, is unacceptable to me.

23. *Ibid.*, p. 43.

24. Maurice Blanchot, *L'Espace littéraire* (Paris: Gallimard, 1955), p. 111.

25. Mallarmé, *Correspondance 1862–1871*, p. 278.

26. According to Robert Greer Cohn, there is a moon in the sky (*Toward the Poems of Mallarmé*, p. 139). This reading seems justified once *lampadophore* is taken in its root meaning, "torch-bearing." If one accepts the wider meaning of the word, "light-bearing," it can be applied to the scintillations of the stars, very high up, as though the onyx fingernails (note that onyx *is* the Greek word for fingernail!) of the allegorical statue of Anguish (that is, Night) reflect, coincide with, the twinkle of the stars. This broader reading of *lampadophore* has one major advantage: it sets up a metaphorical equivalence of exterior and interior, black night and deserted chamber, and thus inaugurates the "mirage" scheme of the sonnet. The room according to Mallarmé's own assertion (*Correspondance 1862–1871*, p. 278) is "sans meuble, sinon l'ébauche plausible de vagues consoles"; in other words, something like a table lamp (with an allegorical statuette?) *may* be dimly outlined by the feeble light entering the room.

27. See Noulet, *Vingt poèmes*, p. 186. The Pausanias reference is to *Description of Greece*, Book VIII, xvii, 6; xviii.

28. In Ovid's narrative of Callisto (*Metamorphoses*, II) the aggressor of the nymph is Jupiter himself—a far cry from Mallarmé's unicorn but only a short sigh from his Faun! —who disguises himself as Diana to seduce the nymph. Mallarmé seems generally to have kept his Ovid handy when writing; in this instance the divergence is rather interesting. Moreover, the story of Callisto follows the accounts of Phaethon's fall and Cygnus' exile in Ovid's narrative.

29. *Ibid.*, p. 191.

30. Mallarmé, *Correspondance 1862–1871*, p. 279.

31. See Gardner Davies, *Mallarmé et le drame solaire* (Paris: Corti, 1959), pp. 41–71.

32. Cohn, *Toward the Poems of Mallarmé*, p. 120.

33. Richard, *L'Univers imaginaire*, p. 183.

34. Lloyd James Austin, "Mallarmé, Huysmans et la 'Prose pour des Esseintes,' " *Revue d'Histoire Littéraire de la France*, 54 (1954), 145–182; and, "Du nouveau sur la 'Prose pour des Esseintes' de Mallarmé," *Mercure de France*, CCCXXIII (1955), 84–104.

35. Georges Poulet, *Les Métamorphoses du cercle* (Paris: Plon, 1961), p. 435.

36. *Ibid.*, p. 434. The quotation can be found in Mallarmé, *Oeuvres complètes*, p. 396.

37. Lloyd James Austin, "Mallarmé et le rêve du 'Livre'," *Mercure de France*, 317 (1953), 102. See also Henri Mondor, *Vie de Mallarmé* (Paris: Gallimard, 1941), p. 683. There are a number of provocative reflections on Mallarmé's Orphism in Manuel de Diéguez, "Jean-Pierre Richard et la critique thèmatique" (a long review of *L'Univers imaginaire*), *Critique*, 19 (1963), 517–535.

38. Jean Starobiniski, "Mallarmé et la tradition poétique française," *Les Lettres*, 3 (1948), 42.

39. Quoted in Walzer, *Essai sur Stéphane Mallarmé*, p. 190.

40. Poulet, *Les Métamorphoses du cercle*, p. 447.

41. *Ibid.*, p. 449.

42. Paul Valéry, *Oeuvres*, I, 626 (Paris: Editions de la Pléïade, 1957).

43. Camille Mauclair, *Le Soleil des morts* (Paris: Ollendorff, 1924 [?]), p. 24.

CHAPTER V.   RILKE: ORPHEUS AND THE DOUBLE REALM

1. Eudo C. Mason, *Lebenshaltung und Symbolik bei Rainer Maria Rilke* (Oxford: Marston Press, 1964), pp. 4, 20–21.

2. Rainer Maria Rilke, *Sämtliche Werke* (Wiesbaden: Insel-Verlag, 1956), II, 528 ("Vergers," no. 23).

3. Rainer Maria Rilke, *Briefe I (1897–1914)* (Wiesbaden: Insel-Verlag, 1950), pp. 324–329 (to Lou Andreas-Salome).

4. Rilke, *Sämtliche Werke*, II, 94.

5. *Ibid.*, p. 111.

6. *Ibid.*, p. 83.

7. *Ibid.*, pp. 92–93.

8. *Ibid.*, p. 134.

9. The following studies contain detailed exegeses of the Elegies: Romano Guardini, *Rainer Maria Rilkes Deutung des Daseins: Eine Interpretation der Duineser Elegien* (Munich: Kösel-Verlag, 1953); Katherina Kippenberg, *Rainer Maria Rilkes Duineser Elegien und Sonette an Orpheus* (Wiesbaden: Insel-Verlag, 1948); Eva Solmitz-Cassirer, *Das Stundenbuch. Die Aufzeichnungen des Malte Laurids Brigge. Die Duineser Elegien. Die Sonette an Orpheus. Die Götter bei Rilke* (Heidelberg: G. Kaester-Verlag [1957]); Jacob Steiner, *Rilkes Duineser Elegien* (Bern and Munich: Francke-Verlag, 1962).

10. Steiner, *Rilkes Duineser Elegien*, p. 195.

11. Rilke, *Briefe II (1914–1926)* (Wiesbaden: Insel-Verlag, 1950), pp. 480–481.

12. *Ibid.*, pp. 482–485.

13. Erich Heller, *The Disinherited Mind* (Cambridge: Bowes & Bowes, 1952), p. 105.

14. *Ibid.*, pp. 128–129. See Martin Heidegger, *Holzwege* (Frankfurt: V. Klostermann, 1950), p. 288.

15. Rilke, *Sämtliche Werke*, I, 544.

16. *Ibid.*, p. 545.

17. *Ibid.*, II, 137–138.

18. *Ibid.*, p. 133–134.

19. Johanna von Freydorf, *Die Sonette an Orpheus von Rainer Maria Rilke als zyklische Dichtung* (Würzburg: Konrad Triltsch, 1937), p. 22.

20. Hans-Egon Holthusen, *Rilkes Sonette an Orpheus: Versuch einer Interpretation* (Munich: Neuer Filser-Verlag, 1937), p. 44.

21. Herbert Marcuse, *Eros and Civilization* (Boston: Beacon Press, 1955), pp. 146–147.

22. Rilke, *Sämtliche Werke*, II, 465.

23. *Ibid.*, pp. 135–136.

24. Paul Valéry, *Oeuvres* (Paris: Editions de la Pléïade, 1960), II, 165, 174.

25. Rilke, *Briefe II*, pp. 406–407.

26. Rilke, *Sämtliche Werke*, II, 467.

27. *Ibid.*, p. 469.

28. *Ibid.*, pp. 520–521.

29. *Ibid.*, pp. 526–527.

30. *Ibid.*, p. 525.

31. Poulet, *Les Métamorphoses du cercle*, pp. 502–503.

32. Rilke, *Sämtliche Werke*, II, 132.

33. *Ibid.*, p. 179.

34. Heidegger, *Holzwege*, pp. 260, 261.

35. Rilke, *Sämtliche Werke*, II, 175–176.

36. *Ibid.*, p. 319.

37. *Ibid.*, p. 157.

38. Rilke, *Briefe II*, p. 374.

39. Rilke, *Sämtliche Werke*, II, 575.

40. *Ibid.*, p. 549.

41. "Doute" (1925) in *Sämtliche Werke*, II, 607.

42. "Vergers," no. 24 in *Sämtliche Werke*, II, 529.

CHAPTER VI. AFTER RILKE:

ORPHEUS, PARADIGM OR PARADOX?

1. Gwendolyn M. Bays, *The Orphic Vision: Seer Poets from Novalis to Rimbaud* (Lincoln: University of Nebraska Press, 1964). See also Georges Cattaui, *Orphisme et prophétie chez les poètes français 1850–1950* (Paris: Plon, 1965), pp. 135–151.

2. Auguste Viatte, *Les Sources occultes du romantisme* (Paris: Champion, 1928).

3. See R. C. Zaehner, *Mysticism Sacred and Profane* (New York: Oxford University Press, 1961), pp. 61–62: "Rimbaud seems to be a case of self-induced psychosis, of preternatural experience deliberately and recklessly sought. His is not a case of 'grace' gratuitously given or appearing unsolicited and one knows not whence. Rather, he seeks to take heaven by storm, and to capture it not by the regular warfare prescribed by the Church but by a surprise attack which was to seize upon the holy place from the quarter in which it would be least prepared, from the approaches of Hell."

4. Arthur Rimbaud, *Oeuvres complètes*, ed. Rolland de Renéville and Jules Mouquet (Paris: Editions de la Pléïade, 1954), p. 219. All references in the text will be to this edition.

5. H. de Bouillane de Lacoste, *Rimbaud et le problème des Illuminations* (Paris: Mercure de France, 1949).

6. Roland Barthes, *Le Degré zéro de l'écriture* (Paris: Editions du Seuil, 1953), pp. 105–111.

7. A good discussion of Anouilh's play in the context of the Orpheus theme can be found in Eva Kushner's *Le Mythe d'Orphée dans la littérature française contemporaine* (Paris, Nizet, 1961), pp. 224–263.

8. Paul Valéry, *Oeuvres II* (Paris: Editions de la Pléiade, 1960), p. 1402.

9. *Ibid.*, p. 1405. See also Valéry, *Oeuvres I* (Paris: Pléiade, 1957), pp. 1539–1540.

10. *Ibid.*, pp. 76–77.

11. *Ibid.*, p. 177.

12. Valéry, *Oeuvres II*, p. 1409.

13. Paul Valéry, *Cahiers* (Paris: Centre National de la Recherche Scientifique, 1958), VII (1918–1921), 668.

14. Jules Supervielle, *Orphée et autres contes* (Neuchâtel: Ides et Calendes, 1946).

15. Georg Trakl, "Passion," *Die Dichtungen* (Salzburg: Otto Müller, 1938), p. 143; Hermann Broch, *Gedichte* (Zürich: Rhein-Verlag, 1953), p. 150 ("Vergil in des Orpheus Nachfolge").

16. Pierre-Jean Jouve, *En Miroir* (Paris: Mercure de France, 1954), p. 135.

17. The novelette *Dans Les Années profondes* relates the encounter with Hélène and her death. See *La Scène capitale* (Paris: Mercure de France, 1961), pp. 157–260.

18. Jouve, *En Miroir* ("Le Thème Nada"), p. 124.

19. Pierre-Jean Jouve, *Les Noces* (Paris: Au Sans Pareil, 1928), p. 155.

20. Pierre-Jean Jouve, "Orphée," *Poésie* (Paris: Mercure de France, 1964), p. 272.

21. *Ibid.*, p. 276.

22. Pierre Emmanuel, *Poésie raison ardente* (Paris: Egloff, 1948), pp. 73–74.

23. *Ibid.*, pp. 78, 77.

24. *Ibid.*, p. 80.

25. *Ibid.*, p. 82.

26. *Ibid.*, p. 83.

27. See Emmanuel's autobiography *Qui est cet homme?* (Paris: Egloff, 1947), esp. chaps. vii and viii.

28. Pierre Emmanuel, *Le Goût de l'Un* (Paris: Editions du Seuil, 1963), pp. 151–154.

29. *Ibid.*, p. 133.

30. Partially in *Qui est cet homme?* pp. 305–309; subsequently in "Notes sur la création poétique," *Journal de psychologie normale et pathologique*, 44 (1951), 261–268; and more recently in "L'Univers symbolique," *Le Goût de l'Un*, pp. 79–97.

31. Emmanuel, *Le Goût de l'Un*, pp. 81–82.

32. Pierre Emmanuel, *Le Poète et son Christ* (Neuchâtel: Editions de la Baconnière, 1942), p. 87.

33. Eva Kushner, *Le Mythe d'Orphée dans la littérature française contemporaine* (Paris: Nizet, 1961), p. 333.

34. Pierre Emmanuel, *Tombeau d'Orphée* (Paris: L. U. F., 1941), pp. 23–24.

35. *Ibid.*, p. 56.

36. *Ibid.*, p. 64.

37. Emmanuel, *Le Goût de l'Un*, p. 153.

38. Kushner, *Le Mythe d'Orphée*, p. 342.

39. Emmanuel, *Tombeau d'Orphée*, pp. 111–112.

40. See Walter A. Strauss, "Albert Camus, Stone Mason," *Modern Language Notes*, 77 (1962), 268–281.

41. Barthes, *Le Degré zéro*, pp. 12–13.

42. See Jean-Paul Sartre's review of *Aminadab* in *Situations I* (Paris: Gallimard, 1947).

43. Maurice Blanchot, *L'Espace littéraire* (Paris: Gallimard, 1955), p. 146. All quotations in the text are from this edition.

44. Maurice Blanchot, *Thomas l'obscur* (Paris: Gallimard, 1950), p. 7.

45. Maurice Blanchot, *Le Livre à venir* (Paris: Gallimard, 1959), p. 244.

46. Blanchot, *L'Espace littéraire*, p. 169.

47. Maurice Blanchot, *L'Arrêt de mort* (Paris: Gallimard, 1948), p. 7.

48. All quotations from *Thomas l'obscur* will be taken from the 1950 Gallimard edition (Paris).

49. Jean Starobinski, "*Thomas l'obscur*, chapitre premier," *Critique*, 22 (1966), p. 513.

50. Geoffrey Hartman, "Maurice Blanchot," in *The Novelist as Philosopher*, ed. John Cruickshank (London: Oxford University Press, 1962), pp. 154, 162.

51. Georges Poulet, "Maurice Blanchot critique et romancier," *Critique*, 22 (1966), 490, 491.

52. Georges Poulet, *Le Point de départ* (Paris: Plon, 1964), p. 168.

53. All quotations from Perse's poetry are from *Oeuvre poétique*, rev. ed., 2 vols. (Paris: Gallimard, 1960).

54. Alain Bosquet, Preface to *Saint-John Perse* (Paris: Seghers, 1960), p. 45.

55. Poulet, *Le Point de départ*, p. 163.

56. "Lettre de Saint-John Perse à un écrivain suédois," in *Honneur à Saint-John Perse*, ed. Jean Paulhan (Paris: Gallimard, 1965), pp. 665, 667.

57. Saint-John Perse, *On Poetry*, trans. W. H. Auden, bilingual ed. (New York: The Bollingen Foundation, 1961), pp. 8–9, 14–15.

58. *Ibid.*, pp. 11, 17.

59. *Honneur à Saint-John Perse*, p. 667.

60. "Evidence obtained under different experimental conditions cannot be comprehended within a single picture, but must be regarded as *complementary* in the sense that only the totality of the phenomenon exhausts the possible information about the objects"; Niels Bohr, "Discussion with Einstein on Epistemological Problems in Atomic Physics (1949)," *Atomic Physics and Human Knowledge* (New York: Science Editions, Inc., 1961), p. 40.

61. Perse, *On Poetry*, pp. 11–12, 17.

62. Charles du Bos, *Approximations*, 5th series (Paris: Corrêa, 1932), p. 237.

63. Martin Buber, *Daniel*, trans. Maurice Friedman (New York: McGraw-Hill, 1964), pp. 55–56; I have modified the translation considerably.

Index of Names